AGAINST BORDERS

Yevgeny Yevtushenko

All these borders—
they
bug me! Nothing
do I know
of Buenos Aires, or
New York
—and I should
know! I should be able to go
to London
and walk around,
and talk to the people,
even if I can't talk so good,
just walking
around. Like a little kid
I want to ride a bus
through Paris
some morning,
and I want an art
that is something
else, is an exciting sound—
like myself!

AGAINST BORDERS

Promoting Books for a Multicultural World

Hazel Rochman

ALA Books / Booklist Publications

American Library Association

Chicago and London 1993

Cover art by Carlos Cortez. Mr. Cortez, a mestizo with Yaqui Indian ancestry, is a leading Chicano artist, well known for his distinctive artwork and for his poetry. Some of Mr. Cortez's artwork has been collected by the Smithsonian Institution.

Text designed by Stuart Whitwell

The paper used in this publication meets the minimum requirements of the American National Standard for Information Sciences—Permanence of Paper for Printed Library Materials, ANSI Z39.48-1984. ∞

Printed on 60-pound Arbor, a pH-neutral stock, and bound in 10 point C1S cover stock by Edwards Bros., Inc.

Library of Congress Cataloging-in-Publication Data

Rochman, Hazel.
    Against borders : promoting books for a multicultural world / by Hazel Rochman.
       p.   cm.
    Includes index.
    ISBN 0-8389-0601-X (alk. paper)
    1. Children's literature—Bibliography. 2. Children—United States—Books and reading. 3. Pluralism (Social sciences)—Juvenile literature—Bibliography. 4. Minorities—Juvenile literature—Bibliography. I. Title.
Z1037.R6 1993
[PN1009.A1]
 011.62—dc20   93-17840

97 96 95 94   5 4 3 2

For Hymie, Danny, and Simon

CONTENTS

ACKNOWLEDGMENTS

Thanks go first to the consultants who helped with the resource lists in Part Two: Raúl Niño, poet, author of the collection *Breathing Light;* Deborah Taylor, Young Adult Services Specialist at Enoch Pratt Free Library in Baltimore and 1992 chair of ALA's Best Books for Young Adults Committee; Phoebe Yeh, children's books editor at Scholastic Books; and Marc Zimmerman, professor in the Latin American Studies Program of the University of Illinois at Chicago and author of *U.S. Latino Literature: An Essay and Annotated Bibliography.* Special thanks to Michael Dorris, author of *A Yellow Raft in Blue Water, Morning Girl, The Broken Cord,* and (with Louise Erdrich) *The Crown of Columbus,* who not only advised on the Native American list, but also contributed the fine introduction to that chapter.

Thanks also to Stuart Whitwell, Managing Editor of *Booklist,* who designed this book with the sensibility of a writer, and to Irene Wood, Audiovisual Media editor at *Booklist,* who compiled the lists of videos included in Part Two. My thanks as well to Dorothy Broderick, Editor of *VOYA,* who worked closely with me on a bibliography on apartheid; Julie Corsaro, school library media specialist at the Edgewood School in Highland Park, Illinois, whose lists on Arab culture (published in *Booklist*) and on the Caribbean (published in *Book Links*) provided valuable help; Mary Frances Wilkens, Operations Manager for *Booklist,* for hours of editorial and production support; and Stephanie Zvirin, Associate Editor in *Booklist*'s Books for Youth, who worked with me on the Jewish American list and on just about everything else.

I am grateful to the following periodicals for permission to reprint excerpts from my articles: *School Library Journal,* for the article "Medusa in the Mall"; *Horn Book Magazine,* for the articles "Booktalking: Going Global" and "Autobiography: Heroes and Monsters"; and the *New York Times Book Review,* for reviews on Roald Dahl's *Boy,* Paula Fox's *The Moonlight Man,* Sue Ellen Bridgers' *Permanent Connections,* Jan Slepian's *Risk N' Roses,* and Lois Metzger's *Barry's Sister.*

The Holocaust resource guide draws heavily on the *Booklist* special issue, June 1, 1989, "Remembering the Holocaust," which included a multimedia retrospective bibliography from every section of the magazine. Like that list, many of the resource guides and annotations draw on material written by all my colleagues at the magazine, especially in the Books for Youth section under our editor Sally Estes. This book is rooted in my daily work as a book reviewer at *Booklist,* where, under the leadership of Editor and Publisher Bill Ott, words and stories get the passionate attention that he gave to every page of this book.

I am grateful to Bonnie Smothers, ALA Books editor, for pushing me hard and for her commitment and expertise.

All errors and omissions are my own.

AN IMMIGRANT'S JOURNEY

> *. . . we live in an age of refugees, of migrants, vagrants,*
> *nomads, roaming about the continent and warming their*
> *souls with the memory of their—spiritual or ethnic, divine*
> *or geographical, real or imaginary—homes.*
>
> *—Leszek Kolakowski*

Since 1984 I have been an assistant editor at the American Library Association's *Booklist*, where I review books for young people. When Bill Ott, Editor and Publisher of *Booklist*, asked me to do a book about promoting multiculturalism for junior high and high school kids, I thought it would be fairly easy. *Booklist* has been publishing fine ethnic bibliographies for years (from "Growing Up Black" to "World Cultures"), and it seemed a good idea to pull them together, update and expand them, and make a book. What I didn't know was how much that "updating" would mean and where it would lead—both for me as an individual and for the book I would eventually write.

The book became a joint project with ALA's book publishing department, and from the beginning Bill, my ALA Books editor Bonnie Smothers, and I have been vehement about two essentials:

- multiculturalism means across cultures, against borders.
- multiculturalism doesn't mean only people of color.

The best books break down borders. They surprise us—whether they are set close to home or abroad. They change our view of ourselves; they extend that phrase "like me" to include what we thought was foreign and strange.

I grew up in South Africa under apartheid, in a police state that tried to destroy multiculturalism. Ethnic purity and total separation were the law. There were borders and barriers everywhere; barbed wire around our homes and in ourselves. Black schools were separate and grossly unequal. "Public" libraries were for whites only. Book and press censorship was fierce. Most contemporary black writers were banned, banished, imprisoned. Radio was state controlled. We had no television at all.

One night about 30 years ago in the backyard of our house in Johannesburg, my husband and I buried some of our books. I held the flashlight, and he dug a hole; then we packed the books in an old tin trunk, covered them with soil, and left them there. We didn't think of it as a metaphor. Afterwards, we didn't think about it at all. The country was ruled by a state of emergency. We knew that the Special Branch of the police might raid our house, and one of the things they always did was search for banned books. We had lots of those, so why ask for trouble?

When we sold our house in a rush shortly before leaving South Africa in 1963, we forgot about the books. We didn't think about them for a long time. That's what happens with secrets, and it can get you into trouble. You get into a habit of not talking about them, even to each other, not thinking about them. Our books are probably there still, though we like to think of some new owners digging them up one day and discovering treasure.

We left South Africa on a one-way passport. Our son Danny was three years old (the same age as my father when he came to South Africa from Latvia before World War I). We weren't allowed back into South Africa until the 1990s; we were stateless. We lived in England for 10 years, first in Leeds, where our son Simon was born; then in London, where we were more rooted with the concentrated South African emigré community than we'd ever felt "back home." Then in 1972 we came to the U.S. and settled in an apartment in Hyde Park, Chicago, where we've been ever since. For years we had no papers (only Simon could lord it over us that *he* was born a British citizen and had a real passport). We had to line up every year at the Immigration Department to get our Certificates of Identity stamped with permission to stay here. Finally in 1982 we became naturalized U.S. citizens.

We haven't suffered the economic hardship of many immigrants who come here today. Ours has been a very different journey from that of our parents and grandparents, who came as steerage passengers to South Africa from Eastern Europe at the turn of the century. Unlike millions of South Africans, our family wasn't broken up by the migrant labor system. We weren't forced into exile with no work and little food, shelter, and medical care. We flew to the U. S. on the wings of our white South African privilege. But traveling has been hard on me and my family. I can't say I feel at home, no more than I felt in Johannesburg. Not if home is a place. Yet, if as immigrant writer Bharati Mukherjee suggests, home is a state of mind, then I do feel a sense of community. Stories have done something to keep me in touch with the people I loved and left behind. My father died last year, but his stories are part of who I am. When I was growing up, I got sick of hearing them ("Yes, yes, I know about Uncle Leopold and the time he lost everything at the races . . ."), just as I see my own kids getting the same glazed look when my husband and I reminisce about "home." But Danny made his grandfather tell him every detail of those old family stories over and over, and Simon has shared them (many versions of them) with his cousins, from Johannesburg to Boston.

Stories—the kind you read as well as the kind you pass along orally—have also brought me close to all kinds of people who would otherwise have remained strangers. Reading is a solitary activity; yet it breaks barriers with the world. Books—reading, talking, arguing, sharing, reviewing books—are my work and my joy, and they have helped me find a home.

When I first started work as a school librarian at the University of Chicago Laboratory School in 1976, the kids and I were strangers. I had this prissy accent. Their media center was jumping with all kinds of books and films and music that seemed to have little to do with the traditional library I was used to in England. I wasn't at all sure this was going to work. But when I started going to classes to talk about books, we got to know each other. Teachers and students felt welcome in the library, and I was at home in the classroom. I was sharing ideas and feelings, talking about what moved me. I was showing what I cared about, who I was, the fears and dreams we had in common. The books were a bond between us.

Anyone who's ever been in a book discussion group knows how small talk and politeness quickly give way to passionate argument. Feelings and ideas burst out of you. I first met my friend Roger Sutton on ALA's Best Books for Young Adults committee. He remembers me yelling at him across the table, "That's cheap, Roger!" when he sneered at a book I dearly loved. I've served on many book selection committees for the American Library Association (including the Newbery Committee) and on the advisory board of the *Bulletin of the Center for Children's Books*; for years I was part of a women's book discussion group in my neighborhood; we have just started a discussion group at ALA headquarters. All of them have helped me feel at home; I have gotten to know people from cultures very different from where I started off. And I have made friends.

In a direct sense, this book is a collaborative effort: not only because Bill and Bonnie harangued and inspired me every time I wanted to settle for something safe and easy; and not only because I have drawn so heavily on *Booklist*'s expertise in writing and design: on bibliographies and reviews—adult, audiovisual, reference, young adult, and children's—and especially on the work of Sally Estes, Ilene Cooper, and Stephanie Zvirin, the editors in the Books for Youth section. Just as important is the talk about books—sometimes laid-back, sometimes fierce—that goes on all the time in our offices and hallways and at coffee and as the mail comes in. When your work is reading, writing, selecting, talking about books, you get close to people very fast. They get to know you, and they make you listen. When you care about what you're reading, arguments can get disturbing. We're not only making a magazine together, but it's a magazine about books. And books matter.

The apartheid government with its rigorous censorship was right about that: books matter. The stories you read can transform you because they help you imagine beyond yourself. If you read only what mirrors your view of yourself, you get locked in. It's as if you're in a stupor or under a spell. Buried.

As an immigrant, I'm glad that I live in a diverse community and that my kids take for granted that differences in skin color and language and culture are not barriers between people. I am still unable to take for granted the freedoms of the First Amendment. In Johannesburg I worked as a journalist, and over many years I saw freedom of thought and expression whittled away, until it was forbidden to criticize the government or even to ask questions about children tortured and detained without trial. The result of that kind of censorship is that most people can shut out, can *not* know, what is happening all around them.

Apartheid has made us bury our books. The Inquisition and the Nazis burned books. Slaves in the United States were forbidden to read books. From Latin America to Eastern Europe and Asia, books have been trashed. But the stories are still here—and they continue to help hesitant immigrants trying to find their way home.

This book tries to break down apartheid. It connects great books from all cultures. There's no doubt that some kinds of Eurocentric books have dominated the mainstream for a long time and that some cultures have been largely ignored. But the best way to promote them is together; not patronizingly as something cute and exotic and apart, but as good books. At first I thought I could organize my book like that, discuss books across cultures and connect them by theme to show and tell that you can lead kids from their own culture and out to the wider world and back again. But my editors, Bonnie and Bill, were always pushing me to find a focus for the discussion, a model for making connections. It doesn't work to make multiculturalism the subject of an anthology or even of a resource book. That's like making LIFE the subject. You have to have a theme and a unity of tone, however complex, so that the book holds together. It can, it must, contain opposites, but it can't be just a hodgepodge. Otherwise, you can just throw in anything you like from anywhere; even the best stews have some organizing principle. Likewise, the best anthologies or collective biographies or studies across cultures have a point of view that shapes the rich diversity and connects people everywhere by common experience.

The focus I found—again drawing on my experience with teachers and students at the Chicago Lab School—was the myth of the epic journey, the universal coming-of-age story. Each of us must go on a vision quest. Each of us must find our way. As Ursula Le Guin says, "We all have the same kind of dragons in our psyche."

People everywhere tell many of the same kinds of stories about that inner quest. The archetype is rooted in the multifarious particularities of ordinary lives. And our artists and writers keep retelling the age-old stories, transforming the heroic adventure, revealing the myth in the mysteries of contemporary experience. There are mythical moments, "primal echoes," in the banal events of our daily lives, in the things that happen to everyone, says the mythologist Wendy O'Flaherty, whose book *Other Peoples' Myths* is full of people telling stories about people telling stories.

With the present rage for cultural literacy, more young people will learn about Theseus, Odysseus, Medea, King Arthur, and the great traditional stories we all share. But there's strong debate about why and how these myths should be taught. The most rigid back-to-basics pedants, ignoring the riches of contemporary writing and of world cultures, insist that the Western classics are all that students should be reading. Just as exclusionary are those who see stories as literal recipes for ethnic self-esteem: Jews should read about Moses to keep in touch with their roots; the myth of the Woman Warrior can help Asian American women feel strong. Then there are those who see all those classical stories as outdated clichés with little meaning for an MTV generation that wants books only about, like, hanging out at the mall.

All these views patronize young people. All ignore the universals of story. With a medicinal approach to reading, they fail to see the myths from many cultures as part of a living tradition. The gorgon and the golem, the dragon and the labyrinth, the cave and the mountain, the trickster and the witch, the genie and the holy grail, the flood and the snake, the wilderness and the promised land—images like these have enduring power to excite and disturb us. They tell us about the mysterious journey that each of us must take, what the mythologist Joseph Campbell calls "the quest to find the inward thing that you basically are." On that journey, each of us must ask: How do I slay the monsters? How can I transform myself? Is my mentor a friend or fiend? What thread will guide me through the labyrinth? Is there treasure in the dark? Who is my lover? Where is my home?

O'Flaherty says that the mythical events in our lives include "rites of passage: the experience of birth . . . the sudden transition from childhood to adulthood, falling in love, marriage, death—our experience of the deaths of others and our contemplation of our own deaths. We encounter these primal echoes also in classical occasions of joy—plunging into the ocean, galloping on a young horse, returning home after a long journey, listening to sublime music, watching a summer thunderstorm in the middle of the night. And the same feeling overcomes us in moments of modern tragedy—the phone call in the middle of the night, news of failure or desertion, an accident, the diagnosis of cancer, a prison sentence."

In the stories of the 1990s, the epic journey may be into the unknown realm of space or through time; it may be a pilgrimage to Mecca, or a discovery about someone you thought you knew. It may be on the road, far from home; it may take you through the maze of a suburban shopping center or through the wilderness of the inner city. It may take you through the dark forest of a distant kingdom or through the tangle of feelings in the human heart. You may make the journey alone, or you may go with a friend or a mentor. Or a stranger may come to town and transform you.

Some of the best YA literature finds the archetype in contemporary teenage experience. I remember sharing Robert Cormier's *I Am the Cheese* with English teacher Sophie Ravin. She showed me that Cormier's cyclist trying to find out about his father is in some ways like Theseus trying to find his father on the journey to Athens, and that in both stories the search for the father is also a search for identity. I can still remember how that flash of recognition increased my pleasure in Cormier and in the myth. It also opened me to making that kind of connection in other books.

Finding these mythic mysteries in stories of contemporary life—enjoying the story while reaching for the metaphor—can illuminate both the modern story and the myth. The same is true of fairy tale. Teenagers are thrilled to discover that stories they thought they knew, thought they'd left behind in childhood, tell truths about our continuing transformation on the journey through the dark.

Reading the archetypal stories across cultures connects us with each other. When Jamaica Kincaid in *Annie John* describes the necessary abyss that develops between a teenager and her loving mother, I recognize my conflict in breaking free from home. When the teenager in Betsy Byars' *Bingo Brown's Guide to Romance* meets his beloved on a perilous journey to the laundrette, I recognize—in the very banality of the detail—that Odysseus is me. When Paula Fox in *One-Eyed Cat* describes the "little worm of mucus" where the eye had been in the injured cat, I shudder at the physical image and at the sense of shameful secrets. When I read how Michael Nava in "Abuelo: My Grandfather, Raymond Acuña," imagined his *abuelo* to be what he needed him to be, I think again about the beloved mentors and role models I have half-known, half-created.

The best stories don't set up heavily symbolic mythic parallels. Nor do they reduce the complex archetype to neat and tidy formula. O'Flaherty calls that kind of shallow story "kitsch mythology," where everything is predictable and homogenous. In the great writers, the words do what the story says, showing that the cadences of the small talk and the concrete images of daily life hold the intense power of myth. "Who am I?" is an archetypal cry that reverberates on the perilous journeys made by mythic characters from ancient Greece to contemporary Southern California. Medusa lives in the mall.

So the idea of myth across cultures became my focus—the search for self that takes us beyond race, color, and geography. This theme, the link to myth, to the journey we all must take, forms a true multicultural bridge; too many lists of so-called multicultural books function only as a well-meaning spotlight—shining brightly but briefly on one cultural island or another, providing overdue recognition, yes, but imposing a different kind of isolation, celebratory but still separate. The islands need a bridge to connect them, and myth offers one way to build that bridge.

But only *one* way. The essays on mythic themes that make up Part One of this book are intended only as flexible models of some ways to connect books across cultures. A teacher or librarian might choose to use or adapt one essay or one part of an essay, or to use one book discussed in an essay and explore its mythic connections in depth. Adapt them, mix them up, dip into them to suit whatever curriculum project you're working on. Or, better yet, build your own bridge. The perilous journey is only one theme, one way of using multicultural literature to connect rather than separate.

I make connections very simply. The last thing you want to do is overwhelm young people with abstract analysis or with pretentious lectures on the labyrinth as symbol of the unconscious or with feel-good moralistic stuff about following your bliss. The focus should be on the story, character, and immediate situation; that's what lures readers into the book. Once inside, they can take it as far as they want to. For many young people, it's an exciting leap of understanding just to discover the universal mythic themes—the hero, the monster, and the perilous journey—in stories of daily experience from all over the world.

If the theme essays in Part One form a bridge that allows us to move easily across cultures and through multiple levels of meaning, then the books included in the resource lists in Part Two are the vehicles that can transport us over the bridge. The lists are organized by culture, place, or historical event. Selected with the advice of expert consultants in each area, they are guides to some of the best materials that will interest kids. They can be used in individual subject areas or across the school, for personal reading or classroom discussion. All the books are in print. Draw on them to focus on one area in the classroom, to construct your own connecting theme, or to update a library collection. Special classroom projects on a particular country or ethnic group can be an important and enriching part of the curriculum, whether the focus is on apartheid, the Holocaust, the changing patterns of immigration, Black History Month, the Native American experience, or an in-depth study of one group.

For example, two dynamic high school librarians at Topeka West High School in Kansas, Mike Printz and Diane Goheen, created a school-wide project on apartheid that reached out from the library to teachers in every department in the school, and even beyond to the parents and the wider suburban community. From Chicago they brought in a great speaker, Prexy Nesbitt, formerly consultant in the U.S. for the government of Mozambique, and 2,000 students crowded the library to hear him in nine workshop sessions. The eminent Mozambique artist Malangatana Ngwenya came to the school and painted murals with the students. In one class, the students read short stories as literature; in another class they dramatized them. Films were shown all week. The kids did research on-line and gave class presentations on various aspects of apartheid and institutionalized racism. They made a video of the week; they wrote poetry and newspaper articles. Mike and Diane's work is a model for junior high and high school projects across the curriculum, and they have presented it in workshops around the country.

What Mike and Diane accomplished, and what this book hopes to aid others in accomplishing, is the real point of multicultural education: to help kids recognize their own particular culture and understand their connection with those who appear different.

Reading makes immigrants of us all—it takes us away from home, but, most important, it finds homes for us everywhere.

BEYOND POLITICAL CORRECTNESS

. . . the merely human
is denied me still
and I am now no longer beast
but saint.

—*Lucille Clifton*

Multiculturalism is a trendy word, trumpeted by the politically correct with a stridency that has provoked a sneering backlash. There are P.C. watchdogs eager to strip from the library shelves anything that presents a group as less than perfect. The ethnic "character" must always be strong, dignified, courageous, loving, sensitive, wise. Then there are those who watch for authenticity: how dare a white write about blacks? What's a Gentile doing writing about a Jewish old lady and her African American neighbors? The chilling effect of this is a kind of censorship and a reinforcement of apartheid.

It's easy to laugh at the lunatic fringe. According to P.C. labeling, I should change my name to Hazel Rochperson. They comfort me that I am vertically challenged (short), my husband is differently hirsute (bald), my mother is chronologically gifted (old), my brother differently abled (brain-injured), and some of my best friends are people of size (fat). Not at all comforting are the same kind of euphemisms from the corporate world: words like downsizing (firing workers). Then there's ethically different (corrupt) and caloric insufficiency (hunger), or a new one for hunger, misnourishment.

But the greatest danger from the politically correct bullies is that they create a backlash, and that backlash is often self-righteous support for the way things are. Whether we are weary or indignant, we wish the whiners would just go away. Or we focus on the absurd and on the names, and then we can ignore real issues of prejudice and hatred that keep people apart. Ethnic cleansing is the current euphemism: it's an attack on multiculturalism, and it isn't funny at all.

In promoting books with young people, we have to resist the extremes: the mindless conformity to the P.C. of multiculturalism but also the backlash. As with that other current fad, whole language, the pretentious jargon is only now catching up with what we've been doing all along—teaching and sharing great books from everywhere, stories that grab us and extend our view of ourselves.

Growing up in South Africa, I didn't think that anyone could write a good story about where I lived. I was an avid reader, but books were about English girls in boarding school or lovers running wild on the windy moors. My romantic dreams came from Hollywood. Gangsters were in Chicago, and poor people were noble heroes struggling far away in the Dust Bowl in Oklahoma. I certainly didn't think that there could be an interesting story about blacks where I lived. They were servants, not individuals like me with complex feelings and difficult moral choices, not like my family and friends, or people in books.

Apartheid didn't seem to have much to do with me. I grew up in a liberal home. I wasn't allowed to make racist remarks. I thought I was a good person. I didn't see what was going on around me. I took it all for granted. I never noticed that there were no black kids my age in my neighborhood; not one black student in my school. I just accepted that the woman who cooked and cleaned for us lived in a room in the backyard. We knew only her first name or referred to her as the "girl"; I never thought that her children lived far away or that she was forced to leave them in order to come and look after me. I remember vaguely that one of her children died. I never asked her about her life. Read a story about her? From her point of view? What point of view?

As editor of *Somehow Tenderness Survives: Stories of Southern Africa*, I included Doris Lessing's "The Old Chief Mshlanga," a story very close to my experience of growing up white and privileged and apart. In the story, the teenage girl calls black people "natives," a derogatory term in Africa, with racist overtones of primitive, uncivilized. The natives were "as remote as the trees and rocks." They were "an amorphous, black mass," and, of course, their language was "uncouth" and "ridiculous." It's as if the white girl is asleep or blind. Then she meets a black man, the old Chief Mshlanga; he once owned the whole district before the whites came and "opened it up." She sees him as a person, not just a native, and that starts waking her up to the world around her. First, it seems quite easy: Why can't they all live together, black and white, without elbowing each other out of the way? But she discovers that you can't just set things right with "an easy gush of feeling, saying: I could not help it. I am also a victim."

She comes of age—as I did under apartheid—with the shocking awareness that the universe you've always taken for granted is evil.

Another story in the collection is from Mark Mathabane's autobiography *Kaffir Boy: The True Story of a Black Youth's Coming of Age in Apartheid South Africa*. Mathabane grew up in the ghetto of Alexandra Township, barely 10 miles from where I lived on a tree-lined Johannesburg city street. But it was another universe, unimaginable to me when I was growing up. Like the overwhelming majority of whites, I never set foot there, and I blocked out any awareness of its daily life.

Until two or three years ago, Mathabane's book was banned in South Africa. You can see why. Not only does he describe the cruel oppression, he makes us see that black child as an individual, like me. Mathabane's family are people. They aren't amorphous saintly victims, nor are they wild savages. They're definitely not the innocent, mysterious primitives in the popular safari-adventure stories of dark Africa. Racism dehumanizes, but a good story defeats the stereotype. It makes us imagine that boy's life in all its complexity and connects it to ours.

It's not just South Africa. Just as I, a white child in Johannesburg, saw the blacks around me as undifferentiated "natives," so Maya Angelou, growing up in segregated Stamps, Arkansas, couldn't see whites as individuals: "People were those who lived on my side of town. I didn't like them all, or, in fact, any of them very much, but they were people. These others, the strange pale creatures that lived in their alien unlife, weren't considered folks. They were whitefolks."

They all look alike. *We* are individuals.

A good book can help to break down those barriers. Books can make a difference in dispelling prejudice and building community: not with role models and literal recipes, not with noble messages about the human family, but with enthralling stories that make us imagine the lives of others. A good story lets you know people as individuals in all their particularity and conflict; and once you see someone as a person— flawed, complex, striving—then you've reached beyond stereotype. Stories, writing them, telling them, sharing them, transforming them, enrich us and connect us and help us know each other.

But it's insulting to say that a book is good *because* it's multicultural. Betsy Hearne, editor of the *Bulletin of the Center for Children's Books*, was appalled at a recent conference to hear people recommend a book only because it was multicultural, as if no further evaluation were needed.

AND YET . . . BEYOND RECIPES AND ROLE MODELS

How do you evaluate books across cultures? Are there special criteria? What are the pitfalls? And in a time of declining book budgets in libraries and school media centers, when librarians do have to select very carefully, how do you balance all the demands of literary quality and popular appeal and intellectual freedom and curriculum support and multiculturalism? And how do you make kids want to read?

Of course, these issues aren't new, and there are no simple answers. As the arguments about political correctness reach a crescendo, I find myself agreeing and disagreeing with everybody. If there's one thing I've learned in this whole multicultural debate, it's not to trust absolutes. I say something and then immediately qualify it with "And yet . . ." And it's usually because I find a book that upsets all my neat categories. That's what good books do: they unsettle us, make us ask questions about what we thought was certain. They don't just reaffirm everything we already know.

Underlying much of the P.C. debate is the demand that each book must do it all. Let's face it, a lot of kids don't read much for fun, especially as they get older. They don't have time. They get their stories, their dreams, their escape entertainment, without effort from TV and video and commercials. For many students, reading isn't a need and a pleasure. It's a drag. Something you do for a grade, if you have to.

The poet Katha Pollitt says that it's because young people read so little that there's such furious debate about the canon. If they read all kinds of books all the time, particular books wouldn't matter so much. If you think that the book you're promoting is the only one kids are ever going to read on a subject—about the pioneers or about Columbus or about the Holocaust or about apartheid—then there's intense pressure to choose the "right" book with the "right" message. If we don't watch out, reading becomes only therapy, only medicine. We start to recommend books because they give us the *right* role models, depending on what's considered "right" in the current political climate.

Censors think that readers treat a story like a recipe or a self-help manual with directions to follow, so that you go out and do literally what you're reading about. I'm not sure what happens when we read. It's mysterious. A story grabs us; a phrase sings and won't let us be; a street or a room gives us a view; the conflict in a character startles us into seeing ourselves in a new way.

The paradox is that if we give young people didactic tracts, or stories so bland that they offend nobody, we're going to make them read even less. For books to give pleasure there has to be tension and personality, laughter and passionate conflict. That's what will grab kids and touch them deeply—and make them want to read.

A good story is rich with ambiguity. You sympathize with people of all kinds. Read Anne Fine's funny YA novels, like *My War with Goggle-Eyes,* and you get swept up into furious family quarrels about relationships and about ideas, where neither side wins. The best books glory in conflict. This is especially so with political themes, where everything can degenerate into propaganda if the characters become mouthpieces for worthy ideas. Susan Sontag uses a wonderful expression: "Literature is a party," she says, "even as disseminators of indignation, writers are givers of pleasure."

The novelist E. L. Doctorow says that one of the things he most admires about George Bernard Shaw is that "he gave the best speeches to the people he disagreed with. . . . You have to allow the ambiguity. You have to allow for something to be itself and its opposite at the same time."

Censors on the left and the right can't allow for ambiguity. One of their constant mistakes is to take what the narrator says, or what one character says, as the voice of the author. The Canadian novelist Margaret Atwood complains, "It's amazing the extent to which readers will think that everything anybody in any of your books says is an expression of your own opinion. Literature just doesn't work like that." If you judge every character to be the author, then you can never allow debate in a book, never have a protagonist who has an ugly or erroneous thought, never have a narrator who's less than perfect—perfect, that is, according to the current fashion.

A library collection does have to satisfy all kinds of requirements. But each book can't do it all. When Walter Dean Myers spoke at the Columbia Children's Literature Institute in 1990, someone in the audience asked him why he wrote a book about black kids playing basketball—it's such a stereotype, why was he feeding it? "Every book I write," he replied, "can't take on the whole African American experience." He said he had written other books in which kids did other things. But, he said, he likes basketball; lots of African American kids like basketball; and this one book is about that world.

One book doesn't carry the whole ethnic group experience. In Sook Nyul Choi's *Year of Impossible Goodbyes,* chosen as an ALA Best Book for Young Adults, the Japanese occupiers of North Korea during World War II, as seen through the eyes of a young Korean girl, are cruel and oppressive enemies. Japan-bashing is a problem in the U.S. now, but that doesn't affect the truth of this story. You could read that book with Yoko Kawashima Watkins' *So Far from the Bamboo Grove,* about a Japanese girl on the run from cruel Koreans after World War II. Or with Yoshiko Uchida's fiction and autobiography about how Japanese Americans were treated here during World War II.

What's more, one writer is not the representative of a whole ethnic group. Maxine Hong Kingston, who wrote the classic memoir *The Woman Warrior,* complains about "the expectation among readers and critics that I should represent the race. Each artist has a unique voice. Many readers don't understand that. What I look forward to is the time when many of us are published and then we will be able to see the range of viewpoints, of visions, of what it is to be Chinese American." Nor does one reviewer speak for a whole ethnic group. Phoebe Yeh, a children's book editor at Scholastic, says that she is a reader before she is Chinese. I'm a Jew, but I can't speak for all Jews. Nor for all South Africans; not even for all South Africans who are anti-apartheid.

And every time an artist or writer does something, it doesn't have to be about her race. Sheila Hamanaka's book *The Journey* is based on her five-panel mural painting. It shows the World War II experience of Japanese Americans, including her own family, who were herded up and sent to concentration camps. It's a story of prejudice and injustice, personal and official, and Hamanaka is passionate about what happened to her people. But some of Hamanaka's books aren't focused on the Japanese American experience at all. *A Visit to Amy-Claire* is a picture book about a family, about sibling rivalry, and the family happens to be Asian American. Recently, Hamanaka illustrated a delightful picture book, *Sofie's Role* by Amy Heath, about a family bakery, and there are no Asian characters at all.

Accuracy and Authenticity

Now, there are people who say that Hamanaka should stick to stories about Asians. Or that Lloyd Alexander's *The Remarkable Journey of Prince Jen* (*Booklist*'s Top of the List winner for fiction in 1991) can't be any good because Alexander can't really know the Chinese tradition. Or that Chinese American Ed Young can't illustrate African American folklore because he can't really know the culture. One of the most violent debates swirling around the issue of multicultural literature relates to accuracy and authenticity.

Of course accuracy matters. You can get a lot of things wrong as a writer, an artist, or a reviewer when you don't know a place or a culture. Junko Yokota Lewis, who's from Japan, has pointed out some important errors in Japanese costume and custom in picture books published in the U.S. For example, she shows that one illustration has characters wearing their kimonos in a style that only dead people are dressed in, another shows characters with chopsticks in their hair; a third depicts food in a manner appropriate only when served to deceased ancestors. I'm from South Africa, so I know that culture better than the average American does, and reviewing a book about apartheid I might find things that others might miss.

And yet . . . that isn't the whole story. Sometimes I worry that I know too much, that I can't see the forest for the trees, that steeped as I am in the South African culture, I can't always know what an American teenager doesn't know. Would an American reader be confused by something that I take for granted? One of the things that does help me is that I no longer live in South Africa, so to some extent I can see things from outside as well as in—from both sides of the border.

So what about those who say that an American can never write about Japan, that men can't write about women? In fact, some take it further. Only Indians can really judge books about Indians, Jews must review books about Jews. And further still, you get the ultimate extreme, blacks should read only about blacks, Latinos about Latinos, locking us into smaller and tighter boxes.

What I hear echoing in that sort of talk is the mad drumbeat of apartheidspeak. Apartheid made laws on the basis of so-called immutable differences. Not only should whites and blacks be kept absolutely apart and educated separately, but among blacks, each "tribe" should be separate, so that Zulus should live only with Zulus and be taught in Zulu about Zulu to do things that only Zulus do. The apartheid planners said that the only work blacks could do was simple manual labor, that science and abstract thinking weren't part of their culture, and that their training should prepare them to be good servants. It's so absurd that it's hard to believe how much of it was carried out, and with untold suffering to millions.

When I went back to South Africa in 1990, I interviewed Nadine Gordimer for *Booklist* at her home in Johannesburg. I asked her if she felt that as a white she could write about black experience, and how she answered those who said she was using black suffering. She got angry. "How does a writer write from the point of view of a child?" she said. "Or from the point of view of an old person when you are 17 years old? How does a writer change sex? How could the famous soliloquy of Molly Bloom have been written by James Joyce? Has any woman ever written anything as incredibly intimate? I mean, how did Joyce know how a woman feels before she's going to get her period?"

Then, in 1992, I interviewed Virginia Hamilton. She spoke about her frustration in not being allowed to write *outside* the black experience. "People won't allow it; critics won't allow it," she said. "If I would do a book that didn't have blacks, people would say, 'Oh, what is Virginia Hamilton doing?' I feel the limitation," she explained. "I'm always running up against it and knocking it down in different ways, whichever way I can. But I know that it's there and will always be there. I mean, there were people who said in the middle of my career, 'Now Virginia Hamilton has finally faced who she is.' Well, how dare they?"

In a wonderful article called "What Mean We, White Man?" Roger Sutton sums it up this way: "Literature, language, is a way to jump out of our own skins. If we cannot reach beyond the bounds of race, ethnicity, sex, sexual orientation, and class, literature is useless, leaving writers few options beyond Joni Mitchell–style confessional lyrics."

And yet . . . only gifted writers can do it, write beyond their own cultures. Fiction and nonfiction are full of people who don't get beyond stereotype because the writer cannot imagine them as individuals. Traveling to foreign places—or reading about them—isn't necessarily broadening. Many tourists return from their experience with the same smug stereotypes about "us" and "them." Too many books *about* other countries, written without knowledge or passion, take the "tourist" approach, stressing the exotic, or presenting a static society with simple categories. Some writers who try to tackle a country's complex political and social issues seem to think that in a book for young people it's fine to do a bit of background reading and then drop into a country for a few weeks, take some glossy pictures, and go home and write a book about it.

There's nothing wrong with writing a book about travel, about how it feels to be in a foreign place, even about finding a foreign place exotic. But don't pretend you're writing about the place or the people there. If the book takes a tourist approach, just touching down from the cruise ship for some local shopping, then you get the kind of nonfiction photo-essay so common in children's literature, where the pictures are arranged so that the child—usually attired in national dress—goes on a "journey," a journey that allows the book to include some colorful scenery and local customs.

Yes, authenticity matters, but there is no formula for how you acquire it. Anybody can write about anything—if they're good enough. There will always be inauthentic or inaccurate books, and defining authenticity on some exclusionary basis or other won't change a thing. The only way to combat inaccuracy is with accuracy—not with pedigrees.

Saints, Role Models, and Stereotypes

The savage savage is a stereotype, but the noble savage is, too. Both are designed to set up borders, to keep "them" far away from "us."

Michael Dorris, who acted as consultant for the Native American list in this book, said in a *New York Times* article about the depiction of Indians in the movie *Dances with Wolves*: "Readers and viewers of such sagas are left with a predominant emotion of regret for a golden age now but a faint memory. In the imaginary mass media world of neat beginnings, middles and ends, American Indian society, whatever its virtues and fascinations as an arena for Eur-American consciousness raising, is definitely past tense." Doris Seale and Beverly Slapin in *Through Indian Eyes: The Native Experience in Children's Books,* show how often Indians are presented as whooping savages in paint or feathers, or as cute, make-believe figures for kids to playact in costume, or as noble savages, generic and distant, as in dusty museum panoramas.

Lionel Trilling said that James Agee's text for *Let Us Now Praise Famous Men,* published in the early 1940s, about poor tenant families in the South, was the most realistic and the most important moral effort of his generation. Even so, Trilling pointed out "a failure of moral realism" in the book. "It lies in Agee's inability to see these people as anything but good. He writes of these people as if there were no human unregenerateness in them, no flicker of malice or meanness, no darkness or wildness of feeling, only a sure and simple virtue, the growth, we must suppose, of their hard, unlovely poverty. He shuts out, that is, what is part of the moral job to take in. What creates this falsification is guilt—the observer's guilt at his own relative freedom."

When I was compiling the stories about apartheid for *Somehow Tenderness Survives,* I struggled at first with that kind of reverential, patronizing guilt. I looked for stories that had the right line—brave, good, strong, beautiful people succeeding in the fight for freedom—and I felt a great deal of pressure to include role-model stories.

But several things stopped me from choosing that kind of propaganda. First, reviewing the books on South Africa for *Booklist,* I had seen too many politically correct anthologies with the right balance and the reverential attitudes, that just weren't being read. You can't harangue people into reading, however worthy the cause. There has to be the pleasure of story, character, passionate conflict, and language if you're going to grab readers and make them want to read on.

Second, I listened to Nadine Gordimer when she came to speak in Chicago. She is politically militant, unequivocally committed to Nelson Mandela and the struggle against racism. But she is just as adamant that the correct attitude doesn't make a good story. She writes about betrayal, as well as courage. About people.

Ethnicity, Universals, and a Sense of Place

Of course it's great to read about your own culture and recognize yourself in a book, especially if you have felt marginalized and demonized. The writer Jamaica Kincaid, who grew up in Antigua, talks about the joy she felt when she first read the books of fellow Caribbean Derek Walcott (the 1992 winner of the Nobel Prize for Literature): "I thought we were just the riffraff of the British Empire until I read this man and thought: 'Oh yes, that is me. That is us.'" Katha Pollitt says that, however much she hates the "self-esteem" argument, she has to admit that it meant something to her when she was growing up to find a female poet in an anthology.

But it isn't always as direct as that. Mark Mathabane remembers reading a battered copy of *Treasure Island* and realizing that there were other possibilities beyond his ghetto township. Similarly, Richard Wright, in *Black Boy,* describes how books gave him "new ways of looking and seeing," offering him hope that there was a world beyond the one in which he was trapped. "It was not a matter of believing or disbelieving what I read, but of feeling something new, of being affected by something that made the look of the world different." I love the Yiddish idiom and the shtetl setting in the stories of Isaac Bashevis Singer: he makes me laugh; he makes me remember my mother's stories and her love of Singer; and he gives me a sense of my family and who I am. But I also get immense pleasure and the shock of recognition when I read Sandra Cisneros' stories in *The House on Mango Street,* about a young Chicana girl, Esperanza, coming of age in Chicago. Esperanza says her great-grandmother "looked out of the window her whole life, the way so many women sit their sadness on an elbow." That image makes me catch my breath. It makes me think of so many women trapped at home. I remember my mother-in-law, an immigrant from Lithuania, well-educated, spirited, but a stranger, who got stuck in the rigid role prescribed for her in Cape Town's Jewish community. She used to sit like that, chin in her hands, elbows on the table, angrily watching us eat the food she'd cooked. And just as I love Cisneros, so non-Jews can find themselves in the humor and humanity of Singer's shtetl stories.

Amy Tan's *The Joy Luck Club* does give you an idea of what it's like to grow up Chinese American, and that is a good reason to read it. It's important for Asian Americans to read about themselves in books, and it's important for everybody else to read good books about them. It does show women struggling for independence, and that does give me pleasure. But it isn't reverential; the people aren't always wise and admirable. The extraordinary success of *The Joy Luck Club* has little to do with our need to know about "other" cultures. This book is a best-seller because, rooted as it is in the Chinese American experience, it explores the complexity and conflict, the love and anger, between mothers and daughters everywhere.

I was on the committee that selected Virginia Hamilton as the 1992 U.S. nominee for the international Hans Christian Andersen Award. When the nomination was announced, some people said that she didn't have a chance of world recognition because foreigners wouldn't understand her, wouldn't read her, wouldn't translate her. She was too idiomatic, too difficult, too local, they said. They were wrong. She won. And, in fact, her books have been widely read in countries like Japan for years.

We're too quick to say, "kids won't read this." We each live in a small world and talk to people like ourselves and reinforce each other, and we think everyone agrees with us. If you choose good stories and if you promote them, it's not true that books in translation or about foreign cultures are only for the "gifted," that young people won't read books with a strong sense of a foreign place. Singer says that the opposite is true, that the more a story is connected with a group, the more specific it is, the better. In an opening note to *When Shlemiel Went to Warsaw*, he says: "In our time, literature is losing its address." That's such a wonderful pun—losing its sense of place, its identity, and because of that, losing its ability to speak, to address an audience. (It's interesting that for him place isn't so much a landscape or a physical environment—"in a village some-where in the Ukraine"—it's really that idiom, that individual voice, rooted in a particular group and their way of life.) Singer says that in writing for children, he's not concerned with using only words that the child will understand. "Unknown words don't stop the child," he says. "But a boring story will." E. B. White said the same about *Charlotte's Web*. "Children are game for anything," he said. "I throw them hard words and they back-hand them over the net. They love words that give them a hard time."

It's obvious that for mainstream young people, books about "other" cultures are not as easy to pick up as *YM* magazine, or as easy to watch as "Beverly Hills 90210." And, in fact, they shouldn't be. We don't want a homogenized culture. If you're a kid in New York, then reading about a refugee in North Korea, or a teenager in the bush in Africa, or a Mormon in Utah, involves some effort, some imagination, some opening up of who you are. In talking about books with kids, I always start with a story set where they are, here and now. Then once they're listening, I move to other cultures, in this country and across the world and back again.

Stories about foreign places risk two extremes: either they can overwhelm the reader with reverential details of idiom, background, and custom; or they can homogenize the culture and turn all the characters into mall babies. There's always that tension between the particular and the universal, between making the character and experience and culture too special, and making them too much the same. On the one hand, we don't want to be bogged down in reverential details about the way of life and the deep mystical meaning of everything the protagonist sees; we don't want to wade through thickets of idiom, background, and culture before we can get to the story. And yet . . . on the other hand, the pleasures of a good story emerge most forcibly from a vividly evoked, particularized setting. Details make a world. Take *Shabanu: Daughter of the Wind* by Suzanne Fisher Staples, about a young Muslim girl living with her nomadic family in the desert of Pakistan. Shabanu has spirit and intelligence and that's dangerous in a girl, especially when at the age of 12 she's promised in marriage to an old man. As we get to care for Shabanu and what happens to her, we imagine what it must be like to be her. At the same time the story is rooted in the particulars of her culture, and the sense of her place is deeply felt. The important thing is that there's no sense of the exotic; the desert is very much there but not as scenery or travelogue. This book is remarkable in showing a sense of individual personality within a tight structure.

Glossaries and Names

When I was compiling *Somehow Tenderness Survives,* both my editor, Charlotte Zolotow, and I were reluctant to have a glossary. We felt that readers would get the meaning of strange words from context. If you know there's a glossary, it makes you stiff and wary, instead of allowing you to give yourself over to the world of the story. What persuaded us that we did need a glossary was the fact that the racist categories and racist insults needed clarification. Americans didn't know that kaffir was the worst insult, the equivalent of *nigger* here; they didn't know that *native* is derogatory. In fact, it's a sign of the shame of apartheid that it has spawned such an exact list of racist names.

This chapter started with a joke about names. And yet . . . what you call people does matter, especially in a society where groups are angry and divided. When Malcolm Little dropped the last name that had been given to his family by slave owners and took on X to stand for the "true African family name that he never could know," he was making a powerful statement about his identity. His renaming was like a rebirth: he was freeing himself from the self-hatred that kept him enslaved. To call a man a "boy," as many whites do in South Africa, is a vicious racist insult. If servants are nameless, they aren't people.

Sensationalism and Sentimentality

Books about apartheid, about slavery, about the Holocaust, can be grim. Do you give young people books about racial oppression and mass suffering? How do you evaluate such books?

Young people want to know about these things, and it is important that they know. But, whether it's fiction or nonfiction, the account shouldn't exploit the violence; it shouldn't grab attention by dwelling on sensational detail. Nor should it offer slick comfort; the Holocaust did not have a happy ending. Nor should it fall back on exhortation and rhetoric; after a while, words like *horror, atrocity,* and *terrible* cease to mean anything.

The best stories tell it from the point of view of ordinary people like Anne Frank, like us. Holocaust accounts like Ida Vos' *Hide and Seek* or Isabella Leitner's *The Big Lie* succeed through understatement, allowing the facts to speak for themselves, true to the Jewish child's bewildered point of view (Why must she wear a star? What does it mean, going into hiding?). There are no gimmicks like time travel or easy escape; no rhetoric, no tears, no hand-wringing about *atrocity* and *horror.* Stories like these defeat stereotype. They overcome the evil institution, not by making the character a heroic role model or a proud representative of the race, not by haranguing us with a worthy cause, but by making the individual a person.

AGAINST BORDERS

I have tried to take all these criteria into account in this book. At first I felt overwhelmed by the demands of political correctness. How was I going to choose the "right" books for the essays and resource lists? The watchdogs from right, left, and center would pounce: How could you put that in? How could you leave that out? Even with my great editors and wise advisers and consultants, there were going to be so many *problems.*

My husband is a long-time apartheid fighter. "Not *problems,*" he said. "*Riches.*"

And that's really the point about the whole multicultural debate. When I lived under apartheid, I thought I was privileged—and compared with the physical suffering of black people I was immeasurably well-off—but my life was impoverished. I was blind, and I was frightened. I was shut in. And I was denied access to the stories and music of the world. Groups like Ladysmith Black Mambazo were making music right there, and I couldn't hear them. I didn't know that in the streets of Soweto there were people like Nelson Mandela with a vision of nonracial democracy that would change my life. I was ignorant, and I didn't know I was ignorant. I thought I was better than someone like Mark Mathabane's mother because she spoke English with an accent; I didn't know that she and others like her were fluent in multiple languages. I didn't know anything about most of the people around me. And because of that I didn't know what *I* could be.

Borders shut us in, in Johannesburg, in Los Angeles and Chicago, in Eastern Europe, in our own imaginations.

PART ONE

Themes

Journeys
Across
Cultures

"And where we had thought to find an abomination, we shall find a god; where we had thought to slay another, we shall slay ourselves; where we had thought to travel outward, we shall come to the center of our own existence; where we had thought to be alone, we shall be with all the world."

—Joseph Campbell

"'Is there anybody there?' said the Traveler, Knocking on the moonlit door."

—Walter de la Mare

THE PERILOUS JOURNEY

"People surprise you." My father, Maurice Fine, always said that. We put those words on his tombstone. The religious authorities wanted us to use an orthodox Hebrew text; they said that his phrase would be misunderstood, that it could imply that people show unexpected evil as well as good. "He meant that, too," we said. "About others and about himself." That continuous transformation, that openness to the unexpected is the essence of the perilous journey.

Everyone has to go on a vision quest. Whether the journey's a physical adventure across the snows of Alaska or a fantasy flight through time and space or a search for identity alone at home, the old stories—from *The Odyssey* to *Exodus* to *Hansel and Gretel*—get retold again and again. On the archetypal journey, you leave home and encounter monsters and undergo trials and rites; you return from the journey transformed into your heroic self. There's an enduring appeal in the action stories of escape and survival, whether on the Underground Railroad or through the sewers of the Warsaw Ghetto or anywhere across the border at dawn. But the hero's journey is also close to home: it may be the turning of a corner to discover a whole new view of what you took for granted. You may be traveling far when you make a new friend or when you break free from a paralyzing view of yourself.

There are endless variations, from Meg's fantastic journey to fight the forces of evil in Madeleine L'Engle's *A Wrinkle in Time,* to Douglas Adams' *A Hitchhiker's Guide to the Galaxy.* Or the quest may take you to a dead end. It may lead you into exile or into the darkness of Hades. Some of the best realistic stories use the journey to emphasize stasis. In Amy Ehrlich's *Where it Stops, Nobody Knows* and in Walter Dean Myers' *Somewhere in the Darkness,* the teenager and parent are rushing all over the place, speeding across the country from one state to another, and imprisoning themselves ever deeper in the labyrinth. In contrast, the teenager in Zibby Oneal's *In Summer Light* seems immobilized, under a spell, lethargic, as she recovers from mononucleosis in her parents' island home; yet she's breaking free from the obsession that has kept her from becoming herself. In many coming-of-age stories, young people wake from innocence (and ignorance) to the truth about themselves and the world they've always taken for granted.

STUCK

Before you can wake from ignorance to truth, from innocence to experience, before you can escape that paralyzing view of yourself, you have to become "unstuck." Perilous journeys usually start in stasis, with the hero-to-be trapped. The poem below expresses the teenager's sense of being stuck. The narrator feels that he's shut in, that everything is happening somewhere else. Home, school, neighborhood, friends, are only something to escape from.

SATURDAY AT THE CANAL
by Gary Soto

I was hoping to be happy by seventeen.
School was a sharp check mark in the roll book,
An obnoxious tuba playing at noon because our team
Was going to win at night. The teachers were
Too close to dying to understand. The hallways
Stank of poor grades and unwashed hair. Thus,
A friend and I sat watching the water on Saturday,
Neither of us talking much, just warming ourselves
By hurling large rocks at the dusty ground
And feeling awful because San Francisco was a postcard
On a bedroom wall. We wanted to go there,
Hitchhike under the last migrating birds
And be with people who knew more than three chords
On a guitar. We didn't drink or smoke,
But our hair was shoulder length, wild when
The wind picked up and the shadows of
This loneliness gripped loose dirt. By bus or car,
By the sway of train over a long bridge,
We wanted to get out. The years froze
As we sat on the bank. Our eyes followed the water,
White-tipped but dark underneath, racing out of town.

Even the happiest person feels that way sometimes, and, in fact, it's a natural stage of breaking away from childhood. As Soto says, "We wanted to get out." For the immigrant child, for someone who feels on the margin, the sense of being stuck outside, with your nose pressed against the pane, may be especially intense. You feel that nothing about you could be worth writing about. For the young person, caught in an unhappy family or a repressive community, the confinement can be overwhelming.

James Baldwin's autobiographical novel *Go Tell It on the Mountain* is candid about the way family conflicts can be a trap that holds you fast. In one scene, teenage John comes home to find that his older brother, Roy, has been stabbed in a gang fight with whites. For a naked moment John sees that his father wishes it were he, John, who had been hurt and not the favored elder son. John meets his sister in the hallway, and he hates the way she's relishing the excitement.

James Baldwin. *Go Tell It on the Mountain.* Gr. 8–12

> "What happened?" he whispered.
>
> She stared at him in astonishment, and a certain wild joy. He thought again that he really did not like his sister. Catching her breath, she blurted out, triumphantly: "Roy got stabbed with a knife!" and rushed into the living-room.
>
> Roy got stabbed with a knife. Whatever this meant, it was sure that his father would be at his worst tonight. John walked slowly into the living-room.
>
> Then his father turned and looked at him.
>
> "Where you been, boy," he shouted, "all this time? Don't you know you's needed here at home?"
>
> More than his words, his face caused John to stiffen instantly with malice and fear. His father's face was terrible in anger, but now there was more than anger in it. John saw now what he had never seen there before, except in his own vindictive fantasies: a kind of wild, weeping terror that made the face seem younger, and yet at the same time unutterably older and more cruel. And John knew, in the moment his father's eyes swept over him, that he hated John because John was not lying on the sofa where Roy lay. John could scarcely meet his father's eyes, and yet, briefly, he did, saying nothing, feeling in his heart an odd sensation of triumph, and hoping in his heart that Roy, to bring his father low, would die.

John goes into his parents' bedroom and picks up his squalling baby sister, Ruth, whom he loves. She stops crying, and he laughs as he whispers to her to run far away from that house as soon as she can. "He did not quite know why he said this, or where he wanted her to run, but it made him feel instantly better." The trouble in that house imprisons the children. John knows he, like his baby sister, must leave.

Politics imprisons teenage Marta in her father's house in Lyll Becerra de Jenkins' autobiographical novel, *The Honorable Prison*, which is set in a Latin American country under military dictatorship in the 1950s.

On the first page Marta is in school:

Lyll Becerra de Jenkins. *The Honorable Prison.* Gr. 7–12

> Today is a day like any other day. From inside the convent we hear the police whistles, shooting, the wailing of an ambulance siren, and silence . . . My classmates look at me and I wonder, whom did they shoot today? Did the military police discover the secret place where my father and his friends gather daily to print their newspaper? Will I see my father this evening?

Because of her father's newspaper editorials attacking the regime, Marta and her family are placed under house arrest in a remote village guarded by an army post. Official terror beats down the country; violence is all around them. Inside their dreary house, Marta and her family struggle to survive. Her father is sick, and the damp climate makes his chest worse. Slowly, as the medicine runs out, the sound of his cough becomes as persistent as his typing; and then there is only his cough, filling the house all the time. Marta loves and admires her father, but at the same time she's angry at the suffering his political ideals have caused them. For brief moments she even wishes he'd die, so that they can go free. As food gets scarce and hope and courage fail, she tries to hold on to her humanity and to understand her father's ideals: "Every individual . . . has a responsibility for the events of his time."

This is the best kind of political fiction. Without preaching, without lessening the monster outside, Jenkins is candid about the conflict inside one girl, stuck in the house. However political the story, however different the culture from our own, the language of intimacy is recognizable to all of us, just as we all feel the conflicting needs for love and freedom, security and adventure.

Sometimes you may think you've left home, but you're just spinning your wheels. You can be as trapped on the street as in the family kitchen.

Rita Williams-Garcia. *Fast Talk on a Slow Track.* Gr. 8–12

Denzel Watson is going nowhere fast in Williams-Garcia's *Fast Talk on a Slow Track.* Growing up in the '90s, valedictorian in his New York City high school, he's always had everything easy. Fast and smooth, he skates through the high school academic and social scene "achieving the most while expending the least." But then he fails at Princeton's summer program for minority students, and he doesn't dare tell his middle-class parents that their "firstborn son and Black man on campus" has decided not to go to college. They hate his summer job selling candy door to door, and they hate the friends he makes on the street. Denzel loves his family, but he laughs at their snobbery. He can't stand the way his dad is always going on about the "struggle" and about "roots." His African name, Dinizulu, embarrasses him. He gets on with whites better than his father does. Yet his failure haunts him. Will he stay on the street or crawl back to college? Who is he? Where is he going?

Denzel locks himself in by refusing to commit to anything. That's one way to do it, but the possibilities are endless: we are our own worst jailers:

LOCKED IN

by Ingemar Leckius

All my life I lived in a coconut.
It was cramped and dark,
especially in the morning when I had to shave.
But what pained me most was that I had no way
to get in touch with the outside world.
If no one out there happened to find the coconut,
if no one cracked it, then I was doomed
to live all my life in the nut, and maybe even die there . . .
A person who chooses to live in a coconut!
Such a person is one in a million!
But I have a brother-in-law who
lives in an
acorn.

Swedish poet Leckius is mocking those who shut themselves off from other worlds and live a "cramped" and fearful existence in the darkness. Nadine Gordimer does the same thing in her short story "Once Upon a Time," showing how white South Africans carefully make their own concentration camp. As the title of the story implies, Gordimer is deliberately playing with images from fairy tales, especially "Sleeping Beauty." A privileged white Johannesburg family tries to shut out the threatening black violence by building higher and higher walls around themselves, walls topped with spikes and lethal barbed wire. They try to shut themselves in and enjoy their gracious home behind a forest of thorns. In a shocking ending, their own child is impaled on the spikes when he tries to climb the wall.

Nadine Gordimer. "Once Upon a Time." Gr. 9–12

The sleeping beauty metaphor also underlies Doris Lessing's brilliant short story "The Old Chief Mshlanga." The protected white child on the southern African farm is blind to the world around her and to the racist evil she's grown up with. It's as if the young girl is under a spell, suspended, her eyes closed. She doesn't see blacks as people; they're just "natives," servants in the background. When she's shocked awake, she recognizes not only the way whites grabbed the land and dehumanized black people, but also that you can't live happily ever after and put everything right again with just "an easy gush of feeling."

Doris Lessing. "The Old Chief Mshlanga." Gr. 8–12

The image of a magic spell is a powerful way of showing someone held fast by obsession. In Zibby Oneal's *In Summer Light,* the teenage girl is so overwhelmed by her artist father and by her resentment of his domineering presence in her life that she's immobilized, unable to develop her own talent and break free. Oneal says that she didn't realize until long after she had written the book that she was retelling the old story of Sleeping Beauty. In her acceptance speech for the 1986 Boston Globe–Horn Book Award, Oneal describes teenage Kate as dozing, "hedged all around by a thorny tangle of childhood memories . . . among the thorns and brambles of the family thicket." Oneal makes a fascinating point about Kate's apparent passivity. "Growing up is not a passive undertaking," she says. Kate's journey is a quiet, dreaming, inward one. It may look as if she's doing nothing compared with the heroes who go off and slay dragons, "but who is to say that the dragons encountered are not equally fearsome or that the arrival at the destination has not been just as dearly won?"

Zibby Oneal. *In Summer Light.* Gr. 7–12

You don't have to stay in one place to get stuck. Sometimes you can be running away so hard that the farther you travel, the deeper and deeper you imprison yourself in the labyrinth. Nina Lewis and her mother, in Amy Ehrlich's *Where It Stops, Nobody Knows,* travel thousands of miles across the country, but they're trapped. Nina has grown up strong and independent, alone with her single-parent mother, Joyce. They love each other, and they give each other space. "We had secrets," Nina says. "But we were so close that we needed our secrets." Nina has never questioned why they have to move so much—always packing up their van and driving to a new town, a new job for Joyce, yet another new school for Nina to blend into. Then, when she's in eighth grade, and they've come down from Alaska to a town in Vermont, Nina gets to like a boy, Sam Gordon, and he makes her ask questions. Why can't she play on the basketball team? Why won't her mother let her make close friends? Why are they always moving? As they rush away from Vermont, then from Utah, then from Venice, California, their journey becomes more and more frantic, their closeness imprisoning. They can no longer

Amy Ehrlich. *Where It Stops, Nobody Knows.* Gr. 5–10

pretend that their "crazy dance" is normal. They hole up in New York City, and Joyce's shattering secret is revealed when the police come.

Ehrlich's thriller is also about the mysteries of intimacy and family bonds. Nina tells the story in a candid, unpretentious voice, and the writing style is simple, accessible at a fifth-grade reading level. Yet it expresses complex feelings and a precise sense of place—a great variety of places, in fact, from the mountains at sunset to a crowded McDonald's parking lot. Sometimes an image fuses outer landscape and inner experience with startling clarity. There's the terror when Joyce breaks down and cries in front of Nina for the first time ever: at a rest-stop, really only a wide spot on the road with overflowing trash-barrels, "she turned off the ignition and threw herself onto the steering wheel like she was throwing herself into someone's arms."

There's no preaching. Everything is dramatized, seen from Nina's sometimes bewildered point of view. All the moving has been hard on Nina, but it's also meant adventure. Living in so many places has made her broad-minded, and she can see beyond the surface clichés of fashion and culture. Unlike those bound by regional stereotypes, she can respond to the kindness of a hippie and to a Mormon and to a lonely child in Brooklyn.

Nina is a survivor, strong and humane, nurtured by Joyce's love. But the story is filled with sadness. Through all the wandering—the Travelodges, the truck stops, the shabby rooms, the freight trains that pass in the night—is the loneliness of those who are far away from home, stuck on the road but going nowhere.

ON THE THRESHOLD

Intense battles are fought in the labyrinth of the family, where mentors and monsters are transformed as the young person comes of age. The most dramatic journey may be the step across the kitchen door to the street outside. Your adventures may be just beginning, but you are already on the threshold of a new view of home and of yourself.

Joyce Carol Oates. "Where Are You Going, Where Have You Been?" Gr. 8–12

Joyce Carol Oates' "Where Are You Going, Where Have You Been?" is one of the most astonishing stories about the teenager's journey. Connie is restless, fighting with her nagging mother ("Who do you think you are?"), hanging out at the mall with her friends. One day, when she's alone at home, a guy, Arnold Friend, comes by in his car. He's dangerous. She's scared he'll come in the house and hurt her. She stands in the kitchen doorway, on the threshold of her parents' home, while he tempts her to come riding with him. Kids get this story, from the familiar nagging cadences of the title, to the terrifying ambiguity of Connie's choice between home and danger. It's also been made into a powerful film, *Smooth Talk*, starring Laura Dern and Treat Williams. Darlene Mc-Campbell, English teacher at the University of Chicago Lab School, says that her classes respond to the immediacy of Connie's conflict and its contemporary setting, to the elemental choice between the safety of home and the lure of danger outside. Kids are also amazed to see how our most casual, daily words hold the intense power of myth.

Oates' story can be used with the poem "Cinderella" by Gwen Strauss. Here Cinderella is transformed, not by a fairy godmother but by passion.

After meeting the prince at the ball, she half wishes she could go back to childhood ("I would go backwards if I could"). Part of her wants to stay stuck on the hearth in the ashes:

> Mother, no one prepared me for this—
> For the soft heat of a man's neck when he dances
> Or the thickness of his arms.

Gwen Strauss.
Trail of Stones.
Gr. 7–12

In Jamaica Kincaid's *Annie John,* the split between mother and daughter, tearingly painful as it is, frees Annie John to make her own way. Growing up on the Caribbean island of Antigua, Annie changes from a happy secure child to a defiant teenager. Annie and her mother used to adore each other. Now they are fighting, and their quarrels are fierce and painful. Kincaid shows the conflict between mother and daughter and the conflict within Annie herself, and we see that Annie rebels because she feels her mother is rejecting her. After one of their wounding quarrels, in which her mother has called Annie a slut for hanging around with boys and Annie has replied, "Well . . . like mother, like daughter," Annie feels an almost physical barrier separating her from her mother:

Jamaica Kincaid.
Annie John.
Gr. 9–12

> I wanted to go over and put my arms around her and
> beg forgiveness for the thing I had just said and to explain
> that I didn't really mean it. But I couldn't move, and when
> I looked down it was as if the ground had opened up
> between us, making a deep and wide split.

Afterwards, alone in her room:

> My heart just broke, and I cried and cried. At that
> moment, I missed my mother more than I had ever
> imagined possible and wanted only to live somewhere
> quiet and beautiful with her alone, but also at that mo-
> ment I wanted only to see her lying dead, all withered and
> in a coffin at my feet.

In Amy Tan's *The Joy Luck Club,* the mother-daughter quarrel has a different focus but reflects the same intense ambiguity about breaking free. This is the world of Chinese Americans, interwoven stories of mothers and daughters, caught between two cultures, their loving bonds and ugly conflicts.

Amy Tan. *The Joy Luck Club.*
Gr. 8–12

Jing-Mei's story exemplifies the burden on the immigrant child who has to succeed for her parent and fulfill all her mother's failed dreams. (The children of Holocaust survivors talk about this same burden to be happy and successful, the need to make up for their relatives' suffering):

> My mother believed you could be anything you wanted
> to be in America. You could open a restaurant. You could
> work for the government and get good retirement. You
> could buy a house with almost no money down. You could
> become rich. You could become instantly famous.
> "Of course you can be prodigy, too," my mother told me
> when I was nine. "You can be best anything . . ."
> America was where all my mother's hopes lay. She had
> come here in 1949 after losing everything in China: her
> mother and father, her family home, her first husband,

and two daughters, twin baby girls. But she never looked back with regret. There were so many ways for things to get better.

We didn't immediately pick the right kind of prodigy. At first my mother thought I could be a Chinese Shirley Temple.

Then her mother decides that Jing-Mei will be a *musical* prodigy, and they start her on piano lessons. But she hates the way her mother pushes her. Part of her wants to fail to spite her mother. After a catastrophe at a public piano recital, they face off:

"You want me to be someone I'm not!" I sobbed. "I'll never be the kind of daughter you want me to be!"

"Only two kinds of daughters," she shouted in Chinese. "Those who are obedient and those who follow their own mind! Only one kind of daughter can live in this house. Obedient daughter!"

"Then I wish I wasn't your daughter. I wish you weren't my mother," I shouted.

The struggle doesn't suddenly end there. She goes on to say:

It was not the only disappointment my mother felt in me. In the years that followed, I failed her so many times, each time asserting my own will, my right to fall short of expectations. I didn't get straight As. I didn't become class president. I didn't get into Stanford. I dropped out of college.

For unlike my mother, I did not believe I could be anything I wanted to be. I could only be me.

Ilene Cooper.
Choosing Sides.
Gr. 4–8

The boy in Ilene Cooper's *Choosing Sides* has to free himself from his father's expectations in order to get on with his life. With considerable pain, Jonathan stands up for himself and tells his father that he doesn't want to play on the basketball team:

"Is this really how you feel about basketball?" he asked in disbelief.

Jonathan nodded mutely and braced himself for what was coming next.

Mr. Rossi merely slumped in his chair, however, and said, "I knew you were frustrated for a while . . . " His words trailed off. Then he asked, "What are you going to do?"

"What do you think I should do?"

Mr. Rossi stayed silent for a long time. "A month ago, I would have forbidden you to quit. But I see you changing every day now, Jon." He shook his head. "I think you know my opinion about playing and doing your best, but you have to make your own choices. And then live with them."

Jonathan leaned forward and tried to explain. "Playing isn't any fun for me, Dad."

"Fun isn't always the most important thing in the world."

"Well, maybe fun isn't what I meant."

Jonathan searched for the right words.

> "Basketball makes me feel like I'm all tied up. My head, my body, my time, too, I guess.
>
> "That's not a good way to feel," Mr. Rossi said.
>
> "No, it stinks," Jonathan murmured.
>
> Mr. Rossi folded and refolded his hands. "It sounds to me as if you've made your decision."
>
> "I guess so." He said it so quietly, he could hardly hear the words himself. He waited to see what else his father would say, but Mr. Rossi just stared at the television set. Finally, Jonathan got up and walked out of the room. He went to the closet and threw on his coat. Then he went outside.
>
> The air was cold, but it felt good on Jonathan's face. He started walking, even though he wasn't sure where he was headed. When he came to a yard where a father and his little boy were making a snowman, Jonathan stopped and watched for a few seconds. Then he forced himself to move on.
>
> Telling his father he was quitting the basketball team was about the hardest thing he had ever done. And he knew that he hadn't heard the end of it—once his father got over the shock. There was also the matter of letting the coach and his teammates know he was off the team. That wouldn't be easy, either. Right now, though, despite all the sad feelings inside of him, there was also a lightness he hadn't felt in a long time.
>
> A whole vacation stretched in front of him, filled with all kinds of possibilities. After his walk, he would ask his mother to call Aunt Janice to confirm the arrangements for his trip. Then he would start on one of those books on his nightstand he'd been longing to read. Jonathan stopped his rambling and headed toward home. There were a lot of things he wanted to do.

Jonathan has literally stepped across the threshold. At the same time, he has also taken a gigantic inner step toward finding his own way home. What gives this story its special power is that Cooper makes clear how hard it is to take that step away from home. There's always loss.

Sometimes the break from innocence can happen from one moment to the next. Avi's *Wolf Rider* is a taut YA thriller in which a boy's life is transformed by a phone call. This is how the book begins:

Avi. *Wolf Rider*.
Gr. 5–10

> The kitchen phone rang three times before Andy picked it up. "Hello?" he said.
>
> A voice replied, "I just killed someone."
>
> "What?"
>
> "I just killed someone."
>
> "I don't understand," said Andy.
>
> "I have to tell . . . "
>
> "Who is this?" Andy demanded.
>
> "I killed Nina."

"You killed . . . Nina," Andy echoed. From across the kitchen his friend Paul—who had just arrived—was staring at him. They were on their way to a party.

The voice said, "What should I do?" It was a male voice, low, flat.

Andy pulled a chair over to the table and sat down. He said into the phone. "I don't get it."

"I killed her," the voice continued. "Now I don't know what to do . . . I loved her."

From that moment, Andy's life is changed. He tries to warn people, but no one believes him. Not the police. Not Nina, who isn't dead—not yet. Not his own father. Andy's alone in a kind of limbo, trying to find what he must do.

ESCAPE

Once over the threshold, the hero's adventures begin, and with adventure comes peril and the need to escape and survive. Filled with risk and excitement, survival stories are always popular, from science fiction and fantasy to physical adventure and war stories, with their clear separation between the good guys and the evil empire.

Stories of rugged adventure often set the individual alone in the wilderness. But even when the perilous journey is a physical one and the trials are cold and hunger and isolation, writers like Jack London and Gary Paulsen combine wild adventure and precise observation with intensely private discovery.

Gary Paulsen.
Woodsong.
Gr. 6–12

In Paulsen's best book, his autobiographical *Woodsong*, he writes about his fierce, beautiful experience with sleds and dogs, first in northern Minnesota where he lives and then in 17 grueling days with his 15-dog team in the Iditarod race. Despite occasional inflated messages about "life" and about "blood," the stories ring with truth. The language is stark as he describes big, near-mystical experiences in the snow and wind; he also shows a lightness of touch and a self-deprecating sense of humor (even about his great vision quest); in fact, there are episodes of outright farce, both in his domestic barnyard and in the Alaskan tundra. He's candid about the boredom and mundane detail (including "gastric distress" from gorging on moose chili) and about the wild hallucinations that come with sleep deprivation. The nature lore woven into the narrative celebrates the special world of the woods: the grouse's eggs that lie cuddled in the nest; the bears hungry beyond caution; the goats whuffing and blowing snot; the high keening wail and whoop of the loon. And always there's the image of Paulsen sleeping in a tent at 35 below, warmed by the dogs jamming into the sides of his sleeping bag. The ending is subtle and astonishing: not wanting to finish the race, barely able to speak to people anymore, he nearly turns the sled around to go back into the tundra: only his wife's shout breaks the spell.

Like adventure stories, many realistic war-refugee stories about kids dramatize the young person having to survive alone without parental protection or adult authority. The appeal of these adventures lies in the romantic side of the secure kid's nightmare: What if I got lost? What if an enemy came and tore apart my home? The bad guys are out there, and we, people like us, the good guys, often civilians, often children, have to get away from them, beat them, survive, escape, triumph in hard times. The English writer Robert Westall remembers World War II in Britain as an exciting time for many civilians. He candidly admits that, despite the fear, there was a thrilling sense of danger in ordinary life, of boring routine disrupted. A good way to introduce world cultures is to read a World War II adventure story, with its apparently clear division between good (us) and evil (them).

Ian Serraillier's *Escape from Warsaw* is an immensely satisfying, romantic account of ordinary young civilians caught up in the war as refugees, forced to fend for themselves without adults. Based on a true story, it's about a family in Nazi-occupied Warsaw. For disrespect to Hitler, the schoolmaster father, Joseph Balicki, is sent to a concentration camp. Then one day the young people, Ruth, Edek, and Bronia Balicki, watch as the Nazis come to take their mother. Edek runs up to the attic where he has a gun hidden:

Ian Serraillier. *Escape from Warsaw.* Gr. 5–7

> The noise in the room below had stopped. Looking out of the window into the street, he saw a Nazi van awaiting outside the front door. Two storm troopers were taking his mother down the steps, and she was struggling.
>
> Quietly Edek lifted the window sash till it was half open. He dared not shoot in case he hit his mother. He had to wait till she was in the van and the doors were being closed.
>
> His first shot hit a soldier in the arm. Yelling, he jumped in beside the driver. With the next two shots Edek aimed at the tyres. One punctured the rear wheel, but the van got away, skidding and roaring up the street. His other shots went wide.

An hour later the soldiers come back and blow up the house. Everyone assumes the young people are killed. When their father escapes from the prison camp and returns to find his home a heap of rubble, the neighbors tell him what happened. His children had not been seen since the explosion. But, in fact, they have worked out a daring escape and are surviving in the ruins of the city.

Another refugee adventure based on a true story, Tamar Bergman's *Along the Tracks,* tells of a small Jewish boy on the run in Russia during World War II. The Holocaust terror is in the background as the cause of the dislocation, but the focus is on the escape adventure, horrifying and savage at times, but exciting and ultimately triumphant. At first, Yankele and his parents are among a mass of refugees rushing across the border from Poland into Russia; but at eight years old, he's separated from them, and for more than four years, he wanders thousands of miles searching for his mother, scavenging, thieving, riding the tracks, sometimes with gangs of abandoned children, often on his own. His narrative voice changes from naive, stubborn child to wild, street-smart tough. The story is full of dramatic scenes to read aloud: the train bombing that separates him from his family in the snow; the facts of what he eats; how he keeps warm; how he tricks the authorities. Junior high readers will enjoy every gritty detail.

Tamar Bergman. *Along the Tracks.* Gr. 6–10

Translated from the Russian with spare beauty, the graphic, interconnected stories in Ephraim Sevela's *We Were Not Like Other People* extend

Ephraim Sevela.
*We Were Not
Like Other
People.*
Gr. 8–12

the survival-adventure genre. For this title, translator Antonina Bouis was chosen as the 1992 U.S. Hans Christian Andersen Award nominee for the international honor list. The stories about a young refugee during World War II combine an intrepid hero and fierce, sometimes cruel action with complex characters, a delight in the absurd, and compassion for human frailty under stress.

The narrator (we never learn his name) dates the end of his childhood to 1937, during the Stalinist purges when he is nine years old and the secret police come for his army-commander father. Over the next eight years, he's alone, often on the run, from the Urals to Siberia and the German front, in orphanages and vocational schools, laboring in factories with other child-adults, scavenging, hungry, many times near death.

He's a liar, a thief, and a survivor, but he's also vulnerable, yearning for home. Most other refugees give him little help: "I thought that the suffering they were going through had made them deaf and that the only thing they could hear was their own footsteps." Yet again and again, like the fairy tale hero, he finds a mentor, usually comic, who restores him physically and shows him what is morally right: "We both decided that there were a few good people in the world," he says of an old soldier who becomes his guide.

Several of Sevela's stories will make riveting read-alouds. There's the Stalinist episode, where the boy is urged to betray his own parents. Or there's the segment about the funny, old geography teacher who refuses to leave the injured boy during an air raid, cursing him affectionately ("Worthless child . . . Icthyosaurus, Neanderthal"), keeping the boy from slipping into unconsciousness by making him imagine a precise journey across the sea from London to Sydney. Or there's the grim scene with the child factory workers in their dormitory, curling up together in fetal positions to keep warm, raging at each other for dreaming aloud about food.

Once an activist Jewish dissident, Sevela now lives in Israel, and the Jewish experience, especially with anti-Semitism, is a quiet thread throughout his work. The prelude is by far the most brutal story, detailing how the narrator helps a fellow child-laborer cut off his hand to avoid the infernal factory. Yet Sevela is neither exploitive nor sentimental. His words are strong and controlled. (A soldier at the front thinks of his near-starving family: "I know things are tight for you. But how can I help? I'm far. We have nothing ourselves.") The surprising twists in plot stem as much from the muddled truth of the human condition as from the accidents of war. The background for the boy's first sexual experience is the burgeoning Siberian harvest ("the grass could grow to the sky") and also the mourning of the women harvesters whose husbands are not coming back. As a child at home, the boy wishes his formidable mother would kiss and hold him; as a refugee, he can never remember any demonstration of affection from her, but at the end when they find each other after the years of separation, it is he, the young man of 17, who stops her from embracing him: "It would have been too much."

There's a compulsion, especially in books for young people, to give these stories a happy ending, to tell stories of heroism, sacrifice, and escape without the context of terror and mass murder. However enjoyable and inspiring and comforting the escape stories of survival and adventure, it's important to place them in context and not to transform the suffering into soap opera. Junior high and high school readers are open to the truth. The Holocaust did not have a happy ending. The concentration camps were extermination camps: the liberators found mounds of tangled corpses. The other pitfall to avoid is that of sensationalism. It's easy to get attention by dwelling on scenes of violence and then adding a self-righteous message. The best war-survivor stories humanize the statistics without exploiting the suffering.

There's the drama of escape but no romantic adventure in Sook Nyul Choi's *Year of Impossible Goodbyes*, an autobiographical novel about a child in North Korea during and after World War II—first, under Japanese military oppression; then, after 1945, under Russian occupation; and finally, on the run across the border. The last third of the book is the most gripping, as 10-year-old Sookan, her little brother, Inchun, and their mother flee from their town, hoping to reach Sookan's father in South Korea. Their guide turns out to be a double agent, and their mother is captured. The two children wander alone through the rain and mud of the rice paddies, filthy, hungry, bruised, sobbing. A few adults help them and show them the way past the dogs and searchlights. To cross the tracks, Sookan and Inchun crawl under a train while it's in the station. To cross a rushing river, they drag themselves across the rungs of a dangerous railway bridge. They tear their backs on the frontier barbed wire. Choi communicates the overwhelming physical experience of these once-protected small children who find themselves suddenly alone. We feel their dazed terror, their exhaustion and weakness, as well as the astonishing determination that somehow gets them across.

So Far from the Bamboo Grove by Yoko Kawashima Watkins, again fictionalized autobiography, is also an escape story about ordinary people caught up in terrible times. As World War II ends, 11-year-old Japanese Yoko and her family, who have been living in North Korea, become refugees, in deadly danger from the soldiers of the new regime. Rooted as this story is in a vividly evoked place with strongly individualized characters, it stands for the refugee experience anywhere—homeless, separated, struggling for food, shelter, safety.

Not only does Watkins vividly depict young people on the run, she does so with complete honesty and a lack of false sensitivity. The ending, like so many in life, is neither happy nor tragic, merely attenuated. The two sisters do manage to get back to Japan, but no one cares much about them there, either.

In Kerop Bedoukian's *Some of Us Survived* and David Kherdian's *The Road from Home*, the theme is again young people's perilous escapes, but the scene has changed from Korea after World War II to the Middle East in 1915, the time of the Turkish massacre of Armenians. Bedoukian remembers himself as a young boy avid to see things, treating the brutal deportation march as an adventure, making a game of following the corpse collectors during a typhus epidemic. The poet David Kherdian speaks with restraint of his mother's experience of the persecution, focusing on the bonds of affection that sustained her and ending with her coming to America at 16 in an arranged marriage.

Whether it's Japan, Korea, Poland, or Turkey, what's compelling in these books is the fact that their young heroes are "like me." What if they came and dragged my mother away to a concentration camp? How would I survive as a refugee?

The teenager in Uri Orlev's *The Man from the Other Side* makes us confront a moral conflict: How much would I risk to help someone else escape? Translated from the Hebrew, Orlev's story (which won the 1992

Sook Nyul Choi. *Year of Impossible Goodbyes.* Gr. 6–10

Yoko Kawashima Watkins. *So Far from the Bamboo Grove.* Gr. 6–10

Kerop Bedoukian. *Some of Us Survived.* Gr. 7–12

David Kherdian. *The Road from Home.* Gr. 7–12

Uri Orlev. *The Man from the Other Side.* Gr. 6–12

Batchelder Award for best book in translation) is a fast-paced escape thriller; it's also about idealism, courage, and betrayal. Marek is a teenager in Warsaw during World War II. He doesn't know much or care about the Jews who've been walled up in a ghetto by the Nazis. At first he thinks it's an adventure to go with his stepfather down into the filthy sewers beneath the city and smuggle food and arms to the desperate Jews. Sometimes they smuggle people out of the ghetto, to save them from the death camps. His stepfather doesn't particularly like Jews, not in the abstract, anyway; most of the time, he does it for money. Then, one day in a church in Warsaw, Marek sees a man cross himself—the wrong way, backward—and he realizes the man is a Jew. Marek helps him hide and keeps him safe and gets to like him. Then when the Jews in the ghetto rise up against the Nazis, the Jewish fugitive wants to be part of that brave and desperate uprising, and he makes Marek take him back through the sewers to join the rooftop battle.

DESCENT INTO HELL

What makes escape stories exciting, of course, is the omnipresent fear of getting caught. History and mythology are full of examples of what happens when you get caught: Hector tortured, humiliated, and brutally killed by a vengeful Achilles; Africans sold to slavery; and our modern symbol of nightmare, a visit from the Gestapo followed by a journey to the camps and the ovens.

Getting caught usually occasions a journey of its own, but it is the very opposite of the Perilous Journey to a new self. Instead, it's a descent into Hell, an enforced journey away from one's destination and toward darkness and imprisonment. The African slave's journey is the archetypal example, in both history and myth: the capture and total exile from family and home; the close imprisonment in chains in the hold of the ship; the labors and suffering in America; and the separation of family and loved ones. Millions died on the way to America and after they arrived. None went back. Then came the second journey, where the individual was able to take some responsibility: the running away (either real or visionary), often with the help of conductors on the Underground Railroad; and, for some, the arrival in the promised land. The first journey, the kidnapping and coming to America, though, means the opposite of adventure. It means being forced apart from family and home and choice. It means being stuck in the deepest hole of all.

Virginia Hamilton. *Many Thousand Gone.* Gr. 5–10

In *Many Thousand Gone,* Virginia Hamilton combines general history with direct quotes from personal slave narratives and biography. Designed as a companion to *The People Could Fly* (discussion follows), the book has the same striking style of illustrations by Leo and Diane Dillon. Sometimes the prose has a spare lyricism, like a story told over and over ("Heard tell that on the other side, a slave is . . . a free man"). Often the telling is more direct, allowing the dramatic facts to speak for themselves: the sheer numbers, the stark despair (like the case of Margaret Garner who killed her child rather than have her captured back into slavery), the grim account of rebellions put down with ruthless barbarity. Hamilton's focus is also on those who escaped and helped others escape: the famous, such as Frederick Douglass, Sojourner Truth, Anthony

Burns, and Harriet Tubman, and also obscure men and women who were slaves and "running-aways," rebels and conductors.

Perhaps the most moving part of the book, though, is when the slaves and escapees speak for themselve. Here Hamilton quotes from *The Interesting Narrative of the Life of Olaudah Equiana, or Gustavau Vassa*, published in London in 1789. At the age of 11, in 1745, he was captured from his home in Benin, Nigeria, sold to slave traders, and taken on a slave ship to the West Indies. Years later he wrote about the ship:

> I was soon put down under the decks and was greeted by such a stench as I had never experienced in my life. I became so sick and low that I was not able to eat, nor had I the least desire to taste anything.
>
> Soon, to my grief, two of the white men offered me eatables and, on my refusing to eat, one of them held me fast by the hands, and laid me across, I think, the windless, and tied my feet, while the other flogged me severely.
>
> I had never experienced anything of this kind before ... (and) in a little time after, amongst the poor chained men, I found some of my own nation ... I feared I should be put to death, the white people looked and acted, as I thought, in so savage a manner. I asked my countrymen if these white people had no country, but lived in this hollow place (the ship)? They told me that they did not, but came from a distant one.
>
> "Then how comes it in all our country we never heard of them?" I asked. They told me because they lived so very far off.

Hamilton says that on that journey across the ocean from Africa to America (it became known as the Middle Passage) 30 percent of the slaves did not survive. Still others tried to drown themselves as soon as the ship docked. Accessible to middle graders, this powerful history will draw older readers, too. It makes us all want to know more, much more, about those many thousand gone.

In *Ajeemah and His Son*, a searing combination of fact and fiction, James Berry describes what it was like to be a slave, to become someone's property. Ajeemah and his son Atu are kidnapped and sold in West Africa, never to see home or family again. After the bitter journey to Jamaica, they are separated forever, sold off to plantations 20 miles apart. Each sustains himself with memories of home, and each dreams of revenge and escape. The son's rebellion ends in heartbreak, flogging, suicide. The father is betrayed, but he survives to marry, sire a daughter, and celebrate when freedom comes.

James Berry. *Ajeemah and His Son.* Gr. 6–10

Like Berry's short story collection, *A Thief in the Village*, this is rooted in his native Jamaica, even as it reaches out to universals. Berry is also a fine poet, and he tells his story with the rhythm, repetition, and lyricism of the oral tradition, recounting the history as passionately as the personal drama of capture, journey, sale, and toil. No reader or listener will forget the kidnapping scene when Ajeemah begs his captors to tell his family what's happened to him: they look at him as if he's crazy, and we know he will never see his loved ones again. Berry dramatizes how a new slave is renamed and broken in; how those bound by family and language are purposely kept separate. We feel the savagery of the system that buys and sells human beings—"He didn't belong to himself." The son's story moves with inexorable tragedy: he nurses a young colt, trains it to full strength, dreams and schemes of riding away on its back. When the horse is confiscated, he breaks its legs and breaks himself.

There's some overwriting at times: in the same paragraph, Berry can slip from stirring poetry to rhetoric about "horror, awe and dread," and he relies too much on words like *terrible* and *awful*, diminishing their impact with overuse. The villain always seems to walk with a "waddle," and there's a contrived plot element about some hidden gold. But there's no sentimentality. Even while he dramatizes the strong individual's power to transcend the plantation whips, Berry shows that the system kept most slave people subservient, "all beaten down, gutted and trampled." The book ends with the joyful wedding of Ajeemah's daughter soon after emancipation. But the son's despairing end underlies all celebration. And Africa is lost.

For some, the descent into Hell ends not in death or despair but in escape, and the escape from Hell is the most dramatic of all because the stakes are highest: the escapee earns another chance to live, to choose, to take his or her own journey.

Jennifer Armstrong. *Steal Away.* Gr. 7–10

In Jennifer Armstrong's *Steal Away*, two unhappy, 13-year-old girls on a Virginia farm in 1855—black slave Bethlehem and white orphan Susannah—disguise themselves as boys and run away together. More than 40 years later, as Bethlehem is dying in poverty in Canada, she calls Susannah to her. Together they tell their story to two young girls who write it down—Susannah's privileged white grandchild, Mary, and Bethlehem's black student, Free. The constant switch back and forth in narrators and in time between the 1850s and the 1890s makes you stop and think about the escape adventure, the friendship, and the enduring racism. Slavery's horrors are there, though understated. Susannah secretly teaches Bethlehem to read, and the girls save each other on their journey north, first alone, and then with the help of the Underground Railroad. Their friendship is never sentimentalized: we see that both must fight the violence in themselves, the desire to dump the other and get away alone. The close parallels between the old women and their young listeners are somewhat contrived, but the writer avoids any sweet resolution, past or present. Armstrong weaves a strong story of doubt and guilt as well as courage and escape.

Virginia Hamilton. *The People Could Fly.* Gr. 5–12

The beautiful title story in Virginia Hamilton's folklore collection *The People Could Fly* is both anguished and hopeful, a fantasy about those who flew away from slavery to freedom, and those who had to stay and who told the story.

> They say the people could fly. Say that long ago in Africa, some of the people knew magic. And they would walk up on the air like climbin up on a gate. And they flew like blackbirds over the fields. Black, shiny wings flappin against the blue up there.
>
> Then many of the people were captured for Slavery. The ones that could fly shed their wings. They couldn't take their wings across the water on the slave ships. Too crowded, don't you know.

Then, when they came to America:

The slaves labored in the fields from sunup to sundown. The owner of the slaves callin himself their Master. Say he was a hard lump of clay. A hard, glinty coal. A hard rock pile, wouldn't be moved. His Overseer on horseback pointed out the slaves who were slowin down. So the one called Driver cracked his whip over the slow ones to make them move faster. That whip was a slice-open cut of pain. So they did move faster. Had to.

The story focuses on a young woman, Sarah, laboring in the fields with a baby on her back. In her suffering she remembers how to fly—and she and others fly away from slavery to freedom. But some could not fly. They had to stay, and they told and retold the story. Hamilton says of some of them in her note, they "had only their imaginations to set them free."

Blending fantasy and history, this story speaks to all of us about courage in the face of oppression. Slaves aren't the only people to use transformation as a means of escaping Hell. This contemporary Palestinian poem describes a prisoner who frees herself with the power of imagination.

THE PRISON CELL
by Mahmud Darwish

It is possible . . .
It is possible at least sometimes . . .
It is possible especially now
To ride a horse
Inside a prison cell
And run away . . .

It is possible for prison walls
To disappear,
For the cell to become a distant land
Without frontiers.

—What did you do with the walls?
—I gave them back to the rocks.
—And what did you do with the ceiling?
—I turned it into a saddle.
—And your chain?
—I turned it into a pencil.

The prison guard got angry.
He put an end to the dialogue.
He said he didn't care for poetry,
And bolted the door of my cell.

He came back to see me
In the morning;
He shouted at me:

—Where did all this water come from?
—I brought it from the Nile.

—And the trees?
—From the orchards of Damascus.
—And the music?
—From my heartbeat.

The prison guard got mad;
He put an end to my dialogue.
He said he didn't like my poetry,
And bolted the door of my cell.

But he returned in the evening:

—Where did this moon come from?
—From the nights of Baghdad.
—And the wine?
—From the vineyards of Algiers.
—And this freedom?
—From the chain you tied me with last night.

The prison guard grew so sad . . .
He begged me to give him back
His freedom.

Paula Fox.
Monkey Island.
Gr. 5–12

In today's world, homelessness is the descent into Hell we most fear. In Paula Fox's *Monkey Island*, 11-year-old Clay Garrity loses his loving home, is abandoned by his parents, and finds himself living on the streets of New York City. When the home is broken there's no place to leave or return to.

Clay sleeps for a month in a crate in a small park in the city. At first he's scared the authorities will find him; then he realizes nobody cares. Fox makes the city both a real place and a mythical underworld. Clay fights for food, warmth, safety, privacy, community. With stony realism, Fox writes about the physical particulars of what it's like to be thrust out on the street. At the same time, her tenderness for Clay and his companions in limbo is like a transforming light that gives their struggle the power of myth. This is no exciting survival adventure; rather, it tells with almost unbearable clarity about a search for home. As his name shows, Clay is everyone. What happens to Clay could happen to me. As he rummages through the garbage, he realizes what the word *away* means. To the joggers and the people who pass him and don't see him, he's *away*.

He's also lucky; two streetpeople look after him. Teenager Buddy and retired teacher Calvin share their place with him in the park and watch over him the best they can. But they are also lost souls in the city inferno. Calvin and Buddy are Clay's companions on his dangerous journey through noise and filth and violence, where people huddle like restless shadows in the dark.

Clay does get help: he finds a home, his mother does come back, and he learns that he can hold on in the storm. In his quiet statement at the end about his journey to school—"I can walk there from home"—he expresses all that it means to have a place to leave from and come back to. His side trip has ended.

Walter Dean Myers' *Somewhere in the Darkness* roots the archetypal themes in a stark social realism: there's the universal father-son quest, from the inner city to the rural South; there are side trips to Hell; and there's a literal and metaphorical escape from Hell.

Walter Dean Myers. *Somewhere in the Darkness*. Gr. 7–12

"I'm your father," a man tells teenage Jimmy Little in the dim hallway of a New York city tenement. They don't know each other. Crab, the father, has been in jail for nine years. Critically ill, he's escaped from the prison hospital. He wants to clear his name, wants his son to love him and believe in him. As they drive to Chicago, then down to Crab's childhood home in Arkansas, the police close in, and Jimmy sees the failure of his father's dreams ("Anything I could have been is gone"). The climax, the moment of truth, is not an expression of love, but a cry of anger: "You don't even know how to be a father."

Running through the story is the misery of prison, "worse than being a slave"; Jimmy thinks of Crab crying, locked in a cell in the darkness. The scenes are cinematic, taut; the hesitant conversation, sometimes warm, sometimes hostile, keeps falling off into silence that holds the dreams of what could have been. The main characters are drawn with quiet intensity, and there are also spare vignettes on the road—a weary stranger on a Chicago bus; a malnourished country child clutching a blonde doll; a glimpse of past segregation; a flash of beauty. As in *Scorpions*, Myers allows no sentimentality, no quick fix of self-esteem. Escape from Hell is hard; prison, both external and internal, looms over everything. Jimmy finds hope in having a loving foster mother to return to and a chance to break free from his own prison dreams.

COMING TO AMERICA

The prison of poverty and persecution and the ravages of war have driven millions of immigrants to undertake the Perilous Journey to America since the late fifteenth century. Stories of the immigrant on the way to the New World—to what the Chinese called Gold Mountain—are a dramatic way to link books across cultures to universal themes. As an escape from hell and as a heroic quest, fiction, history, myth, and folklore tell of the journey to America.

The Great Famine in Ireland drives Peggy O'Driscoll to leave for America in Marita Conlon-McKenna's *Wildflower Girl*. Peggy's story started in *Under the Hawthorn Tree* when her parents died, and she walked with her older brother and sisters across the country in search of food and a home. Now, at 13, prospects are bleak; she leaves Ireland behind and takes up the offer of a free passage across the Atlantic to Boston in the 1850s. Of course, she's brave, resourceful, spirited, and loving, but there's no easy rags-to-riches success formula. The facts of this docunovel will fascinate kids, and the story will make fine reading for any classroom unit on nineteenth-century immigration: the wrenching leave-taking; the excitement and misery of the long, cramped, stormy journey in steerage ("five stinking, rotten, smelly, disgusting weeks"); the struggle for work as a skivvy and then as kitchen maid in a grand house; the aching homesickness. Peggy's a survivor. The hardship, fear, and loneliness are always there, as well as the promise of something better.

Marita Conlon-McKenna. *Wildflower Girl*. Gr. 5–7

In Russell Freedman's enthralling photo-essay *Immigrant Kids*, the experience of the children who immigrated to the U.S. during the largest European influx, 1880–1920, is presented through a lucid text and

Russell Freedman. *Immigrant Kids*. Gr. 5–9

stirring period photographs. Freedman shows the journey by steerage, the terrifying health inspections on Ellis Island, and then how these immigrant kids lived, learned, worked, and played, most of them in crowded ethnic neighborhoods in the big cities. There were painful conflicts as the kids became Americans and as their parents clung to Old World customs and beliefs; some children rejected their parents and were ashamed of them. The photographs are unforgettable, including several by Lewis Hines and Jacob Riis that depict the crowded tenements and the sweatshops where children worked.

Karen Hesse. *Letters from Rifka.* Gr. 5–8

Karen Hesse's *Letters from Rifka* is about a Jewish immigrant girl escaping with her family from the Russian pogroms and coming through Ellis Island to America. In letters to her cousin back "home" in Russia, 12-year-old Rifka tells of her journey to America in 1919: the dangerous escape over the border, the journey through Europe and across the sea to the new country. Rifka gets ringworm and has to stay behind in Belgium for nearly a year while her parents and brothers go on to America. The best part of the book is about her time on Ellis Island, in limbo, waiting to see if the authorities will declare her infection-free. The epistolary format is occasionally contrived, though it is moving to discover that she's writing everything in the margins of her beloved copy of Pushkin. The letters do allow her to bring in memories of what she left behind, including the racist persecution. Based on the experience of Hesse's great-aunt, the narrative flashes occasionally with lively Yiddish idiom: "You are bored?" her mother says to Rifka, "So I'll hire you a band." What raises it above docunovel, though, is the emerging sense of Rifka's personality. Bald from the ringworm, poor and needy, she proves she's no greenhorn; she has a gift for languages, she's brave and clever, and if she talks too much, so be it.

Olga Levy Drucker. *Kindertransport.* Gr. 6–12

Olga Levy Drucker's autobiographical *Kindertransport* tells how, at the age of 11 in 1938, she was sent by her Jewish parents from their home in Nazi Germany to safety in England. In her quiet, candid account, Drucker describes how the rising anti-Semitism of the era invaded her assimilated, affluent home ("I was never inside the synagogue that had been burned the night the Nazis took Papa away."). Most of the book is about her six years as an evacuee in England, cared for at boarding school and in a series of foster homes, some dreary, some less so, until finally she moves in with a family filled with life and love. The viewpoint is occasionally awkward, but Drucker writes with spare truth about how a refugee adjusts and what's both lost and gained. She worries about her family, but as time passes their reality slowly fades: "What was real was school, the War, and surviving from day to day." The blitz is scary; it's also fun. The Holocaust is far away. When she hears that her parents have made it to New York, her relief is mixed with resentment that she's going to have to leave the life she's made in England. In the final, heartbreaking reunion in America in 1945, she searches for her parents on the station platform, not sure if they'll know her; that's when she allows herself to feel what she's had to repress, and, for the first time, she grieves for her grandmother dead in the camps. The afterword describes the recent fiftieth reunion of the Kindertransport, where Drucker learned she had been one of 10,000 children, 9,000 of whom never saw their parents again.

In Hilda Perera's novel *Kiki,* based on the experience of unaccompanied refugee children who came to the U.S. from Cuba in the 1960s, the immigrant boy goes through the same stages as Drucker: first, hard times; then adjustment in a loving, comfortable foster home; then anger when his parents arrive four years later and want him to go back to being like them. Translated by Warren Hampton and Hilda Gonzalez from a popular Spanish novel, this frank, first-person immigration story is both funny and poignant. Kiki (Jesús Gómez) is eight years old when he's sent with his older brother and cousins from Cuba to his grandfather in Miami. The old man can't cope with the children, and Kiki has a hard time at first, alienated and poor. His first foster home is with a Cuban family in the Everglades. Then he's moved to a rich Anglo family, where he's so happy that he begins to forget his Cuban roots. Kiki gets so comfortable in his new home that he's not at all pleased to see his parents when they eventually make it to Miami four long years after him. He loves them, but he hates the return to poverty and separateness, the insistence on speaking Spanish, the endless reminiscences of "home." Perera manages to show the poverty with realism but no sense of squalor, and she makes no heavyhanded comment about Kiki's contempt for Cuban ways. Nor does she offer any simple happy ending: it's hard to be a refugee, hard to be caught between your parents' culture and the lure of the mainstream. A note at the end says Kiki's story is based on the experience of 14,000 unaccompanied Cuban children who came secretly to Miami in the 1960s. Every immigrant family will recognize the conflict.

Hilda Perera. Kiki: A Cuban Boy's Adventures in America. Gr. 4–8

"Most Americans think that Arabs live in the desert and ride camels." Such pervasive stereotypes are countered in Brent Ashabranner's timely book *An Ancient Heritage: The Arab-American Minority*, based on informal interviews with a wide variety of Arab Americans and illustrated with lively black-and-white photographs by Paul Conklin. Also included is a brief history of Arab culture and Arab immigration to the U.S. Ashabranner and Conklin, who have worked together on such excellent ethnocultural essays as *The Vanishing Border*, demonstrate their usual empathy for their subjects, a warming combination of personal involvement and unobtrusive background research. The book shows what's special about Arab American culture: what various groups left behind in the strife-torn Middle East ("I left a country that once was beautiful and part of me will always be sad"); why they came here; why they stay; and how they live—students, teachers, shopkeepers, artists, doctors, etc., from Boston and Detroit to Portland and New Orleans. At the same time, readers will see how Arab Americans are like all immigrant groups: the differences among generations; the need to live in two cultures; for some, the memory of pain and dream of return, even while they work hard and enjoy their good fortune in America. This enjoyable introduction to a unique ethnic minority demonstrates its rich contribution to our national culture.

Brent Ashabranner. An Ancient Heritage. Gr. 5–12

The account of the boat people from Asia and how they came to America after the Vietnam War is powerfully presented in Brent and Melissa Ashabranner's *Into a Strange Land: Unaccompanied Refugee Youth in America*. The harrowing personal story that opens the book makes you wonder if the escape is into safety or into Hell.

Brent and Melissa Ashabranner. Into a Strange Land. Gr. 5–12

Tran is on a boat crowded with refugees from Vietnam. They are all strangers to him. He remembers how three days ago he had been delighted when his father had told him they were going fishing. But his father had tricked him. He given him a small plastic bag, put Tran on the boat, and watched him leave. In the darkness, "Tran cried out to his father, but one of the men standing beside him gripped him roughly by the shoulder. 'Do not make noise,' he said."

Tran is sick, terrified, and desperate.

> It was not until the third day that Tran opened the plastic bag, although it had not been out of his hand, even for a moment. Some of his clothes were in the bag, and there was an envelope. He opened it and found a picture of his family that had been taken last year. He was in the picture with his mother and father, his two sisters, and his brother, Sinh.
>
> A letter from his mother was also in the bag. The letter said she was sorry they could not tell him he was going away. She said the boat would take him to a refugee camp in a place called Thailand. She told him to tell the people who ran the camp that he wanted to go to America. She said she hoped someday the whole family could come or at least his brother when he was older.
>
> Tran held the letter in his hand and stared at it. He knew about refugees. You could not live in Vietnam and not know about them. He had even thought that someday he might be a refugee, but had never imagined that he would leave Vietnam without his family.

In this book and in numerous others, Ashabranner combines the immediacy of oral history with a general view of the issues. Neither sentimental nor exploitative, his work is always candid about suffering as well as hopeful that people can help. His great achievement is to give an individual face to those the society labels "alien."

Fran Leeper Buss. *Journey of the Sparrows.* Gr. 7–12

Fran Leeper Buss' *Journey of the Sparrows* brings the refugee journey right here now. Nailed into a crate in the back of a truck, 15-year-old Maria and her sister and little brother endure the cruel journey across the border from Mexico and then north to Chicago. There they struggle to find work—cleaning, sewing, washing dishes—always careful to remain "invisible" so that the authorities won't arrest them as illegal aliens and send them back. Maria can read and write, and she has an artistic gift. "You're the one who'll save the family," her father told her before he died, murdered in El Salvador. Maria's greatest trial comes when—like a contemporary Harriet Tubman—she must make the journey back again down south to save her baby sister and smuggle her across the border. She's sustained by her memories of her father, her family here, and the Chicago community that helps her. Use this story with some of the photo-essays about illegal aliens and migrant workers or with accounts of the Underground Railroad.

READING THE MAP

Coming to America has traditionally been an arduous, life-changing journey, but for most of the immigrants we've just discussed, there was never any doubt about which direction to travel, or whether they should go at all. Many were driven out of their old homes by poverty or persecution, and they left seeking a new home, a better way of life, a New World. But when you're already in the New World, and it's no longer possible, as Huck Finn put it, to "light out for the territories," the question of where to go on your vision quest becomes a very real one. For some of us in the late twentieth century, the biggest problem with taking a Perilous Journey is knowing how to read the map.

In "On the Rainy River," one of the interconnected stories in Tim O'Brien's novel *The Things They Carried*, the narrator is not sure whether the map is directing him to run away or return home. The story is based on O'Brien's own experience as a grunt, a foot soldier, in Vietnam—the very image of Hell (and of forced servitude) for an entire generation of American youth. In simple prose, both poetic and casual, he remembers trying to run from his country to escape the draft. He tries to cross the river into Canada. All the mythical elements of the journey—the mentor, the crossing, the confrontation with the monster, and the return—are set here in a contemporary context. Rooted as it is in the particular facts of small-town America, this story vividly portrays the modern dilemma: Where do you go to find yourself?

Tim O'Brien. *The Things They Carried.* Gr. 8–12

O'Brien's narrator gets his draft card in the summer of 1968. He's 21, just graduated from Macalester College in St. Paul, near his home town in Minnesota. He's top of the class, ready for Harvard. Then he's told to go to war. He's against the war—not in any fiercely militant way—he just believes we shouldn't be in Vietnam, and he wants to get on with his life. "Driving up Main Street, past the courthouse and the Ben Franklin store," he begins to think of running away to Canada, and he faces his fear. He's afraid of dying; he's also afraid of being thought a coward, of being exiled from home, from the "mainstream life" he was born to ("I loved baseball and hamburgers and cherry cokes."). He tries to run away. He gets right to the border, and there he meets an old man who takes him out fishing on the Rainy River and stands vigil. But Tim can't cross over the river. He drives home. He goes to war, not as a hero, but as he says, "because I was embarrassed not to."

O'Brien says you can tell a true war story if it embarrasses you. If it makes you feel uplifted, reconciled, comforted, it's repeating a very old and terrible lie. All good writing is "embarrassing" in that sense. It won't let you settle comfortably. It upsets the way you're used to looking at the world, and it disturbs what you'd like to believe about yourself. It won't let you escape into easy lies or get stuck in cliché.

Tracing the Perilous Journey across cultures and over centuries, from Trojan warriors to Vietnam grunts, shows us the way a universal human theme keeps rising to the surface of our shared experience, bringing us together as our differences transform the theme again and again. But the theme keeps reappearing. We are all confronted with the need to embark on a journey; sometimes the path is obvious, other times murky. But the general direction is always the same: away from home. We may find new homes, but we'll never recapture the home of our youth. The poet and novelist Louise Erdrich states quite clearly that you can't go home again. "Going home for most people is like trying to recapture childhood. It's an impossible task; you're not a child, and unless your parents have, by some grace of God, grown up with you, it's almost impossible to go back and stay and live."

THE HERO
AND THE MONSTER

I went up one step.
Just like me.
I went up two steps.
Just like me.
I looked out the window.
Just like me.
I saw a monkey.
Just like me.

—*Traditional children's rhyme*

The best hero stories expand our view of what is ordinary. Of course, any classroom unit on the Hero can bring in the great epic stories from many cultures, as well as biographies of famous people everywhere, from Joan of Arc and Martin Luther King, Jr., to the Wright brothers and Diego Rivera, people who have pushed against borders and changed the world. But kids are also drawn to stories about people who aren't famous or exceptional at all, stories that make the reader ask, "What would I have done?"

The answer isn't simple. Just as many old fairy tales reveal that the beast is really a prince, so there are stories that discover the monster in each of us and show how we are continually transforming ourselves as we come of age. If you hate your brother, is he the monster or are you? Is it friend or fiend who lures you over the threshold of your parents' kitchen door? The moment of transcendence may come when you reach beyond yourself and see, not that the other is perfect, but that the other is like you. When you love the Beast, he becomes a prince, and you become beautiful.

Why is the Beast in stories so often more interesting than the hero? Why do we love scary tales of the dark? Why do kids ask for books about monsters—the more dangerous and nightmarish the better? Whether it's the Wicked Witch of the West in *The Wizard of Oz* or Frankenstein's demon or the wolf in *Lon Po Po* or the Hairy Man or the Devil, the best monster stories speak to what Virginia Hamilton calls "our most secret, fearful heart."

Each of us has so many possibilities. The best stories, mythic and contemporary, fiction and nonfiction, help us imagine all our selves. It's a joyful surprise in a classroom unit on myth to show that, in *Bingo Brown's Guide to Romance* by Betsy Byars, the All-American boy Bingo Brown is, in fact, a universal hero in search of "quiet manhood." Though he's rooted in the domestic, Bingo is on his own Perilous Journey. "In the old days," bemoans Bingo, "when a boy asked his mom for a new challenge, she sent him to the Crusades or out West to look for gold." Instead of the Crusades, Bingo's mother sends him to the laundromat to wash the family's clothes. What's more, he encounters his true love, Melissa, in the supermarket on his quest with a grocery cart through Produce and into Health Supplies. Bingo dreams of a manly life, but he's bound by the muddled and the mundane. He has trouble with "mixed-sex conversation." He's trapped by desire and confusion "for eternity, maybe even infinity." This funny, tender story will bring home to kids how the great hero stories relate to our daily lives.

Betsy Byars. Bingo Brown's Guide to Romance. Gr. 5–8

The experience of ordinary people is as much part of history as the roles of the heroic leaders and generals. Warwick Hutton's recent picture book version of *The Trojan Horse* will fascinate teens because he tells the story not from the traditional viewpoint of Achilles, Hector, Helen, and Priam, but through the eyes of the common people of Troy, families with kids who find this strange wooden horse on the beach, take it into the city, and end up as refugees fleeing their burning homes.

Warwick Hutton. The Trojan Horse. Gr. 2 and up

Most accounts of the civil rights movement focus on such inspiring events as the stirring speeches of Dr. Martin Luther King, Jr., or the history-changing act of Rosa Parks, who refused to give up her seat on a segregated bus. Young people today want to know about the movement's famous leaders, but they also want to read about what it was like to be young at that time.

In Ellen Levine's *Freedom's Children*, a fine collection of oral histories, 30 African Americans who grew up in the 1950s and 1960s talk about what it was like for them in Alabama, Mississippi, and Arkansas: sitting in, riding at the front of the bus, integrating schools, being threatened by beatings, arrest, even death. Levine provides a clear framework, organizing the personal accounts into chapters first on what segregation was like and then on the stages of the struggle, from the Montgomery bus boycott and the freedom rides to Bloody Sunday and the Selma Movement. In each chapter, she introduces the individual stories with a general view of the political scene, and she provides a detailed chronology and who's who. But it's the dramatic immediacy of the first-person accounts that will hold kids fast: Claudette Colvin tells what it was like for her at 15 in 1955 to be the first—before even Rosa Parks—to refuse to give up her seat on the bus. Several people remember what it was like to sit in and demand to be served in an all-white restaurant ("You would have thought we had walked in nude, or had three eyes."). They remember the sense of solidarity with white freedom riders who risked their lives, and several recall personal meetings with Dr. Martin Luther King, Jr. Above all, they communicate what it was like to find courage they didn't know they had and to transform themselves and the world around them.

Ellen Levine. Freedom's Children. Gr. 6–12

Yvette Moore's YA novel *Freedom Songs* tells the civil-rights story through the eyes of ninth-grader Sheryl, whose 19-year-old Uncle Pete becomes

Yvette Moore.
Freedom Songs.
Gr. 6–12

a freedom rider. On Good Friday morning 1963, Sheryl and her parents and brothers drive down from Brooklyn, New York, to their family in North Carolina. Sheryl loves the South—for her it means fun and an endless summer with her cousins—and she's swept up in the singing and togetherness in the old wooden church in the woods. But she loses her innocence when she's yelled at for using a whites-only water fountain in Hodges' Five-and-Ten (the store owner washes out the fountain with ammonia), and she faces the Jim Crow reality of her cousins' daily segregation. Then, at the Easter Sunday family dinner, Uncle Pete, home from college, announces that, instead of picking tobacco that summer, he's going to join the freedom riders, helping to encourage voter registration. Some relatives argue fiercely with him. They don't want trouble, don't want him challenging the segregation laws by sitting in. Sheryl's father keeps quiet. But Sheryl finds herself on her feet, crying, and shouting, "Do it! Do it, do it, do it! *Do it!*"

The writing in this first part has a poetic intensity, shifting quietly from the teasing chatter among the cousins to the stark, understated confrontation in the store, and then to biblical metaphor and cadence as Sheryl discovers her commitment. The action sags when Sheryl and her parents return to Brooklyn. They hear about the marches on the news and by phone from relatives—snarling dogs and sheriffs, injury and jailing. What keeps the story focused is Sheryl's identification with her uncle. When he dies in a bomb explosion, and the family returns south for the funeral, a simple image captures Sheryl's grief and her transformation: she goes to sleep on his made-up bed, which still has the imprint of his last late-afternoon nap. Sheryl walks into the county courthouse with her aunts and uncles when they try to register to vote. And, finally, she comes back to Hodges' Five-and-Ten, where she supports the students at a nonviolent, lunch-counter sit-in. A bitter joke is played out in the inevitable confrontation between black customer and white waitress:

> "I'd like a Coke and fries, please."
> "We don't serve nigras."
> "A Coke and fries will do, thank you."

As the protestors are insulted, beaten, and dragged away to prison, Sheryl joins the singing that gives them strength, allaying fear, quelling hate. "The singing couldn't stop but pressed on deep into the night." With other young people, and with her uncle as model, Sheryl has found the strength to reach beyond herself and confront the monster of bigotry.

James Baldwin.
Notes of a Native Son.
Gr. 8–12

Sheryl's lunch-counter confrontation is like a scene in the great 1955 essay, *Notes of a Native Son*, where James Baldwin dramatizes his own struggle not to let the monster of racism and hatred enter and destroy him.

Baldwin remembers himself, 19 years old, attending his father's funeral in 1943, when race riots had broken out in Harlem. Driving to the funeral through streets filled with glass, he was frightened of the raging bitterness that had helped to kill his father. The bitterness, the monster, was racism. Baldwin had been away from home for a little over a year then, working in New Jersey, where he suffered vicious discrimination. Restaurants, bars, bowling alleys, diners, places to live—he was always being asked to leave, always hearing the refrain, "We don't serve Negroes here."

He describes one particular night, when his simmering rage boiled over. Baldwin and a friend had gone into a diner. The counterman asked them what they wanted. "A hamburger and coffee," he said, and as usual, he was told, "We don't serve Negroes here." This time, though, he lost control. Leaving the diner, he walked into a glittering, fashionable restaurant and sat down at a table. All his fury flowed toward the little, frightened waitress, who repeated, as if she'd learned it somewhere else, "We don't serve Negroes here." Baldwin picked up the only thing he could find—a glass of water—and hurled it at her. The shattering of the glass against a mirror behind the bar shocked Baldwin into seeing what he'd done and what he had become. Afterwards he went over and over what had happened, appalled to discover not only that he could have been murdered, but also that he could have committed murder.

Baldwin writes about himself with such drama and simplicity that this piece will move even junior high readers and introduce them to a writer of great depth and passion. And writing like that can move those who thought that an essay was the last thing they'd want to read. In much of his fiction and nonfiction, Baldwin wrote about the dual fight to keep himself free of the bigotry out there, and of the hatred and despair in himself.

At the time of slavery the confrontation was often secret, the journey hidden, the heroism uncelebrated. And that distinction between the public celebrity and the quiet hero is very much an issue in our time of media hype and fleeting fame. The great abolitionist and ex-slave Frederick Douglass confronts this issue with painful clarity in his letter to Harriet Tubman, who had undertaken more than 20 dangerous journeys to bring out more than 300 people on the Underground Railroad.

> The difference between us is very marked. Most of what I have done and suffered in the service of our cause has been in public and I have received much encouragement at every step of the way. You, on the other hand, have labored in a private way. I have wrought in the day—you in the night. I have had the applause of the crowd and the satisfaction that comes of being approved by the multitude, while the most you have done has been witnessed by a few trembling, scared and foot-sore bondmen and women, whom you have led out of the house of bondage and whose heartfelt "God Bless You" has been your only reward. Excepting John Brown—of sacred memory—I know of no one who has willingly encountered more perils and hardships to serve our enslaved people than you have.

Harriet Tubman's courage was transcendant, a model for all. Often, though, heroic models for teens come not only from history but also from popular culture. Take sixth-grader Frankie Wattleson in Avi's "Who Was That Masked Man, Anyway?" With his glasses perched over his mask, Frankie tries to be a Master Spy, "ruthless, clear-eyed, brave, and smartly dressed." In the last chaotic months of World War II, Frankie's brother has come home wounded and depressed; school's a bore; and a lodger has taken Frankie's room. Only his beloved radio serials make any sense. He tries to transform his life into a script from "Captain Midnight," "Superman," and "The Lone Ranger." The whole future of the free world depends on the outcome of Frankie's adventures, which he embarks on with his trusty sidekick, Mario, from across the street. Their crucial quest is to get rid of the Evil Scientist (that is, the lodger) so that Frankie can get his room back and his own radio. Then, in a grim outburst that runs

Avi. *"Who Was That Masked Man, Anyway?"* Gr. 5–7

counterpoint to all the Superman fun and games, Frankie's brother tells him what war was really like: mess, slaughter, and babble.

Avi tells the whole story through dialogue. There's not even a "he said" to show who's speaking, though a different typeface sets off the radio excerpts. Yet the characters and the parody are so sharp, the fast-paced scenes so dramatic, that readers will have no trouble following what's going on. In fact, they might enjoy acting out parts of the story or making up their own contemporary scripts. Avi is tuned into the way kids play. The joy of this novel is the way it mocks heroic stereotypes and celebrates our common dreams. Even while Frankie faces the truth about heroes, the farce of his ordinary life outdoes his make-believe adventures.

Michael Dorris. *A Yellow Raft in Blue Water*. Gr. 9–12

In Michael Dorris' *A Yellow Raft in Blue Water*, fifteen-year-old Rayona, half-Indian, half-black, doesn't want adventure. Instead, she wants desperately to be ordinary. She longs for a cozy suburban family with a dog named Rascal and a Daddy mowing the lawn. But, in fact, her father's long gone, and her desperate mother, Christine, takes Rayona back to the Montana reservation that Christine left as a young girl—back to Christine's mother, fierce Aunt Ida. Like Avi, Dorris works with and revitalizes the popular dreams we all share, the visions of good and evil formed from soap operas or country western songs. Bill Ott said in *Booklist* that Dorris' story embraces familiar themes (coming of age, the shackles of familial love, the burden of pride) but does so in a manner all its own. Dorris tells the tale through the alternating voices of his three heroines: teenage Rayona, much loved but repeatedly abandoned, vulnerable yet somehow indomitable; Christine, Ray's mother, confident she was "bound for something special" but only too aware that she might be "hard for destiny to locate"; and Aunt Ida, "who's lived for fifty-seven years and worn resentment like a medicine charm for forty." Ott says that Dorris' evocation of place (the barren landscape of the Montana reservation, in particular) mirrors his characters' inner lives, especially the unflinching stubbornness that both keeps them apart and allows them to survive.

This is how Rayona describes the homecoming, as she, her mother, and her grandmother meet on the barren land. Aunt Ida is mowing the lawn near her house with the speakers of a Walkman plugged into her ears; off-key but loud, she accompanies the tape:

> "*I've been looking for love in all the wrong places,*" she booms out, and then something makes her notice us. At first, she pretends not to have seen anything out of the ordinary, and goes back to her pushing.
>
> "*Looking for love in too many faces,*" she shouts, then stops again and drops her forearms on the handle of the mower. Finally she glances over her shoulder and sighs as she pulls off the headset.
>
> "Well, what did the cat drag in," she says in Indian, in a voice as scratchy and knotted as a fir tree. "My favorite thing, a surprise visitor."
>
> "I came home, Aunt Ida." Mom stands in the yellow field, her hair blowing across her face like dark string, the green garbage bags full of Seattle clothes at her feet. She's nervous. The wind rises, filling her blouse like a kite and outlining her short, square body. I have a sudden, sure sense that for Mom this is an important moment, a beginning or an end of something, and she's scared to find out

which. I have the idea to walk over to her, punch her on the arm, and tell her to lighten up, but I stay put and watch as though I'm seeing this scene on an old movie and a commercial could come along any time.

The music leaking out of Aunt Ida's earphones is tinny and low, but it fills the air around us and we listen. I think it's the Oak Ridge Boys or a group like that, but it's a song I don't know. Hearing that tune gives us all something to do, though, while we wait for what Aunt Ida will say. She's taking her time, giving Mom a chance to put in another word more if she wants.

"Give me three good reasons why I should be glad to see you." Aunt Ida's forehead bends into a frown. She pulls a red kerchief from her hip pocket and wipes her mouth.

Mom doesn't move. She doesn't even relax her scared smile. She tenses as though she's thought of an answer but she's not sure it's right. Then she gives it a try anyway, as if this is a quiz show and she's out to stump the stars.

"One, Mother, I'm your daughter, your only living child."

Aunt Ida doesn't like to hear this. Her face twists as if Mom has punched her below the belt or whacked her from behind when she wasn't looking.

"Two, I need someplace to stay."

But three is a raging curse, and Christine abandons Rayona there with the grandmother who doesn't know her and doesn't want to.

With dark humor Dorris shows that Rayona is, in fact, on a vision quest —as we all are; that destiny does locate her mother; that her grandmother is a wise old medicine woman, even if the spirits she communes with talk through her Walkman or on People's Court on television.

In Brock Cole's *Celine*, Chicago teenager Celine watches television, too, zapping with the remote control though cartoons, soaps, and commercials to the televangelists with their blow-dried hairdos. Like a 1980s Holden Caulfield, she's trying to find truth and intimacy in a phony, conformist culture, where slick images echo each other with banal repetition. "I do know about teen suicide, as a matter of fact. Just last night," she reports, "I watched a reporter interview two other reporters about the effect of reporting teen suicide on teen suicides." Cole captures the way we speak, the way we look, what we watch, and he relates this to the enduring metaphors of the inner quest for identity.

Brock Cole.
Celine.
Gr. 7–12

Celine's divorced parents are off somewhere, and she's living with her shallow young stepmother in a rented loft in a Chicago walk-up. Celine finds herself taking care of her neighbor, Jacob, a second-grader caught up in the pain of his parents' separation. It's the free use of the TV that first attracts Jake to Celine's apartment, that and her honesty. He's straight with her, too; when she wonders if she can fly, he reminds her that she has dirty feet. Their domestic scenes together are funny, both wild and gentle, as they talk, play, and watch television, surrounded by the clutter of junk-food carry-outs and bathed in the glow of commercials that promise "we will never have a moment's worry, because our lost credit cards will be replaced anywhere in the world at a day's notice (some restrictions may apply)."

Celine and Jake are two unlikely outsiders, far apart in age, who make a home together in the wasteland of the modern city. Like Dorris, Cole reveals the strangeness and the mythic in ordinary things. The surreal is rooted in precise observation of the physical world—Celine enjoys eating in the busy deli under the tracks of the Chicago el; she exults in the perfect mechanism with which a human arm fits into the shoulder socket. However, that beauty can shift to nightmare. In a scene as hallucinatory as anything in Hades, yet close to many teens' experience, Celine is trapped at a party, her way blocked by a doorway that "seems to bulge with people and hilarity." The uproar makes conversation, even thought, impossible. ("I think . . . " she tries to say. "You stink?" asks the person next to her. "I think!" she shouts.)

When another girl asks Celine, "Can I make you up?" she's talking about cosmetics. But Celine is an artist, and she does make herself—with charcoal and paint and the power of her imagination. Alone in her apartment, stripped naked, in silence (the television off), working with passionate concentration on an idea that's been with her for a long time, she begins to create her self-portrait as Celine-Beast, confronting her image and transforming it. Like Zibby Oneal in *In Summer Light*, Cole dramatizes what it's like to create: the work and the drudgery, the terror of commitment, as well as the exhilaration. Without elitism, without a word of jargon, he shows that art is neither copying nor escape, but discovery.

Cole's wit gives readers the same sense of discovery, casually mocking the clichés and transforming them into myth. In an interview with *Booklist*, Cole noted that while television plays such a great role in people's lives, it seldom makes its way into books. "What fascinates [Celine] is the trash," he said. "It shapes people's perceptions of the world and the way they view themselves. Celine says that people try to pattern their behavior after roles they've picked up on television. And she does it herself in a self-mocking way."

There's a strong physical sense of Chicago in the novel. Cole spoke about the contemporary myth of the city. "I love Chicago," he said. "A lot of places in the book are real. What fascinates me about cities is that they tend to be the focus of a lot of destructive energy. The great American myth, of course, is the rural myth, but what symbolizes the reality of the American world for me is the destruction of the urban life. I think of the city not only as a place where a lot goes on, but also as a place where all kinds of destructive forces are rearing themselves up— racism, poverty, the destruction of the environment, the confusion of our purposes and direction. European cities seem to me more livable. Here I feel that we're always right on the edge of something. It's a fascinating place; it's kind of a hellish place, too."

Sandra Cisneros.
*The House on
Mango Street.*
Gr. 8–12

Also rooted in the city of Chicago, Sandra Cisneros' *The House on Mango Street* has the same rich ambiguity. The story is about the coming-of-age of Chicana (Mexican American) Esperanza. Her complicated feelings about her great-grandmother are captured in the exquisite piece "My Name." For Esperanza her great-grandmother is part hero, part victim; she's part role model, part warning.

> In English my name means hope. In Spanish it means too many letters. It means sadness, it means waiting. It is like the number nine. A muddy color. It is the Mexican records my father plays on Sunday mornings when he is shaving, songs like sobbing.

It was my great-grandmother's name and now it is mine. She was a horse woman, too, born like me in the Chinese year of the horse—which is supposed to be bad luck if you're born female—but I think this is a Chinese lie because the Chinese, like the Mexicans, don't like their women strong.

My great-grandmother. I would've liked to have known her, a wild horse of a woman, so wild she wouldn't marry. Until my great-grandfather threw a sack over her head and carried her off. Just like that, as if she were a fancy chandelier. That's the way he did it.

And the story goes she never forgave him. She looked out the window her whole life, the way so many women sit their sadness on an elbow. I wonder if she made the best with what she got or was sorry because she couldn't be all the things she wanted to be. Esperanza. I have inherited her name, but I don't want to inherit her place by the window.

At school they say my name funny as if the syllables were made out of tin and hurt the roof of your mouth. But in Spanish my name is made out of a softer something, like silver, not quite as thick as sister's name—Magdalena—which is uglier than mine. Magdalena who at least can come home and become Nenny. But I am always Esperanza.

I would like to baptize myself under a new name, a name more like the real me, the one nobody sees. Esperanza as Lisandra or Maritza or Zeze the X. Yes. Something like Zeze the X will do.

Writing like this will grab kids everywhere with its poetry and candor about the roots that give you strength and also hold you too tight, the immigrant culture that's rich and also oppressive. Read aloud almost any page from this novel. The combination of lyricism and harsh fact, the loving, angry young voice, can help kids confront their own conflicts, hesitancies, the lies that tell truth in the world they're trying to understand. With tenderness and fury, Cisneros evokes the experience of a young girl growing up in Chicago's Mexican American community, strengthened by her rich tradition, but also oppressed by it and needing to transform herself. Any number of the pieces in this book will surprise YA readers into facing their own conflicts, their own family stories, the constraints imposed on them by gender and ethnicity, the heroes and monsters they find around them, on the street, and across the dinner table.

In Maxine Hong Kingston's fiercely honest autobiography *The Woman Warrior*, the teenager growing up female and Chinese American in California listens to the adults "talking-story" from the old country and knows she can be a heroine, a swordswoman. She hears the story of the woman warrior, Fa Mu Lan, who took her father's place in battle, fought gloriously, and returned alive from war to settle in the village. That old story is an inspiration: "Perhaps women were once so dangerous that they had to have their feet bound." Yet at the same time Kingston's immigrant culture gives her another message, telling her to submit herself to a subservient woman's role. She resists by making herself into a hero who is a kind of monster, thus fighting the constraints of her immigrant culture, the ghosts of tradition, and the alien values of the United States. Her parents try to marry her off to one of the new immigrants, the FOBs, Fresh-off-the-Boats:

Maxine Hong Kingston. *The Woman Warrior*. Gr. 9–12

The girls said they'd never date an FOB. My mother took one home from the laundry, and I saw him looking over our photographs. "This one," he said picking up my sister's picture.

"No. No," said my mother. "This one," my picture. "The oldest first," she said. Good. I was an obstacle. I would protect my sister and myself at the same time. As my parents and the FOB sat talking at the kitchen table, I dropped two dishes. I found my walking stick and limped across the floor. I twisted my mouth and caught my hand in the knots of my hair. I spilled soup on the FOB when I handed him his bowl. "She can sew, though," I heard my mother say, "and sweep." I raised dust swirls sweeping around and under the FOB's chair—very bad luck because spirits live inside the broom. I put on my shoes with the open flaps and flapped about like a Wino Ghost. From then on, I wore those shoes to parties, whenever the mothers gathered to talk about marriages. The FOB and my parents paid me no attention, half ghosts half invisible, but when he left, my mother yelled at me about the dried-duck voice, the bad temper, the laziness, the clumsiness, the stupidity that comes from reading too much. The young men stopped visiting; not one came back. "Couldn't you just stop rubbing your nose?" she scolded. "All the village ladies are talking about your nose. They're afraid to eat our pastries because you might have kneaded the dough."

But she can't stop at will anymore. She has vampire nightmares, and she becomes terrified that she's turning into a monster. Wanting to be a hero and believing you're a monster is the universal teen identity crisis, an emotional condition impervious to the artificial borders of culture or race. The fight to kill the monster within is at the heart of many fine YA novels.

Virginia Euwer Wolff. *Probably Still Nick Swansen*. Gr. 7–12

In *Probably Still Nick Swansen* by Virginia Euwer Wolff, Nick struggles to overcome his view of himself as a monster: in his crisis he descends into the abyss, and he emerges from his trials reborn.

Nick is in Room 19, the special-ed class in his high school. He likes his teacher, Mr. Norton, and he's learning things, and he especially likes Shana. She used to be special-ed, too, but she did so well she got moved "up" to regular classes. She also seems to like Nick, so he wonders if he dare ask her to the prom.

The prom was coming, and Nick was thinking about it. He couldn't remember any Room 19 kids going to a prom, but somebody might have. Why couldn't you just up and go to the prom? Why couldn't he just go to the prom with Shana? No rule said you couldn't. It began as a sort of thought in his head one day, and pretty soon it was a bigger thought. . . .

Nick decided to do what he maybe shouldn't do. He might be really sorry, but there was nobody to talk to about it, so he brushed his teeth very hard, practiced saying it to the bathroom mirror nearly twenty times, and then walked to school early and hung around his locker until he could say it really. It was Monday.

"Hi, Shana. You want to go to the prom?" It came out faster than he thought it would. Suddenly he thought he needed a haircut. And he suddenly hated the braces on his teeth. He wished he wasn't so skinny.

"Hi, Nick. You're kidding."

He had to say something. "No. You want to go to the prom?" He should have been a football player, or at least baseball.

She stood next to her locker, with one foot propped on the edge of it, balancing a load of books in her arms. Her face was joking, he thought. But then she said, "Sure. Really? Are you asking me to the prom?"

Suddenly he had all kinds of guts. "Sure. You want to go with me?" So that's how they ask girls to proms, he discovered. They just do it. It just comes out of their mouths. He almost laughed.

"Gee." She made a face. "I've got these tests this week." She squinted and shrugged at the same time. "But yeah. Yeah, sure. I want to go."

"You really do?"

"I really do."

He knows that for things to go right for him he has to plan very carefully, make lots of lists, do things step by step. He earns extra money, rents a tuxedo, buys a corsage to match her dress, and every night he practices how to dance. At last the big night comes . . . and Shana stands him up.

In his despair, Nick wonders if he is just the "drooler" some of the other kids call him. He goes through a dark and terrible time. He's in the abyss. When he does find the strength to carry on, it's like a rebirth: "He felt as if he'd gone to another country and come back with somebody else's thoughts . . . Or maybe he'd slid down inside himself and come back out, and he was still Nicholas Swansen." Sometimes you just need to be by yourself to try to find out what was going on. The pain isn't minimized. There's no easy release. He talks with Shana. She tells him that what they both have is minimal brain dysfunction. He asks her if it went away when she moved up. She tells him it doesn't go away.

Nick's world is drawn without condescension. He's funny and brave, as determined to be independent as any teenager. What Wolff manages to do is make you feel Nick's special problems and at the same time see how much he is like you: asking someone to the prom, keeping hovering parents at bay, trying to get an injured dog to the vet, fearing everyone will know you're a monster. With her unobtrusive evocation of the heroic journey, Wolff universalizes Nick's experience and connects him to us.

In Paula Fox's *One-Eyed Cat*, a boy in a loving home feels that he has become a monster. His guilty memory weighs on him and poisons everything.

Paula Fox.
One-Eyed Cat.
Gr. 5–12

Ned Wallis is the only son of a minister. He knows he is loved by his gentle father and his witty, irreverent mother. His mother is ill, crippled with rheumatoid arthritis; when the pain is very bad and his father is lovingly attending to her, Ned must tiptoe around the house. He feels her pain "as if his own bones were turning into water." For Ned's birthday, his uncle gives him an air rifle, but his father forbids him to use it, and it is put away in the attic. Ned feels he must try it just once. That night he takes the gun, and, outside in the moonlight, he shoots at something that moves, a "dark shadow." Some time later, when he's working for a neighbor, old Mr. Scully, they notice a wild cat in the yard, and they see that there's something wrong with it.

> The cat was as gray as a mole and its fur was matted. As it peered toward the house, it shook its head constantly as though to clear away something that made seeing difficult.
>
> "What's the matter with him?" Ned asked.
>
> "Hunger," replied Mr. Scully. "No. Wait a minute. There is something wrong."
>
> "One of its eyes is shut tight."
>
> The cat came closer to the house.
>
> "The eye isn't there," Ned said. "There's just a little hole." He felt a touch of fear.
>
> Mr. Scully pressed against the counter. Ned could feel his breath.
>
> "You're right." Mr. Scully said. "The cold does that to them sometimes, and he looks big enough to have been born last year. Or else someone used him for target practice. A boy would do that. A living target is more interesting than a tin can . . ."
>
> "Hunting will be hard for him now," [Mr. Scully said]. "These cats live pretty good off rodents until the ground freezes over. I'll keep food out for him. Maybe he'll manage."
>
> Ned didn't think he would. He'd seen the gap, the dried blood, the little worm of mucus in the corner next to the cat's nose where the eye had been.

Ned feels responsible for the cat's pain. He feels he is in limbo, separated from his parents who believe he is loving and good. He feels locked in. And then his mother shares her own dark secret with him and helps to set him free.

Leonard Everett Fisher. *Cyclops*. Gr. 2 and up

It would be great to pair *One-Eyed Cat* with Leonard Fisher's picture book *Cyclops*, which makes the savage, one-eyed monster seem less a monster and more a victim. The Cyclops Polyphemus is, oddly, much like his adversary, the heralded Odysseus, who is portrayed not unlike you and me: sometimes violent and boasting but also bewildered, frightened, and alone. Pictures and words show that it's all in the perspective, in how you see it, with which eye. Like a close-up in a monster movie, the front cover shows the Cyclops' head almost filling the frame, its huge, white, rolling eyeball in the center, while the men crane their necks to look up at him, close and crowded in the lurid firelight of the cave. On the back cover you see a helpless man being lifted in the giant's fist toward that eye. It's scary all right, but Fisher doesn't sensationalize Homer's classical story.

It begins conventionally with Odysseus and his Greek warriors on their way home from triumph in Troy. The gods punish them with a storm that blows them onto a strange island. They find a cave filled with food and then are trapped inside by a huge giant, Polyphemus, who boasts that he heeds neither humans nor gods. He grabs the men for his dinner, two at a time, but clever Odysseus works out a plan. They blind the giant and escape by tying themselves underneath his sheep.

The words say one thing but the pictures say a lot more. Except for the opaque eyeball, there's almost no white in the double-page spreads, no borders, no space. We feel the Greeks' claustrophobic terror. Yet Polyphemus has an aquiline nose, a sensitive mouth, a neatly trimmed beard and fingernails. We're told that he wakes "roaring with rage," but the pictures show him gently stroking his sheep. In the final painting, he sits at the water's edge, his hands covering his face, wounded and solitary.

"The stories they would tell of his defeat would last forever." Kids will feel themselves caught between pity and terror. Older readers may see that all explorers tell tales of triumph over monstrous dangers. Can we ever know the whole story?

In Peter Dickinson's powerful science fiction story *Eva*, monster and hero blend to make a new creature who will save the world.

Peter Dickinson.
Eva.
Gr. 7–12

Teenage Eva wakes up in the hospital after an automobile accident that nearly killed her. She discovers that the scientists have saved her life by implanting her neuron memory into the body of a chimpanzee. This is the scene where she first becomes conscious of what's happened to her:

> Eva willed her eyes to open.
> For an instant all she seemed to see was nightmare. Mess. A giant spiderweb, broken and tangled on the pillows, with the furry black body of the spider dead in the middle of it. And then the mess made sense.
> She closed her right eye and watched the brown left eye in the mirror close as she did so. The web—it wasn't broken—was tubes and sensor wires connecting the machines around the bed to the pink-and-black thing in the center. She stared. Her mind wouldn't work. She couldn't think, only feel—feel Mom's tension, Mom's grief, as much as her own amazement. Poor Mom—her lovely blue-eyed daughter . . . Must do something for Mom. She found the right keys.
> "Okay," said her voice. "It's okay, Mom."
> "Oh my darling," said Mom and started to cry. That was okay too. Mom cried easy, usually when the worst was over. Eva stared at the face in the mirror. She'd recognized it at once, but couldn't give it a name. Then it came. Carefully she pressed the keys. She used the tone control to sound cheerful.
> "Hi, Kelly," said her voice.
> Kelly was—had been—a young female chimpanzee.

Then Eva must learn to integrate her human consciousness with her chimp nature and instincts. As well as the drama of her changed identity, there are fascinating ideas here about what we're doing to our planet and how to save it. Vermont librarian Grace Green calls this powerful novel a combination of *National Enquirer* and creation myth.

Scientific fact can be as monstrous as myth. David Bodanis' *The Secret House* is a scientific account of the seething hidden life in an ordinary home—from the electric force fields in the wall sockets to the armies of bacteria and mites on your face, your robe, the kitchen table. There are things you might not want to know: what happens to your skin when you shave or apply antiperspirant; what the milk in your refrigerator might look like to a miniaturized diver; what a greasy hair follicle looks like

David Bodanis.
The Secret House.
Gr. 7–12

magnified. The sense of an invisible seething world is as scary as nightmare, as monstrous as Frankenstein.

Shame and nightmare invade an ordinary house in *Mary Reilly* by Valerie Martin. Set in late Victorian London, it's a quiet, harrowing retelling of the Jekyll and Hyde story, seen from the point of view of the young housemaid, Mary Reilly. She escapes her abusive father and finds work as a maid for the generous, kindly Dr. Jekyll. He's gentle to her. But what troubles him so terribly? What secret experiment is he conducting in his laboratory? And what is his relationship with the vicious and violent young man, the evil Mr. Hyde, who creeps into the house late at night? One day, while Mary's making up the fire in the drawing room, the doctor comes in and seems strangely disturbed. He asks her: "Are you ever frightened, Mary?" Well, of course, she says.

Valerie Martin.
Mary Reilly.
Gr. 8–12

"What is it that frightens you?" he asks her.

She mentions the usual things, and her own memories of child abuse. And then there's a long pause.

"'Are you ever afraid of yourself, Mary?' Master said."

It's wonderful entertainment, of course, thrilling horror, but it's also disturbing. That last question is at the heart of why the Jekyll and Hyde story has survived so long. Who is my double? Am I a monster?

The Beast is the exciting center of the great *Beauty and the Beast* story, which is continually told and retold in versions across time and cultures.

In Robin McKinley's *Beauty*, an honorable, studious young woman sacrifices herself for her father and comes to live with the Beast alone in his great castle. She finds everything is laid on for her—a luxurious room, gardens, clothes, books. Her first night there, she meets the Beast:

Robin McKinley.
Beauty.
Gr. 6–12

> I caught a gleam of dark-green velvet on what might have been a knee in the shadowed armchair. "Good evening, Beauty," said a great harsh voice.
>
> I shivered, and put a hand to the door-frame, and tried to take courage from the fact that the Beast—for it must be he—had not devoured me at once. "Good evening, milord," I said. My voice was misleadingly steady.
>
> "I am the Beast," was the reply. "You will call me that, please." A pause. "Have you come of your own free will to stay in my castle?"
>
> "I have," I said, as bravely as I could.
>
> "Then I am much obliged to you."

They talk and eventually he shows himself to her—huge and horrifying—but he speaks gently, and she loses some of her fear:

> "If you wanted someone to talk to," I said, "why didn't you keep my father? He knows many more interesting things than I do."
>
> "Mmm," said the Beast. "I'm afraid I specifically wanted a girl."
>
> "Oh?" I said nervously. "Why?"
>
> He turned away from me, walked back to the doorway, and stood, head bowed, hands clasped behind him. The silence squeezed at my heart. "I am looking for a wife," he said, heavily. "Will you marry me, Beauty?"

And every night after dinner at the moment of parting, he asks her the same question: "Will you marry me, Beauty?"

Once Beauty sees the Beast as beloved, he becomes beautiful. And then she's beautiful. They create each other, transform each other, when she reaches beyond herself.

In his 25-volume Monsters of Mythology series, Bernard Evslin shows that the monsters of mythology are right here with us in the 1990s. From *Amycus* and *The Hydra* to *Scylla and Charybdis,* his vital retellings of the great myths evoke their fierce power and mystery. He goes beyond a simplistic cultural literacy definition (Who was Amycus?) to an imaginative re-creation of the elemental stories, their dark terror and heroic struggle. In prose that is both scholarly and playful, poetic and down to earth, he's not only true to the transcendant drama of the themes, but also informal and colloquial at times, speaking with immediacy to kids today. Angry Hera has a hate list, and Zeus' slimy sons are near the top. The rhythmic narrative is filled with action, danger, and character ("And Scylla, burning with excitement, feeling herself go drunk on sea-wind and moon-flash and weird song, howled back at the rock"). With the monster as the focus, each volume reaches out to a wide range of stories with settings from Arcadia to Hades, so that Jason and Proteus appear in the story of the brass-headed monster, Amycus; Hercules and Iole battle the Hydra; and Ulysses narrowly escapes between Scylla and Charybdis.

Bernard Evslin. *Amycus.* Gr. 5–12

These are also glowing art books, profusely illustrated with color reproductions of ancient, classical, and modern art in various media that show the mythical incidents and their moods, metaphors, and archetypal patterns (from an Indian ceremonial wolf mask and a Blake engraving to a modern glass sculpture of a polar bear encased in ice and Klimt's painting *The Kiss*). There are occasional dull patches, but the 25 titles in this series—most of them Hellenic, two Norse, two Celtic—all written by Evslin, are great for storytelling, reference, and above all, personal reading and visual pleasure.

Discussing the supernatural monster stories in her collection *The Dark Way,* Virginia Hamilton says, "Whether it be monster, gorgon, trickster, ghost, imp, fairy, elf, devil, phantom, or witch—all of these twitch, they change, nightmaring, slumbering there . . . all are eager to leap into our existence, into the corners of our imaginations, into our fearful or caring thoughts."

Virginia Hamilton. *The Dark Way.* Gr. 4 and up

Hamilton finds "frightful fun" in the Russian witch Baba Yaga as much as in the African American Wiley and the Hairy Man, in the shrieking Irish Banshee and the Japanese prankster Tanuki, in the Haitian tricksters Malice and Bouki, and in Yama, the God of Death, who ruled over the underworld in the mythology of India. "I really think there are universals in those kinds of materials," Hamilton said in an interview I conducted with her for *Booklist.* "I mean I love Baba Yaga. It's not my culture, but it's a wonderful tale."

I asked Hamilton why we like those scary tales of darkness:

> Well, what I discovered in doing *In the Beginning* is that people have the same mind about certain things. They have the same fears and the same need for order. Creation stories come out of the need for making sense of the universe, and *The Dark Way,* which is based on our fears and anxieties, is the same thing. It is attempting to bring

us from an outside chaotic place into the place of safety where stories can be told. I think that's the whole idea of telling stories around the fire. In the beginning, people would come inside the cave where the fire was and tell about what happened . . . I think it's very necessary for a kid to read scary books and tell scary tales where it's warm and safe. I mean, American folklore is full of terror—all folklore is. It takes the chaos out of the world. That's what language does. And that's what writing has always done for me. It's ordered the world and made it safe. You come inside from outside . . .

It's a sign of Hamilton's great strength as a writer that she can re-create these supernatural monsters from all over the world and also show in her contemporary stories how each of us must wrestle with the fiend in the dark.

Virginia Hamilton. *Cousins.* Gr. 5–8

In her novel *Cousins,* the war between hero and monster is fought within one family, within one person.

Something about her Gram brings out the best in Cammy, but her cousin Patty Ann brings out the worst. Beautiful and smart, goody-goody Patty Ann is queen of the summer day camp in their small Ohio town, *and* she can sit on her hair. Cammy wishes her cousin would just vaporize, like on "Star Trek." One day her hatred for her pretty cousin bursts out. She tells Patty Ann that the kids have discovered her ugly secret: the beauty is bulimic ("junk-and-sick") beneath her lovely face. Cammy tells her she looks like death, and she describes how disgusting Patty Ann will look in her coffin:

> "You look like death," Cammy told her. "Like you are going to a funeral, which is your own."
>
> Once she got started, she couldn't stop herself. She saw Patty Ann's mouth turn down. "You look like a skeleton. I've never seen anybody that bony outside of a Halloween white cardboard skeleton."
>
> "You are so jealous just because I can sit on my hair and I get all A's," Patty Ann remarked. "I got my picture in the paper for never having below a B plus, and you have never had your picture in the paper." She said this while looking out of the window and swinging her legs. Her voice was up high on itself but still husky.
>
> "They'll pin your eyelids back with glue and make your eyeballs look down at some toy piano in your lap. They'll break your fingers to curl them so it looks like you are playing the keys."
>
> Cammy even shocked herself with her own meanness.

That's a macabre, funny scene, with all the drama of a raging quarrel. But then there's a fatal accident at day camp, and Cammy finds meanness—and courage—where she never expected to.

The three cousins in this story are all individuals, but at the same time each of the girls represents a different part of the same person. Hamilton says she didn't know when she began writing the novel which one of the girls would turn out brave and which one would turn out mean. The transformations are astonishing, and yet in the story they seem inevitable. Heroes and monsters are rooted in myth, as well as in daily life.

OUTSIDERS

Glory be to God for dappled things . . .
All things counter, original, spare, strange.

— *Gerard Manley Hopkins*

The lone gunfighter in Jack Schaefer's *Shane* is a strong outsider. So is the high school senior in Cynthia Voigt's *The Runner*, fierce and alone and determined that no one will box him in. So is Wolf Woman Running in the Sioux transformation myth, who leaves her cruel husband and runs with the wolves for eight winters. So is Sojourner Truth, who escaped from slavery and fought all her life to free others. Many outsider stories are about suffering: the abused orphan in *Jane Eyre*; the victims of a cruel practical joke in Brock Cole's *The Goats*. For the objects of racism, being thrust outside is fact as well as feeling. Ida Vos, in Nazi-occupied Holland, is forced to wear a yellow star; later she's wrenched from her parents and forced into hiding. Yoshiko Uchida's Japanese American family is herded into a concentration camp in Utah. In James Berry's *Ajeemah and His Son*, the West African father kidnapped with his son and sold into slavery across the sea is told that he does not even belong to himself.

The outsider theme—both heroic and painful—has elemental appeal for teens as they struggle with their often conflicting needs for identity and community: what Paula Fox calls "the pain of the conflict between the wish to be different and the horrid suspicion that one is too different." Sandra Cisneros captures the yearning and conflict about independence and belonging in *The House on Mango Street*. With lyrical power and fierce emotion, with tenderness and fury, she evokes the experience of a young girl growing up in Chicago's Mexican American community, strengthened by her rich tradition, but also oppressed by it and needing to transform herself. Just about every coming-of-age story touches in some way on the outsider theme. Whether it's a nineteenth-century classic like Mary Shelley's *Frankenstein* or a contemporary YA novel like Jerry Spinelli's *There's a Girl in My Hammerlock*, outsider stories move us to see our own fears and strengths in those that appear to be different—and to see what connects characters who live in different centuries, who come from different ethnic backgrounds, whose lives seem totally unrelated.

Charlotte Brontë.
Jane Eyre.
Gr. 8–12

Look at *Jane Eyre,* for example. This is a novel with enduring appeal for young people. Jane is an orphan living with her rich relatives who don't want her. Her cousin John beats and bullies her, and one day she rebels and fights back. As punishment, her Aunt Reed orders the servants to take Jane away to the red room and lock her in there. No one sleeps in the large and stately room. It is all red: red drapes, red carpet, huge bed, and furniture of darkly polished old mahogany. But worst of all, it is the room Jane's uncle died in. And as she sits there in the gathering dark and thinks about how she's hated in that house, she's terrified her uncle's ghost will come:

> My heart beat thick, my head grew hot; a sound filled my ears, which I deemed the rushing of wings; something seemed near me; I was oppressed, suffocated; endurance broke down; I rushed to the door and shook the lock in desperate effort. Steps came running along the outer passage; the key turned, Bessie and Abbot entered,
> "Miss Eyre, are you ill?" said Bessie.
> "What's that dreadful noise! It went quite through me!" exclaimed Abbot.
> "Take me out! Let me go into the nursery!" was my cry.
> "What for? Are you hurt? Have you seen something?" again demanded Bessie.
> "Oh! I saw a light, and I thought a ghost would come." I had now got hold of Bessie's hand, and she did not snatch it from me.
> "She has screamed out on purpose," declared Abbot, in some disgust. "And what a scream! If she had been in great pain one would have excused it, but she only wanted to bring us all here; I know her naughty tricks."
> "What is all this?" demanded another voice peremptorily; and Mrs. Reed came along the corridor, her cap flying wide, her gown rustling stormily. "Abbot and Bessie, I believe I gave orders that Jane Eyre should be left in the red-room till I came to her myself."
> "Miss Jane screamed so loud, ma'am," pleaded Bessie.
> "Let her go," was the only answer. "Loose Bessie's hands, child: you cannot succeed in getting out by these means, be assured. I abhor artifice, particularly in children; it is my duty to show you that tricks will not answer; you will now stay here an hour longer, and it is only on condition of perfect submission and stillness that I shall liberate you then."
> "Oh, aunt! Have pity! Forgive me! I cannot endure it—let me be punished some other way! I shall be killed if—"
> "Silence! This violence is almost repulsive"; and so, no doubt, she felt it. I was a precocious actress in her eyes: she sincerely looked on me as a compound of virulent passions, mean spirit, and dangerous duplicity.

Despite Jane's desperate sobbing, she's locked in again, and in her terror, she falls unconscious. Like so many protagonists in contemporary YA fiction, Jane grows up poor and alone, trying to hold on to her belief in herself. Her first job is as a governess in a rich great house. She falls in love with the master of the house, dark, brooding Mr. Rochester. But his house hides an agonizing secret.

This story grabs young people with the outsider theme, the love story, the house that holds a dark secret: all are picked up again in popular stories like Daphne Du Maurier's *Rebecca* and countless Gothic love stories. High school kids who've enjoyed *Jane Eyre* are also moved by Jean Rhys' slim, intense novel, *Wide Sargasso Sea*, which startles you into seeing what drove the madwoman into the attic. What made her a monster? Who is the outsider?

There's a similar powerful ambiguity in Bette Greene's *Summer of My German Soldier*, a landmark children's novel about prejudice and abuse in World War II Arkansas. Patty Bergen's parents don't like her. Her father beats her. She feels lonely and ugly and alone. Only the family's strong black housekeeper, Ruth (another outsider, at least in the mainstream, middle-class world), loves Patty and makes her feels she's worthwhile. One day Patty is in her father's store when some German prisoners of war held in a camp near town are brought in to buy hats for their work in the fields. She talks to a young prisoner, Anton Reiker, and they like each other. When he escapes, she hides him.

Bette Greene. *Summer of My German Soldier.* Gr. 6–10

This book makes you ask all kinds of questions, especially about racism. Patty is Jewish. The town is full of prejudice—against Jews, against blacks, and especially during the war, against Germans. But Anton isn't a Nazi—he's a loving, sensitive man who helps Patty believe that she's a "person of value." Can Patty's Jewish father be like a Nazi in his need to inflict pain?

Mary Downing Hahn's World War II story *Stepping on the Cracks* also makes you rethink categories that once seemed clear and certain. Margaret's brother is away fighting the Nazis in Europe. She worries about him, but otherwise things seem pretty much the same at home in small-town Maryland. She and her bossy friend, Elizabeth, think their war is with Gordy, the scary class bully. But Gordy is covering up some grim secrets: his older brother, Stuart, is an army deserter, and Gordy is hiding him in the woods. Should the girls help Stuart or turn him in? He's a pacifist, he's against war—does that mean he's a sissy, a coward, a traitor? Suddenly Margaret questions things that she's taken for granted. Hitler must be stopped. Her own brother could die. Yet, as she gets to know and like Stuart, he makes her ask, How could anyone point a gun at a human being and pull the trigger? Stuart, like most outsiders in literature, functions as an educator, offering the insider another way to see the world. As in the best political fiction, there are no simple messages; everything is rooted in story and character.

Mary Downing Hahn. *Stepping on the Cracks.* Gr. 5–8

Barbara Gehrts' outsider story *Don't Say a Word*, translated from the German, is about an anti-Nazi family in a Berlin suburb. It's based on the writer's own experience —as so many of these World War II stories are. The restrained, first-person narrative quietly tells of mounting suffering under tyranny. The narrator dreads that her older brother in the army may die for a cause they hate. One day her father's underground activities are discovered, and the Gestapo comes for him. Her Jewish friend down the street writes her a letter before committing suicide with her family when they know they're being sent to the death camps.

Barbara Gehrts. *Don't Say a Word.* Gr. 6–12

In Linda Crew's *Children of the River*, a Cambodian refugee in Oregon today can't forget the wartime atrocity she left behind. Sundara wants to fit in with the crowd in her high school. She likes blond football star

Linda Crew. *Children of the River.* Gr. 6–10

Jonathan MacKinnon, and she'd like to say yes when he asks her to go to the movies. Four years ago, when she was 13, she ran away with her aunt's family from the Khmer Rouge massacres in her country. Now in America, her Cambodian relatives stick to the old ways—no dating allowed; no talking to white boys. Sundara is caught between feeling too American at home, not American enough at school. Worst of all are her memories of her country and her guilt and sorrow about those she left behind. How can she think about trendy clothes when she doesn't know if her parents are alive? How could she have parted from her mother in anger? Sundara tries to find a way to be American without giving up her Cambodian self.

This book doesn't go into heavy messages about "the immigrant experience." Even if it is partly a docunovel, its focus is on the *story*—an individual, like me, trying to fit in with the group without losing her identity. No analysis, no preaching, just her personal conflicts, as specific as you can get. And that's the most important message, anyway—when you see Sundara as an individual, she's no longer a stereotype.

Jacqueline Woodson. *Maizon at Blue Hill.* Gr. 5–10

Jacqueline Woodson's *Maizon at Blue Hill* captures that outsider experience when the young person leaves the security of a familiar group and finds herself suddenly a "minority," the "other." Seventh-grader Maizon Singh, black and smart, reluctantly leaves her Brooklyn neighborhood, her best friend, and her beloved grandmother to take up a scholarship in a private Connecticut girls' boarding school. The classes are small, the place is beautiful, most people are quite nice to her, and her grades are A+. But she can't fit in. For the first time in her life, she's a "minority," and she hates it. She's furious with those whites who fear her as something different; she's not entirely at ease with the small group of rich black girls who tell her not to mix at all ("We have to stick together"), and she closes herself off from her funny, free-spirited white roommate. Contrary to all our formula expectations, Maizon doesn't finally find her place there and settle down. She can't take the loneliness, and she leaves to go back home.

Woodson's story frankly confronts issues of color, class, prejudice, and identity without offering Band-Aids of self-esteem. We're not just told that Maizon's smart: she thinks and reads, and one of the best scenes here is her class discussion of Toni Morrison's *The Bluest Eye*, about a dark-skinned, brown-eyed girl who cannot see her own beauty. Good readers could go on from Maizon to Lorene Cary's *Black Ice*, with its candid recollections of being one of the first black recruits in an eastern prep school.

M. E. Kerr. *Fell.* Gr. 6–12

As well as race, social class can make you an outsider. M. E. Kerr has always integrated political themes in her novels about contemporary American teenagers. In *Fell*, she combines a story of romance, mystery, and wit with serious implications of class conflict and personal betrayal—and she does it with a light touch. The book begins in Kerr's favorite resort setting of Seaville, New York. Fell is a policeman's son involved with the rich crowd on the hill, including a girl whose daddy disapproves of Fell's blue-collar background—he'd like Fell to be "heir to a fortune and descended from William the Conqueror." Fell is sensitive, smart, sexy, funny, and a gourmet cook. He nurtures his family, including his recently widowed mother, who is over the limit on every charge card in her purse, and his five-year-old sister, Jazzy, who plays rags-to-riches games with her paperdoll, Georgette:

Jazzy's game was to have Georgette discover that her real parents were millionaires. She would dress Georgette in her poor clothes and serve her macaroni, or shredded wheat, or a few raisins. Then Georgette's real family would come by to claim her, and she'd be dressed in her other clothes and sit down to "fwogs'" legs or champagne and caviar.

Kerr both understands those kinds of dreams and undercuts them. She gives you the formula situation, and just as you get comfortable with it, she startles you awake. When Fell is paid $20,000 to impersonate a rich neighbor's son at an elite prep school, it's like a dream come true, especially when he's chosen for the snob secret society that runs the school like "the Master Race." In Fell's unaffected voice, Kerr shows how the school reflects the world of privilege, with its power politics, prejudice, lunacy, and ritualized tyranny. And underlying it all is the ache of unfulfilled dreams.

Gender can also make you an outsider. A recent court case in a Chicago suburb involved a teenage girl suing for the right to be on the boys' wrestling team. Jerry Spinelli imagines such a scene in a funny YA novel, *There's a Girl in My Hammerlock.*

Jerry Spinelli.
There's a Girl in My Hammerlock.
Gr. 5–9

Maisie Brown goes out for junior high wrestling—to the consternation of her brother, the boys on the team, and most of the school. She's not sure why, at 105 pounds, she wants to learn monkey-rolls, double arm tie-ups, and all the other holds and escapes. Maybe it's because she didn't make the cheerleading squad. Maybe she's chasing Eric DeLong, the boy she loves, who's on the team. Her mother supports her all the way, but her best friend dumps her, and kids snigger and point: Is she oversexed? Or is she the best hunk in the eighth grade? Eric couldn't care less about her, especially after she beats him at basketball: "Can a boy like a girl he loses to?"

Spinelli uses the situation for all the fun he can get, while at the same time he raises important questions about gender roles and personal independence. There are hilarious scenes to read aloud. Here's how Maisie describes being in love: "Classes? Subjects? Forget it. The capital of Canada is Eric DeLong. Twelve times twelve equals Eric DeLong. The action word in a sentence is called Eric DeLong."

This is how you try to make the scale show your leanest weight: "Don't even drink water. Your body's a one-way street—everything out, nothing in. Go to the bathroom as much as you can. Cut your hair if you have to. Trim your nails. Blow your nose. Clean out your ears, your belly button. Forget your deodorant. Whatever it takes—so when you step on that scale, you're not over."

Humor is a powerful weapon, and one of its best uses is as a means of undercutting stereotypes. The absurdity of apartheid, the babble of ethnocentrism, the reverence for the noble savage, the contempt for the poor, the ethnic slur—all the outsider stereotypes, whether damning or praising, can be turned around with comedy. Here are two poems—one by an Ojibwa, one by an Appalachian. Both poets mock their own group's prevailing stereotypes. The humor is bitter, and while the poets are clearly angry, seeming almost to spit out their words, the irony in their voices takes the edge off the stridency of their messages. That's how humor works—sneaking up on you and then sticking a knife between your ribs.

SURE YOU CAN ASK ME A
PERSONAL QUESTION
by Diane Burns

How do you do?
  No, I am not Chinese.
No, not Spanish.
  No, I am American Indi—uh, Native American.
No, not from India.
  No, not Apache.
No, not Navajo.
  No, not Sioux.
No, we are not extinct.
  Yes, Indin.
Oh?
  So that's where you got those high cheekbones.
Your great grandmother, huh?
  An Indian Princess, huh?
Hair down to there?
  Let me guess. Cherokee?
Oh, so you've had an Indian friend?
  That close?
Oh, so you've had an Indian lover?
  That tight?
Oh, so you've had an Indian servant?
  That much?
Yeah, it was awful what you guys did to us.
  It's real decent of you to apologize.
No, I don't know where you can get peyote.
  No, I don't know where you can get Navajo rugs real cheap.
No, I didn't make this. I bought it at Bloomingdale's.
  Thank you. I like your hair too.
I don't know if anyone knows whether or not Cher is really Indian.
  No, I didn't make it rain tonight.
Yeah. Uh-huh. Spirituality.
  Uh-huh. Yeah. Spirituality. Uh-huh. Mother
Earth. Yeah. Uh-huh. Uh-huh. Spirituality.
  No, I didn't major in archery.
Yeah, a lot of us drink too much.
  Some of us can't drink enough.
This ain't no stoic look.
  This is my face.

OBSERVATIONS

by Jo Carson

Mountain people
can't read,
can't write,
don't wear shoes,
don't have teeth,
don't use soap,

and don't talk plain.
They beat their kids,
beat their friends,
beat their neighbors,
and beat their dogs.
They live on cow peas,
fatback and twenty acres
straight up and down.
They don't have money.
They do have fleas,
overalls,
tobacco patches,
shacks,
shotguns,
foodstamps,
liquor stills,
and at least six junk cars in the front yard.
Right?
Well, let me tell you:
I am from here,
I'm not like that
and I am damned tired of being told I am.

Ethnic and cultural stereotypes are finally about ethnocentricity—a way to keep "them" from ever becoming like "us." It isn't just how we look that gives birth to stereotypes and the ethnocentric way of life. It's also about how we talk. Somehow foreign languages always sound like babble. Dramatic examples of ethnocentrism can make kids laugh and can make them stop to think about their own false perceptions of "us" and "them."

In Paula Fox's *Lily and the Lost Boy,* Lily and her American family are living on a Greek island for several months. They are visitors but not tourists. They live among their Greek neighbors and struggle to learn Greek; by the time they leave, everyone in the village knows them. The landscape, the history, and the daily way of life enrich Lily's view of herself. There's a poignant moment when she faces her own prejudice, her ethnocentricity. A local man, Mr. Kalligas, has always been especially friendly to the American family; he's a warm, excited, slightly comic figure who acts as guide and brings them all the news in his funny broken English. After an accident in which a child has been killed, he tells Lily quietly about the grieving family:

Paula Fox. *Lily and the Lost Boy.* Gr. 6–9

> She and Mr. Kalligas were speaking in Greek. He had always until that moment spoken English with her. She hadn't realized it until she had thought, how well he speaks! Of course, it was his own language! He was a different man in Greek, not comical at all.

Ethnocentricity is no contemporary phenomenon; the more isolated we are, the more we want to divide the world into "us" and "them." And even as the early explorers helped break through our geographical isolation, they were unable to journey beyond their own narrowness. In Rhoda Blumberg's *The Remarkable Voyages of Captain Cook,* the English explorer, on one of his trips to the Pacific in the eighteenth century, stops on a Tahitian island. He's shocked by the Tahitian religious

Rhoda Blumberg. *The Remarkable Voyages of Captain Cook.* Gr. 6–12 practice of human sacrifice: "He told one of the chiefs that he was shocked because an innocent man had been murdered; that in England anyone who killed another person would be hanged. The chief was as horrified. Hanging someone! What a gruesome custom! How dare the English criticize a religiously inspired human sacrifice!"

It hasn't changed all that much in 200 years. When South Africans think of Chicago, they think of gangsters and Al Capone. With the same kind of distortion, the American popular imagination has generally mythologized Africa as a dark, primitive jungle populated with outlandish tribes. According to this view, some brave white explorers "discovered" the continent and brought civilization to a few outposts. Now noble savages give respite to the jaded sophisticates of the West, and rugged individualists find adventure and/or meaning confronting lion and elephant with their trusty native guides. In the South African history textbooks, I was taught about the "Kaffir Wars" from the whites' point of view of "opening up" darkest Africa to the light of Christianity and Western civilization. When the blacks win, it's a massacre; when the whites win, it's a brave victory against desperate odds.

Simi Bedford.
Yoruba Girl
Dancing.
Gr. 9–12

There's a surprising reversal of the colonial encounter in Simi Bedford's adult autobiographical novel *Yoruba Girl Dancing,* a story of culture shock. Throughout her childhood, Remi has been petted and protected, surrounded by comfort and servants, in her grandparents' home in Lagos, Nigeria. But when she's six years old, her stern father ships her off to be educated at a posh girls' boarding school in England. She faces moronic stereotypes and racism. Here's her first encounter in the dorm when the matron introduces her and tells the kids to welcome the new girl who has come all the way from Africa:

> She motioned me forward and I stepped into the room
> and into a silence in which no one breathed. My room-
> mates stood in a row. They examined me from top to toe;
> until now we could not have imagined each other... they
> resembled neither the goose girls nor princesses of my
> reading. We looked at one another in sheer disbelief.

They ask her questions, and when the bell goes off for dinner, one of the girls grabs her hand. Then another girl shouts out:

> 'Let go of her hand.'
> 'The black comes off,' she declared in a voice of doom.
> 'If you touch her the black will rub off on you and very
> soon you will be black all over too.'

At first, when they ask her about life in darkest Africa, she tells them about the big house in Lagos, but she soon finds out that was not the way to keep their interest. What they required, avidly, was life in the African wild. Her experience of such being nil, she's forced to invent, and she discovers an unexpected source—the Tarzan movies she sees on the weekends.

> By and by my father metamorphosed into a tribal chief-
> tain whose frequent duty it was to leave his house in Lagos
> in order to make ceremonial visits to his ancestral village
> deep in the heart of the jungle, and when I was in Africa
> I used to accompany him, naturally, with the rest of the

household. Papa would have been amazed to hear, as I sat by the fire toasting crumpets, how frequently he led his villagers out on a leopard hunt with only his spear to protect him. Mama, Grandma and Patience would have been equally astounded to hear that only the day before they had been sitting in the open around a snake stew supper.

Tough, dynamic, and resourceful, Remi grows up savvy, wise, and proud of both her African heritage and her English education.

We become outsiders in many ways—usually ways over which we have no control. Race, gender, social class, family, and geography can make outsiders of anyone, no matter how passionately they may wish to be inside. On the other hand, sometimes we make outsiders of ourselves, deliberately using our behavior to define us as different. In *The Runner*, one of Cynthia Voigt's best YA novels, the protagonist, Bullet, is an angry outsider and a racist. He's strong, hard, alone, contemptuous of the weak; smart but suspicious of books and talk; prejudiced against blacks. A champion runner, he runs 10 miles a day, every day, and he is the Maryland state champion, but only cross-country, never on a track. In everything, he is proud that "he ran himself." He is angry much of the time, locked in a struggle with his bullying father. It's 1967 and he'll have nothing to do with what he regards as the trendy political issues in his high school—Vietnam, the draft, integration. We watch Bullet struggle with change. He overcomes his prejudice, partly through a challenging relationship with a black runner, experiencing, not sloganizing, that black is beautiful. But he remains fierce and apart, determined that no one will box him in. On his eighteenth birthday, Bullet enlists, knowing it's not for any heroic ideal, but to break free of his father and to choose for himself the box that fits him best. Voigt is raising—without didacticism—important ideas of the individual and society and being "young at a difficult time in time." She makes us see the stubbornness and the confusion, but also the strange nobility, in choosing to become an outsider.

Cynthia Voigt. *The Runner.* Gr. 7–12

Some of the most powerful outsider stories are those about loners who find each other. In Brock Cole's *The Goats*, two solitary kids become close friends. The book opens with a practical "joke" at a summer camp on Lake Michigan. A boy and a girl from Chicago, Howie and Laura, are the victims. Shy and awkward, they are the outsiders, the goats. The other kids take their clothes and leave the pair marooned for the night on a small island. The campers mean to come back later and spy on them. It's all supposed to be a traditional camp joke; even the counselors half go along with it. Shocked, freezing, terrified, Howie and Laura decide to get away from the island and from the camp. They make it to the shore. As they hide, they struggle to find food, clothes, and shelter. And they take care of each other. The friendship after the isolation is intensely moving, even more so because Cole writes with such control. One night they sleep over at another camp where the kids are kind to them. Howie and Laura meet the next morning at breakfast:

Brock Cole. *The Goats.* Gr. 6–9

> She found him the next morning sitting alone and slightly apart at breakfast. He was eating something white and fluffy, covered with syrup. He ate very neatly, like a cat. She felt a sudden raging tenderness toward him. She

was so glad he was there. She wanted to roughhouse; to throw her arms around him and wrestle him to the ground. She bet she could do it. She was bigger than he was. She couldn't, of course. He wouldn't mind, but the other kids would think they were crazy. She contented herself with sliding along his bench and bumping his hip with hers as hard as she could. He smiled at her and bumped back.

"Yuck!" she said. "What's that?"

"Grits. It's made out of corn. Did you ever have it before?"

She shook her head.

"Me neither. It's pretty good, though. You just put lots of syrup on it. It's Milo's specialty. You want some?"

"I don't know. Can I try some of yours?"

"Sure. This is my seconds, actually." He gave her his spoon and leaned his head on his fist so he could watch her eat. He couldn't seem to stop smiling.

It is appropriate to end the outsider chapter with a quote that is as much about friends as it is about outsiders. Great books are never "about" one theme, no more than individuals are defined by a single characteristic. Outsiders, friends, monsters, journeys, survival—all the archetypal themes commingle freely, not only in *The Goats*, but also in ourselves.

FRIENDS AND ENEMIES

I loved my friend.
He went away from me.
There's nothing more to say.
The poem ends,
Soft as it began—
I loved my friend.

—*Langston Hughes*

"When I take that journey and go down there and slay those dragons, do I have to go alone?" Bill Moyers once asked Joseph Campbell. Even though the epic journey is a personal one, companions and mentors can help you find your way. Sometimes the hero's companion is a member of the family. Sometimes it's a friend. It may be a stranger who turns out to be a friend, or it may be a friend who changes to an enemy. Unlike family ties, friendships not only begin, they can also end.

Whether the focus is on the conflict between family and friend, the search for identity and courage, the joy of sharing, or the shock of betrayal, stories about friendship are of universal interest to young people. There's no more natural way to see across cultures than to recognize in stories from everywhere your own yearning for a friend you can trust or a group you can belong to. Some of the best friendship stories show how love and hurt get all mixed up, how you make friends and lose them and sometimes keep them for a lifetime. You share good times, danger, secrets. A friend you've grown up with moves away. You've hurt someone who depends on you, and you wish you could go back and put things right. You find a friend in your family. Someone you laughed with is now laughing at you. A friend lets you down. Or throws you a lifeline. Is it friend or enemy who exposes you to a dark corner inside yourself? Friends help you know who you are. They can also transform you.

Like Brock Cole's *The Goats*, Katherine Paterson's Newbery Medal–winner *Bridge to Terabithia* is as much about outsiders as it is about friends.

Katherine Paterson. *Bridge to Terabithia.* Gr. 5–8

Ever since first grade, Jess Aarons has been that crazy little kid who draws all the time. Then last year he won the sprint race at recess, and now he's training hard to be the fastest runner in the fifth grade. He wants to win. But then a new girl called Leslie Burke comes from the Washington suburbs to live on a farm near Jess. At school, she crosses over to the boy's side of the playground and beats Jess in a crucial race. At first he's furious with her, but then they become close friends. They make their own secret place—a castle stronghold they call Terabithia—deep in the woods where no one can come and mess up their games. As in Avi's *"Who Was That Masked Man, Anyway?"* these friends make a secret world through their play. Jess doesn't care that the other kids think Leslie is weird, or that they tease him for playing with a girl, though he wishes his Dad didn't think he was a sissy. Then Leslie is killed in a storm. Jess is devastated, but Leslie's friendship has transformed him, and he finds the strength to bring others to Terabithia.

Walter Dean Myers says that when kids write to him about his books, what they talk about most is the friendship between his characters, whether the book is the funny neighborhood comedy *Fast Sam, Cool Clyde, and Stuff,* or the stark novel about a Harlem teenager in Vietnam, *Fallen Angels,* or a grim, inner-city story like *Scorpions.*

Walter Dean Myers. *Scorpions.* Gr. 5–10

A strong friendship across cultures is at the center of *Scorpions,* where 12-year-old Jamal is struggling to survive on the dangerous inner-city streets. He's a nice kid, and he cares about his mother and his younger sister and his best friend, Tito. But there's too much against Jamal, and no one to help. His big brother, Randy, is in jail for shooting a man in a hold-up, and his mother can't find the money for an appeal. One of Randy's old gang members gives Jamal a gun. He's scared of the gun. He hides it. He agrees with Tito that he should get rid of it. But it's so tempting to keep it and feel powerful in a dangerous world:

> Every thought he had about the gun was bad. It had made so much trouble, had hurt them so much. But there was something else, too. Something deep in him that he thought Tito knew about, had maybe known about even before he did. That was the part of him, a part that was small and afraid, that still wanted the gun.

The gun and the gang pull Jamal one way; his friendship with Tito pulls him another way. The scenes between Jamal and Tito are funny and tender and then increasingly desperate, until Tito gets drawn into Jamal's trouble, and the police send him back to Puerto Rico to live with his father. The parting of the two friends at the end of the book is heartbreaking.

There's the same sense of sadness in this oft-anthologized poem:

WE REAL COOL

by Gwendolyn Brooks

The Pool Players
Seven At the Golden Shovel

We real cool. We
Left school. We

Lurk late. We
Strike straight. We

Sing sin. We
Thin gin. We

Jazz June. We
Die soon.

Brooks' relentless emphasis on "We" makes you think about why people join gangs. The contemporary idiom of this poem, the jazz rhythm, and the deceptively simple, entirely monosyllabic text compel kids' attention. The search for community and belonging, for friends, makes even more shocking the truth of the last line. In fact, almost every word can be read ironically, including each word of the title. Are *We* tough or desperate, friends or enemies? A good poem to read with this is Brooks' "Song in the Front Yard" about a child in a protected home longing for adventure and risk. What myths of comradeship, what needs, underlie gang wars?

Alex Kotlowitz's *There Are No Children Here: The Story of Two Boys Growing Up in the Other America* is a moving nonfiction account to read with Brooks' "We Real Cool" and with Myers' *Scorpions*. In fine journalistic style, both quiet and passionate, Kotlowitz tells of the two years he spent following the lives of two brothers, Lafeyette and Pharoah Rivers, in the Chicago Henry Horner Homes in the inner city. He saw the brothers "struggle with school, attempt to resist the lure of gangs, and mourn the death of friends, all the while searching for some inner peace." This account gives a human face to the statistics—one in every three children in Chicago lives in poverty—and shows what it's like to grow up where your schoolmates are shot on the way to class.

Walter Dean Myers makes a bitterly ironic comment on those inner city wars in his novel *Fallen Angels.* Seventeen-year-old Richie Perry has left the violent streets of Harlem for Vietnam, and at first he mouths clichés about fighting to keep the streets of America free. But Richie isn't sure how he got to be a soldier in Vietnam. He wouldn't have joined the army if he'd seen anything else to do. When he figured he couldn't afford college, he just didn't want to be in Harlem anymore. What he does know now is that he is nearly always afraid. As he faces his uncertainty about why he is fighting or who the enemy is, friendship is what sustains him. This story is about Richie and the other young men on his squad, who find themselves in a nightmare of rain and mud and slaughter. Richie says that the war seems to be about "hours of boredom, seconds of terror." There's the frenetic moment in the helicopter after a battle, where wounded Richie sees that his friend is dead, zipped into a bodybag.

And there's the elemental scene when Richie kills a soldier and finds the enemy is himself: "I looked up into the face of the Cong soldier. He was young. No more than a teenager. He looked scared and tired, the same as me. I squeezed the trigger of the sixteen and watched him hurtle backward."

Erich Maria Remarque's German classic *All Quiet on the Western Front,* about German teenage soldiers during World War I, is very like *Fallen Angels* in its story about high school kids who find themselves fighting in a war they know nothing about against an enemy just like them. In spare,

Alex Kotlowitz.
*There Are No
Children Here.*
Gr. 9–12

Walter Dean
Myers. *Fallen
Angels.*
Gr. 7–12

Erich Maria
Remarque. *All
Quiet on the
Western Front.*
Gr. 8–12

laconic style, accessible to most junior high and high school readers, a young soldier tells the story of himself and his school classmates in the trenches. Terse heartbreaking scenes communicate the boys' loss of innocence as they face the facts of war. The narrator talks about his schoolmaster, who exhorted the boys in his classes to "join up" and fight. Then he talks about a classmate, Joseph Behm, who died in agony in No Man's Land:

> There was, indeed, one of us who hesitated and did not want to fall into line. That was Joseph Behm, a plump, homely fellow. But he did allow himself to be persuaded, otherwise he would have been ostracized. And perhaps more of us thought as he did, but no one could very well stand out, because at the time even one's parents were ready with the word "coward"; no one had the vaguest idea what we were in for. . . .
>
> Strange to say, Behm was one of the first to fall. He got hit in the eye during an attack, and we left him lying for dead. We couldn't bring him with us, because we had to come back helter-skelter. In the afternoon suddenly we heard him call, and saw him crawling about in No Man's Land. He had only been knocked unconscious. Because he could not see, and was mad with pain, he failed to keep under cover, and so was shot down before anyone could go and fetch him in.

The narrator attacks those who sent young boys to their deaths with talk of glory:

> While they continued to write and talk, we saw the wounded and dying. While they taught that duty to one's country is the greatest thing, we already knew that death-throes are stronger. But for all that we were no mutineers, no deserters, no cowards—they were very free with all these expressions. We loved our country as much as they; we went courageously into every action; but also we distinguished the false from true, we had suddenly learned to see. And we saw that there was nothing of their world left. We were all at once terribly alone; and alone we must see it through.

Or there's the scene where the boys visit their wounded schoolmate Kemmerich and realize he is dying. His leg has been amputated. One of the boys, Muller, covets the dying boy's boots—not because Muller does not feel grief for his friend, but because Kemmerich will not use his legs again, and good boots are scarce.

An eighth-grade social studies teacher, Rita Headrick, first told me to read *All Quiet on the Western Front*. She was teaching a unit on early-twentieth-century history, and she wanted to humanize the history by having the kids read fiction about the period. We included adult classics like John Steinbeck's *Grapes of Wrath* and Betty Smith's *A Tree Grows in Brooklyn* as well as YA titles like Mildred Taylor's *Roll of Thunder, Hear My Cry*. Dorothy Strang in the English department got involved, and each student chose a book to write about as history for social studies class and as literature for English class. Rita wanted to include *All Quiet on the Western*

Front. I'd never read it—though I didn't dare tell her that—and I resisted her; too dull, foreign, difficult, I thought. But she persuaded me, and I was astonished at how accessible it was and how contemporary. We bought bright new paperbacks and promoted it—and many kids chose that novel and were profoundly moved by it. In fact, it was so successful that Remarque's novel is now required reading for the course.

A boy and his high school friends are also fighting on the front in Grigory Baklanov's *Forever Nineteen*. Translated from the Russian, the novel is based on Baklanov's own experience as a teenager fighting the Germans somewhere in the Ukraine during World War II. He writes about the ordinary young soldier's experience of the muddle and waste of war. The battle scenes are vivid, with vignettes of bloody action and empty glory. The protagonist, Treyakov, doesn't even last through one battle, and most of the story takes place in the hospital ward of a small town where he's recovering from his wounds. Lying awake, he doesn't know if it's his wounds or his soul that bother him, but he can't help thinking about the loss, the futility. In his quiet introduction, Baklanov says that all 20 boys in his high school class were sent to the front. Only he returned.

Myron Levoy's *Alan and Naomi* is a beautiful story of a wartime friendship, where a Jewish boy in New York City during World War II is moved to reach beyond himself and try to help Naomi, a disturbed Holocaust refugee. Alan's parents ask him to help Naomi, who lives in the upstairs apartment. She's been mentally disturbed since she watched her father beaten to death by Nazis in France. Alan doesn't want to go near her:

> I won't do it. I have enough problems the way it is. Some of the guys call me sissy sometimes! . . . I got one friend on the block, that's all. And he'll quit on me! She's a girl! And she's crazy . . .
>
> Dad, I can't! It's not fair! Don't make me do this. *Please!*

But his father makes an appeal:

> No , we can't force you. But—allow me one but. In our life, Alan, sometimes when we're young, sometimes when we're old, in our life, once or twice, we're called upon to do something we can't do . . . . Why do we do it? It's a mystery. Maybe to prove that what we are is something a little more than what we think we are.

Reluctantly Alan agrees, and he visits Naomi daily, talking to her through his old puppet. After days and days of compulsively tearing paper, she finally begins to answer him through her doll.

Although Alan and Naomi are only 12, junior high and high school readers are moved by the horror of Naomi's experience, by Alan's moral struggle to find meaning in the overwhelming evil of the Holocaust, by the depth of their unlikely friendship, and by the integrity of the bleak ending.

The title says it all in Ilse-Margret Vogel's memoir *Bad Times, Good Friends*. Up to now, this has been a largely untold story: the experience of ordinary Germans who hated Hitler and tried to survive and befriend each other, doing what they could in daily life to undermine the Nazi war effort. This memoir is about the last years of the war, when Vogel,

Grigory Baklanov. *Forever Nineteen*. Gr. 7–12

Myron Levoy. *Alan and Naomi*. Gr. 6–10

Ilse-Margret Vogel. *Bad Times, Good Friends*. Gr. 8–12

about 30 years old, is living in Berlin as an artist. She's in touch with others like herself, who hide in the crowds of the city, always balanced on the edge of danger between the Nazi threat around them and the Allied bombardment from the skies. Vogel makes you feel how you can get used to a wilder and more desperate norm. There's a sense of recklessness, and of barely contained chaos, in the madness outside and sometimes in Vogel herself. Yet with all the fierce action—even in episodes of rape and pillage—the writing is controlled, totally without hype or empty heroics. The structure is a little too loose, each chapter focusing, more or less, on a particular friend, circling back sometimes to tell more about someone we met earlier. Vogel doesn't tell much about her inner life, but her friends are memorable characters: awkward, strange, endearing, ugly, mysterious—the gifted forger, the draft evader, the fugitive Jew. In one of the best episodes she's asked to hide a man she can't stand; he's an anti-Nazi, and he's in danger. Where does her duty lie? Readers will find this quiet account a moving contrast to the usual escape-adventure World War II story with its clear separation into "us" and "them." Even when it's difficult to pinpoint good and evil, though, we respond to the bond shared by friends.

**Sheila Gordon.
Waiting for the Rain.
Gr. 7–12**

Sheila Gordon's *Waiting for the Rain* is about an interracial friendship that is broken by apartheid. The story begins with what seems to be a strong relationship. Two boys—the white Afrikaans farmer's nephew, Frikkie, and the black foreman's son, Tengo, have been playmates since childhood. Frikkie wants things to remain the same (one day he'll own the farm, and Tengo will be his bossboy), but Tengo comes to resent the way things are under apartheid. He wants an education, and he forces his parents to let him go to school in Soweto, near Johannesburg. He does brilliantly in his studies, but he can't ignore the seething rebellion around him. At first he's reluctant to join the school boycott. But as the violence gets worse and police and soldiers shoot at demonstrators and arrest his classmates without trial, he joins the street battles. When Tengo and Frikkie meet again, they're on opposite sides.

With its compelling friendship theme, you could use this book with junior high readers as a starting point for a discussion of apartheid. Young people have been at the forefront of the contemporary apartheid struggle. School boycotts, pitched street battles, police terror, and prison without trial are a part of common teenage experience. Here it's clear that personal friendship can be wrenched apart by politics.

**Rafik Schami. *A Hand Full of Stars*.
Gr. 7–10**

Rafik Schami's *A Hand Full of Stars*, which won the 1991 Batchelder Award for best book in translation, also sets friendship against a background of political terror. In contemporary Damascus, an Arab teenager writes in his journal about himself, his family, his friends, and his love, while in the background, government violence mounts, coup follows coup, and he is drawn into secret and dangerous resistance. With warmth and comedy, the journal entries focus on the characters in the boy's narrow street, where "poverty smothers our dreams," but there's a rich, vital multicultural community. The narrator's family is Catholic, his best friend is Muslim, the barber is Armenian, the assistant comes from Persia, and the boy's beloved elderly mentor tells him stories from everywhere. Schami is a Syrian now living in Germany.

An Armenian boy comes to America from the Middle East in this comic baseball poem in which friends are formed on the ball diamond, through the narrator's bumbling and laughter:

HOW I LEARNED ENGLISH

by Gregory Djanikian

It was in an empty lot
Ringed by elms and fir and honeysuckle.
Bill Corson was pitching in his buckskin jacket,
Chuck Keller, fat even as a boy, was on first,
His T-shirt riding up over his gut,
Ron O'Neill, Jim, Dennis, were talking it up
In the field, a blue sky above them
Tipped with cirrus.
    And there I was,
Just off the plane and plopped in the middle
Of Williamsport, Pa. and a neighborhood game,
Unnatural and without any moves,
My notions of baseball and America
Growing fuzzier each time I whiffed.

So it was not impossible that I,
Banished to the outfield and day dreaming
Of water, or hotel in the mountains,
Would suddenly find myself in the path
Of a ball stung by Joe Barone,
I watched it closing in
Clean and untouched, transfixed
By its easy arc before it hit
My forehead with a thud.
    I fell back,
Dazed, clutching my brow,
Groaning, "Oh my shin, oh my shin,"
And everybody peeled away from me
And dropped from laughter, and there we were,
All of us writhing on the ground for one reason
Or another.
    Someone said "shin" again,
There was a wild stamping of hands on the ground,
A kicking of feet, and the fit
Of laughter overtook me too,
And that was important, as important
As Joe Barone asking me how I was
Through his tears, picking me up
And dusting me off with hands like swatters,
And though my head felt heavy,
I played on till dusk
Missing flies and pop-ups and grounders
And calling out in desperation things like
"Yours" and "take it," but doing all right,
Tugging at my cap in just the right way,
Crouching low, my feet set,
"Hum baby" sweetly on my lips.

Baseball is also the bridge to friendship in Chaim Potok's *The Chosen*, where two teenage players begin as angry rivals and end up as close friends. The story begins with a very competitive baseball game between two rival Jewish schools, one of them Hasidic, in Brooklyn during World

Chaim Potok.
The Chosen.
Gr. 6–12

. . . .

War II. Being good at baseball is as important to the boys as a top grade in Talmud, because it is a sign of being a strong, patriotic American. In the tight excitement before the first pitch is thrown, Reuven chats to a teammate about the game and the rival Hasidic team:

> "You're looking good out there, Reuven," he told me.
> "Thanks," I said.
> "Everyone is looking real good."
> "It'll be a good game."
> He stared at me through his glasses. "You think so?" he asked.
> "Sure, why not?"
> "You ever see them play, Reuven?"
> "No."
> "They're murderers."
> "Sure," I said.
> "No, really. They're wild."
> "You saw them play?"
> "Twice. They're murderers."
> "Everyone plays to win, Davey."
> "They don't only play to win. They play like it's the first of the Ten Commandments."

The Hasidic team arrives, but they don't look murderous at all: Orthodox, self-righteous, dressed in their traditional clothes. But as the game goes on, the Hasidic's intense hostility is communicated; tension rises, and Reuven, the other team's pitcher, feels it:

> Standing on the field and watching the boy at the plate swing at a high ball and miss, I felt myself suddenly very angry, and it was at that point that for me the game stopped being merely a game and became a war. The fun and excitement was out of it now. Somehow the yeshiva team had translated this afternoon's baseball game into a conflict between what they regarded as their righteousness and our sinfulness. I found myself growing more and more angry, and I felt the anger begin to focus itself upon Danny Saunders, and suddenly it was not at all difficult for me to hate him.

Danny, at bat, slams a line drive back to the pitcher's mound, smashing Reuven's glasses and nearly blinding him.

Afterwards, Danny visits Reuven in the hospital to try to apologize. At first Reuven drives Danny away, but he comes back and they talk, candidly facing the violence they had both felt. "I don't understand why I wanted to kill you," Danny says, and Reuven admits that he could have ducked but wouldn't allow himself to duck a drive off Danny's bat. And from that intense rivalry, even hatred, from that honest confrontation, a close friendship grows that sustains both boys through some hard times.

Friendship can reach across generations. Truman Capote's autobiographical story *The Thanksgiving Visitor* is based on his experience as a small boy living with elderly relatives in rural Alabama during the Depression. Buddy is relentlessly bullied by Odd Henderson, who is 12 years old but only in second grade. Odd sees Buddy as a sissy and torments him so that Buddy has nightmares and hates school. Odd's father is in

Truman Capote.
*The
Thanksgiving
Visitor.*
Gr. 6–12

. . . . . .

jail, and the family is struggling in poverty. Buddy says you might have felt sorry for Odd if he weren't so hateful.

Buddy's friend is his 60-year-old cousin, Miss Sook Faulk. Shy, innocent, a little childlike, she understands him perfectly. He confides in her about the bullying, and she suggests he ask Odd for Thanksgiving dinner. When Buddy won't, she does. At the party, Buddy finds a wonderful opportunity for revenge and compassion.

The intensity between friends, the anger that can destroy you if you don't confront it, is also the subject of this great eighteenth-century poem:

THE POISON TREE

by William Blake

I was angry with my friend: .
I told my wrath, my wrath did end.
I was angry with my foe:
I told it not, my wrath did grow.

And I water'd it in fears,
Night and morning with my tears;
And I sunned it with smiles,
And with soft deceitful wiles.

And it grew both day and night,
Till it bore an apple bright;
And my foe beheld it shine,
And he knew that it was mine,

And into my garden stole
When the night had veil'd the pole:
In the morning glad I see
My foe outstretch'd beneath the tree.

There's the same candor about the transformation of enemies and friends in Maurice Gee's scary thriller set in New Zealand during World War I. *The Fire-Raiser* dramatizes the secret fury of a pyromaniac and relates it to the mob violence let loose in the community by jingoism and war. Four kids start off hostile and ugly and end up working together as friends to stop the burning.

Maurice Gee.
The Fire-Raiser.
Gr. 6–12

At times you're right there with the fire-raiser, his pleasure and power ("Flame filled the inside of his head. It ran along his arteries. It licked around his bones."). At other times you're with the wise, quirky schoolteacher, coping with meanness and cruelty, trying to give his students hope. But most of the action focuses on four town kids. Kitty and Noel are the children of the sensible baker; Phil's a street-kid, smelly and smart; Irene's the butt of playground teasing because she's upperclass. These kids find themselves in deadly danger from a villain who is "silent, quick, and mad." Gee makes some attempt at psychologizing about why the fire-raiser Marwick became the way he is, but, fortunately, most of that is left mysterious. Marwick's mother, fierce, punishing, patrician, is straight out of old-fashioned melodrama; she's "witch and spider." What makes this story special is the combination of terror and dailiness. Gee gets the kids exactly right, with an ambiguity rare in YA books. He shows in every beautiful sentence how complicated feelings can be, how ally and foe can shift, in the classroom, in the adult community, and on the battlefields in Europe.

Jan Slepian. *Risk N' Roses.* Gr. 6–10

Jan Slepian's YA novel *Risk N' Roses* captures the powerful attraction of a dangerous friend. Slepian dramatizes an essential teen conflict: How do I choose between home and the street? Does it have to be my father or my friend?

Skip Berman has always been her father's good girl. In fact, she's had to be especially good to make up to her parents for her older sister, Angela, who's mentally slow. Skip's duty to her sweet, simple sister is like a weight around her neck.

Then Skip falls under the spell of Jean, an exciting girl she meets on the playground. Skip abandons her sister and follows Jean into wildness and daring. With three other girls, they break into an abandoned house and form a secret club. Jean dares Skip to steal from the Five-and-Ten.

For Skip it's a thrilling, dazzling time. "I'm Jean's best friend." she tells herself. "We're best friends."

From the street, Skip comes home to angry scenes about her sister Angela. Always Angela. Skip tries not to hear the same old arguments between her parents, arguments about Angela, like the steps of a dance. Always Angela. Always guilt. What Skip likes about Jean is that Jean doesn't care; she doesn't feel guilty about anything. She's like the leader of a wolf pack, untamed. And Skip discovers a taste for cruelty in herself when she's with Jean: it's exciting. And in the shadows lurks the omnipresent threat: What if the pack turns on me?

Then Jean makes a cruel plan, and Skip must choose—her sister or her friend. When Skip does break with Jean, it's like waking from a fever. But Skip knows her father doesn't know her; she is beyond trying only to please him. Her sister is the same pain in the neck she's always been. And the street still calls.

Betrayal is the other side of friendship. The intense bond can turn to hatred. Sometimes it's hard to know why. Perhaps having been so close to someone, you know how to get them where it hurts.

Margaret Atwood. *Cat's Eye.* Gr. 9–12

In *Cat's Eye,* Canadian writer Margaret Atwood dramatizes what many of us would rather forget about growing up female—the cruelty of little girls to each other, especially girl *friends*. She takes the ages around nine through twelve—the misnamed "latency" years—and remembers that far from being a calm cheery time, for some girls it was filled with ferocious power games and fierce obsession.

Elaine is an outsider, and she can't get things right, can't understand all the clues. Her three "best" friends, led by Cordelia, correct her for her own good:

> On the window ledge beside mine, Cordelia and Grace and Carol are sitting, jammed in together, whispering and giggling. I have to sit on a window ledge by myself because they aren't speaking to me. It's something I said wrong, but I don't know what it is because they won't tell me. Cordelia says it will be better for me to think back over everything I've said today and try to pick out the wrong thing. That way I will learn not to say such a thing again. When I've guessed the right answer, then they will speak

to me again. All of this is for my own good, because they are my best friends and they want to help me improve.

In the morning at the bus stop they're waiting:

> Once I'm outside the house there is no getting away from them. They are on the school bus, where Cordelia stands close beside me and whispers into my ear: "Stand up straight! People are looking!" Carol is in my classroom, and it's her job to report to Cordelia what I do and say all day. They're there at recess, and in the cellar at lunchtime. They comment on the kind of lunch I have, how I hold my sandwich, how I chew. On the way home from school I have to walk in front of them, or behind. In front is worse because they talk about how I'm walking, how I look from behind. "Don't hunch over," says Cordelia. "Don't move your arms like that."

Elaine wishes she could hate them:

> With enemies you can feel hatred, and anger. But Cordelia is my friend. She likes me, she wants to help me, they all do. They are my friends, my girl friends, my best friends. I have never had any before and I'm terrified of losing them. I want to please.

Atwood acknowledges another disturbing truth: adults can do nothing about it. "You don't have to play with them," her mother says. "There must be other little girls you can play with instead."

"They're my friends," Elaine says miserably.

Queen of the Sixth Grade, one of the titles in Ilene Cooper's fine Kids from Kennedy Middle School series, also captures that desire to be one of the in-group, a desire so all-consuming you're willing to compromise the best in yourself, just so the kids will like you and won't exclude you. The overwhelming fear is that you'll be the outsider, the one they sneer about, the friendless one. Robin knows that Veronica is cruel, but Veronica's a leader and Robin wants to be liked by her. In this scene, Veronica sets up the outsider, Gretchen, for public humiliation:

Ilene Cooper. *Queen of the Sixth Grade.* Gr. 4–7

> Then, when the class was almost over and the girls were sprawled out on the grass, listening to Coach's announcements, Gretchen raised her hand.
>
> Coach Brown peered at her over his glasses.
>
> "Yes?"
>
> Gretchen stood up. "Coach, uh, I want to show the class my tumbling act."
>
> "Your tumbling act?" he repeated.
>
> Robin closed her eyes.
>
> "Yes, I've been practicing."
>
> The coach was nonplussed, but he glanced at his watch. "We have a minute or two before we're dismissed. Go ahead."
>
> Gretchen moved slowly to the front of the class. She stood there for a moment, looking heavier and more awkward than ever. Then she got down on her hands and knees and did a somersault. As she lopsidedly rolled over,

her fat thighs quivered like melting Jell-O. The edge of
her underpants, caught in the elastic of her shorts, winked
out at the class.

Veronica had been whispering to some of the girls, who
snickered and passed on the joke to whoever was sitting
next to them. By the time Gretchen righted herself and
tried a cartwheel—her thick legs never even left the
ground—a couple of the kids were stuffing their hands in
their mouths to hold in the laughter, while others didn't
even try to hide their hilarity.

Coach Brown didn't know exactly what was going on,
but he knew enough to be angry. "That's enough,
Gretchen. I don't know why ... " The bell clanged noisily
and everyone got up and ran indoors, laughing and
screaming.

Robin knew she should be mad at Veronica, but her fury
was directed at Gretchen, who was walking toward the
locker room, her head down.

"How could you do that?" she yelled at Gretchen. A few
of the other stragglers turned and then looked away.

Gretchen looked at her with tired eyes. "Veronica said
she'd let me into the club."

Kids will recognize the truth of Robin's misery and anger: she's furious
not at the tormentor, but at the victim, who is so close to what Robin
fears she herself could be.

Like Cooper, Phyllis Reynolds Naylor, in her funny, poignant coming-
of-age series about motherless Alice, is right on target with the contemporary peer scene, even as she dramatizes the age-old patterns of shame
and transformation. In *The Agony of Alice*, Alice goes through sixth grade
in an agony of humiliation, longing for a female role model to show her
how to behave. Her father tries his best, but he can't help her with things
like buying her first bra, and the Sears Catalog only confuses her. She's
grateful when the girlfriend of her older brother, Lester, talks to her
about pantyhose and about how to take care of her cuticles ("I didn't
even know I *had* cuticles."). She longs to be in the class of glamorous Miss
Cole and hates her teacher, pear-shaped Mrs. Plotkin. But Mrs. Plotkin
proves kind; she knows Alice at her worst and likes her. Alice begins to
accept herself; a cousin helps her buy a bra; her period comes, and it's
no big deal; she reaches out to comfort her brother in trouble, and they
have "an entire conversation without being rude to each other once."
Although the resolution is a little too easy, Naylor's characters are drawn
with subtlety and affection, and there's no heavy moralizing. Alice has
just a glimpse of Miss Cole's shallow behavior. Mrs. Plotkin delivers few
homilies besides telling Alice that her "agonies" happen to everyone.
This wonderfully funny and touching story will make readers smile with
wry recognition.

In *All But Alice*, the once-klutzy outsider has made it into the popular
group, her ears pierced, her brand names correct. The trouble is that
her life gets boring. But if the agony's gone now, the comedy's as rich as
ever. Alice would like to conform, but who comes first? Family? Friends?
The sisterhood? Her confusion and her fear of embarrassment come
together in a beautifully understated climax on the school bus, when she
defies the crowd and risks her popularity for a friend.

Phyllis Reynolds
Naylor. *The
Agony of Alice*.
Gr. 5–8

Phyllis Reynolds
Naylor. *All But
Alice*.
Gr. 5–8

One of the great pleasures of friendship (and of reading) is that it shows you alternatives to the patterns of home. This is especially satisfying for a young immigrant caught between two cultures. But everyone can remember astonishment at spending time in a friend's home and discovering that things you thought were written in stone aren't important to other families at all.

In Lensey Namioka's warm, funny *Yang the Youngest and His Terrible Ear,* two friends who can't live up to the pressures of their rigid families help each other find self-acceptance. Newly arrived in Seattle from Shanghai, nine-year-old Yingtao fails his musical family because he has a terrible ear—he's tone deaf. No amount of practicing can help. When he plays second violin in the Yang family string quartet, the screeches make his musician father screw up his face in pain. Yingtao does begin to fit in at school when he makes the baseball team with the help of his friend Matthew. The trouble is, Yingtao's father disapproves of baseball; his son should be practicing for the upcoming recital. American Matthew has the opposite problem: he's a gifted violinist, but his father thinks he's a nerd for playing music instead of baseball. As the recital draws near, the friends work out a plan for Matthew to "bow sync" for Yingtao from behind a screen. The lighthearted, first-person narrative captures the bewilderment of the immigrant experience and the confusion about customs and language. There are also some poignant moments—the ache for home in China, the sting of prejudice, the wish to be part of the family music. But self-acceptance triumphs as Yingtao realizes that his great eye for the ball "made up for having a terrible ear."

Lensey Namioka. Yang the Youngest and His Terrible Ear. Gr. 4–7

Richard Peck's YA novels dramatize teenage friendship with poignancy and wit. In *Remembering the Good Times,* Buck remembers his friendship with Trav and how they both loved the same girl, their classmate Kate. Trav is brilliant, intense, driven—he later commits suicide—and the book is about personal suffering; it is also a witty commentary on the way we live now. There's Rusty, new to their Midwest school: "Because I'm from California," she said, "so I'm flexible." The three friends ask her what schools are like in California:

Richard Peck. Remembering the Good Times. Gr. 6–10

> Rusty leaned back in the chair. "Basically optional," she said. "You've got your burnouts and your Vals and your heads and your modified heads and your granola people. You've got your Souls, your Anglos, your low-riders, your boat people. Everybody's in little boxes." She paused. "Like here, come to think about it, but the climate's better."
>
> "I meant academically," Trav said.
>
> Rusty thought about that—thought about Trav, maybe. "It's there if you want it, but most people are majoring in personal image. Basically, it's too easy. Even with a room-temperature IQ you can pull down a couple of A's for the report card. That's enough to mellow out most parents. So then you think, Why worry?"

There's a lot of preening, just showing off, in youthful friendship, but there's also safety, knowing that you have somewhere to go for help when you need it.

Like a good friend, a story can make the world bigger.

LOVERS AND STRANGERS

I want to feel myself in you when you taste food, in the arc
of your mallet when you work.
When you visit friends, when you go
up on the roof by yourself at night.
There's nothing worse than to walk out along the street
without you. I don't know where I'm going.
You're the road and the knower of roads,
more than maps, more than love.

—Rumi

The transformation of falling in love has inspired stories and poetry that reach young people across time and space and language. Whether it's Cathy and Heathcliff running wild on the moors in defiance of convention and authority; or Tristan betraying his father-friend for his love, Isolde; or Romeo and Juliet doomed by the family feuds that imprison them, the stories and songs reveal a fragile intimacy so powerful that it reaches out to the universe.

Love stories are also about strangers and about leaving home. The stranger who comes to town may kill the dragon that lays waste the land. Or the stranger may be the dragon that destroys truth and beauty. Either way, the stranger is mysterious and powerful, revealing a whole new view of the universe, moving you away from home.

Whether satyr or siren, the exciting newcomer can come from far away or can be someone you've known all your life who is suddenly transformed. The dull girl everyone's ignored since kindergarten can become a powerful stranger when she finds a new sexy self (that's what happens in the story "Waiting" in *The Leaving* by Nova Scotia writer Budge Wilson). The stranger can be the boy next door, who turns into a handsome prince. The awakening of love can make you a stranger to yourself.

The exquisite lines from the poem by the Persian poet Rumi that begin this chapter are in Ruth Gordon's anthology *Under All Silences: Shades of*

Love, which fuses feelings and ideas in exciting paradox. Translated by John Moyne and Coleman Barks, Rumi's poem roots myth in the everyday world, so that the banal words "I don't know where I'm going" evoke the archetype of the journey, and the glorious image "the arc of your mallet" makes us see the universal cycle in the particulars of daily work.

Drawn from ancient Egypt and medieval Japan, as well as from contemporary Europe, Russia, the U.S., and other times and places, the poems in this world anthology celebrate love that both holds and frees you, emotions so deep that the lover lacks words for them. The Russian Yevgeny Yevtushenko is breathless in "Waiting," beginning with "My love will come" and imagining how she will run upstairs "in from the pouring dark" and into his arms; e.e.cummings is equally giddy as he celebrates the very fact of love:

> love is the air the ocean and the land . . .
> the truth more first than sun more last than star.

There's also yearning and melancholy. And, always, there's surprise, as when May Sarton describes opening a letter from someone you love:

> There was your voice, astonishment,
> Falling into the silence suddenly.

A common theme across cultures is that of love threatened by prejudice and by rigid barriers and community taboos. The setting can be as contemporary as Leonard Bernstein's musical *West Side Story*, where the love between Puerto Rican Maria and Anglo Tony is destroyed by New York City gang wars. Or it can be as old as Romeo and Juliet in Verona.

Romeo and Juliet is the Shakespeare play that touches teenagers most directly, with its themes of love at first sight, secret trysts, and passionate young love destroyed by old hatred. When Romeo and Juliet first meet, they see each other as individuals. Only after that do they learn each other's names. She's a Capulet, he's a Montague: their families are bitter enemies. Juliet asks:

> What's Montague? It is nor hand nor foot,
> Nor arm nor face, nor any other part
> Belonging to a man. O be some other name.
> What's in a name? That which we call a rose,
> By any other name would smell as sweet.

Her cry when she hears who he is ("Prodigious birth of love it is to me / That I must love a loathed enemy") expresses the powerful metamorphosis that passion has caused in the young lovers and in their world.

There are many parallels with *Romeo and Juliet* in the Aztec story "The Smoking Mountain," which has been passed on orally in Mexico among the Náhuatl-speaking people for seven centuries. One version is beautifully retold in *Stories from the Days of Christopher Columbus* by Richard Alan Young and Judy Dockrey Young. The young lovers are from warring kingdoms. A princess named Yoloxóchitl ("Red Flower") is the most beautiful young woman in the Red Kingdom. One day she hears a young man singing on a distant shore, and forgetting danger and custom, she paddles past "the painted boundary pole" in the lake. The singer is Tépetl

("Strong-like-the-Mountain"), prince of the White Kingdom. They fall in love, but their parents forbid their marriage, and the young couple run away. Even in exile they find no home. Even the great Aztec god Feathered-Serpent cannot make the kings change heart. "I cannot change what men and women feel in their hearts," he says. "Only men and women can do that for themselves." When the lovers ask the god to keep them together forever, they are transformed: she into a huge new mountain that looks like a woman lying on her side, Ixtaccíhuatl ("Reclining Woman"). Kneeling beside her is a volcano, which the Aztecs called Popocatépetl ("The Smoking Mountain").

Nadine Gordimer. "Country Lovers." Gr. 7–12

Apartheid drives the young lovers apart in Nadine Gordimer's story "Country Lovers." A white farmer's boy, Paulus, and a black farm laborer's daughter, Thebedi, play closely together as children. As teenagers they're supposed to part; he's sent away to school where he takes an interest in white girls. But at a deep level he's bonded to Thebedi, and in the summer holidays they meet often and make love in secret. They have to hide their relationship because the law, known as the Immorality Act, forbids love and sex across the color line. When she has a baby—who's very light-skinned—he poisons it. He denies the best in himself, commits murder, to fit in with white supremacy. The best in him, his loving self, is killed by apartheid.

There's a trial of sorts. This is how the story ends:

> The verdict on the accused was "not guilty."
> The young white man refused to accept the congratulations of press and public and left the Court with his mother's raincoat shielding his face from photographers. His father said to the press, "I will try and carry on as best I can to hold up my head in the district."
> Interviewed by the Sunday papers, who spelled her name in a variety of ways, the black girl, speaking in her own language, was quoted beneath her photograph: "It was a thing of our childhood, we don't see each other anymore."

That word *see.* These two young people have had to go backwards; they've had to learn not to know.

In the July 1992 issue of *Horn Book*, a teacher, Susan Moran, writes of her success in using this story with her eighth-grade English class. She quotes ones student's sensitive comment:

> What makes this so awful for me, knowing that this baby was soon to die, is how tenderly Gordimer describes the baby. Every detail makes the reader want to take it up, to protect it. I want to smooth down the fine hair, to rub that little cheek. I also notice how the sentences kind of come in a rush, as if the narrator is out of breath just trying to get it all out . . . It's sort of how I feel as I read it—out of breath, so afraid of what is going to happen next.

Judith Ortiz-Cofer. "American History." Gr. 8–12

Racism separates two teenagers before they can become really close in Judith Ortiz-Cofer's short story "American History," from the collection *Iguana Dreams.* The narrator is 14-year-old Elena, a first-generation American from a Puerto Rican immigrant family living in "El Building" in Paterson, New Jersey. From her bedroom window she can see into the kitchen of the house next door. She watches her classmate Eugene, a shy Anglo boy newly arrived from Georgia, who reads at the kitchen table. They get to know each other at school and walking home; they like each other and make plans to study together. But when Elena comes to Eugene's house, his mother shuts the door on the Puerto Rican girl: Eugene cannot associate with "you people." Ortiz-Cofer tells it quietly, weaving in the universal clichés: "It's nothing personal," as she describes how Elena's innocent world is transformed into a gray and ugly limbo.

Several books set lovers against a background of turbulent political times. Even if the warring groups don't focus on the young lovers, the outside conflicts deeply affect the intimate relationships.

Frances Temple's gripping novel *Taste of Salt: A Story of Modern Haiti* is simply told in the voices of two Haitian teenagers who find political commitment and love. Woven into the story are real events of the late 1980s, and the priest-leader, Aristide, appears as a quiet, charismatic figure who calls for democratic change. Djo's in the hospital from a terrorist fire-bombing that killed his friends. Jeremie's a convent girl who's been sent by Aristide to record Djo's story. Haltingly, Djo tells her of his early life on the streets as a shoeshine boy and of the hope he found in Aristide's shelter for boys. Then he remembers how he was kidnapped and spent three years in limbo as an indentured laborer in the sugarcane fields of the neighboring Dominican Republic, and how he escaped. For a time in the hospital, Djo hovers near death, and at his bedside Jeremie writes her story for him, though her educated voice doesn't have the vital Creole idiom of Djo's longer lyrical narrative. The main characters are idealized, but their grim circumstances are not. The combination of dramatic action, romantic interest, and vivid storytelling will grab even the most apolitical teens. The ending, when Djo remembers the firebombing of the boys' shelter, is like a cry. The title is from a Haitian story: everyone needs a taste of salt; otherwise you can become a zombie with neither insight nor will. We feel the struggle of this couple to reach beyond themselves.

Frances Temple. *Taste of Salt.* Gr. 7–12

Minfong Ho's *Rice without Rain* is set during the revolutionary turmoil of Thailand in the 1970s. Seventeen-year-old Jinda finds her love and personal commitment beset by politics and terror. After two years of drought, the harvest is bitter. Jinda's sister has no milk, and her baby starves to death. Then a group of radical students comes from Bangkok to work for the summer in Jinda's valley, and she and student leader Ned fall in love. He encourages the landless farmers in the rent-resistance movement, and Jinda's father is imprisoned. She follows Ned to Bangkok, but she's bewildered and bored by his fervent politics; her only interest in the demonstration he's organizing is that it might help free her father. The demonstration ends in massacre by the military, and Jinda returns home to find that her father has died in prison. There are some caricatures (the ruthless rent collector, for example), but author Ho, a Thai teacher who now lives in New York, doesn't neatly resolve the tension between the political and the personal. Though Jinda's love for Ned begins with skipped heartbeats and shy glances, it breaks the formula. They can't resolve their differences, and they part, he to join the Communist guerrillas in the fight for justice and equality, she to stay with her village to "grow things and be happy." The violence is quiet, never exploited, and the atrocity is balanced by the birth—in the last chapter—of a new baby for Jinda's sister. The birth is described in all its

Minfong Ho. *Rice without Rain.* Gr. 7–12

bloody exhilarating struggle, and with the baby "strong and sweet with the pulse of life" finally comes the rain.

Patrick Raymond. *Daniel and Esther.* **Gr. 8–12**

The plot of Patrick Raymond's *Daniel and Esther* could have been melodrama. Hitler's on the loose in Europe, and in a progressive boarding school in the idyllic English countryside, young teenager Daniel (problem child of rich, uncaring parents) falls passionately in love with beautiful Esther. He's in agony when she has to go back and forth to her parents who are fighting the Fascists in Austria. The melodramatic elements are controlled by the complex characterization, by the spare, poetic style that distills the hit and miss of conversation, and by Daniel's hesitant voice. He's brash yet bumbling and vulnerable. He's also blinded by his egotism and immaturity ("Was it very exciting?" he asks a wounded Spanish civil war veteran) and, above all, by his refusal to face the coming darkness. Esther knows much more than he does—she speaks each English word "as if she's had to pay for it"—but she's far from the pure, idealized victim of so many Nazi persecution stories. Daniel sees that she's prickly, vain, and giggly, as well as sensitive and suffering. When they finally kiss, the flame is as strong as the fire in Europe. Their parting is captured in an image that also evokes the Krystallnacht (night of broken glass) of the Nazi persecution of the Jews: "I looked down the river where, because of my tears, the water and sky were like broken glass." When war comes, he's in New York, she's somewhere in Austria, and his most intense memory is of a fragile moment when he suddenly saw her—and saw her see him—as older, wiser, more beautiful. With a cry, he faces the truth at last: "I just wanted you to come back."

What nearly all these stories express is the longing for an absent lover. That's a compelling theme that reaches beyond culture.

DISTANCES OF LONGING

by Fawziyya Abu Khalid

When you go away and I can't
follow you up with a letter,
it is because the distance
between you and me
is shorter than the sound of Oh,
because the words are smaller
than the distance
of my longing.

Paul Goble. *Love Flute.* **Gr. 3 and up**

In Paul Goble's *Love Flute*, rooted in a legend of the Plains Indians, a young man longs for the woman he loves, but he's too shy to woo her. He's brave in battle and a leader in the buffalo hunt, but he's afraid to speak to her, though he wants to stand with her in the tent of his blanket and whisper his love. Sad and lonely, he wanders far away into the forest, where two great Elk Men with branching antlers bring him a flute that the birds and animals have made for him. When he plays it, the harmony of nature is in his melodies, and he speaks straight to the heart of the girl he loves. Goble's illustrations, finely drawn and brilliantly colored, create a world that is precisely detailed and magically transformed, silent and yet vibrating with energy. Words and pictures convey the lover's yearning and desire and also the thrilling power he shares with the living world around him. In a fascinating note, Goble talks about related myths of the love flute and about the conventions of courting in a tepee village, where there was very little privacy and the lovers would stand in plain view, whispering together with the man's blanket wrapped around them.

For the mythic hero on a quest in a strange land, the reward for killing the monster is often marriage with the captive princess. That story can be reduced to shallow romantic formula with the girl passively waiting to be rescued while the man kills the monsters, proves himself, and comes home to her. But in many contemporary stories, girls are free to go on quests for themselves, just as boys are now free to stay home and worry about their feelings and their relationships. In fact, the best stories have always revealed that complex truth. Marriage is a metaphor for our happiness once we have slain our dragons and found who we are. If the quest is an inner one, then it may be as dark in your father's house as in the belly of the whale.

You can't invent a myth to fit a political creed. Most of the feminist fairy tales now being written to order may have a worthy message, but they're boring and literal, with little terror and mystery, little sense of the stranger. Yes, it's fine that the girl goes out and kills the dragon, but that's just a variation of formula. The best stories about feisty heroines move beyond message. There's "Marie Jolie," the Cajun fairy tale retold by J. J. Reneaux in *Cajun Folktales.* Here the independent girl is forced to marry the devil, but she outsmarts him. The storytelling is vital, with shivery fear and humor.

Or there's the wild beautiful story "White Wolf Woman," told by the Zuni Indians, about a maiden who escapes from her Navajo captors and finds her way home through the wind and snow with the help of a great white wolf. The wolf gives her the freedom and strength that brings her home. But the people in her village treat her like a stranger. When she's old and frail, she crawls out alone into the hills, and with a howl of freedom she changes into a white wolf:

Teresa Pijoan. "White Wolf Woman." Gr. 7–12

> A blood-curdling howl reverberated across the land. The howl of freedom flowed from her lips as her body changed into that of a white wolf. Her legs gained strength. Her eyes glowed silver-blue. She loped along the hills to freedom.

This age-old story is clearly an example of what the Jungian feminist Clarissa Pinkola Estes calls the Wild Woman archetype, a celebration of woman's strength, intuition, and creativity. Another story in Pijoan's collection, "Wolf Woman Running," is also about a woman who runs with wolves.

Katherine Paterson's strange and beautiful retelling of an old Russian fairy tale, *The King's Equal,* also plays with the formula in ways that deepen the story's resonance rather than simply inheriting the characters and their roles. It is a long magical story, not simply of virtue rewarded but of virtue so clever and strong it can change the world. A greedy and arrogant young king can't wear his crown until he finds a woman who is his equal. He exploits his people and lays waste the land, sneering at all the prospective brides his counselors parade before him, though the women are the most beautiful, wise, and wealthy in the kingdom. Rosamund is a poor goatherd before she befriends a hungry wolf, who transforms her into the bride the king wants—except she won't have the king. She shows the ruler that he's beneath her and sends him away to

Katherine Paterson. *The King's Equal.* Gr. 2 and up

be a goatherd. He learns humility and also how to sing and play and make his daily bread. Then he's her equal. Occasionally the message is spelled out, but the prince is a great villain, and his comeuppance is wonderfully satisfying. The paintings by the Russian illustrator Vladimir Vagin are lush and romantic, with richly colored, elaborately detailed costumes and interiors. The story is told in chapters with rhythm, repetition, and immediacy, and with dramatic confrontations and reversals that make it great for reading aloud. This is a picture book with appeal far beyond the youngest children.

Although Paterson and others embellish and transform the traditional romantic formula, they also rely on it. The lovers meet, they fight, they make up. We know and enjoy those old patterns, and we desperately want the lovers to live happily ever after. In fact, it is precisely because we crave the formula—often in spite of ourselves—that any change has such power to disturb and break the spell.

Wuthering Heights begins like a fairy tale. Heathcliff is a mysterious stranger. The father asks young Catherine and her brother, Hindley, what they would like him to bring them from his journey to the city, but instead of their gifts, he returns with the wild little foundling Heathcliff. The father dotes on Heathcliff, and Hindley is jealous. An intense bond develops between Cathy and Heathcliff as they run wild on the stormy and desolate moors. Then the father dies, and Hindley becomes head of the family. He abuses Heathcliff, denies him education, and banishes him to the stables. Catherine feels all Heathcliff's pain and fury, but she betrays the best in herself and marries the gentleman landowner Edgar Linton. In an unforgettable scene, Heathcliff overhears Cathy talking to the housekeeper, Nelly Dean, about how it would be degrading to marry Heathcliff. He runs away. He doesn't hear Cathy go on to declare her love for him:

> My great miseries in this world have been Heathcliff's miseries, and I watched and felt each from the beginning; my great thought in living is himself. If all else perished, and he remained, I should still continue to be; and if all else remained, and he were annihilated, the Universe would turn to a mighty stranger. I should not seem a part of it. My love for Linton is like the foliage in the woods. Time will change it, I'm well aware, as winter changes the trees—my love for Heathcliff resembles the eternal rocks beneath—a source of little visible delight, but necessary. Nelly, I am Heathcliff—he's always, always in my mind— not as a pleasure, anymore than I am always a pleasure to myself—but, as my own being.

When Heathcliff returns later, he's a strong and vengeful stranger. Their love is, in some sense, transcendant, but there is no fairy tale ending. We feel their pain all the more acutely because the formula has left us unfulfilled.

In another story of love and revenge, *The Owl Service*, Alan Garner draws on Celtic myth for a terrifying contemporary adventure. Two teenage boys in a Welsh valley love the same girl, and as their intense feelings mount, the three find themselves acting out an old legend of love and rivalry. The legend has repeated itself for generations, always

Emily Brontë.
Wuthering Heights.
Gr. 8–12

Alan Garner.
The Owl Service.
Gr. 7–12

ending in violent disaster. Then, in a heartrending scene, one of the boys transcends revenge and breaks the cycle.

Carson McCullers goes against the romantic myth of lovers forever joined. In "The Ballad of the Sad Café," she tells a haunting story in which the lovers remain strangers "from different countries." The separation between the lovers is as strong as their passion.

Carson McCullers. "The Ballad of the Sad Café." Gr. 9–12

In a dreary, small, southern town, "lonesome, sad, and like a place that is far off and estranged from all other places in the world," one very old house is boarded up. In that house, a tragic love triangle was once acted out. Miss Amelia owned the house. She was solitary, rich, and harsh, with the bones and muscles of a man. Long ago she had been married very briefly to Marvin Marcy, who was "bold and fearless and cruel." He loved her wildly, but she hit him if he came near her, and he left town. Years later, a stranger came to town, a small hunchback who said he was her cousin Lymon, and Miss Amelia fell in love for the first time in her life and took him in. Then Marvin Marcy returned, on parole from the penitentiary, and cousin Lymon fell in love with him.

McCullers writes about the solitude of love, the obsession, the mystery:

> There are the lover and the beloved, but these two come from different countries. Often the beloved is only a stimulus for all the stored-up love which has lain quiet within the lover for a long time hitherto. And somehow every lover knows this. He feels in his soul that his love is a solitary thing. He comes to know a new strange loneliness . . .
>
> Now the beloved can also be of any description. The most outlandish people can be the stimulus for love. A man may be a doddering great-grandfather and still love only a strange girl he saw in the streets of Cheehaw one afternoon two decades past. The preacher may love a fallen woman. The beloved may be treacherous, greasy-headed, and given to evil habits. Yes, and the lover may see this as clearly as anyone else—but it does not affect the evolution of his love one whit. A most mediocre person can be the object of a love which is wild, extravagant, and beautiful as the poison lilies of the swamp.

For George Bernard Shaw, it's not obsession but reason and common sense that get in the way of formula. His version of the Pygmalion story doesn't have a romantic ending. In his play *Pygmalion*, the ex-flower girl Eliza Doolittle will never marry the teacher, Henry Higgins, who made her a lady; the last thing she's going to do is spend her life with her bossy mentor. In contrast, the enormously popular musical version of Shaw's play, *My Fair Lady*, reduces the original disturbing Pygmalion myth by patching on a happily-ever-after ending.

Marilyn Sachs also explores the Pygmalion myth in the YA novel *The Fat Girl*. Like Shaw, she disturbs the romantic formula and tells an uncomfortably truthful story about power and control. The person who thinks he can create another human being is trying to be a god; he can't control human destiny, not another person's, not his own. At first Jeff feels revulsion for Ellen, the fat girl in his class; then he becomes obsessed with her, and he helps her to lose weight and feel comfortable with herself. But he wants to keep controlling her, making her his princess. He tells her what to wear, how to make up her face, who to talk to. When

Marilyn Sachs. *The Fat Girl.* Gr. 7–12

she tries to assert herself, he won't allow it. The honesty of Sachs' characterization adds depth to her story: Ellen is no great beauty, no great intellect, no princess. Jeff would like to make her what she can never be, what she doesn't want to be. She's just an ordinary girl.

There are lots of good YA stories about friends who transform each other and who fall in love without playing god. In *Just Friends*, Norma Klein brings sex and character and conversation into the old formula YA romance about the girl who discovers she loves the boy next door after all. Harry Mazer's *I Love You, Stupid!* is a funny, honest story about loving the girl next door: awkward high-school senior Marcus, a virgin obsessed with girls, confides in his good friend, Wendy; they decide to have sex, and he discovers that he loves her. In Marilyn Singer's *The Course of True Love Never Did Run Smooth*, Becky has a brief infatuation with a handsome newcomer, but then she discovers that she loves her long-time friend, Nemi, the boy next door, who is short, smart, funny, vulnerable—and sexy.

Sue Ellen Bridgers. *Permanent Connections.* Gr. 7–12

Sue Ellen Bridgers challenges romantic formula in *Permanent Connections.* Seventeen-year-old Rob has the kind of rich suburban home that Rayona dreams about in *A Yellow Raft in Blue Water,* but Rob's rootless and bitterly unhappy there. The book's opening will be instantly recognizable to teens—Rob wakes up in the night and hears his parents arguing about him. He's hostile, into drugs, always on the edge of trouble. But he shuts out his parents' expectations and his own fears. When his uncle breaks his hip on the old southern family farm, Rob is sent to help out for a few months, and he hates it—the shabby farm, the unnerving forest quiet, the boring little town. Rob wants easy answers. He thinks his passionate love affair with classmate Ellery will fill the void inside him, but it isn't enough. "You expect too much," Ellery tells him, unable to cope with his desperate need. Much of the novel takes place at night, in the black nothingness that is a descent into hell, and Ellery quotes Rob a line from Sylvia Plath that catches the novel's mood: "You have seen me through that black night when the only word I knew was NO." In the end, what helps Rob most is his transformed relationship with his father.

John Rowe Townsend. *Downstream.* Gr. 8–12

Several good YA novels capture the intensity of the primal rivalry between father and son, when those who have been closest become strangers. John Rowe Townsend, in *Downstream,* writes about the frenzy of adolescence with understatement and control. Seventeen-year-old Alan is drifting, lonely, vaguely aware of his parents' not very happy marriage. Then he falls in love with his beautiful, 23-year-old tutor Vivien, and his sexual excitement transforms his world. She rejects him; she's gentle with his awkwardness and tells him firmly that she likes older men. When he finds her in bed with his father, he is wild with fury. Spying, eavesdropping, alternately aroused and disgusted, he plots frenzied revenge and brings about a shocking confrontation. "I never want to see you again," his father tells him, and he moves in with Vivien. Alan's mother tells him, "You've broken up your own home." Townsend captures both the father's rage and the son's thwarted passion and humiliation, but he also portrays the son's emerging independence as the madness works itself out and he is left drained and calm. In a story of discovery and betrayal, the greatest surprise is Alan's mother: her husband and son have always regarded her as a nagging, small-minded housewife, but she turns out to be the strong one; realistic and dour, she knew about her husband's affair all along—there'd been others, he'd be back. Alan must make his own way home.

In Margaret Mahy's *The Catalogue of the Universe*, set in New Zealand, it's the girl who's obsessed with her father. Angela has grown up beautiful and confident with her strong, loving unmarried mother, but she yearns for the father she has never known. She tracks him down, follows him from afar, stand outside his house, and dreams that she "might turn out to be the daughter he's always longed for." But it doesn't work out like that, and in her pain she reaches out to Tycho, the homely boy who has always loved her. In an intense scene, he squeezes himself into a telephone booth where she is phoning her mother, and half-angrily declares his love for Angela, while people outside are banging to use the phone:

Margaret Mahy.
The Catalogue of the Universe.
Gr. 7–12

> "All right!" he said at last, "But I'll tell you two things first. I don't know what's happened, but I do know this—whatever your father thinks—if he is your father, that is—your mother loves you." The words were stiff but defiant, as if Tycho knew he were offering yet another piece of unwelcome information. "And I'm crazy about you," he added as they stared woodenly at one another. "You're all I think about when you're not there," he went on in a matter-of-fact way, as the banging on the door was repeated, "and you're all I think about when you are. So there!"

Tycho has always shared with Angela his excitement for science and the history of ideas, but he thinks of himself as short and strange looking; when she tells him she admires his brilliant, searching mind, he replies (only half-joking): "I'd rather be tall." This is a funny, tender, and passionate love story about the thrill of real love and the search for ideas that include science and mystery. The jokes about romantic formula intensify the pain and the loving.

There's a similar combination of humor and melancholy in Ron Koertge's *The Arizona Kid*. Like Rob in *Permanent Connections*, the teenager Billy leaves home for another place, has a love affair, undergoes trials with a loving mentor, and returns home with a new sense of himself.

Ron Koertge.
The Arizona Kid.
Gr. 8–12

Tenth-grader Billy feels stuck in the identity he's acquired in Bradleyville, Missouri. Everyone knows him. He has to get away, go somewhere new, to make himself new. He leaves home to spend the summer with his uncle Wes in Tucson, Arizona. Billy knows that Wes is gay, and at first he feels a bit awkward about that:

> Let's face it, I'd had some doubts. Of course he was my dad's brother, and Dad and I'd had some man-to-man talks about being gay. But still, it wasn't just going to a new place to live for a while with somebody I'd only talked to on the phone and thanked for the presents. It was going somewhere new to live with somebody who was really different from me. Somebody who was homosexual.
>
> Believe me, I hadn't told anybody in Bradleyville High School. They just wouldn't have understood.

Billy also feels awkward about himself.

> That was one of the reasons I wanted to come to Tucson. Sure, it was a learning experience and a chance to travel and a way to work at a racetrack and to see if being a vet

appealed to me. But I also wanted to do *something*. Have a real girlfriend, maybe. Or at least meet a girl who also wanted to do something. Or at least wouldn't mind if I did something, and if I did, wouldn't tell the world.

In Bradleyville, everybody knew everybody else's business . . . And they knew me—Billy Kennedy, the shrimp. Good grades, good outside shooter, fair shortstop, sense of humor, okay guy in general. Virgin.

Billy and his uncle Wes soon get to be friends, and they're comfortable with each other. They laugh a lot, and Billy is able to talk openly with Wes about things he would have been shy about with most other people. He falls in love with a feisty girl, Cara Mae. His uncle gives him condoms and warns him about safe sex.

One night when Wes and Billy get back home from their respective dates, they talk and Billy asks his uncle a question:

"I forget sometimes," I said slowly, "that we're not just guys sharing an apartment and all that. Roommates. I forget we're different."
"Well, you're right. We are."
"Will you not get mad if I ask you something else?"
"Who knows?"
"Do you kiss these guys?"
"Sometimes."
"Yuk."
"Do you kiss Cara Mae?"
"Well, sure."
"Yuk," he said.

Billy's coming-of-age journey follows the classic pattern. When he goes back home to Bradleyville, he is transformed, not only by having had a girlfriend but also by having known his uncle and a wider world. The issues are serious in Koertge's book, but the tone is light. He enjoys subverting formula.

Francesca Lia Block's *Weetzie Bat* also upsets our expectations. This gentle punk fairy tale doesn't feel like a love story at first, but beneath the weirdness and the unconventionality is a touching story of love, friendship, and family.

Dirk is the best-looking guy in high school:

He wore his hair in a shoe-polish-black Mohawk and he drove a red '55 Pontiac. All the girls were infatuated with Dirk; he wouldn't pay any attention to them. But on the first day of the semester, Dirk saw Weetzie in his art class. She was a skinny girl with a bleach-blonde flat-top. Under the pink Harlequin sunglasses, strawberry lipstick, earrings dangling charms, and sugar-frosted eye shadow she was really almost beautiful . . .

They go to clubs dressed in sunglasses and leather, jewels and skeletons, fur and silver, and they eat the best pastrami burritos and bagels and turkey platters in Hollywood. Dirk is gay, and as he and Weetzie get a little older, they each find a boyfriend. He finds Duck, and Weetzie finds My Secret Agent Lover Man. They all set up house together;

Francesca Lia Block. *Weetzie Bat.* Gr. 9–12

they make a baby, and they make movies. But then grief and darkness enter their dream house, and all their love has to be very strong.

Because this is a beautifully told love story, it is enjoyed by teenagers everywhere, whether or not they are able to idenify with Weetzie's on-the-fringe life-style. As New Yorker Norma Klein has said: "Perhaps the way one *didn't* grow up always seems more exotic. When I was a teenager, one of my favorite series of books was the Betsy, Tacy, and Tib novels by Maud Hart Lovelace, about three little girls growing up in turn-of-the-century Minnesota. The details of small-town life that Lovelace described were as wonderfully exotic to me as the New York City background of my books may seem to my readers."

Exotic and different, yes, but also the same. *Weetzie Bat*, like Norma Klein's New York stories and Ron Koertge's midwestern novels, has a strong sense of place; yet all these books have immediate appeal for those teenagers everywhere who are thinking about, confused about, and talking about (or just wanting to talk about) love, friendship, sex, and intimacy.

As with race and color, differences of fashion and style and values can make people strangers. Stereotypes about those who wear dreadlocks or gold earrings or army fatigues can prevent people from knowing each other. When you first read a book like *Weetzie Bat*, you might say to yourself, "What *is* this?" But as you are drawn into the book's culture, you discover that what appears to be bizarre can also be beautiful and delicate and cozily domestic, "a collage of glitter and petals." When you first read *Wuthering Heights*, you also wonder what strange house you've landed in. Like the narrator Lockwood, you're mystified: Why is there such raging hatred in this house? What is Heathcliff's story? Why can't Cathy's ghost rest? One of the great things about reading a good book is that it draws you into its special world and makes you stay there and listen. Whether the lovers are part of the melancholy of the Sad Café or the political storm of Haiti, you see the landscape and the characters in all their aching strangeness, and the writer's voice and rhythm echo in your head. And that changes your world.

FAMILY MATTERS

Happy or unhappy, families are all mysterious. We have only to imagine how differently we would be described— and will be after our deaths—by each of the family members who believe they know us.

—*Gloria Steinem*

Stories can break down borders by taking us to places around the world—or right into the house next door. One of the first ways you leave home is to go into other families (in real life and in story) and see variations on what you thought was written in stone: how a family jokes, how they fight, who they are, how they see their neighbors.

Each family is an intimate private world. Every time you go into someone else's home you glimpse another universe. Your friend's family doesn't watch TV while they eat dinner. They don't lock the door when they go to the bathroom. They don't have any pets. They make so much noise, so much mess. Her father is gay. His *abuelo* lives with them. Her mother works nights. In Sandra Cisneros' story "My Lucy Friend Who Smells Like Corn," the little girl would like to live in her friend's house where all the sisters share a bed "some at the top and some at the feets" instead of sleeping like she does "alone on a fold-out chair in the living room." Stories can take us right into the intimacies of family life, whether it's the scene in D. H. Lawrence's *Sons and Lovers* where the children huddle in the dark fearful that their father will hit their mother, or the lyrical passages in *I Know Why the Caged Bird Sings* when Maya Angelou celebrates her love for her brother, Bailey.

Some of the most powerful stories show how an outside monster invades the home and savages the elemental rites and relationships: that's what happens in Toni Morrison's *Beloved* when the mother cuts her own baby's throat rather than have her captured as a slave. Personal experiences in the family also reach outwards from home to the wider community. As Michael Dorris shows in *Morning Girl,* the young girl overcomes her prejudice and jealousy about her brother and gets to see him as a person, like herself.

Family members may go along with you on the heroic journey, especially brothers and sisters, though parents, grandparents, and other relatives are often there, too, as mentors or memories, as friends or enemies or both. Stories about families in all their variety are part of every theme, whether the people are Amy Tan's mothers and daughters caught between cultures in *The Joy Luck Club*, or the loving if unconventional household in Francesca Lia Block's *Weetzie Bat*, or the teenager and the old lady in Margaret Mahy's *Memory* who make a home together in the wasteland of the city. The focus in this chapter is on particular family relationships and how they transform you.

FATHERS

THOSE WINTER SUNDAYS
by Robert Hayden

Sundays too my father got up early
and put his clothes on in the blueblack cold,
then with cracked hands that ached
from labor in the weekday weather made
banked fires blaze. No one ever thanked him.

I'd wake and hear the cold splintering, breaking.
When the rooms were warm, he'd call,
and slowly I would rise and dress,
fearing the chronic angers of that house,

Speaking indifferently to him,
who had driven out the cold
and polished my good shoes as well.
What did I know, what did I know
of love's austere and lonely offices?

The physical immediacy of this scene—the boy lying in bed and hearing his father doing the chores around the house—draws you right into the poem. The detail, "and polished my good shoes as well," is heartbreaking in its particularity. The son's repeated cry for what can't be undone ("What did I know, what did I know?") is a counterpoint to the almost classical constraint of the father, "of love's austere and lonely offices." Everyone who has woken up to family rows and resentments will recognize the unhappiness in the home. But while we feel the "chronic angers" in that house, we also know the unspoken love.

There's the same ambivalence in Sandra Cisneros' "Papa Who Wakes up Tired in the Dark" in *The House on Mango Street*. Esperanza rages against the macho culture that oppresses her; yet, at the same time, she sees her father's struggle, his weariness, and she loves him. Again, the particularity of the details, the sense of the father gone in the early morning before the family wakes, is what reaches out to the universal.

In Suzanne Fisher Staples' *Shabanu*, a Newbery Honor book, both father and daughter are bound tight by the rules of their Muslim society.

Suzanne Fisher
Staples.
*Shabanu:
Daughter of the
Wind.*
Gr. 7–12

The father carries out his traditional role of keeping her in line, even as he feels for her suffering. For Shabanu, living with her nomad family in the Cholistan Desert of Pakistan, the journey is reversed: marriage—at age 12—is not love and happily ever after, but the end of freedom. Terrified at the prospect of an arranged marriage to an older man, the 12-year-old girl tries to run away, but her father must bring her back.

Shabanu has spirit and intelligence, and that's dangerous in a girl. She has grown up with her loving family traveling across the desert, where life is hard, yet she wouldn't live anywhere else. She especially loves one of the camels in the family herd, Guluband. She teaches him to dance, and riding him is the grandest thing on Earth. When he's sold to get a dowry for herself and her older sister, Shabanu's grief nearly overwhelms her.

She accepts that she must marry at 12, though she doesn't want to and she's scared. She quite likes the young man originally chosen for her, but then a wealthy older man—older than her father—wants her, and she's promised to him. He's decent, powerful, a religious leader; she knows the marriage will really help her family. She also knows she'll be his fourth wife. He may love her, at least at first, but his other wives will be jealous; they'll despise her as a desert girl and treat her as a servant. She tries to run away before the wedding, but she can see that, like Guluband, she's been betrayed and sold.

As many of us do, Shabanu finds a mentor in the extended family. Her Aunt Sharma lives differently. When her husband beat her for bearing only sons, she left him, built up her own herd of goats and sheep, as well as her courage. It's Sharma who shows Shabanu that she has a choice and who tells her that no one can reach her inner self.

This book is remarkable in showing a sense of individual personality within a tight structure. Through Shabanu's first-person, present-tense narrative, we see the diverse, complex inner lives of her family, as well as their strictly defined cultural roles. Her father is as trapped as she is, loving her proud spirit, suffering even as he battles her into submission.

Again, as with Hayden and Cisneros, the particulars of Shabanu's world universalize her sorrow. There's no false sense of the exotic, only a precise sense of place. This is where she lives. She is rooted in her culture, and she is like us. Shabanu's culture shuts her in, but inside she can be free.

Paula Fox. *The
Moonlight Man.*
Gr. 7–12

Paula Fox's *The Moonlight Man* has the same tension between father and daughter. Catherine must free herself from the father she thought was a mentor. She leaves him behind; he is in limbo, stuck. And yet, the gifts she has received from him continue to enrich her life. As always, Fox intensifies her coming-of-age story with mythic images of quest and transformation.

"Where was he? Where was her father?" For three weeks of the summer vacation, 15-year-old Catherine has been stranded at her boarding school, waiting for her father to come and get her. It's to be their first long time alone together since her parents divorced 12 years ago. He finally calls, disarming, apologetic as always, and she crosses on the ferry to meet him in Nova Scotia, where they spend a month in a cottage near the sea.

He has always been an exciting, romantic figure to her, a moonlight man. She hasn't known much about him from their snatched infrequent meetings. But always "Catherine wanted to do what her father wanted her to do." Now she hopes for a "splendid journey."

Two days after her arrival she discovers he's an alcoholic, a shambling monster in chaos that terrifies and disgusts her. After a night of drinking, he makes her drive his sodden friends home. The next morning, bitterly ashamed, he promises to stop drinking and charms her into forgiving him. Alone together, they begin to know each other. Her father cooks and reads aloud; he talks about books he loves and places where he promises to take her. Catherine sees that she astonishes him and that he likes her. They laugh a lot. Sometimes he lectures her, challenging slick responses (What does she mean she "had" "The Ancient Mariner" in school?). But in unguarded moments she sees his sadness. He is a failed writer, disappointed, drowning.

A few days before they leave, he gets drunk again. She finds him at an illegal still, on his hands and knees, barking for the company like a dog. When he comes round, she rages at him, hurls cruel insults: he's nothing but a "moonshine man." Though she soon pities and forgives him, their relationship is changed. Facing her own cruelty ("she hadn't known she had it in her to be so mean") and the illusions that have kept her helpless, she begins to take responsibility for her actions.

Catherine's father is like the Ancient Mariner bum who staggers after her on a New York sidewalk. She and her father are at times as helpless as the crazy old crone they find shut up in the dark rural cottage down the hill. All that Catherine discovers in her summer retreat is also part of home and school and within herself: danger and affection; monstrosity and laughter; moonlight and glaring sun.

Her father's way of seeing, his questioning of the familiar, will always be part of her, and so will her knowledge that they love each other. She has seen him dumb, helpless, insensible; she has also seen him struggle to see the truth. The novel's astonishing ending bares the painful ambiguity of that struggle: in reply to Catherine's tired cliché, "See you," as they part at the airport, he kisses her and whispers, "Not if I see you first."

In facing the truth about her father, Catherine has found who she is. This is a classic example of what Campbell means by the father quest as a search for the hero's identity. When Catherine asks "Where's her father?" her question means "Who am I?"

In Robert Lipsyte's *One Fat Summer*, 14-year-old Bobby Marks knows that his father has no confidence in him. "He's always afraid I'll get hurt, or do a bad job and embarrass him." Bobby is overweight, and summer makes him more of an outsider than ever:

Robert Lipsyte.
One Fat Summer.
Gr. 6–10

> I always hated summertime. When people take off their clothes. In winter you can hide yourself. Long coats, heavy jackets, thick sweaters. Nobody can tell how fat you really are. But in the summertime they can see your thick legs and your wobbly backside and your big belly and your soft arms. And they laugh.

This story has some of the best descriptions of the pleasures and pains of overeating, including a moment of truth as Bobby argues with his alter ego, Captain Marks, at the refrigerator:

> I hit the refrigerator the minute I got back to my house. Didn't even think about it. Jerked back the metal handle, pulled open the door, let the sweet cool blast wash over

my body, then plunged into the racks of food. I had one hand on a glass bowl of chocolate pudding and the other on a package of salami when a voice said, "Put it down."

"Says who?" said I.

"Says you, " said Captain Marks.

"C'mon," I said, "one slice of salami isn't going to hurt, one spoonful of chocolate pudding."

"Since when," said Commander Marks, "have you ever stopped at just one of anything?"

But one summer Bobby slims down as he sticks to an exhausting job, stands up to his father, and finds his own definition of a strong hero.

Bruce Brooks.
What Hearts.
Gr. 8–12

A stepfather is the focus of hostile competition in Bruce Brooks' four connected stories in *What Hearts*. Like all Brooks' protagonists, the boy Asa is smart and sensitive and trying to stay in control. In the unforgettable first story, Asa's stepfather-to-be forces the seven-year-old onto a solitary roller coaster ride, and the surreal images of jerking and whirling out of control—the terror and the thrill—recur throughout the book. As Asa and his fragile mother move seven times in the next three years, the boy deliberately sets up his own carefully ordered plans, only to find his personal journey aborted again and again by the adults around him. As in *Midnight Hour Encores,* Brooks deliberately plays with formula and then shocks you out of it.

Barbara Ann Porte. *I Only Made Up the Roses.* **Gr. 6–10**

In Barbara Ann Porte's *I Only Made Up the Roses,* the negative father figure is replaced by a loving stepfather who helps to free the young girl from painful rejection. When Cydra's absent father lets her down, she's immobilized, stuck fast, until her stepfather comes home and undoes the ugly spell.

Cydra remembers how when she was in third grade she had romantic dreams about meeting her Real Father. She thought about him in capital letters to distinguish him from Daddy, her loving stepfather:

> My Real Father . . . was a total stranger to me and had never shown the slightest interest in altering that condition.

But she pesters her mother, and they track down her Real Father, and he says he'll come and take Cydra to dinner. All excited, she gets dressed up and waits—then he calls to say he can't come:

> After hanging up, I tried to decide what to do. I could change my clothes, have milk and cookies, do my homework. I couldn't seem to get the order right, and when I tried to stand, it seemed I moved in slow motion. I was still sitting there that same way half an hour later, when Daddy got home.

She tries to act natural, but when he bends to kiss her, she starts crying and she just can't stop. He picks her up and sits down and holds her in his lap and rocks them back and forth until eventually she stops crying.

> Daddy stood me up, got a dishtowel, wet it, and washed my face in the kitchen. "Don't budge," he said, then got Mother's hairbrush from her dresser and redid my hair. He plaited it into a single braid, which he pinned on top of my head.

"There," he said, looking down at me, "that's better. Now then, what's the problem, Cyd?"

He had posed that question to me since I've known him: What's the problem, Cyd? Usually it has the effect of seeming to reduce my problems to manageable proportions, but not that time.

I tried to tell him. "My father doesn't love me. He doesn't love me at all. He doesn't seem to care anything about me." I was struck again as I said it by its awful enormity.

"I see," he said, understanding at once which father we were discussing. Before I could start crying again, he swooped me up and sat me on a shelf above the kitchen counter so that I was eye to eye with him.

"Cydra, look at me," said Daddy. I looked at him. "If someone were to ask me what child I wanted, exact and in every detail, you would be that child . . . Really." Then he lifted me from where I was and set me down. "Would you do me the honor," he asked, "of joining me for dinner?"

Cydra is part of a dynamic extended family. She and her mother are white, and Daddy, her stepfather, is black, as is her little brother. Cydra tells the family stories that are woven into her identity, as well as the history of African Americans and stories from all over the world that belong to all of us. Hers is a family that works, and that is richer for its diversity.

There's another positive father mentor in Ron Koertge's *The Boy in the Moon*, about midwestern high school senior Nick. "The good thing about my dad, though—one of the good things—is that he isn't a creep; he doesn't run his eyes all over girls and drool and make motorboat sounds. He looks at them with actual admiration; he smiles with complete delight." Nick's sensitive, first-person narrative is candid about male sexuality and feeling. In a very funny scene, Nick and his worried father discuss condoms. Nick's embarrassed not so much because they're talking about sex, but because he still hasn't done anything, and he knows his father wants him to "get out there and *be responsible.*"

Ron Koertge.
The Boy in the Moon.
Gr. 9–12

The pain of children separated from their fathers is at the center of Rachel Isadora's picture book, *At the Crossroads*, which was *Booklist*'s Top of the List pick as best picture book of 1991. This is an example of a picture book that can be used with older students. Set in contemporary South Africa, it's a story of joyful reunion that also reveals its wrenching opposite: the central monstrosity of apartheid was the breakup of family life by the migrant labor system. The system forced men to come to the white areas for work and forbade them from bringing their families with them.

Rachel Isadora.
At the Crossroads.
Gr. 2 and up

In a simple text with glowing, double-spread watercolor paintings, a boy tells how he, his brother and sister, and their friends celebrate their fathers' anticipated arrival home after 10 months of working in the mines. Home is a shanty town in the dusty veld, without electricity or running water. It looks like a slum in one of the so-called homelands, remote and barren, where millions have been forcibly resettled, far from the mines and cities. Yet despite the hardship, the huddle of shacks is a community. Swirling color, energy, and laughter burst out from the gray, uniform lines of the corrugated iron huts.

Isadora has been there, and her sensitive portraits, crowded street scenes, and impressionistic landscapes vividly portray South Africans in their country. Early in the morning people wait at the watertap to fill the buckets they will carry home on their heads. After school they party at the crossroads; the children play improvised instruments and sing over and over again, "Our fathers are coming home!"

Then it gets quieter, and the fiery sunset merges with the light and smoke of the township braziers. As darkness falls, only six children stay on at the crossroads. They wait and wait together, through the long still night, and we feel how they have waited all year. "It's a long way from the mines."

This book is a celebration, but in the joyful reunion is all the leaving. Under apartheid the mythic journey is distorted. It is not the young people who are leaving on a journey of discovery, but the young people who are abandoned by fathers who are forced to break up their homes.

MOTHERS

> *Yet my mother's life provides me with a good road map into the next generation, if for no other reason than that the detours and dead ends are marked for me. She taught me to hold America to its promise. She had great expectations and no intention of letting her adopted country off the hook. But she also taught me what any Jewish mother knows: a country, just like a child, needs a shove in the right direction sometimes.*
>
> —*Faye Moskowitz*

Literature is filled with stories about mothers, about the clashing, confusing welter of emotions stirred by the bond between a mother and her children. In the most elemental sense, of course, there is no archetypal journey without a mother—to bring us into the world, to nurture and protect us, to prepare us for the journey we must all take, to await our return. Inevitably, though, there are competing emotions: protecting becomes smothering, preparing becomes forbidding, letting go becomes casting away. Below we touch only a few examples of how these emotions are explored in fiction and autobiography. The list is limitless—somewhere, either on stage or off, there is a mother in every story.

Toni Morrison.
Beloved.
Gr. 10–12

In Toni Morrison's great novel *Beloved*, runaway slave Sethe knows that there will be no archetypal journey for her child; she cuts her baby's throat rather than have it captured to suffer slavery as Sethe has. In the novel, Beloved is that baby, come back after the Civil War as a ghost, a very real person, moved into the house of the mother who murdered her. When Charlene Hunter-Gault interviewed Morrison on Public Television's "McNeil-Lehrer Report," Morrison read from the scene in which Sethe tries to get Beloved to understand why Sethe had to murder her, her own beloved child. Sethe wants to make Beloved know that worse than that, far worse, was what she would suffer as a slave, what her grandmother died of, what other slaves knew:

That anybody white could take your whole self for anything that came to mind. Not just work, kill, or maim you, but dirty you. Dirty you so bad you couldn't like yourself anymore. Dirty you so bad you forgot who you were and couldn't think it up. And though she and others lived through and got over it, she could never let it happen to her own. The best thing she was, was her children. Whites might dirty Her all right, but not her best thing, her beautiful, magical best thing—the best part of her that was clean.

Morrison also spoke about why she made the ghost Beloved so real, a person living in the household. Morrison said that she wanted to show that that's what your past is like: you cannot deny it; it's seated right there with you at your dinner table.

The death of a baby is also central to Pam Conrad's *Prairie Songs*, but here it underscores both the harshness of a woman's life in pioneer times as well as the way a mother's love can drive an entire family. The young girl Louisa loves the wide space of the Nebraskan prairie, and she feels safe in her isolated sod house with her loving pioneer family. Louisa looks up to the beautiful cultured doctor's wife, Emmeline, who comes from New York City, shares her books with Louisa, and teaches her to love poetry. But Emmeline can't get used to the harsh frontier life, especially to the loneliness. When she becomes pregnant, she gets more and more fragile and uncontrolled. Then a shock brings on the birth prematurely. Louisa's mother helps the doctor, and the birth is long and painful. The baby is born dead.

Pam Conrad. *Prairie Songs.* Gr. 6–12

Afterwards Louisa's mother comes home in the middle of the night. "She just came and stood stone still in the middle of the room." Louisa and her little brother, Lester, hear their mother sobbing as she tells their father how it was.

> "Momma?" Lester's whisper seemed to shatter the air in the room, as if he had given away the secret that we were listening. "Momma? The baby died?"
>
> "Yes, sweetheart." She walked slowly to our beds and sat down near Lester. Her hair was down her back, and her face was all swollen. "The baby died. He was just too weak and little to live. Come," she said, drawing back the blankets. "Come let me feel how alive you are."
>
> I sprang up, too, and both Lester and me went into her arms. She was trembling and began to rock us. I felt Poppa gather the blankets up around the three of us, and I closed my eyes. We rocked slowly in big rocking movements, back and forth, as vast as the Milky Way, as wide and as far as the prairie.

In Conrad's story the loving embrace holds the family so close they can reach out to the stars. In contrast, the conflict and loneliness inside a home can imprison you, whether the captor is the Wicked Stepmother or your resentment of your sister.

Family life was imprisoning for *Ms.* magazine founding editor Gloria Steinem. In her memoir "Ruth's Song (Because She Could Not Sing It)," she talks about how she grew up in poverty, caring—alone—for her mentally ill mother. Sometimes she protected herself by imagining that

Gloria Steinem. "Ruth's Song (Because She Could Not Sing It)." Gr. 9–12 this wasn't her mother at all; she had been adopted and one day her real parents would find her. Only much later could she see the sadness and waste of her mother's life and understand that many women shared that confinement. "But at least we're now asking questions about all the Ruths and all our family mysteries," Steinem says.

Tobias Wolff. *This Boy's Life*. Gr. 8–12

Tobias Wolff remembers a similar dream of escape. In his autobiography *This Boy's Life*, he describes himself growing up Catholic with the stepfather he hates and the mother he loves in a small town in the Seattle area in the 1950s. He's a liar and a thief, wild and ugly at times; yet he wishes he weren't such a mess: he dreams that he's a scholar-athlete, a boy of dignity, a success. Like Gloria Steinem, like many of us, he has a secret dream that he's really adopted and that one day his true father will find him. Then suddenly it seems as if his dream has come true. His rich uncle in Paris offers to adopt him: he could live in France and travel and go to a fancy school. He could get away.

But he knows he could never leave his mother:

> I was my mother's son. I could not be anyone else's. When I was younger and having trouble learning to write, she sat me down at the kitchen table and covered my hand with hers and moved it through the alphabet for several nights running, and then through words and sentences until the motions assumed their own life, partly hers and partly mine. I could not, cannot, put pen to paper without having her with me. Nor swim, nor sing. I could imagine leaving her. I knew I would, someday. But to call someone else my mother was impossible.
>
> I didn't reason any of this out. It was there as instinct.

That's the positive side of staying home. Like Conrad's embrace, it gives you the strength to make your own way. It's hard to find a more heartfelt statement of love, the emotion expressed in the simplest words, the physical facts, and the enduring memory. Every reader will have someone's voice or touch they remember like that. Whom do you think of when you tie your shoelaces? When you ride a bike? When, as Yeats says, you are climbing "to the heights of sleep"?

Wolff is just as open about those he hates. This is a candid, beautiful memoir, funny and disturbing, dark and tender. It has one of the best dedications, that breaks all the rules, with Wolff getting his revenge at last: "My first stepfather used to say that what I didn't know would fill a book. Well, here it is."

Yet, looking back now, Wolff knows that things weren't really as simple as that. Maybe his mother, even though she loved him, wouldn't have minded him going to Paris, so that she wouldn't have to be stuck in a bad marriage. "The human heart is a dark forest," Wolff says, bringing new vitality to one of the archetypal images from fairy tale.

The monster can be sitting right next to you at the dinner table. Nothing shows this better than an intense family quarrel.

Anne Fine. *My War With Goggle-Eyes*. Gr. 6–10

A teenager's rage against her mother and prospective stepfather gets wonderfully comic treatment in *My War with Goggle-Eyes* by the British writer Anne Fine. The personal feelings get mixed up with the political argument, and both matter. A young British girl, Kitty, hates her mother's boyfriend, Gerald. She calls him Goggle-Eyes because of the way he looks at her mother's legs. He's a conservative—a political

Neanderthal, she calls him—and he disagrees with the peace activism of Kitty and her liberal mother.

Along with the family quarreling and her reluctantly growing affection for Goggle-Eyes, there's an ongoing serious debate about nuclear disarmament.

> "So," [Goggle Eyes] said. "You're all mixed up in it as well."
>
> Though I had no idea what he was talking about, I got the feeling he was speaking to me.
>
> "Mixed up in what?"
>
> "You know," he said, grinning. "The Tattered Banner Brigade. Close Down the Nuclear Power Plants. Ban the Bomb."
>
> Fine, I thought. Lovely. Terrific for me. My mother's busy upstairs turning herself into some simpering Barbie doll for the sort of man she'd usually take a ten-mile hike to avoid, and I'm stuck downstairs with the political Neanderthal.
>
> "I'm in the antinuclear movement, yes . . ."
>
> "Nuclear power's been invented now," he said. "And we have nuclear bombs. You can't just pretend that we haven't. You can't disinvent them."
>
> "You can't disinvent thumbscrews either," I snapped. "Or gas chambers. But you can dismantle them. And you *should*."
>
> He spread his hands.
>
> "But why? Nuclear weapons are our best defense."

The author is clearly against nuclear weapons, but she indulges in some wicked insider's mockery of the peace movement's self-righteousness and muddle. She shows that politics and ideas don't have to be heavy and preachy, and that they are always mixed up with each individual's personal life. The teenager here is trying to save the world, even as she's jealous and worried about the new man in her mother's life.

GRANDPARENTS

> *He represented a kind of masculinity from which I was not excluded by reason of my intelligence or, later, my homosexuality. It was exactly those qualities that separated me from the boisterous athletic boys who were my peers. Fat, myopic, and brainy, I escaped sissyhood only because of the aggressive gloominess I shared with my grandfather.*
>
> *—Michael Nava*

Michael Nava, the mystery writer, says that in childhood he felt like a monster who kept people away. In his memoir "Abuelo: My Grandfather, Raymond Acuña," he tells how the Mexican Catholic mother and grandmother who raised him couldn't handle his moodiness. They had no idea what to do with him. And he couldn't tell them—because he

Michael Nava. "Abuelo: My Grandfather, Raymond Acuña." Gr. 8–12 didn't understand himself—how he hurt. He felt he was no one's child. When, at age 11, he was sexually molested by an adult family member, he felt cast off completely. It was his grandfather, a Yaqui Indian, to whom the boy was drawn. His grandfather was the only person in the family who read for pleasure. Solitary and secretive, intelligent and apart, he seemed to the boy like the adult he would become.

Nava writes with such control, with such uncompromising honesty, that neither quote nor paraphrase can get across the complexity of what he has to say. In the simplest words, he tells of change, of reversal, of how his view of his grandfather was clouded, how he realized later that he hadn't understood the old man, and how in the end, his grandfather's model of self-denial and courage helped free Nava to live differently. "It isn't necessary for me to live the same kind of life because he did it for me."

Writing like this will certainly help an isolated gay kid, but it also speaks to anyone who feels imprisoned in an unhappy home. Further, it can be a stimulus for creative writing about family, bringing depth and subtlety to the usual role-model character. Nava shows that there's a vital interaction between what the grandfather is and what the boy needs him to be. His grandfather helped Nava to find his way out of the labyrinth.

Berlie Doherty.
Granny Was a Buffer Girl.
Gr. 7–12

Stories passed along from one generation to another can become family folklore, personal versions of myth. In Berlie Doherty's *Granny Was a Buffer Girl*, winner of England's Carnegie Medal, a contemporary teenager in a working-class English family tells the story of her grandmother and finds some of the same patterns in her own life. The love story of the grandmother, Dorothy, is filled with the yearning of the Cinderella fairy tale and the harshness of class differences. It begins in the 1920s with six-year-old Dorothy playing the sleeping princess in a children's street game. She dreams of romance and hopes for a handsome prince, but the boy who wakes her with a kiss in the game is her playmate Albert, "snotty-nosed and big-limbed."

When she's 17, Dorothy gets a job as a buffer girl polishing silverware in one of the big cutlery firms in town. At the annual staff ball, her first dance, she dances all night long with the boss's son, Mr. Edward, and dreams about his love. But when he looks for her in the firm the next day, he doesn't know her among the rows of buffer girls. Her arms and body are protected by newspaper, her face is blackened with the hot metal dust from her polishing machine. Cinderella is not recognized by the rich prince. It's her neighbor Albert she marries.

Two generations later Jess' own love story echoes her Granny's. Jess meets a man at a disco and loves him, but he isn't what he seems.

M. E. Kerr.
Gentlehands.
Gr. 7–12

A grandfather proves a false mentor in M. E. Kerr's classic YA novel *Gentlehands*. Teenage Buddy is the son of a policeman in a small seaside town, and he is in love with one of the socially elite summer visitors, Skye Pennington. In a funny family quarrel, which takes place in the bathroom, Buddy's father and mother tell him that they are worried about him, especially because he's suddenly spending all his money on clothes. "She's not our class," Buddy's father tells him. But Buddy likes Skye, and he wants to impress her. He starts taking her to visit his grandfather. Buddy's family has never had much to do with the old man. He lives alone in a big elegant house with books, paintings, and antiques, all of which impress Skye. Buddy likes talking to his grandfather, learning how to pour wine and listen to opera. Then a shocking secret is revealed that stretches back to the Holocaust.

Hero becomes monster as the drama of the grandfather's Nazi past is revealed. Buddy faces the anti-Semitism in his community and confronts his own shallow values. Kerr takes on big moral issues, and she does it without didacticism. She lets the story tell it, and it's a disturbing story. The book still inspires controversy. Some critics remain outraged that Kerr made the Nazi grandfather so "nice." Kerr brings monstrosity very close to home.

BROTHERS AND SISTERS

BROTHER
by Mary Ann Hoberman

I had a little brother
And I brought him to my mother
And I said I want another
Little brother for a change.

But she said don't be a bother
So I took him to my father
And I said this little bother
Of a brother's very strange.

But he said one little brother
Is exactly like another
And every little brother
Misbehaves a bit he said.

So I took the little brother
From my mother and my father
And I put the little bother
Of a brother back to bed.

Hoberman's delightful poem will appeal to every age group. Reading it aloud gets across the desperate tone of voice and the repetition emphasizes that the rhyming word play is with "other."

Many old stories juxtapose the rich, greedy, arrogant brother, who gets his comeuppance, against the poor, naive, virtuous one, who helps the witch and gets rewarded in the end. That's what happens in the Japanese folktale, "Why Is Seawater Salty?" which is retold by Yoko Kawashima Watkins in *Tales from the Bamboo Grove.* Another story with that pattern is *Boots and His Brothers,* a Scandinavian tale retold by Eric Kimmel. The British writer Diana Wynne Jones mocks this tradition in her delightful fantasy *Howl's Moving Castle.* The heroine Sophie, the eldest of three sisters, gives up without trying: "Everyone knows you are the one who will fail first and worst," she thinks to herself, "if the three of you set out to seek your fortunes." Why bother stepping out into the unknown if failure is certain?

Along with the competitive stories about ugly sisters and bossy brothers, there's also the "Hansel and Gretel" kind, where the kids band together against the cruel outside. And many stories, traditional and contemporary, show a bonding between siblings in the closest kind of friendship,

Louise Erdrich.
Love Medicine.
Gr. 9–12

In Louise Erdrich's "The Red Convertible," one of the interconnected stories from the novel *Love Medicine,* Lyman loves his older brother, Henry. They have grown up close friends on the Chippewa reservation, comfortable together. When they manage to afford a car, a red convertible, they drive it from North Dakota all the way to Alaska, and it's a journey of pure happiness. Then Henry goes to Vietnam for two years, and he returns home a wreck. "When he came home, though, Henry was very different, and I'll say this: the change was no good." The comfort is gone. Henry is jumpy and mean. It's as if his former self is asleep. To get his brother out of his deep depression, Lyman secretly bashes up the red convertible they both love. For a while his plan works; Henry comes out of himself and repairs the car. But the suffering is too deep, and even a brother's love can't bring Henry back from the dead. The title of the story with its pun on transformation is an example of mythic metaphor that grows right out of the story and enriches it.

Klaus Kordon.
Brothers Like Friends.
Gr. 6–10

East Berlin in 1950 is the setting of Klaus Kordon's *Brothers Like Friends,* the story of seven-year-old Frank and his older half-brother, Burkie, the very best of friends. Frank's father never came back from the war. Their Jewish neighbor survived by hiding in a cellar for three years. Now Frank and the other kids play in a "cave" in a bombed-out building down the street. At 14, Burkie's a soccer star, though his mother wishes he wouldn't play. In an exciting game in which he scores like a champion, he is critically hurt. He swears Frank to secrecy, until it's too late—Burkie dies, and Frank blames himself. The story's episodic at times, especially as the neighborhood scene is set and many people come and go, but once the focus is on the soccer game, the injury, and the grief, readers will be held by the tautness of the narrative and the universality of the drama. Kordon never exploits the intense emotion and offers no false comfort. The main characters are beautifully drawn: not only the brothers, but also their strong mother and her new lazy lout of a husband, who tries but can't really get beyond his own comfort. Through Frank's viewpoint, there's a sense of grown-up secrets, conversations overheard and half-understood. Despite an occasional awkwardness, the translation has a clear, informal simplicity that both deepens and controls the sorrow. In a quiet afterword, Kordon says the story is based on the loss of his own brother.

Margaret Mahy.
The Changeover.
Gr. 6–12

Margaret Mahy's *The Changeover* is a family story, a fantasy, and a love story. The place is New Zealand, but, more universally, it's a world not quite right, an incipient chaos beneath the familiar order, what Mahy calls an "inexplicable tremble." Laura's little brother, Jacko, is dying. Neither his mother nor the doctors can find out what's wrong with him. But Laura knows that he is possessed by an ancient unseen evil and only she might be able to save him. She is helped by a mysterious young man who loves her and who helps her change over into her powerful self. Jacko needs Laura, but Laura needs Jacko, too, because only through saving her brother does Laura find herself and explore her supernatural powers. Becoming a witch to save your little brother is a perilous journey indeed.

Virginia
Hamilton. *Sweet Whispers,*
Brother Rush.
Gr. 7–12

A sibling torn between love and resentment is often the narrator for stories about mental disability. In Virginia Hamilton's *Sweet Whispers, Brother Rush,* Tree loves her mentally disabled older brother, Dab, and while their mother is away working as a nurse, often for days at a time, Tree cares for Dab. She sees that he eats and bathes; sometimes she even has to remind him to sit down as he paces restlessly about. Then Tree sees her uncle's ghost, and he takes her back into the past, where she discovers harsh secrets about her mother.

In Lois Metzger's *Barry's Sister*, Ellen Gray hates her little brother. An only child until the age of 11, she is furious that her mother is pregnant. When the baby's born with ataxic cerebral palsy—"Barry would never walk or talk properly, and might not think right, either"—Ellen feels she's responsible for a monster. She had wanted to kill the baby, but she "only wrecked him." She can't bear to touch Barry. She's repulsed by his drooling, spitting, snoring. In her guilt and rage, she lies, cheats, steals, gives up studying, and leaves the softball team. She hangs out with kids who treat visiting her brother like seeing a horror movie, "now playing at a theater near you." ("How about a seizure? I want to see that!") Even in the midst of all the fury, however, there are quiet, aching moments. Barry whimpers when Ellen leaves one day, and she doesn't know why. "You don't get it, do you?" her mother says. "He loves you. He's all relaxed because of you."

Lois Metzger. *Barry's Sister*. Gr. 5–12.

Ellen swings from rejection to devouring love. She overcompensates, identifying with Barry, focusing her life on him. Barry needs her. She must never let him down. She must be perfect. As she works daily with his therapist, we feel Ellen trying to imagine how it feels to be Barry, to have the connection damaged between brain and muscle. She wonders whether his body, like the body of a woman Oliver Sacks described in *The Man Who Mistook His Wife for a Hat*, is "blind and deaf to itself." Everything becomes focused on Barry and his condition. Ellen is just Barry's sister.

The emotional therapy talk is occasionally overdone, and Ellen's neat, linear transformations from anger to depression to overcompensation to equilibrium have little to do with the messy adjustments of real life. As Ellen returns to friends, school, romance, and laughter, though, it is clear that loving Barry has changed her. She used to run from trouble, but now she has no illusions that things are easy. As she gets close to a friend and looks at her family as individuals, she accepts that everyone is "somewhat handicapped." Her journey to empathy has been hard.

Michael Dorris' historical novel *Morning Girl* juxtaposes the outer and inner journey. It starts off with a brother and sister in a family and moves out to a global journey. Morning Girl wishes she didn't have a younger brother, Star Boy. He's just a noisy intruder, disturbing her closeness with her parents. Then, in a moment of shared grief, she suddenly sees her brother as a person. She recognizes his pain and that it's like her own, and he sees that she sees him. The reflections go on and on throughout the story, reaching from brother and sister to the wider family, their Native American community, and their island world. "I watched the way you watch when you know you want to remember," Star Boy says when he's thinking of telling a story about his experience. In another shining moment, Morning Girl finds herself by looking into the dark brown circles of her father's eyes.

Michael Dorris. *Morning Girl*. Gr. 5–9

In alternate first-person narratives, perfect for reading aloud, the brother and sister tell of incidents in their growing up on an island: quarrelling, coming together, withstanding tropical storm and public ridicule. The characters are more idealized than in *A Yellow Raft in Blue Water*, Dorris' adult novel, but there's no reverential talk about vision quests or what Dorris has called the "basketweaving and mysticism" stereotype of Native American culture. Yet, like teenage Rayona in *A Yellow Raft*, these young people do go on quests to find themselves. They come of age in harmony with the rich opposites of their world. We see them grow from separateness to security, and then each finds the strength to be alone.

The shock of the ending comes quite casually. Columbus "discovers" them. The year is 1492, and he names the place the "Indies." First we see the encounter through Morning Girl's friendly eyes: she welcomes the strange visitors, laughing at their dress and language, sure "that we could find ways to get along together." But the book ends with a passage quoted from Columbus' diary. Through the conqueror's ethnocentric view, these people we have come to know in all their rich complexity appear to be "a people very poor in everything." They have neither weapons nor religion. He's sure they will make good servants, and he will teach them to speak.

Discovery is the fact and metaphor of this story. What Dorris does is to connect the way a sister sees her brother with the way we view any outsider, with the way Columbus sees the Indians. At first, Star Boy's just her brother, a nuisance, an obstacle in her way; then she gets to see him as a person. Columbus cannot make that discovery. Despite his brave world voyage, he is bound by the racism he set out with; he can't see the "other" as like himself. He can't imagine the lives of others. He's stuck at home.

FINDING THE WAY HOME

The human heart is a dark forest.

—Tobias Wolff

In the old stories, when the hero goes on the perilous journey to kill the monster, sometimes he finds a god. Or the opposite can happen: when he looks for the gold in the labyrinth, sometimes a monster rears up from the dark. Some of the best autobiographies tell stories that show this ambiguity: the stumbling onto secrets, the surprise that opens you up to the discovery of love and terror, of lies that tell truth—out there in the world and in yourself. The "life story," whether in fiction or in fact, is always about these discoveries and how they enable individuals to find their way home.

It can be a great stimulus for kids' personal writing to read about how all kinds of people have made crucial choices and discoveries and transformed themselves. Sometimes it can be a literal identification. For example, an isolated gay kid can get immense comfort from a book like *A Member of the Family: Gay Men Write about Their Closest Relations.* The South African "Coloured" (mixed race) writer Peter Abrahams remembers the joy he felt when he first read black American writers like Langston Hughes and Countee Cullen and recognized their struggle with race. But it may not be as direct as that. Stories of all kinds of people beyond the street where you live can help you discover wide possibilities in yourself.

Young adults are fascinated with how memory works and how family myths grow and why some things stick in our minds and won't go away. Mary McCarthy, in *Memories of a Catholic Girlhood,* tells a wonderful story about the muddle of memory.

Mary McCarthy.
Memories of a Catholic Girlhood.
Gr. 9–12

> My own son, Reuel, for instance, used to be convinced
> that Mussolini had been thrown off a bus in North Truro,
> on Cape Cod, during the war. This memory goes back to

. . . . .

119

one morning in 1943 when, as a young child, he was waiting with his father and me beside the road in Wellfleet to put a departing guest on the bus to Hyannis. The bus came through, and the bus driver leaned down to shout the latest piece of news: "They've thrown Mussolini out." Today, Reuel knows that Mussolini was never ejected from a Massachusetts bus, and he also knows how he got that impression. But if his father and I had died the following year, he would have been left with a clear recollection of something that everyone would have assured him was an historical impossibility, and with no way of reconciling his stubborn memory to the stubborn facts on record.

Young adults like to read about childhood experience and to write about their own memories. What bores them is nostalgia, that view of childhood as a time of sweet innocence and bliss. Yet we all have distant memories of pure happiness and security.

John Updike.
Self-Consciousness.
Gr. 9–12

In his memoir *Self-Consciousness,* John Updike remembers the physical sensation of being out of the rain—but *just* out—"I loved doorways in a shower," he says. We all remember that feeling of cozy safety. But Updike's no sentimentalist. He knows that even as a young, protected child he sensed pain and guilt—the dead sparrow on the lawn, the leering bully on the playground. In fact, the pleasure of shelter was intensified *because* there was danger; you were safe now in contrast with the tumult outside.

Eudora Welty.
One Writer's Beginnings.
Gr. 8–12

But even the most sheltered home can hide a monster. Eudora Welty, in *One Writer's Beginnings,* talks about herself as a child in the shelter of a happy, loving home in Jackson, Mississippi, listening to adult stories. Growing up, she says, she had to learn to listen for the unspoken as well as the spoken—and to know a truth, she also had to recognize a lie.

She tells a story about her childhood. Every night when her mother came out to the sleeping porch to say goodnight, Eudora would grab her and ask, "Where do babies come from?" The mother tried, and she didn't fib, but something always seemed to come up to interrupt them, and she just couldn't tell.

Then Welty goes on: "Not being able to bring herself to open that door to reveal its secret, one of those days, she opened another door."

Eudora is given permission to play with the treasures in her mother's bottom bureau drawer, and she finds there one day two polished buffalo nickels, embedded in white cotton. She rushes to her mother and asks if she can run out and spend them:

> "No!" she exclaimed in a most passionate way. She seized the box into her own hands. I begged her; somehow I had started to cry. Then she sat down, drew me to her, and told me that I had had a little brother who had come before I did, and who had died as a baby before I was born. And these two nickels that I'd wanted to claim as my find were his. They had lain on his eyelids, for a purpose untold and unimaginable. "He was a fine little baby, my first baby, and he shouldn't have died. But he did. It was because your mother almost died at the same time," she told me. "In looking after me, they too nearly forgot about the little baby."

She'd told me the wrong secret—not how babies could come but how they could die, how they could be forgotten about.

Welty comments:

The future story writer in the child I was must have taken unconscious note and stored it away: one secret is liable to be revealed in the place of another that is harder to tell, and the substitute when nakedly exposed is often the more appalling.

You think you're after gold, and it turns to ashes. You think you have a clear purpose, and you know where you're going. But secrets can leap out at you.

Also set in the deep South, this autobiographical poem quietly reveals secrets about the author's parents.

DOCTOR

by Betsy Hearne

Riding roadward
Pa and I paid calls.
He cured sick men
and I kept company.
We sang and played,
pretended rich,
talked snooty what we'd do
with money.

He aged less than I.
We watched car-lights
gobble up black dragon macadam;
watched the southern sun
drink the road grasses' water
till they curled and crackled;
heard silence suck up afternoons
while worried family friends
swatted flies and children,
and he fixed bones and wounds.

Long later I found hearts he lanced,
and learned the crack in the man,
and knew my mother's pain,
waiting at home.

That word *crack* explodes like a shot, and a revelation.

The harsh secret can leap out of yourself. Some of the most moving immigrant stories show how the monster of prejudice becomes internalized as self-hatred, how the desire to be "mainstream" makes you see yourself as a stranger.

Milton Meltzer's autobiography, *Starting from Home,* fuses his personal story with the social and political conditions of the time. Growing up as

**Milton Meltzer.
Starting from Home.
Gr. 6–12**

a child of Jewish American immigrants in Worcester, Massachusetts, Meltzer remembers how he sometimes longed to be one of the "un-hyphenated" people, a "real" American. His father works as a window washer during the hard times of the Depression, and one time Milton is on a date with his all-American girlfriend, sharing a soda in the drugstore. He sees his father washing the big plate-glass window in the store across the street. When they pass by his father with his squeegee, pole, and pail, Milton pretends he doesn't know him.

It's a powerful story, all the more moving because Meltzer tells it without pushing for easy resolution. He shows the boy infected with ugly social values, facing the monster in himself.

**Richard
Rodriguez.
*Hunger of
Memory.*
Gr. 8–12**

Richard Rodriguez in *Hunger of Memory* writes with the same candor about his sense of shame in being a Mexican American outside the Anglo culture.

> Thirteen years old. Fourteen. In a grammar school art class, when the assignment was to draw a self-portrait, I tried and I tried but could not bring myself to shade in the face on the paper to anything like my actual tone. With disgust then I would come face to face with myself in mirrors. With disappointment I located myself in class photographs—my dark face undefined by the camera which had clearly described the white faces of classmates. Or I'd see my dark wrist against my long-sleeved white shirt.
>
> I grew divorced from my body. Insecure, overweight, listless. On hot summer days when my rubber-soled shoes soaked up the heat from the sidewalk, I kept my head down. Or walked in the shade. My mother didn't need anymore to tell me to watch out for the sun. I denied myself a sensational life. The normal, extraordinary, animal excitement of feeling my body alive—riding shirt-less on a bicycle in the warm wind created by furious self-propelled motion—the sensations that first had excited in me a sense of my maleness, I denied. I was too ashamed of my body.

**Piri Thomas.
"The Konk."
Gr. 5–8**

Piri Thomas, in his autobiographical story "The Konk" about growing up Puerto Rican in New York 50 years ago, treats the theme of self-rejection with gentle comedy. Ashamed of his curly hair, at 14 he goes to a barbershop to have his hair straightened. But the barber gets distracted by a numbers runner and leaves the konk on top too long. For a short time, Piri is proud of his lanky straight hair, but by the time he gets home, his locks are like wires of black spaghetti, and everyone laughs at him:

> I walked slowly over to the sofa and plunked down heavily on it, feeling old and tired at fourteen and wondering why my strong young legs refused to hold me up.
>
> Poppa shook his head. He knew what my hurting was all about. Momma sat down by my side and caressed my wilted, abused hair. Then hugging me close, she allowed my tears of hurt and shame to be absorbed by her big momma breasts. She whispered to me, "Hijo, what have you done to your beautiful hair?"

"Oh, Moms," I whispered back. "I just didn't want to be different any more. I'm so tired of being called names. I ain't no raisinhead or nothing like that."

Momma hugged me very closely and said out loud, "Don't you ever be ashamed of being you. You want to know something, negrito? I wouldn't trade you for any blanquitos."

The next day found me playing stick ball with a red bandana around my forehead, sporting the baldest head in town.

Growing up poor in Appalachia in the 1960s, Cynthia Rylant felt the same kind of shame at being outside the mainstream. In her autobiography, *But I'll Be Back Again*, she talks about how she longed for the kind of house she read about in magazines:

> I was ashamed of where I lived and felt the world would judge me unworthy because of it. I wouldn't even go to the library in the nearby city because I felt so unequal to city kids. Consequently, I lived on comic books for most of my childhood, until I moved into drugstore paperback romances as a teenager.
>
> As long as I stayed in Beaver, I felt I was somebody important. I felt smart and pretty and fun. But as soon as I left town to go anywhere else, my sense of being somebody special evaporated into nothing and I became dull and ugly and poor. . . .

Cynthia Rylant. *But I'll Be Back Again.* Gr. 5–9

Rylant is honest about contradictory feelings. She describes the visit of the New Orleans Symphony to her small town and what it meant to her. It was a curse, making her ashamed of herself. It was also a gift, giving her a glimpse of another world she could reach for:

> I wanted to be somebody else, and that turned out to be the worst curse and the best gift of my life. I would finish out my childhood forgetting who I really was and what I really thought, and I would listen to other people and repeat their ideas instead of finding my own. That was the curse. The gift was that I would be willing to write books when I grew up.

The painful experiences helped to transform her into a writer.

Sometimes the very act of coming home reveals the grief that separates the traveler from his or her family. In "The Story of My Life," Anna Bender, a Chippewa girl sent away to boarding school for seven years to become part of the white world, tells how she comes home a stranger. She can't find her way home.

Anna Bender. "The Story of My Life." Gr. 6–12

> I had no reason for wanting to go home except that other students went to theirs. I seldom heard from my parents and was so young when I came away that I did not even remember them. . . .
>
> How miserable I felt when the time came to go! It was to me the leaving of a home instead of returning to one. The trip was very pleasant at first for there was a crowd of us returning, but when we got to Chicago I was made sad

and lonely again by the departure of my friends. From St. Paul I had to travel all alone, not for long as my home was just fifty miles from there.

My mother met me at the station bringing with her my two younger sisters and two younger brothers whom I had never seen. They greeted me kindly but they and everything being so new and strange that I burst into tears. To comfort me my mother took me into a store close by and bought me a bag of apples. As the house was only about a mile from the station we all walked home into the woods while my sisters tried to cheer me up by telling me about places we passed and the good times they had. . . .

As we gathered around the table later a great wave of homesickness came over me. I could not eat for the lump in my throat and presently I put my head down and cried good and hard, while the children looked on in surprise. When my father returned from work he greeted me kindly but scanned me from head to foot. He asked me if I remembered him and I had to answer no. He talked to me kindly and tried to help me recall my early childhood, but I had never known many men and was very shy of him. At last he told me I had changed greatly from a loving child to a stranger.

There's not a word of self-pity. Yet Bender's quiet personal account of returning home to strangers expresses the sadness of her people's exile in their own country, far from home.

Beverly Cleary.
A Girl from Yamhill.
Gr. 7–12

In her autobiography, *A Girl from Yamhill,* Beverly Cleary, author of the Ramona books and other beloved children's stories, also tells quiet, sad secrets of being a stranger in the family. Growing up an only child in a stable home in Portland, Oregon, during the Depression, she was the center of her mother's world, and yet she always knew she couldn't please her mother. She didn't know why—she still doesn't understand why—and it still hurts. The pain is particularly acute in the powerful final scene at the Greyhound station, when Cleary's leaving home for college:

My father kissed me goodbye; my mother did not. I boarded and found a seat on the station side where I looked down on my parents standing together, seeming so sad and lonely. We waved without smiling. We could not smile, any of us.

As the bus pulls out, the pain of separating is partly because she'll miss them and partly because she sees what they've lost in the hard times of the Depression—her lively mother had no outlet for her energies other than her daughter; her father had given up the farm he loved and was forced to work long days confined in the basement of a bank. But Cleary's enduring sorrow is more basic: "Somehow, I felt, I should have made Mother happy. I ached to love and be loved by her."

For teenagers raised on the ebullient Ramona and Henry Huggins books and other beloved Beverly Cleary classics (books that many still return to as "thumbsucking" reading when they need comfort), it can be surprising to learn about the underlying complexity and sadness in Cleary's family life.

There was a different kind of terror, difficult choices to be made, sorrows to be endured, in the young life of another popular children's writer, Roald Dahl. The autobiographical stories in *Boy* are as frightening and funny as Dahl's fiction. They feel as if they have been told as family folklore, honed down to essential incident and sharp detail. They have the intense drama and simplicity of the fairy tale, as well as its unequivocal extremes of good and evil.

Roald Dahl. *Boy.* Gr. 5–12

In real life the witch won. Mrs. Pratchett, the mean and filthy sweet-shop lady, watched with relish as the headmaster-giant ferociously caned eight-year-old Roald Dahl and his four friends for putting a dead mouse in her candy jar. No wonder so much of Dahl's widely popular (and sometimes ghoulish) fiction has children and small creatures inflicting gruesome punishment on disgusting and malignant adults.

Dahl explains in the introduction that he is not writing a boring history of his entire life, but only about those things—comic, painful, unpleasant—that he has never been able to forget. After a brief sketch of his early years and his Norwegian father's death when Roald was four, the division is clear: home, in Britain, was "totally idyllic"; school was misery. There were vacations in Norway, feasts and mischief in his close, large, wealthy, and almost entirely female family, led by his indomitable and beloved mother. But from the age of 9 to 18, he endured the harsh rigor of select English boys' boarding schools, where, as in Dickens' novels of childhood, grotesque adults wielded savage power over helpless and innocent students.

Dahl does not patronize himself as a child. What "Boy" saw was the truth. "We hated her and we had good reason for doing so," he says of Mrs. Pratchett. The matron who ruled the school dormitories was an "ogre." The horror of the ritualized, sadistic beatings by masters and prefects remains with him: "I couldn't get over it. I never have got over it."

The comedy, too, is close to the macabre, as when his nose hangs by a thread after a farcical automobile accident. He admires Thwaite, the doctor's son, who knows about "scabs and when they were ready to be picked off," explains why spit makes candy change color and tells long stories about how licorice is made from rat's blood.

Remembering, Dahl is in quiet control, chatting to his readers, explaining a few historical differences, illustrating each incident with scraps of his weekly letters home, his mediocre report cards, small ink drawings, and family photographs with captions in longhand like "me seven months." The tension between this casual commonsense tone and the lurking demonic terror gives these tales their power.

For a black child in apartheid South Africa, the demon is the law. There's no shelter in the storm, no doorway like Updike's. Several powerful autobiographies show how that law affects individual lives. The apartheid monster invades the home, distorts its most intimate relationships, tears apart its secrets.

In Peter Abrahams' story "Crackling Day," the child must learn to lie in order to survive. He must keep secret his belief in himself. Like Richard Wright in *Black Boy*, he has to pretend that he accepts the whites' view of him, that he's of no value.

Peter Abrahams. "Crackling Day." Gr. 7–12

When he's new to the country area where he's staying with his Aunt Liza and his Uncle Sam, Peter doesn't know he's supposed to act subserviently to whites, drop his eyes before them, call them "baas," master. He tells how he learns a bitter lesson when he attacks a white bully who calls him racist names. That night the white boy's father comes to the tiny shack and forces Uncle Sam to beat Peter until he breaks down and promises that he will never lift his hand to a white person. After the whites have gone, the suffering continues:

> Uncle Sam flung the thong viciously against the door, slumped down on the bench, folded his arms on the table, and buried his head on his arms. Aunt Liza moved away from him, sat down on the floor beside me, and lifted me into her large lap. She sat rocking my body. Uncle Sam began to sob softly. After some time he raised his head and looked at us.
>
> "Explain to the child, Liza," he said.
>
> "You explain, "Aunt Liza said bitterly. "You are the man. You did the beating. You are the head of the family. . ."
>
> With me in her arms, Aunt Liza got up. She carried me into the other room. The food on the table remained half eaten. She laid me on the bed on my stomach, smeared fat on my back, then covered me with the blankets. She undressed and got into bed beside me. She cuddled me close, warmed me with her own body. With her big hand on my cheek, she rocked me, first to silence, then to sleep . . .
>
> The next night Uncle Sam brought me an orange, a bag of boiled sweets, and a dirty old picture book. He smiled as he gave them to me, rather anxiously. When I smiled back at him, he seemed to relax. He put his hand on my head, started to say something, then changed his mind and took his seat by the fire.
>
> Aunt Liza looked up from the floor, when she dished out the food.
>
> "It's all right, old man," she murmured.
>
> "One day . . ." Uncle Sam said.
>
> "It's all right," Aunt Liza repeated insistently.

That home is battered, but despite the demon's invasion of the family, the loving bonds hold. The boy does not succumb to self-hatred. Instead, he transcends it. He grows up to write this story and so metaphorically finds his way home. From the monstrosity Abrahams makes a story of truth and beauty. He finds the god in the heart of hell. Abrahams' act of writing about it, making a story that tells how it was with such quiet intensity, is a powerful act. He makes us see. We cannot not know. No wonder the South African censors banned his story.

Gcina Mhlope's autobiographical story "The Toilet" is *about* the act of writing, of making a story under appalling conditions. As a young girl new to the city, she is living illegally in a white area, secretly sharing her sister's room in a white family's backyard where her sister works as a servant. The sisters are irritable with each other, confined and edgy. Gcina has to leave early and come back late so that no one sees her, and she finds shelter in a public toilet in a nearby park. It becomes her study and she begins to write there—poetry, a journal.

Gcina Mhlope. "The Toilet." Gr. 7–12

> Then one morning I wanted to write a story about what had happened at work the day before. . . . I had to write about it and I just hoped there were enough pages left in

my notebook. It all came back to me, and I was smiling when
I reached for the door, but it wouldn't open—it was locked!

I think for the first time I accepted that the toilet was
not mine after all. . . . Slowly I walked over to a bench
nearby, watched the early spring sun come up, and wrote
my story anyway.

Mhlope has set herself free with the radiance of her imagination.

You can link these apartheid experiences with the chapter in Yoshiko
Uchida's memoir *The Invisible Thread*, in which she tells how the U.S.
government broke up her home and herded her Japanese American
family into a concentration camp during World War II. For five months
they were interned with other Japanese Americans in a cluster of stables
and barracks in Tanforan, California. Then they were moved to a camp
in Topaz, Utah. On the way there, they marveled at normal life:

Yoshiko Uchida.
*The Invisible
Thread.*
Gr. 6–9

> Long after Tanforan was behind us, we continued to
> stare out the window, drinking in sights we had missed for
> five months. Houses, gardens, stores, cars, traffic lights,
> dogs, white children riding bicycles. All these ordinary
> things seemed so strange and wonderful to us.

Uchida talks about the cruel deprivation of their civil rights:

> There had yet been no freedom marches or demonstra-
> tions of protest. No one had yet heard of Martin Luther King,
> Jr. No one knew about ethnic pride. Most Americans were
> not concerned about civil rights and would not have sup-
> ported us had we tried to resist the uprooting.
>
> We naively believed at the time that cooperating with
> the government was the only way to prove our loyalty and
> to help our country. We did not know then, as we do today,
> how badly our leaders betrayed us and our country's
> democratic ideals.
>
> They had imprisoned us with full knowledge that their
> action was not only unconstitutional, but totally unneces-
> sary. . . .
>
> How could America—our own country—have done this
> to us, we wondered.

Many Holocaust memoirs capture that sense of the secure child caught
up in a monstrous racist storm that invades the home; even parents
cannot shelter you. The enduring hold of *The Diary of Anne Frank* for
young readers is that she is so ordinary. Like any teenager, she fights with
her mother, resents her sister, finds romance with an interesting boy. But
the flames of the Nazi dragon lay waste the world, and we know that this
girl who is so like us will disappear in the death camps, never to find her
way home. While in hiding in a secret annex with her family and some
other Jews, Anne keeps a diary, recording what she sees outside as well
as the daily happenings in their cramped hiding place:

Anne Frank. *The
Diary of Anne
Frank.*
Gr. 5–12

Wednesday, 13 January, 1943
Dear Kitty,

> Everything has upset me again this morning, so I wasn't
> able to finish a single thing properly.

It is terrible outside. Day and night more of those poor miserable people are being dragged off, with nothing but a rucksack and a little money. On the way they are deprived even of these possessions. Families are torn apart, the men, women, and children all being separated. Children coming home from school find that their parents have disappeared. Women return from shopping to find their homes shut up and their families gone.

She falls in love with teenage Peter, whose family is also in hiding with the Franks:

Sunday, 27 February, 1944

Dear Kitty,

From early in the morning, till late at night, I really do hardly anything else but think of Peter. I sleep with his image before my eyes, dream about him and he is still looking at me when I awake.

I have a strong feeling that Peter and I are really not so different as we would appear to be, and I will tell you why. We both lack a mother. His is too superficial, loves flirting and doesn't trouble much about what he thinks. Mine does bother about me, but lacks sensitiveness, real motherliness.

Peter and I both wrestle with our inner feelings, we are still uncertain and are really too sensitive to be roughly treated. If we are, then my reaction is to "get away from it all." But as that is impossible, I hide my feelings, throw my weight about the place, am noisy and boisterous, so that everyone wishes that I was out of the way.

He, on the contrary, shuts himself up, hardly talks at all, is quiet, day-dreams and in his way carefully conceals his true self.

But how and when will we finally reach each other? I don't know quite how long my common sense will keep this longing under control.

Anne is experiencing first love, the glorious human rite of passage, and that, more than any statistic, personalizes the sorrow of the six million gone. Her individual struggle to grow up and find her way home is aborted. Her home is ashes.

Ida Vos. *Hide and Seek*. Gr. 4–9

Ida Vos' *Hide and Seek*, an autobiographical story, translated in simple direct style from the Dutch, has the same sense of nightmare invading an ordinary middle-class home. It's about a Jewish child in Holland under the Nazi occupation, and it will reach a younger audience than *The Diary of Anne Frank*. You feel the small child's bewilderment as she tries to make sense of the madness, the absurdity of racism. We feel her rising terror. Why can't she sit on a public bench? Why must she go to a special school? Where did they take her grandparents, her friend? Why must she change her name? What does it mean, "going into hiding?" With a foster family, Vos survives the war, and some of the most powerful vignettes are about the return of her relatives from the camps. There's her grandfather, who compulsively goes through the neighbors' garbage, stealing moldy bread. Or there's Miep, who returns from Auschwitz and covers up the number tattooed on her arm.

Primo Levi, in *Survival in Auschwitz,* his stark account of the 10 months he spent in the Nazi death camp, sets the realistic, immediate, almost banal detail within universal myth. In the first chapter, "The Journey," he tells how at the age of 24 he's crammed with 650 men, women, and children into a transport train to "nothingness." The train stops finally in the dead of night "in the middle of a dark silent plain." He describes the prisoners' "metamorphosis" in "hell," as they lose their companions, their clothes, their hair, even their names, and undergo the "true initiation" of being tattooed with a number. The "rites" to be learned and carried out are infinite and senseless. The initiation involves a total transformation.

With brilliant insight, Levi imagines how he and the other Jewish prisoners must appear to the civilians as "untouchables":

> They think, more or less explicitly . . . that as we have been condemned to this life of ours, reduced to our condition, we must be tainted by some mysterious, grave sin. They hear us speak in many different languages, which they do not understand and which sound to them as grotesque as animal noises; they see us reduced to ignoble slavery, without hair, without honour and without names, beaten every day, more abject every day, and they never see in our eyes a light of rebellion, or of peace, or of faith. They know us as thieves and untrustworthy, muddy, ragged and starving, and mistaking the effect for the cause, they judge us worthy of our abasement.

The blame-the-victim racism he describes is startlingly familiar today and so is the terminology. Whether in South Africa or Eastern Europe or Germany or the United States, people use the same clichés. The objects of revulsion always seem to speak in grotesque-sounding foreign languages; they deserve what they get because they are lazy, dirty, and physically disgusting; and they are nameless.

But one person, an Italian civilian worker, sees Levi as an individual. Lorenzo Perrone saves Levi's life, first with the food he brings, but also because he helps Levi hold on to the belief that people can be good and therefore it is worth trying to live on. He sees Levi as a person.

> I believe that it was really due to Lorenzo that I am alive today; and not so much for his material aid, as for his having constantly reminded me by his presence, by his natural and plain manner of being good, that there still existed a just world outside our own, something and someone still pure and whole, not corrupt, not savage, extraneous to hatred and terror; something difficult to define, a remote possibility of good, but for which it was worth surviving. . . . Thanks to Lorenzo, I managed not to forget that I myself was a man.

Levi's account of the ordinary hero who retains his humanity, who finds community, even in the inferno, confronts the worst and the best in all of us. It is also perhaps the most vivid example possible of how a writer uses autobiography to describe the process of finding your way home. For Levi, home is the will to live.

Primo Levi.
Survival in Auschwitz.
Gr. 9–12

Malcolm X and
Alex Haley. *The
Autobiography of
Malcolm X.*
Gr. 7–12

For Malcolm X, finding his way home meant fighting the enemy out there and in himself. The dramatic changes in his life—from top student to street hustler, from prison inmate to leading voice in the Nation of Islam, from separatist to pan-Africanist who came to accept brotherhood with all individuals of goodwill—speak to many African Americans who feel they must act out their lives as if they were living among enemies. Until his life was cut off by assassination, he was always transforming himself, whether on his pilgrimage to Mecca or in the streets of Harlem. It's that image of self-transformation that gives his *Autobiography of Malcolm X* mythic force. He speaks with a fierce wit that is rooted in daily experience, in African American history, and in the universal images of the heroic journey.

> Thicker each year in these ghettoes is the kind of teenager that I was—with the wrong kind of heroes, and the wrong kind of influences. I am not saying that all of them become the kind of parasite that I was. Fortunately, by far most do not. . . . I believe that it would be almost impossible to find anywhere in America a black man who has lived further down in the mud of human society than I have; or a black man who has been any more ignorant than I have been; or a black man who has suffered more anguish during his life than I have. But it is only after the deepest darkness that the greatest joy can come; it is only after slavery and prison that the sweetest appreciation of freedom can come.

As Walter Dean Myers shows in his biography *Malcolm X: By Any Means Necessary,* Malcolm spoke to the voiceless because he had walked in their shoes, calling on them to free themselves from the slavery of self-hatred and from wanting to be part of the mainstream that rejected them.

While there are young people today who wear X baseball caps only to identify with Malcom's rage against "white devils," there are also many who read the *Autobiography* and see that it's possible to move beyond racism. In *Malcolm X: In Our Own Image,* a collection of essays edited by Joe Wood, a young student at Spelman College speaks eloquently about the transformations in her own life and what Malcolm X means to her. "Just look at what he was able to become," she says.

Maya Angelou.
*I Know Why the
Caged Bird Sings.*
Gr. 7–12

Malcolm X was a reader. Some of the most stirring passages in his story are about what he finds in books, about his longing to study more, to know languages. In her autobiography *I Know Why the Caged Bird Sings,* Maya Angelou also talks about how books transform her life.

She says that Shakespeare was her "first white love":

> It was Shakespeare who said, "When in disgrace with fortune and men's eyes." It was a state with which I felt myself most familiar.

Angelou describes how at age eight she was raped by her mother's boyfriend. The man was killed, and, as a result of the trauma and guilt, Maya stopped talking. She was punished, beaten, ignored, but nothing helped. Then she was sent to stay with her strong grandmother in a segregated neighborhood in Stamps, Arkansas. There an aristocratic woman, Mrs. Flowers, who made Maya feel "proud to be Negro," helped her break her silence. Mrs. Flowers invited Maya to her home, and read aloud to her from Dickens: "It was the best of times, it was the worst of times." She lent Maya poems to read aloud and recite, and showed her the power and beauty of the human voice. Looking back, Angelou says:

> I have often tried to search behind the sophistication of years for the enchantment I so easily found in those gifts. The essence escapes but its aura remains. To be allowed, no invited, into the private lives of strangers, and to share their joys and fears, was a chance to exchange the Southern bitter wormwood for a cup of mead with Beowulf or a hot cup of tea and milk with Oliver Twist. When I said aloud, "It is a far, far better thing that I do, than I have ever done . . ." tears of love filled my eyes at my selflessness.

In that sharing, Angelou felt that Mrs. Flowers was throwing her a "lifeline," freeing her from the grim confines of her private sorrow. The best books can do that. James Baldwin said of *I Know Why the Caged Bird Sings* that it moved him like books did when he was a child, a time when people in books were more real than the people around him.

The sense of universal connection is at the heart of the most surprising autobiographical story I know. The scientist Lewis Thomas, in his essay "A Long Line of Cells," goes along with all the conventions even as he changes the whole genre. He was asked to give one of a series of talks on memoir at the New York Public Library. Other speakers—Russell Baker, Toni Morrison, Annie Dillard— spoke about their lives and their writing. But as his editor William Zinsser notes, Thomas is a cell biologist, and he thinks of himself as a collection of cells. So, when he talks about his early life, he begins with his prenatal experience. "To begin personally on a confessional note, I was at one time, at my outset, a single cell." Much of the reader's pleasure comes from surprise. Thomas seems to go along with the pattern, and then he shocks you into thinking in a new way. When Thomas talks about his "humble" ancestors, they turn out to be very humble indeed: "What sticks in the top of my mind is another, unavoidable aspect of my genealogy . . . It is a difficult and delicate fact to mention . . . That first of the line, our n-granduncle, was unmistakably a bacterial cell."

Now there's a vision of journey and transformation to answer the ethnic cleansers, the border patrollers. Lewis' amazing autobiography makes us imagine the beginning of life on Earth. He brings us out of the tight labyrinth into the shining light under one sky, and he takes us all the way home—to the single cell that was our common beginning.

Lewis Thomas.
"A Long Line of Cells."
Gr. 8–12

PART TWO

Resources

Going
Global

"I am an American writer, in the American mainstream, trying to extend it . . .my literary agenda begins by acknowledging that America has transformed me. It does not end until I show how I (and the hundreds of thousands like me) have transformed America.

The agenda is simply stated, but in the long run revolutionary. Make the familiar exotic; the exotic familiar . . .

The most moving form of praise I receive from readers can be summed up in three words: I never knew. Meaning, I see these people (call them Indians, Filipinos, Koreans, Chinese) around me all the time and I never knew they had an inner life. I never knew why they schemed and cheated, suffered, felt so strongly, cared so passionately."

—*Bharati Mukherjee*

RACIAL OPPRESSION

The Holocaust

How could the Holocaust happen? Who is guilty? Could it happen again? More than half a century later, survivors, writers, and artists continue to confront these enduring questions with graphic realism and moral intensity. The best books do it without either cant or sensationalism. They do not try to give us an upbeat resolution. They address the horror of the topic and force us to remember:

- the facts—that in the Nazis' deliberate genocide, six million Jews were murdered for only one reason: because they were Jews.

- the experience—the ghettoes, the transports, the camps, the crematoria, and, for the few survivors, the attempt to return home.

- the consequences—that the Holocaust changed forever our view of humanity: in the words of survivor Bruno Bettelheim, these "unimaginable" things were done "by average people to average persons."

- the responsibility—that we must never again look away from racist evil.

OVERVIEW

Chaikin, Miriam.
A Nightmare in History.
1987. Clarion, $14.95 (0-89919-461-3); paper, $7.95
(0-395-61580-1).

Gr. 6–9. Illustrated with searing documentary photographs, this stark, readable account introduces young people to the history of anti-Semitism, the rise of Hitler, the Warsaw Ghetto uprising, the death camps, and the enduring consequences.

"I thought one
should talk
about these
things in a quiet
voice."

—Ida Fink

Dawidowicz, Lucy S.
The War against the Jews, 1933–1945.
1975. Free Press, $29.95 (0-02-908030-4); Bantam, paper,
$13.95 (0-553-34532-X).

Gr. 10–12. This long, detailed history of Nazi destruction of European Jewry describes the rise of anti-Semitism, the genocide, and the ways in which Jews and the rest of the world reacted to this systematic annihilation.

Epstein, Helen.
Children of the Holocaust.
1979. Penguin, paper, $8.95 (0-14-011284-7).

Gr. 9–12. Epstein discusses how the experiences of concentration camp survivors have become a disturbing heritage for their children, who feel the parents' survivor guilt and the driving need to compensate for all that's been lost.

Fink, Ida.
A Scrap of Time and Other Stories.
Trans. by Madeline Levine and Francine Prose. 1987.
Schocken, paper, $6.95 (0-8052-0869-0).

Gr. 7–12. Many of these Holocaust stories about young people who survived tell of the moments when Nazi terror invaded ordinary homes. Translated from the Polish, this is spare but powerful short fiction. Fink's novel *The Journey* is an intense story of two young Jewish sisters who flee the ghetto in disguise in 1942 and try to survive in wartime Germany. They find enemies and informers and also rare friendship.

Frank, Anne.
Anne Frank: The Diary of a Young Girl.
Trans. by B. M. Mooyaart. 1952. Doubleday, $21.95
(0-385-04019-9); Pocket/Washington Square Press,
paper, $3.95 (0-685-05466-7).

Gr. 5–12. Translated from the Dutch, this is the classic journal, kept by Jewish teenager Anne during the two years she, her family, and several others hid from the Nazis in a secret annex in Holland.

Warsaw Jews,
captured after the
uprising

Gilbert, Martin.
The Holocaust: A History of the Jews of Europe during the Second World War.
1986. Holt, $24.95 (0-03-062416-9); paper, $14.95 (0-8050-0348-7).

Gr. 8–12. Gilbert draws on records and testimonies of survivors to produce an accessible, massive, detailed, chronological overview of the attempt to annihilate the Jews of Europe.

Hersey, John.
The Wall.
1950. Knopf, $25 (0-394-45092-2); Random/Vintage, paper, $9.95 (0-394-75696-7).

Gr. 8–12. A long, harrowing, ultimately triumphant novel of the heroic resistance of a group of Jews facing death by the Nazis in the Warsaw ghetto.

Kerr, Judith.
When Hitler Stole Pink Rabbit.
1972. Putnam/Coward-McCann, $8.95 (0-698-20182-5); Dell, paper, $3.25 (0-440-49017-0).

Gr. 4–7. Based on the author's own experiences as a child, this story tells how a German Jewish girl and her family left their home in Berlin just before Hitler came to power in 1933. The sequel, *The Other Way Round*, describes their adjustment in England.

Kerr, M. E.
Gentlehands.
1978. HarperCollins, $16.89 (0-06-023177-7); paper, $3.50 (0-06-447067-9).

Gr. 7–12. In one of the great YA novels, teenage Buddy tries to impress a rich beautiful girl by taking her to visit his grandfather.

Buddy's family has never had much to do with the old man. He lives alone in a big elegant house with books and paintings and antiques. He knows about opera. He's kind to animals. Then Buddy discovers that the grandfather he has just come to know and admire is a Nazi war criminal.

Kertész, Imre.
Fateless.
Trans. by Christopher C. Wilson and Katherine M. Wilson. 1992. Northwestern Univ., $58.95 (0-8101-1024-5); paper, $12.95 (0-8101-1049-0).

Gr. 9–12. "Buchenwald's weather was cooler that Auschwitz's." Written from the point of view of a teenager, both innocent and immensely experienced, this autobiographical novel, translated from the Hungarian, strips away rhetoric and shows how a boy survived in the shadow of the chimneys. Kertész allows no false comfort (hatred is what he feels for everyone when he returns) and no heroics. Survival means taking one step after another.

Koehn, Ilse.
Mischling, Second Degree: My Childhood in Nazi Germany.
1977. Greenwillow, $12.88 (0-688-84110-4); Penguin/Puffin, paper, $4.95 (0-14-034290-7).

Gr. 7–12. For her own protection in Nazi Germany, Ilse Koehn's parents kept from her that she was part Jewish. In diary form she tells of joining the Hitler Youth movement and of the two years she spends in a paramilitary girls' camp in occupied territory. A vivid, immediate account of what it was like to be a young German at that time.

OF MICE AND CATS

Leitner, Isabella.
Fragments of Isabella: A Memoir of Auschwitz.
1978. Dell, paper, $3.95 (0-440-32453-X).

Gr. 8–12. In a haunting, impressionistic account of her brutal experiences, Leitner conveys what she and her sisters endured after they were rounded up as teenagers and transported to the Polish extermination camp, a story she continues in *Saving the Fragments.* Leitner has also written a spare, simplified version for younger readers, *The Big Lie.*

Levi, Primo.
The Drowned and the Saved.
Trans. by Raymond Rosenthal. 1988. Summit, $17.95 (0-671-63280-9); Random/Vintage, paper, $8.95 (0-679-72186-X).

Gr. 9–12. Discussing what it was like in the transports, the camps, even the crematoria, an Auschwitz survivor talks with candor about the enduring questions of guilt and survival. In all his books, translated from the Italian, such as *Survival in Auschwitz* and *The Reawakening,* Levi bears powerful witness.

Meltzer, Milton.
Never to Forget: The Jews of the Holocaust.
1976. HarperCollins, $13.89 (0-06-024175-6); paper, $6.95 (0-06-446118-1).

Gr. 6–12. This compact, eloquent history is based on personal accounts of the ghettos and camps.

Orlev, Uri.
The Island on Bird Street.
Trans. by Hillel Halkin. 1984. Houghton, $13.95 (0-395-33887-5).

Gr. 5–7. Set in the Warsaw ghetto, Orlev's novel, translated from the Hebrew, portrays the experiences of a young boy who escapes a Nazi round-up and waits steadfastly for his father to return.

Orlev, Uri.
The Man from the Other Side.
Trans. by Hillel Halkin. 1991. Houghton, $13.95 (0-395-53808-4).

Gr. 6–12. Through the maze of filthy sewers under Nazi-occupied Warsaw, teenage Marek helps his rough Polish stepfather smuggle food and arms to the desperate Jews in the walled-up ghetto. Orlev's fast-paced thriller is also about moral conflict, courage, and betrayal. The story has none of the sentimentality that pervades so many children's books about the Holocaust. While Marek's first-person account is unequivocal about the evil of the Nazi genocide, the misery of the crowded ghetto, and the stirring events of the brave uprising, it also bears witness to the way hunger and fear affected individual behavior. The Jews weren't an amorphous mass of victims and heroes. Some were brave, some weren't, some were traitors. Many Poles were anti-Semitic, many were indifferent, but some transcended prejudice.

Reichel, Sabine.
What Did You Do in the War, Daddy? Growing Up German.
1989. Hill & Wang, $17.95 (0-8090-9685-4).

Gr. 8–12. In a desperate attempt to come to terms with her shame and fury about the Nazi past, German Reichel (who now lives in the U.S.) talked to her parents and others of their generation and confronted her own memories of home and school in post–World War II Germany.

> "It's not who did what to whom that matters. What matters is that it was done at all. That it keeps being done."
>
> —Cynthia Voigt

Reiss, Johanna.
The Upstairs Room.
1972. HarperCollins/Crowell, $12.95 (0-690-85127-8); paper, $2.95 (0-06-447043-1).

Gr. 6–9. With the honesty of Anne Frank, the author recalls her childhood experiences hiding from the Germans who occupied her native Holland in World War II. She makes us imagine what it was like to be confined for over two years in a small, cramped room.

Richter, Hans P.
Friedrich.
Trans. by Edite Kroll. 1987. Penguin/Puffin, paper, $4.95 (0-14-032205-1).

Gr. 6–9. Translated from the German, this is an unforgettable story of the persecution of the Jews in Nazi Germany and how it affected two families, one Jewish, the other not.

Rogasky, Barbara.
Smoke and Ashes: The Story of the Holocaust.
1988. Holiday, $16.95 (0-8234-0697-0); paper, $9.95 (0-8234-0878-7).

Gr. 6–12. Passionate and controlled, Rogasky's detailed history combines eyewitness accounts, statistics, and commentary. The 80 graphic photographs, many of them taken by Nazis at the time, add to the power of this account.

Siegal, Aranka.
Upon the Head of the Goat: A Childhood in Hungary, 1939–1944.
1981. Farrar, $14.95 (0-374-38059-7); NAL, paper, $2.25 (0-451-12084-1).

Gr. 6–10. A powerful memoir that documents the destruction of Siegal's family at the hands of the Nazis. At the end they are on the train to Auschwitz. The book was adapted into a memorable filmstrip distributed by SRA School Group.

Spiegelman, Art.
  Maus: A Survivor's Tale.
    1986. Pantheon, paper, $9.95 (0-394-74723-2).

    Gr. 7–12. In this grim autobiography and its brilliant 1991 sequel, *Maus II: A Survivor's Tale,* Spiegelman takes the comic book to a new level of seriousness, portraying Jews as mice and Nazis as cats. Depicting himself being told about the Holocaust by his Polish survivor father, Spiegelman not only explores the concentration-camp experience, but also the guilt, love, and anger between father and son.

Vishniac, Roman.
  A Vanished World.
    1983. Farrar, $63 (0-374-28247-1); paper, $19.95
      (0-374-52023-2).

    Gr. 7–12. Vishniac's photographic documentary of ghetto life in Poland just prior to World War II reveals unemployed, boycotted, impoverished, pious people trying to carry on their familiar way of life—just before most of them were lost to the Nazi death camps.

Voigt, Cynthia.
  David and Jonathan.
    1992. Scholastic, $14 (0-590-45165-0).

    Gr. 8–12. Without false comfort, Voigt confronts issues of survivor guilt and enduring racism. Jon's cousin, David, a disturbed Holocaust survivor, moves in with the Jewish extended family, and all their lives are darkened forever. The enduring questions are made personal: Could I do that to others? Could others do that to me?

"'This is Mrs. Helsloot,' says Mother. 'She has come to take you. You are to go into hiding.'

'Going into hiding?' Rachel doesn't know what her mother means. 'I'm not going with her,' she replies.

'My dear, you must.'

'Why haven't Papa and you told us? And what does going into hiding mean?'

'Going into hiding is this: you hide from the Germans,' her mother explains. 'It is becoming too dangerous to wait here at home until they come get us. Go along. Esther and you will sleep one night at Mrs. Helsloot's. Tomorrow she will bring you to a village nearby. Papa and I will be there, too. Come, dear, get your scooter and go along.' Mother says it in such a special way that Rachel has to listen."

—Ida Vos

Vos, Ida.
Hide and Seek.
> Trans. by Terese Edelstein and Inez Smidt. 1991. Houghton,
> $13.95 (0-395-56470-0).

> Gr. 4–9. Why must Rachel wear a yellow star? This autobiographical story, translated from the Dutch, about a young girl's experience under the Nazi occupation is told in a series of spare vignettes that will move readers to imagine, "What if it happened to me?"

Wiesel, Elie.
The Night Trilogy: Night, Dawn, The Accident.
> Trans. by Stella Rodway. 1987. Hill & Wang, paper, $9.95
> (0-374-52140-9).

> Gr. 6–12. In *Night*, a stark autobiographical account, translated from the French, Wiesel describes the nightmare of being taken as a young boy with his father and other Hungarian Jews to the Buchenwald concentration camp, where he watched his father break down and die.

RIGHTEOUS GENTILES

Within the scope of Holocaust literature and film, certain themes stand out. The role of "righteous Gentiles" is definitely one of them. Raoul Wallenberg, Oscar Schindler, Miep Gies, and many others, whose courage is commemorated in Israel at the Yad Vashem memorial, stood up against the Nazis, bringing aid, rescue, comfort, and inspiration to Jews and others at the mercy of Hitler's "final solution." The bravery of these men, women, and children comes clear in the accounts listed below.

Bierman, John.
Righteous Gentile: The Story of Raoul Wallenberg.
> 1981. ADL, $12.95 (0-686-95084-4).

> Gr. 8–12. This account documents the wealthy, influential Swedish diplomat's efforts to save 100,000 Hungarian Jews and investigates his mysterious disappearance in 1945.

Gies, Miep and Gold, Alison Leslie.
Anne Frank Remembered: The Story of Miep Gies Who
Helped Hide the Frank Family.
> 1987. Simon & Schuster, paper, $7.95 (0-671-66234-1).

> Gr. 7–12. Gies hid Anne Frank and her family, and this affecting memoir adds fresh perspective to the classic diary.

Innocenti, Roberto and Gallaz, Christophe.
Rose Blanche.
> 1986. Stewart, Tabori & Chang, $15.95 (1-55670-207-8).

Gr. 5–7. A powerful picturebook/novel for older children, this focuses on a young girl who discovers a concentration camp in the woods near her town and begins carrying food to its inhabitants.

Keneally, Thomas.
Schindler's List.
1982. Penguin, paper, $8.95 (0-14-006784-1).

Gr. 8–12. A novel based on the life of a German business owner who shielded his Jewish workers in Poland from death in Nazi concentration camps.

Lowry, Lois.
Number the Stars.
1989. Houghton, $12.95 (0-395-51060-0); Dell, paper, $3.50 (0-440-40327-8).

Gr. 5–7. This novel of two Danish girls, one Jewish, the other not, highlights the way Danes protected their Jewish citizens from the invading Nazis. 1990 Newbery Medal winner.

Meltzer, Milton.
Rescue: The Story of How Gentiles Saved Jews in the Holocaust.
1988. HarperCollins, $13.95 (0-06-024209-4); paper, $6.95 (0-06-446117-3).

Gr. 6–12. Drawing heavily on personal accounts, Meltzer looks back at those brave people—ordinary men, women, children, priests, even whole villages—who risked their lives to aid the Jews.

THE OTHER VICTIMS

In addition to the six million Jews murdered by the Nazis, five million Gentiles were also killed. They included Gypsies, homosexuals, the disabled, Jehovah's Witnesses, and political prisoners. German pastor Martin Niemoller, who spent years in the camps, spoke eloquently about what happened: "The Nazis came first for the Communists. But I wasn't a Communist, so I didn't speak up. Then they came for the Jews, but I wasn't a Jew so I didn't speak up. Then they came for the trade unionists, but I wasn't a trade unionist so I didn't speak up. Then they came for the Catholics, but I was a Protestant so I didn't speak up. Then they came for me. By that time there was no one left."

Butterworth, Emma Macalik.
As the Waltz Was Ending.
1982. Four Winds, $13.95 (0-02-716190-0); Scholastic/Point, paper, $2.95 (0-590-33210-4).

Gr. 7–12. Butterworth, now a U.S. citizen, recalls six years of her Catholic girlhood in war-torn Vienna. Her anti-Nazi father is conscripted. Jewish friends are persecuted. When the Russians enter Vienna, Emma is raped.

"The first question that the Levite asked was, 'If I stop to help this man, what will happen to me?' But then the good Samaritan came by. And he reversed the question. 'If I do not stop to help this man, what will happen to him?' That is the question before you."
—Martin Luther King, Jr.

Friedman, Ina.
The Other Victims: First-Person Stories of Non-Jews Persecuted by the Nazis.
1990. Houghton, $14.95 (0-395-50212-8).

Gr. 5–9. Survivors of "undesirable" Gentile groups persecuted by the Nazis—including Gypsies, gays, Jehovah's Witnesses, artists, dissenters, the disabled, and kidnapped foreign workers—tell their stories. The style is flat, but the facts are riveting and not easily available elsewhere.

> "Wherever they burn books, they will also in the end burn human beings."
>
> —Heinrich Heine

Gehrts, Barbara.
Don't Say a Word.
Trans. by Elizabeth D. Crawford. 1986. Macmillan/Margaret K. McElderry, $13.95 (0-689-50412-8).

Gr. 7–12. An autobiographical novel, translated from the German, about an anti-Nazi Gentile family in a Berlin suburb quietly portrays mounting suffering under tyranny, as teenage Anna's father is arrested by the Gestapo, her brother dies in battle, and her Jewish girlfriend commits suicide with her family.

Mumford, Erika.
"The White Rose: Sophie Scholl, 1921–1943." In **The Music of What Happens.**
Ed. by Paul B. Janeczko. 1988. Orchard, $14.95 (0-531-05757-7).

Gr. 7–12. A long, dramatic poem based on the true story of the student resistance movement, called the White Rose, organized by Hans and Sophie Scholl in 1941. The Scholls were subsequently caught and executed. Read this with Hermann Vinke's *The Short Life of Sophie Scholl.*

Plant, Richard.
The Pink Triangle: The Nazi War against Homosexuals.
1986. Holt, paper, $10.95 (0-8050-0600-1).

Gr. 8–12. Plant frames his history of the Nazi attempt to exterminate gay men against the poignant story of his own flight from Germany and his return more than 30 years later.

VIDEOS

Bambinger.
Beacon Films. 1984. 26min. $149.

Gr. 8–12. Although 12-year old Sammy is initially resentful of the Jewish refugee's arrival, the boy's self-centered complacency turns to compassion when the refugee's family is killed on route from war-torn Europe to join him.

The Life of Anne Frank.
Films for the Humanities and Sciences. 1987. 25min. $149.

> Gr. 7–12. Portions of Anne Frank's diary are read against stills and footage of the family's hideout to trace the poignant story of the suffering and fate of one family during the Holocaust.

A Matter of Conscience.
The Media Guild. 1989. 34min. $345.

> Gr. 7–12. The horror of the Holocaust reverberates in this effective dramatization in which a teen discovers that his beloved grandfather was a guard at a Nazi concentration camp. The plot is similar to that of M. E. Kerr's novel *Gentlehands.*

Voices from the Attic.
Direct Cinema. 1988. 57min. $250.

> Gr. 10–12. A return to her family's Polish village and to the cramped attic where her relatives survived for more than a year grippingly personalizes the Holocaust for this filmmaker and child of a survivor.

Witness to the Holocaust.
The Anti-Defamation League. 1984. 7 programs on 2 videos. (each 20min.). $100.

> Gr. 9–12. Simply told reminiscences of survivors, telling archival stills and footage, and atmospheric music and sound effects record the history of the Holocaust.

Apartheid

Many white South Africans openly admired Hitler. The Nazi doctrine with its talk of ethnic purity and Aryan superiority was inspiring stuff to them.

There had always been gross inequality between the races, ever since the Europeans "discovered" the Cape and grabbed the land from the blacks. But when the Nationalist Party came to power after World War II, they set about codifying the inequality. Racism was the law. They called it "Apartheid" (pronounced "A-part-hate"), which is Afrikaans for apartness, or separate development. There was no deliberate genocide to compare with the Holocaust, but hunger, prison, family separation, and exile were common experience. Apartheid was sanctified by the Dutch Reformed Church; the whites told themselves they had a divine mission to care for the inferior blacks and to defend racial purity against "barbarism."

A system of laws was introduced that made blacks foreigners in their own country. Although they made up 75 percent of South Africa's population, blacks were given 13 percent of the land. Don Mattera remembers in his autobiography, *Sophiatown,* how he saw bulldozers raze his home and his whole urban community. It was like a bombing. The people of Sophiatown were "relocated," the place was renamed Triomf (Triumph), and whites moved in. Beverley Naidoo's YA novel *Chain of Fire* focuses on the same kind of forced removal in a rural community. Altogether about three-and-a-half million blacks found themselves dumped in places they'd never seen; they were told these barren places were their "homelands." Few crops grew in what rapidly became rural slums; many people died of starvation and disease. There were no jobs in those homelands. Family life was broken up as the men were forced to come alone to the cities to work.

The Population Registration Act arbitrarily classified everyone by color. If you were black, you had to carry a pass, a document that showed you had permission to work in a white area, and you had to produce it for any policeman. The demand, "Kaffir, where's your pass!" was a daily bureaucratic insult. The famous singer Miriam Makeba says in her autobiography that being arrested for pass offenses was part of ordinary life; everyone went to jail many times. Mark Mathabane's account of a pass raid on his parents' shack in Alexandra is like something out of the Holocaust: doors bashed in in the middle of the night, people dragged away to prison for not having their papers in order. He was forced to witness the humiliation of his father before the sneering police.

In their madness to keep the races separate, the government introduced the Immorality Act, which made it a crime to have sex across the color line. People went to jail for it. Some committed suicide in shame. In Nadine Gordimer's story "Country Lovers," a baby is murdered because its light color reveals the relationship between a white teenage father and a young black woman.

Education was separate and unequal, designed to prepare blacks mainly for menial work. In setting up "Bantu education," Dr. Hendrik Verwoerd, who later became prime minister, put it plainly: "There is no

> "They say that apartheid is dead; but the blacks haven't been invited to the funeral."
>
> —Archbishop Desmond Tutu

Above left: The people of Mogopa, forced from their ancestral land, 1984. **Right:** Houses set on fire by vigilantes in squatter camp, Cape Troy, January 1988.

place for the native in European society above the level of certain forms of labor."

In the 1960s and 1970s, while the civil rights movement in the U.S. was challenging official segregation, South Africa moved in the opposite direction. Peaceful protest, as at Sharpeville, was met by massacre. Suspects, including thousands of children, were tortured and held indefinitely in prison without trial. It was against the law to write about what happened to them or to say where they were. Nelson Mandela was sentenced to life in prison.

Then in 1976, young township students led the Soweto uprising. It started a great upheaval that, with the help of world pressure, eventually led to the chance for a new South Africa.

At last things are changing. No more passes, no more Immorality Act, no more removals. Mandela and most other political prisoners are free. There's hope. People are talking to each other about how we can live together.

And yet, racist oppression is still a bitter reality. At the time of this writing:

- Nelson Mandela has addressed the United States Congress, but he cannot vote in his own country. Neither can the Nobel Peace Prize–winner, Archbishop Desmond Tutu.

- While whites still enjoy a high standard of living, many blacks have neither land, nor shelter, nor enough to eat. A pathologist, Dr. Jonathan Gluckman, has revealed, with documentation and slides, that the police are torturing and murdering numbers of black prisoners, just as they killed activist leader Steve Biko in 1977.

- The schools have been desegregated, but South African style. *If* a white school wants to, and *if* the overwhelming majority of white parents agree, then the school is allowed to admit blacks. My old school has chosen not to.

Yet, despite the history of fierce censorship and terror, despite apartheidspeak that declared new meanings for words like *home* and *immorality,* South Africans have continued to write about their lives with honesty and passion. Their books reach a world audience. Perhaps because South Africans had no television until 1976 (and even now it's state controlled), they've had to tell stories. Perhaps it was all that secrecy that made the stories intense and quiet. Censorship made books matter.

Until very recently blacks in many areas, including Pretoria, could not use the public library. Gcina Mhlope tells of how she hid in a public toilet in a white area and transformed it into her writer's study. But, for every artist who has found her or his voice, there must be thousands, whether fighting on the barricades or just trying to feed their families, who have not been able to find the space or the privacy—the room of their own—to develop their talent and tell their stories.

NONFICTION

The Anti-Apartheid Reader: South Africa and the Struggle against White Racist Rule.
Ed. by David Mermelstein.
1987. Grove, paper, $15.95 (0-394-62223-5).

Gr. 7–12. A large collection of newspaper articles, speeches, interviews, book excerpts, and statistics provides a broad introductory resource on the apartheid society and resistance to it. Included are famous texts, such as the Freedom Charter, Mandela's court statement, Tutu's Nobel Peace Prize speech, as well as summaries of the racist laws, detailed accounts of the various uprisings, and discussions of issues like health, education, forced removals, and the role of women. There's also a section on U.S. foreign policy.

Benson, Mary.
Nelson Mandela: The Man and His Movement.
1986. Norton, paper, $8.95 (0-393-30322-5).

Gr. 9–12. This is not only a fine political biography of the great South African leader, but also a history of black struggle in his country and of the long outlawed (now unbanned) resistance movement, the African National Congress.

Beyond the Barricades: Popular Resistance in South Africa.
1989. Aperture, $24.95 (0-89381-375-3).

Gr. 7–12. Documentary photographs by 20 leading South African photographers take you to the barricades and reveal widespread protest and suffering, including the detention and torture of children. With background notes and personal accounts, and with a foreword by the Reverend Frank Chikane.

Biko, Steve.
I Write What I Like.
1979. HarperSanFrancisco, paper, $8.95 (0-06-250055-4).

Gr. 8–12. Articles by the young leader of the Black Consciousness Movement, who was murdered in 1977 while under interrogation in prison, demonstrate clearly why the white power structure feared him enough to kill him.

du Boulay, Shirley.
Tutu: Voice of the Voiceless.
1988. Eerdmans, $22.50 (0-8028-3649-6).

Gr. 7–12. This moving biography of the defiant, outspoken archbishop of Cape Town and Nobel Peace Prize winner integrates Desmond Tutu's personal story and his liberation theology with a strong sense of what it's like to live under apartheid. To this day, Tutu remembers his astonishment when, as a child, he saw the white Anglican priest Trevor Huddleston raise his hat in greeting Tutu's mother.

Finnegan, William.
Crossing the Line: A Year in the Land of Apartheid.
1986. HarperCollins, paper, $10.95 (0-06-091430-0).

Gr. 8–12. Finnegan, a California surfer, went to South Africa for personal adventure, but when he took a job in a "Coloured" (mixed race) high school in the throes of boycott and violence, he learned what apartheid was like for young people—the suffering and the commitment.

Women who lost their homes at Crossroads protesting outside the gates of Parliament after a futile meeting with government ministers.

From South Africa: New Writing, Photographs, and Art.
Ed by David Bunn and Janet Taylor.
1988. Univ. of Chicago, $47.50 (0-226-09035-8); paper,
$16.95 (0-226-08036-6).

Gr. 8–12. Written by those fighting at the barricades, this collection of poems, speeches, articles, stories, novel excerpts, and graphics expresses a people's sorrow and protest as well as a vision of nonracial liberation. The editors' introduction points out how far this post-Soweto culture is from the mysterious, primitive stereotypes in *Out of Africa.*

> "People
> are people
> through other
> people."
>
> —Xhosa proverb

Fugard, Athol.
"Master Harold . . . " and the Boys.
1982. Penguin, paper, $4.95 (0-14-048187-7).

Gr. 7–12. A famous play about a white South African teenager ("the master") who lashes out at two older black men ("the boys") who have long treated him as a younger brother: he takes out on them his anger and frustration and reveals the inherited hatred that poisons their world. An Afrikaner from the rural Cape, Fugard says that he first woke up to the evil of apartheid when, as a young boy, he spat in the face of a black man.

Gordimer, Nadine and Goldblatt, David.
Lifetimes under Apartheid.
1986. Knopf, $30 (0-317-47546-0).

Gr. 7–12. With both arms in casts above the elbow, a teenager, released from detention, stares at the camera: opposite is a quote from a Nadine Gordimer novel: "It's about suffering. . . . It's strange to live in a country where there are still heroes." Prose excerpts from one of South Africa's greatest writers accompany 60 searing photographs.

Harrison, David.
The White Tribe of Africa: South Africa in Perspective.
1982. Univ. of California, $35 (0-520-04690-0); paper, $14.95
(0-520-05066-5).

Gr. 8–12. Harrison's sympathetic exploration of the attitudes of Afrikaners makes use of many personal anecdotes and photographs. The author describes their travails of the past in the Great Trek and the Boer War, their rise to power, and their efforts to consolidate that power and ensure the survival of their culture.

Holland, Heidi.
The Struggle: A History of the African National Congress.
1990. Braziller, $19.95 (0-8076-1238-3); paper, $10.95
(0-8076-1255-3).

Gr. 7–12. This lively popular history of South Africa's leading protest movement integrates crucial events (at Sharpeville, Rivonia, Soweto, etc.) and biographies (Mandela, Luthuli, Tambo, etc.) with a historical account of the black struggle against apartheid. Author Holland finds hope in the ANC's unwavering commitment to nonracial democracy.

Hoobler, Dorothy and Hoobler, Thomas.
Mandela: The Man, the Struggle, the Triumph.
1992. Watts, $13.95 (0-531-15245-6).

Gr. 6–12. The Hooblers' YA biography sets the great leader's personal story within the politics of his country. The authors discuss his early life, his struggle, and his imprisonment, as well as details of his release, Winnie Mandela's trial, and the tour of the United States. Contemporary problems of internal violence and the transition to democratic rule are also addressed.

Hope, Christopher.
White Boy Running.
1988. Farrar, $17.95 (0-374-28925-5).

Gr. 9–12. After 12 years in London, this talented novelist returns home to observe the whites-only 1987 election; he weaves together his family's and his country's history in an account that brings out the absurdity as well as the terror of apartheid. Hope is also the author of *A Separate Development*, a sardonic novel about Harry Moto, who finds himself branded as "Coloured" and forced to live apart from his family.

Lelyveld, Joseph.
Move Your Shadow: South Africa, Black and White.
1985. Times Books, $18.95 (0-8129-1237-3); Penguin, paper, $8.95 (0-14-009326-5).

Gr. 8–12. Winner of the Pulitzer Prize, this in-depth personal profile by a *New York Times* correspondent lets the white racists convict themselves through their own words and actions. Lelyveld emphasizes the gap between superficial concessions and legalized brutality.

Magubane, Peter.
Soweto: The Fruit of Fear.
1986. Eerdmans/Africa World Press, $29.95 (0-86543-041-1); paper, $14.95 (0-86543-040-3).

Gr. 7–12. The 1976 Soweto uprising of schoolchildren is dramatically documented by an acclaimed South African photojournalist in pictures of violent confrontation and sorrow. The photos show street battles with heavily armed police and soldiers facing teenagers using sticks, stones, and ash-can lids. Magubane is also the author/photographer of *Black Child*, winner of the Coretta Scott King Award.

Makeba, Miriam and Hall, James.
Makeba: My Story.
1988. NAL/Plume, paper, $10.95 (0-452-26234-8).

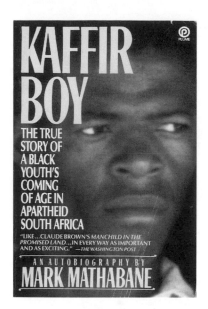

"A huge throng of handcuffed black men and women, numbering in the hundreds, filled the narrow streets from side to side. The multitude, murmuring like herds of restless cattle, was being marched by scores of black policemen and a dozen or so white ones, some of whom had fierce police dogs on leashes, toward a row of about ten police vans and trucks parked farther down the street. More handcuffed men and women were still filing out of the yards on either side, swelling the ranks of those already choking the streets. It seemed as if the entire population of Alexandra had been arrested."

—Mark Mathabane

Gr. 8–12. In a colloquial, present-tense narrative, the popular South African singer Miriam Makeba tells her story with warmth and candor, beginning with her childhood and coming-of-age under apartheid. She goes on to describe her international success after arriving in the U.S., her relations with the famous, including Harry Belafonte; her marriage to the radical Stokely Carmichael; and her unsuccessful attempt to make a home in Guinea. Makeba's story rings with authenticity, whether she's describing her bewilderment as a UN delegate, the suffering of her people and her bitter sense of exile from them, or her unashamed pride and delight in her music.

Malan, Rian.
My Traitor's Heart: A South African Exile Returns to Face His Country, His Tribe, and His Conscience.
1990. Atlantic Monthly Press, $19.95 (0-87113-229-X);
Random/Vintage, paper, $10.95 (0-679-73215-2).

Gr. 9–12. Afrikaans journalist Malan, great-nephew of apartheid's first prime minister, returns to his country after years of living in the U.S. He investigates a number of murders—in Soweto, in the police torture chambers, on the farms, in the gold mines, in the "homelands"—and relates the tangled stories of why people kill each other to politics, history, culture, myth, and to his own quest for home.

Mallaby, Sebastian.
After Apartheid: The Future of South Africa.
1992. Times Books, $22 (0-8129-1938-6).

Gr. 9–12. In accessible, journalistic style, Mallaby conveys the excitement of a country where people are talking about such basics as how to make a constitution and build an economy. He ridicules the crude rhetoric that a black government in South Africa would mean communism and chaos, and he also argues that the fear of a right-wing backlash is exaggerated.

Mandela, Nelson.
No Easy Walk to Freedom.
1965. Heinemann, paper, $7.95 (0-435-90782-4).

Gr. 8–12. A collection of Mandela's speeches and articles, this includes accounts of his court trials and writing from his time underground, as well as his famous speech to the court before he was sentenced to life imprisonment.

Mathabane, Mark.
Kaffir Boy: The True Story of a Black Youth's Coming of Age in South Africa.
1986. NAL, paper, $9.95 (0-452-25943-6).

Gr. 8–12. *Kaffir* means *nigger* in South Africa. This searing autobiography, a best seller in the U.S., was banned in South Africa until recently. Mathabane tells of growing up in poverty and fear in the ghetto of Alexandra township near Johannesburg and of the near miracle by which he came to college in the U.S. on a tennis scholarship. In *Love in Black and White*, he and his white American wife, Gail, talk about their marriage and the taboos that still surround interracial relationships, even in the U.S.

Mattera, Don.
Sophiatown: Coming of Age in South Africa.
1989. Beacon, paper, $10.95 (0-8070-0207-0).

Gr. 9–12. In a painful story, Mattera describes his growing up in the vital, multiracial Johannesburg ghetto of Sophiatown in the 1950s, his change from murderous gang leader to political activist,

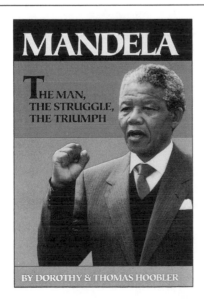

"I have fought against White domination, and I have fought against Black domination. I have cherished the ideal of a democratic and free society in which all persons live together in harmony and with equal opportunities. It is an ideal which I hope to live for and to achieve. But if needs be, it is an ideal for which I am prepared to die."

—Nelson Mandela

and his anguish at watching the razing of his home and community by the bulldozers of the apartheid authorities.

Meer, Fatima.
Higher Than Hope: A Biography of Nelson Mandela.
1990. HarperCollins, $19.95 (0-06-016146-9); paper, $10.95 (0-06-092066-1).

Gr. 8–12. This authorized biography by a longtime family friend and fellow activist describes the Mandelas' personal lives ("I felt I was more or less raised by the police," says daughter Zindzi) and also the history of the anti-apartheid struggle and the role of the ANC.

"Bulldozers, like the terrible· bombs of war, had razed our homes, our hopes and dreams, and what little love and comfort and peace Sophiatown had given us."

—Don Mattera

Modisane, Bloke.
Blame Me on History.
1990. Simon & Schuster, $21.95 (0-671-70794-9); paper, $9.95 (0-671-70067-7).

Gr. 9–12. Less graphic and more analytic than *Kaffir Boy*, but just as candid, this autobiography is the cry of a brilliant, vital man who grows up black in the slums of Johannesburg and tries to resist the apartheid view of him as less than human.

Mphahlele, Ezekiel.
Down Second Avenue: Growing Up in a South African Ghetto.
1959. Peter Smith, $21.50 (0-8446-4451-X); Faber, paper, $6.95 (0-571-09716-2).

Gr. 9–12. The author, now a university professor, describes his childhood and youth in the country and city slums, where his education, his sense of community, and his pride in himself helped him to survive vicious racism and his own bitterness.

Paton, Jonathan.
The Land and People of South Africa.
1990. HarperCollins, $14.95 (0-397-32361-1).

Gr. 6–12. Paton attacks white versions of history (that show courageous whites fighting off hordes of fierce, heathen black warriors) and discusses his country as a multicultural community in all its vitality and terrible conflict. Part of the fine YA Portraits of the Nations series.

Peace, Judy Boppell.
The Boy Child Is Dying: A South African Experience.
1986. HarperSanFrancisco, $11.95 (0-06-066482-7).

Gr. 6–12. Written from the viewpoint of a liberal Christian American who spent eight years in South Africa, these vignettes of the dailiness of cruelty and suffering vitalize the statistics and rationalizations and show the price both whites and blacks pay for living under apartheid.

The Penguin Book of Southern African Verse.
  Ed. by Stephen Gray.
    1989. Penguin, paper, $8.95 (0-14-058510-9).

    Gr. 8–12. Dennis Brutus, Mazisi Kunene, Mongane Serote, and Jeremy Cronin are among the wide range of contemporary poets collected here. There are translations, classics, poetry from the oral tradition, and contemporary pieces.

Russell, Diana.
  Lives of Courage: Women for a New South Africa.
    1989. Basic, $22.95 (0-465-04139-6); paper, $12.95 (0-465-04141-8).

    Gr. 8–12. Interviews with 60 women who have been actively involved in the anti-apartheid struggle give a direct account of their experiences, which range from life in Soweto to forced removals to the "homelands," and from marriage across the color bar to civil disobedience.

Sachs, Albie.
  Running to Maputo.
    1990. HarperCollins, $19.95 (0-06-016468-9).

    Gr. 9–12. A terrorist bomb took his right arm and blinded him in one eye, but South African lawyer-activist Sachs recovered to continue his fight for a nonracist South Africa. With humor and spirit, he describes his first year of recovery and his struggle to come through without hatred or self-pity.

Sparks, Allister.
  The Mind of South Africa.
    1990. Knopf, $24.95 (0-394-58108-3); Ballantine, paper, $15 (0-345-37119-4).

    Gr. 9–12. Writing as personal witness, political analyst, and historian, a leading Johannesburg liberal journalist looks at his country's history, past and present, focusing on daily life and how people see themselves.

Thompson, Leonard.
  A History of South Africa.
    1990. Yale, $29.95 (0-300-04815-7).

    Gr. 10–12. Scholarly, authoritative, and highly readable, this history of South Africa includes a lot about precolonial societies and points out that indigenous southern Africans were not blank stereotypes for white invaders to civilize or victimize.

Williamson, Sue.
  Resistance Art in South Africa.
    1990. St. Martin's, paper, $35 (0-312-04142-X).

"In my writing —as opposed to my life —I'm only interested in the personal. I'm not interested in the abstraction of politics because that's got nothing to do with literature. Politics is just something causal, but the life comes from inside."

—Nadine Gordimer

Gr. 7–12. From T-shirts and banners to sophisticated paintings, drawings, and sculpture, this contemporary collection blends politics and art.

Women under Apartheid.
  1980. Africa Fund, paper, $7 (0-317-36678-5).

Gr. 7–12. These 100 heartbreaking photographs, combined with informative text, depict the lives of black women, focusing on the migrant labor system and resettlement laws and their devastation of home and family life. The book is derived from a UN exhibition prepared by the International Defence and Aid Fund for Southern Africa. A set of the black-and-white photographs is available for exhibition. *Children under Apartheid* is a companion volume.

Woods, Donald.
  Biko.
  1983. Peter Smith, $15.95 (0-8446-6037-4); Holt, paper, $10.95 (0-8050-1899-9).

Gr. 7–12. White journalist Woods was a close friend of Biko, the leader of the Black Consciousness Movement who was murdered in prison. This biography (which provided the background for the movie *Cry Freedom*) is both a personal testimony to Biko and a fierce indictment of the apartheid system.

> "I had learned that if one cannot call a country to heel like a dog, neither can one dismiss the past with a smile in an easy gush of feeling, saying: I could not help it, I am also a victim."
>
> —Doris Lessing

FICTION

Abrahams, Peter.
  Mine Boy.
  1948. Heinemann Educational Books, paper, $7.95 (0-435-90562-7).

Gr. 7–12. Young Xuma comes from the country to the slums of Johannesburg, where he finds work in the gold mines and manhood in resistance, and where the girl he loves is destroyed by self-hatred. Abrahams' powerful autobiography, *Tell Freedom* (1954), includes a joyful chapter about his discovery of black American writers like Langston Hughes and Countee Cullen and how much that helped him as a struggling "Coloured" (mixed race) writer.

Brink, André.
  A Dry White Season.
  1980. Penguin, paper, $8.95 (0-14-006890-2).

Gr. 9–12. A liberal Afrikaans novelist writes of a white teacher who thinks that apartheid hasn't much to do with him until the experience of a black family in the Soweto riots draws him into confrontation with the regime and with his own family. This was made into a fine feature film.

Gordimer, Nadine.
  Crimes of Conscience.
    1991. Heinemann, paper, $8.95 (0-435-90668-2).

    Gr. 8–12. Part of the African Writers series, this small retrospective collection of 11 great short stories introduces teens to the Nobel Prize–winning writer, who shows with candor how racism affects people's personal lives.

Gordimer, Nadine.
  My Son's Story.
    1990. Farrar, $19.95 (0-374-21751-3); Penguin, paper, $9.95 (0-14-015975-4).

    Gr. 10–12. A searing story told from the point of view of a "Coloured" teenager who sees how apartheid experience brings out love, betrayal, and courage in his family—"what was there to be discovered."

Gordon, Sheila.
  Waiting for the Rain.
    1987. Orchard, $12.95 (0-531-05726-7); Bantam, paper, $3.50 (0-553-27911-4).

    Gr. 7–12. A YA novel about two boys who have grown up on a South African farm. White Frikkie, nephew of the farm owner, joins the army. Black Tengo, son of the farm foreman, goes to the city, desperate to get an education, and he's drawn into the struggle against the white government.

Thembalihle School at the former Gandhi settlement in Inanda near Durban. All the kids attending this school come from nearby Bhambayi squatter shacklands.

Isadora, Rachel.
At the Crossroads.
1991. Greenwillow, $13.95 (0-688-05270-3).

Gr. 2 and up. In a stunning picture book, Isadora captures the vitality of a South African shantytown, where celebration bursts out from the gray corrugated iron huts in the dusty veld. As the men return home from long months at the mines, the outstretched arms of fathers and waiting children express all the pain of family separation. The simple text with glowing double-spread watercolor paintings tells a story of joyful reunion that also reveals its wrenching opposite—the pain of families separated by migrant labor. A *Booklist* Top of the List winner as the best picture book of 1991.

Maartens, Maretha.
Paper Bird.
1991. Clarion, $13.95 (0-395-56490-5).

Gr. 5–9. Translated from the Afrikaans, this is a moving story of 12-year-old Adam growing up in poverty in a black township, threatened by violence from the police and from the local thugs. His younger sisters and his pregnant mother rely on him for support. On a dangerous journey to earn money in the city, he finds companionship and courage.

Naidoo, Beverley.
Chain of Fire.
1990. HarperCollins, $12.95 (0-397-32426-X).

Gr. 6–10. Through the experiences of 15-year-old Naledi, this YA novel by South African exile Naidoo dramatizes the apartheid atrocity that made blacks foreigners in their own country: the forced removal of more than three million blacks to barren, overcrowded "homelands" many of them had never seen.

Paton, Alan.
Cry, the Beloved Country.
1948. Macmillan/Collier, paper, $4.95 (0-02-053210-5).

Gr. 7–12. This classic novel is about the agonizing plight of a black country parson, the Reverend Stephen Kumalo, who comes seeking his son, Absalom, in the city and discovers that Absalom is condemned to hang for the murder of a white man.

Sacks, Margaret.
Beyond Safe Boundaries.
1989. Dutton/Lodestar, $13.95 (0-525-67281-8);
   Penguin/Puffin, paper, $3.95 (0-14-034407-1).

Gr. 6–12. Growing up in a Jewish liberal home in South Africa, teenage Elizabeth disapproves of apartheid, but she thinks it doesn't have much to do with her—until prison and murder invade the intimacy of her family. A powerful YA novel that raises troubling moral questions, this is one of the best stories about the white experience.

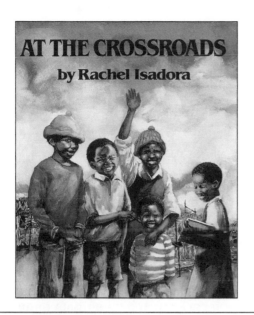

"A rooster crows. Down the road we see two bright lights. We hear the rumble of a truck. We jump up. It stops at the crossroads.

Our fathers have come. 'Wake up, Zolani!' 'Our fathers are here!' 'Our fathers are here!' "

—Rachel Isadora

Silver, Norman.
  No Tigers in Africa.
    1992. Dutton, $15 (0-525-44733-4).

    Gr. 7–12. Selwyn Lewis, a white teenager newly arrived in England from Jo'burg, denies his racism. But he's haunted by guilt that he caused the death of a black teenager. He didn't pull the trigger, but he feels it was his fault. This YA novel is uneven, but what will haunt readers is the universal moral issue, the connections made between this ordinary family and those ordinary people who went along with slavery and with the Holocaust. In a mad world that seems normal, Selwyn comes to realize that the system is to blame. And so is he.

Slovo, Gillian.
  Ties of Blood.
    1990. Morrow, $22.95 (0-688-08925-9); Avon, paper, $5.95 (0-380-70902-3).

    Gr. 9–12. This very long, dramatic, fast-paced docunovel about two anti-apartheid families—one black, one white—blends fiction, current history, and autobiography with a strong focus on the conflict and idealism of individual young people over four generations. The best part is about the schoolchildren's uprising in Soweto. Slovo's mother, Ruth First, was killed by a letter bomb. Another daughter, Shawn Slovo, made the exquisite film *A World Apart*, about her childhood conflict with a mother who was fighting for a righteous cause but was unable to be there for her own children.

Somehow Tenderness Survives: Stories of Southern Africa.
  Ed. by Hazel Rochman.
    1988. HarperCollins, $12.95 (0-06-025022-4); paper, $3.25 (0-06-447063-6).

    Gr. 7–12. This YA anthology, which brings together 10 stories and autobiographical accounts by southern African writers, including

Abrahams, Gordimer, Havemann, Jacobson, Lessing, Mhlope, Mathabane, and Wicomb, vividly evokes what it means to come of age under apartheid. The title is from a poem by Dennis Brutus that begins "Somehow we survive / and tenderness, frustrated, does not wither."

Williams, Michael.
Crocodile Burning.
1992. Dutton/Lodestar, $15 (0-525-67401-2).

Gr. 7–12. For Sowetan teenager Seraki Nzule, getting a role in a township musical is a chance to escape from the shambles of school, the poverty, the thugs, the weakness of his parents; and he can block out his fear for his older brother, detained in jail for months without trial. Then the musical moves to Broadway and Seraki finds himself in New York. The first-person narrative conveys the vitality as well as the sorrow of the dusty township streets, and kids will like the vivid re-creation of what it's like to put on a show. Also, the Sowetans' homesickness and their disappointment in America produce a compelling reversal.

VIDEOS

A Chip of Glass Ruby.
Films for the Humanities & Sciences. 1988. 20min. $149.

Gr. 9–12. Clips from the film version of Gordimer's story of a Muslim Indian family in South Africa in the 1950s are interwoven with comments by the author on her craft and on the political unrest in her country.

Maids and Madams.
Filmakers Library. 1985. 52min. $195.

Gr. 10–12. From comfortable white homes where black domestics work to the overcrowded dwellings where they live, the effects of apartheid are revealed through the eyes of the servants and the words of the women they serve.

Senzeni Na?
Pyramid. 1990. 30min., $325.

Gr. 11–12. A case of mistaken identity catapults a meek black worker into prison and leads to a decisive moment of truth in this taut drama that chillingly shows the casual yet calculated brutality visited upon political activists in South Africa.

Six Feet of the Country.
Coronet. 1977; released 1980. 29min. $250.

Gr. 10–12. A black hired man's attempt to retrieve his brother's body for burial underscores the harsh inhumanity of apartheid in this moving adaptation of Nadine Gordimer's short story.

ETHNIC U. S. A.

African Americans

African American literature is flourishing. There's no way all the good titles—adult and young adult, fiction and nonfiction—could be included on any resource list; this is just a selection. Autobiography, poetry, and historical fiction are especially rich genres here. There's also an increasing complexity in contemporary YA stories, which reach beyond simple role models to confront issues of color, class, prejudice, and identity without offering Band-Aids of self-esteem. As Deborah Taylor, head of young adult services at Enoch Pratt Free Library in Baltimore, says, "It's great that YA books no longer have to show us as perfect." Many coming-of-age stories combine individual conflict with a stark social realism and also reach out to universal myth. Styles vary from soaring rhythms to the sparest poetry. Some of the best writers show a humane acceptance of people in their struggle and hope for the power of their love. From Sojourner Truth to James Baldwin and Malcolm X to Virginia Hamilton, the struggle is not only with the racism in society, but also with personal hatred and despair.

There's also laughter, stretching back to the old subversive trickster tales. Dick Gregory says in *Talk That Talk* that once the white establishment got around to designating a Black History Month, "it would be the month of February, with all them days missing."

Of course, this list will help promote Black History Month and special curriculum projects about African Americans. But these are great books for all of us, about all of us, all year long. You don't need a special month to make you want to read some of America's best writers.

NONFICTION

Aaron, Henry and Wheeler, Lonnie.
I Had a Hammer.
> 1991. HarperCollins, $21.95 (0-06-016321-6); paper, $5.50 (0-06-109956-2).

> Gr. 7–12. Aaron, who broke Babe Ruth's home run record, tells of his love of baseball and also of the racial hatred he encountered. A significant sports biography that tells as much about America and baseball in general as it does about Aaron in particular.

Angelou, Maya.
I Know Why the Caged Bird Sings.
> 1970. Random, $19.45 (0-394-42986-9); Bantam, paper, $4.95 (0-553-27937-8).

> Gr. 7–12. In her lyrical autobiography, Angelou tells how, despite its segregation, Stamps, Arkansas, became her refuge after she was raped at age eight and went home to stay with her strong grandmother and beloved brother. This first in a series of Angelou's personal stories remains the best and the most accessible to junior and senior high school students.

Baldwin, James.
Notes of a Native Son.
> 1955. 3rd ed. Beacon, paper, $9.95 (0-8070-0907-5).

> Gr. 8–12. Spare candid essays, some of them autobiographical. In the great title piece, Baldwin confronts the hatred out in society and inside himself, relating it to his separation from his father.

Cary, Lorene.
Black Ice.
> 1991. Knopf, $19.95 (0-394-57465-6).

> Gr. 7–12. A triumphant account of Cary's experiences at a New Hampshire prep school captures her struggle to succeed and maintain her identity in a long-time bastion of upper-class white males.

Children of Promise: African-American Literature and Art for Young People.
Ed. by Charles Sullivan.
> 1991. Abrams, $24.95 (0-8109-3170-2).

> Gr. 5–12. The image of African Americans in literature and art from slavery times through today is the subject of this fine, well-illustrated anthology.

Collier, James Lincoln.
Duke Ellington.
> 1991. Macmillan, $12.95 (0-02-722985-8).

> Gr. 5–7. The author of critically acclaimed adult jazz biographies adapts his adult Ellington book for younger readers, preserving

---

"I have ploughed and planted and gathered into barns . . . and ain't I a woman? I could work as much and eat as much as a man . . . and bear the lash as well! And ain't I a woman?"

—Sojourner Truth

the essence of Ellington the man, the composer, and the elegant performer.

De Veaux, Alexis.
Don't Explain: A Song of Billie Holiday.
1980. HarperCollins, $12.89 (0-06-021630-1); Writers and Readers, paper, $7.95 (0-86316-132-4).

Gr. 8–12. In jazz-flavored lyric form, De Veaux beautifully and tenderly evokes jazz singer Billie Holiday—her life (including her struggle with heroin), the times in which she lived, and her music.

Growing Up Black: From Slave Days to the Present.
Ed. by Jay David.
1992. Rev. ed. Avon, paper, $9 (0-380-76632-9).

Gr. 8–12. This compelling collection of autobiographical accounts of 25 African Americans will introduce readers to some of the best black writers—from Frederick Douglass to Audre Lorde, Claude Brown, John Wideman, and Lorene Cary—and will help students write with candor and control about their own memories.

Haley, Alex.
Roots.
1976. Doubleday, $21.95 (0-385-03787-2); Dell, paper, $5.95 (0-440-17464-3).

Gr. 8–12. Haley traces his ancestry back to Kunta Kinte, who was kidnapped as a slave in Gambia, West Africa, in the mid-1700s.

Hamilton, Virginia.
Many Thousand Gone: African Americans from Slavery to Freedom.
1993. Knopf, $16 (0-349-828-739).

Gr. 5–10. A companion volume to *The People Could Fly*, illustrated in the same style by the Dillons, this recently published account draws on actual slave narratives to produce history that is personal and authentic.

Hamilton, Virginia.
The People Could Fly.
1985. Knopf, $16.95 (0-394-86925-7).

Gr. 5–12. Dramatically retold African American folktales range from fantasy, fun, and horror to history and true escape narratives, with splendid illustrations by Leo and Diane Dillon. The title story is anguished yet hopeful, a fantasy about both those who flew away from brutality to freedom and those who stayed behind and told the story.

Hansberry, Lorraine.
A Raisin in the Sun.
1959. NAL/Dutton, paper, $3.99 (0-451-16137-8).

Gr. 9–12. Hansberry's candid drama focuses on the vital bonds of a Chicago black family that suddenly inherits money in the 1950s.

Haskins, James.
Black Music in America: A History through Its People.
> 1987. HarperCollins/Crowell, $12.95 (0-690-04460-7).

>> Gr. 6–12. A readable overview of black music and the influence it has had on both black and white culture in America.

Haskins, James.
Thurgood Marshall: A Life for Justice.
> 1992. Holt, $14.95 (0-8050-2095-0).

>> Gr. 6–9. This illuminating, in-depth portrait of the first African American Supreme Court justice reveals the late Marshall as a man who devoted his life to fighting racism and segregation through the U.S. legal system.

> "I began to think back to Nat Turner, Harriet Tubman, Sojourner Truth, John Brown, Fred Douglass—folks who left no buildings behind them—only a wind of words fanning the bright flame of the spirit down the dark lanes of time."
>
> —Langston Hughes

Hirshey, Gerri.
Nowhere to Run: The Story of Soul Music.
> 1984. Times, $17.95 (0-8129-1111-3).

>> Gr. 7–12. Told through anecdotes and interviews with James Brown, Aretha Franklin, Diana Ross, Michael Jackson, and many others, this is the story of soul music in the northern cities and in the South, "a restless music that rarely sat down to study on itself."

Hughes, Langston.
The Big Sea.
> 1940. Thunder's Mouth, paper, $11.95 (0-938410-33-4).

>> Gr. 8–12. The first part of Hughes' autobiography integrates some of his great poetry with his life story. His parents were separated, and as a teenager Hughes broke with his rich, powerful father who hated his own people. Hughes made his own way and became one of the great figures of the Harlem Renaissance and an enduring voice in American literature.

I Am the Darker Brother: An Anthology of Modern Poems by Negro Americans.
Ed. by Arnold Adoff.
> 1968. Macmillan/Collier, paper, $4.95 (0-02-041120-0).

>> Gr. 6–12. In this and other fine anthologies of black poetry, including *Black Out Loud* and *Celebrations*, poet Adoff has collected some of the outstanding African American poets, from Langston Hughes and Robert Hayden to Mari Evans and Gwendolyn Brooks.

Katz, William Loren.
Breaking the Chains: African-American Slave Resistance.
> 1990. Atheneum, $14.95 (0-689-31493-0).

>> Gr. 7–12. Basing his text largely on slave testimony, the recollections of white slaveowners, and public records, Katz details the harshness of slave life and the many forms of resistance.

Kotlowitz, Alex.
There Are No Children Here: The Story of Two Boys Growing Up in
the Other America.
1991. Doubleday, $21.95 (0-385-26526-3).

Gr. 9–12. A compelling account of two inner-city Chicago children,
Lafayette and Pharoah Rivers, and their daily struggle with the
sadness and violence of their neighborhood wasteland.

Langstaff, John.
Climbing Jacob's Ladder: Heroes of the Bible in
Afro-American Spirituals.
1991. Macmillan/Margaret K. McElderry, $13.95
(0-689-50494-2).

All ages. This companion to *What a Morning! The Christmas Story in
Black Spirituals* is a vibrant celebration, both a testimony to the
musical heritage of African Americans and a practical resource for
music teachers and their students. Ashley Bryan uses swirling bands
of color to give visual form to the vigorous, up-tempo rhythm of
some familiar hymns.

Lemann, Nicholas.
The Promised Land: The Great Black Migration and How It
Changed America.
1991. Knopf, $24.95 (0-394-56004-3).

From *Many Thousand Gone*, Knopf, 1993

"No more auction block for me,
No more, no more,
No more auction block for me,
Many thousand gone.
No more peck of corn for me,
No more, no more,
No more peck of corn for me,
Many thousand gone.
No more pint of salt for me,
No more, no more,
No more pint of salt for me,
Many thousand gone.
No more driver's lash for me,
No more, no more,
No more driver's lash for me,
Many thousand gone."

—Spiritual sung by black soldiers
fighting in the Civil War

Gr. 9–12. Combining personal interviews and political analysis, Lemann's account of how the great black migration from the South fundamentally changed America also discusses why the war on poverty did not succeed and why the civil rights movement yielded only partial victories.

Levine, Ellen.
Freedom's Children: Young Civil Rights Activists Tell Their Own Stories.
1993. Putnam, $15.95 (0-399-21893-9).

Gr. 6–12. In this fine collection of oral histories, 30 African Americans who were children and teenagers in the 1950s and 1960s talk about what it was like for them in Alabama, Mississippi, and Arkansas: sitting in, riding at the front of the bus, integrating schools, braving arrest and violence, even death.

Lyons, Mary.
Sorrow's Kitchen: The Life and Folklore of Zora Neale Hurston.
1990. Macmillan, $13.95 (0-684-19198-9).

Gr. 7–12. As folklorist, writer, and anthropologist, Hurston celebrated black pride, attacking what she called the "sobbing school of Negrohood." Other leaders of the Harlem Renaissance accused her of ignoring black suffering and playing up the "minstrel image" to please whites. She died poor and alone in 1960. Today her books, such as *Their Eyes Were Watching God,* are enjoying an enthusiastic revival. Lyons' biography for young adults includes long excerpts from Hurston's work and is a good place to start.

McElroy, Guy C. and Gates, Henry Louis, Jr.
Facing History: The Black Image in American Art, 1710–1940.
1990. Bedford Arts, $50 (0-938491-39-3); paper, $24.95 (0-938491-38-5).

Gr. 8–12. This glowing art book examines the changes in the way blacks have been depicted—from "happy" slave and comic grotesque to worker, hero, and symbol of urban life—in works by American artists of all races.

McKissack, Patricia and McKissack, Fredrick.
A Long Hard Journey: The Story of the Pullman Porter Strike.
1989. Walker, $17.95 (0-8027-6884-9).

Gr. 5–9. This sympathetic study of the first organized black labor movement in the U.S. was the winner of the 1990 Coretta Scott King Award. Also by the McKissacks is the biography *Sojourner Truth.*

Myers, Walter Dean.
Now Is Your Time: The African-American Struggle for Freedom.
1991. HarperCollins, $17.95 (0-06-024370-8); paper, $10.95 (0-06-446120-3).

Gr. 6–12. Slaves, soldiers, inventors, political leaders: Myers traces the path of African Americans—some in his own family—inter-

"Sometimes, I feel discriminated against, but it does not make me angry. It merely astonishes me. How *can* anyone deny themselves the pleasure of my company? It's beyond me."

—Zora Neale Hurston

weaving the history with brief sketches of influential and ordinary people. Winner of the 1992 Coretta Scott King Award.

The Negro Almanac: A Reference Work on the Afro-American.
Ed. by Harry A. Ploski and James Williams.
1990. 5th ed. Gale, $110 (0-8103-7706-3).

Gr. 6–12. Thoroughly revised and updated, the 33 chapters cover in detail every aspect of the black experience in America. This is the most important contemporary reference work in the field.

Oates, Stephen.
Let the Trumpet Sound: The Life of Martin Luther King.
1982. NAL, paper, $10.95 (0-452-25627-5).

Gr. 8–12. One of the many fine biographies of the great civil rights leader, Martin Luther King, Jr., who became a national symbol of freedom and justice.

Parks, Rosa and Haskins, Jim.
Rosa Parks: My Story.
1992. Dial, $16 (0-8037-0673-1).

Gr. 6–10. A straightforward, uncompromising autobiography, with many photographs, this is told with the same kind of unflinching honesty and dignity that Rosa Parks displayed one fateful day in 1955 when she refused to give up her seat on a segregated bus.

Patterson, Lillie.
Martin Luther King, Jr., and the Freedom Movement.
1989. Facts On File, $15.95 (0-8160-1605-4).

Gr. 7–12. This political biography of King is also a dramatic account of the civil rights movement he helped lead, beginning with the

Montgomery bus boycott in the mid-1950s, through the sit-ins, freedom rides, the march on Washington, his Nobel Prize, the confrontation in Selma, Alabama, and the Voting Rights Act of 1965.

Russell, Bill and Branch, Taylor.
Second Wind: The Memoirs of an Opinionated Man.
1979. Ballantine, paper, $2.75 (0-345-28897-1).

Gr. 7–12. The superb Boston Celtics basketball star who made playing defense an art speaks with wit and candor about growing up in Oakland, California, withstanding racism and his own rage, and about the joy of the game.

"If Shakespeare can compare all life to a stage, maybe it's not odd to believe that part of the play can take place on a basketball court."

—Bill Russell

Russell, Sandi.
Render Me My Song: African American Women Writers from Slavery to the Present.
1991. St. Martin's, $18.95 (0-312-05288-X).

Gr. 9–12. With scholarship and vitality, Russell's informal literary history introduces the lives, works, and individual voices of great women writers. The order is chronological and individual chapters are devoted to giants like Zora Neale Hurston, Gwendolyn Brooks, and Toni Morrison.

Shake It to the One You Love the Best: Play Songs and Lullabies from Black Musical Traditions.
Ed. by Cheryl Warren Mattox.
1990. Warren-Mattox, paper, $7.95 (0-9623381-0-9).

All ages. An outstanding collection of 16 play songs and 10 lullabies featuring 11 full-color paintings. The songs are accompanied by source notes and historical information, as well as descriptions of the games or activities associated with them.

Talk That Talk: An Anthology of African-American Storytelling.
Ed. by Linda Goss and Marian E. Barnes.
1989. Simon & Schuster/Touchstone, $24.95
(0-671-67167-7); paper, $12.95 (0-685-28034-6).

Gr. 6–12. Nearly 100 stirring stories, from animal tales, legends, raps, and sermons to personal "truth tales" and biographies, by storytellers that include Nikki Giovanni, Zora Neale Hurston, Dick Gregory, and Langston Hughes, with commentaries from historians and folklorists.

Walker, Alice.
In Search of Our Mothers' Gardens: Womanist Prose.
1983. HBJ, $16.95 (0-15-144525-7).

Gr. 9–12. Walker speaks as a woman, mother, writer, and feminist. This collection includes her accounts of her experiences in the civil rights movement and also her famous Zora Neale Hurston essays, which helped spark the revival of interest in that long-neglected writer.

Webb, Sheyann, and Nelson, Rachel West.
Selma, Lord, Selma: Girlhood Memories of the Civil Rights Days.
   1980. Univ. of Alabama, $12.95 (0-8173-0031-7).

   Gr. 6–12. Rachel and Sheyann remember themselves at eight years old in those days of tension in Selma: marching, singing, demonstrating, being set upon by troopers, going to meetings, and talking about those who had been jailed or beaten or killed.

Williams, Juan.
Eyes on the Prize: America's Civil Rights Years, 1954–1965.
   1986. Penguin, paper, $11.95 (0-14-009653-1).

   Gr. 9–12. A companion volume to a PBS series, this heartfelt, illustrated, sociohistorical account covers the period in detail, including civil rights legislation, landmark court orders, the marches and boycotts, and the leaders of the mass protest movement.

Wilson, August.
Fences.
   1986. NAL, paper, $6.95 (0-452-26048-5).

   Gr. 7–12. The Pulitzer Prize–winning play about a black father who cannot overcome the jealousy he feels toward his son for having the baseball career he was denied by racism.

Wright, Richard.
Black Boy.
   1945. HarperCollins, $19.95 (0-06-014761-X); paper, $4.95
      (0-06-080987-6).

   Gr. 7–12. This classic autobiography is by one of the great naturalistic American writers. Dramatic, intense, and immediate, it includes

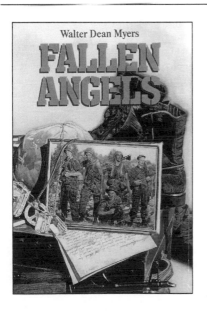

"Captain Stewart came round with a television crew, and we were all filmed. First they got us cleaning our weapons. Then they asked each one of us why we were fighting in Nam . . .

Lieutenant Carroll said that we had to demonstrate that America stood for something, and that's what we were doing . . . .

I said that we either defended our country abroad, or we would be forced to fight in the streets of America, which everybody seemed to like.

Then the news team got to Peewee and asked him why he was fighting in Vietnam.

'Vietnam?' Peewee looked around like he was shocked or something. 'I must have got off on the wrong stop. I thought this was St. Louis.' "

—Walter Dean Myers

searing scenes of confrontation. Wright is forced to mask his pride in himself, yet he refuses to let the white South break his spirit.

X, Malcolm and Haley, Alex.
The Autobiography of Malcolm X.

1965. Amereon, $21.95 (0-89190-216-3); Ballantine, paper, $5.95 (0-345-35068-5).

Gr. 7–12. Malcolm Little, who became Muslim Malcolm X, evolved from being a teenage dope peddler and the unrelenting enemy of all white men to a black leader who understood the real barriers that keep the races apart.

FICTION

Armstrong, Jennifer.
Steal Away.

1992. Orchard/Richard Jackson, $14.95 (0-531-05983-9).

Gr. 7–10. Two unhappy 13-year-old girls on a Virginia farm in 1855—black slave Bethlehem and white orphan Susannah—disguise themselves as boys and escape together. More than 40 years later they tell their stories to two young girls. The compelling escape adventure makes you think about friendship and about the enduring legacy of racism.

Baldwin, James.
Go Tell It on the Mountain.

1953. Dell, paper, $5.99 (0-440-33007-6).

Gr. 8–12. In a powerful autobiographical novel, teenage John struggles with inner religious conflict and with his rigid evangelist father in 1930s Harlem. His fight with his father is also about the black man's view of himself.

Brooks, Bruce.
The Moves Make the Man.

1984. HarperCollins, $14.95 (0-06-020679-9); paper, $2.95 (0-06-447022-9).

Gr. 7–12. Jerome, the first black to integrate a white school, knows the moves you need to survive—in basketball and with people—but his fragile white friend, Bix, refuses to learn how to fake.

Childress, Alice.
Rainbow Jordan.

1981. Putnam/Coward-McCann, $14.99 (0-689-32500-1); Avon, paper, $2.95 (0-380-58974-5).

Gr. 7–12. Despite an irresponsible mother, sexual pressure from her boyfriend, and an uncertain future, 14-year-old Rainbow is a survivor. Childress is also the author of the popular YA novel, *A Hero Ain't Nothin' But a Sandwich*.

TALKING BACK

Guy, Rosa.
  The Disappearance.
    1979. Delacorte, $9.95 (0-385-28129-3); Dell, paper, $3.25
      (0-440-92064-7).

    Gr. 7–12. Inner city teenager Imamu Jones is given a foster home
    with a kind, middle-class black family. But when their little girl
    disappears, Imamu must find her—to save himself from being the
    accused. A fine mystery.

Guy, Rosa.
  The Friends.
    1973. Holt, $10.95 (0-03-007876-8); Bantam, paper, $2.95
      (0-553-26519-9).

    Gr. 7–12. Recently moved from the West Indies, Phyllisia feels the
    hostility of her Harlem classmates. The only one offering her friend-
    ship is ragged Edith, whom Phyl despises for being dirty and poor.

Hamilton, Virginia.
  Cousins.
    1990. Putnam/Philomel, $14.95 (0-399-22164-6).

    Gr. 5–8. Cammy hates her beautiful, sweet, smart cousin Patty Ann.
    Then there's a terrible accident at day camp, and Cammy finds
    meanness—and courage—where she never expected to. The story
    is full of surprise; the characters are about us all.

Hamilton, Virginia.
  The House of Dies Drear.
    1984. Macmillan, $14.95 (0-02-742500-2); paper, $3.95
      (0-02-043520-7).

Gr. 5–10. Thomas knows there are secrets in the great old house in Ohio where his family has recently moved. More than 100 years ago the house was a station on the Underground Railroad, which provided shelter for runaway slaves on their way to freedom in Canada. Thomas' discovery of the slaves' secret signs and codes is one of the enduring appeals of this fine mystery.

Hamilton, Virginia.
Sweet Whispers, Brother Rush.
1982. Putnam/Philomel, $12.95 (0-399-20894-1); Avon, paper, $3.50 (0-380-65193-9).

Gr. 7–12. Tree loves her mentally disabled brother and cares for him while their mother is away working. Then Tree sees her uncle's ghost, and he takes her back in the past, where she discovers harsh secrets about her mother. A poetic, multilayered story that shows Hamilton at her best.

Lipsyte, Robert.
The Contender.
1967. HarperCollins, $12.89 (0-06-023920-4); paper, $2.95 (0-06-447039-3).

Gr. 7–12. Alfred Brooks, high school dropout, scared of a local gang, finds his way to Donatelli's Gym, a boxing club in Harlem, and there he becomes not a champion, but a contender. "It's the climbing that makes the man."

Lyons, Mary.
Letters from a Slave Girl: The Story of Harriet Jacobs.
1992. Scribner's, $14.95 (0-684-19446-5).

Gr. 7–12. Based on the autobiography of the slave Harriet Jacobs, this tells her story in the form of fictionalized letters. Like a quiet memoir or diary, the letters to Jacob's dead and distant loved ones reveal the thoughts and feelings of a person whom the slave system regards only as property. To escape sexual molestation by her master, the continual threat of the auction block, and separation from her children, she hides for seven years in a tiny garrett. The letter format both distances the cruelty and personalizes the sorrow. This would be a fine book to pair with *The Diary of Anne Frank.*

Marshall, Paule.
Daughters.
1991. Atheneum, $21.95 (0-689-12139-3).

Gr. 9–12. Marshall's stories of black women as daughters, mothers, wives, friends, and lovers illuminate how we all come of age. Her classic first novel *Brown Girl, Brownstones* focuses on a high school girl who questions the roles imposed on her. In *Daughters,* Ursa MacKenzie makes some hard and lonely decisions about her life, as her memories swing between the West Indian island where she spent her youth and her current home in New York City.

VOICES OF ANGER, MEN OF COMPASSION

James Baldwin

Malcolm X

Moore, Yvette.
  Freedom Songs.
    1991. Orchard, $14.95 (0-531-05812-3).

    Gr. 6–12. New York teenager Sheryl loves visiting her family in rural
    North Carolina, but in 1963 she faces the Jim Crow reality of her
    cousins' daily segregation. Then her young Uncle Pete's life is
    endangered when he joins the freedom riders. One of the few
    novels that deals with what it was like to be young at that time.

Morrison, Toni.
  Beloved.
    1987. Knopf, $24.95 (0-394-53597-9); NAL/Plume, paper,
      $9.95 (0-452-26446-4).

    Gr. 10–12. The ghost of the child Beloved comes back to haunt the
    mother who murdered her, in an exquisite though demanding
    novel that dramatizes the agony and violence of slavery.

Morrison, Toni.
  Jazz.
    1992. Knopf, $21 (0-679-41167-4).

    Gr. 10–12. A passionate, lyrical story about love and loss, remaking
    your life, and being African American in the late 1920s, when
    Harlem was in its prime. Morrison also takes us back to the fields
    of Virginia at the turn of the century and the years of race riots and
    the steady stream of African Americans moving north in search of
    less-backbreaking, better-paying work and the protection and
    liveliness of a large black community.

Myers, Walter Dean.
Fallen Angels.
> 1988. Scholastic, $12.95 (0-590-40942-5); paper, $3.50
> (0-590-40943-3).
>
> Gr. 7–12. Richie Perry, 17, isn't sure how he got to be in Vietnam.
> But when he figured he couldn't afford college, he just didn't want
> to be in Harlem anymore. Richie and the other young men in his
> squad find themselves in a nightmare with "hours of boredom,
> seconds of terror."

Myers, Walter Dean.
Scorpions.
> 1988. HarperCollins, $12.95 (0-06-024364-3); paper, $2.95
> (0-06-447066-0).
>
> Gr. 5–10. Twelve-year-old Jamal is struggling to survive on the cold,
> dangerous, inner-city streets. He cares about his mother and sister
> and his best friend, Tito. But there's too much against him and no
> one to help. Then someone gives Jamal a gun. A Newbery Honor
> book.

Myers, Walter Dean.
Somewhere in the Darkness.
> 1992. Scholastic, $14.95 (0-590-42411-4).
>
> Gr. 7–12. In a stark, contemporary story, teenage Jimmy finds his
> own way when his father breaks out of prison and they drive across
> the country. Jimmy confronts his father's failure and his own false
> dreams.

Naylor, Gloria.
The Women of Brewster Place: A Novel in Seven Stories.
> 1982. Penguin, paper, $4.50 (0-318-37688-1).
>
> Gr. 9–12. Naylor writes with conviction and beauty about seven
> black women who take different roads to Brewster Place, a street
> that once meant hope and upward mobility to white immigrants
> but is now a dead end for blacks.

Sanders, Dori.
Clover.
> 1990. Algonquin, $13.95 (0-945575-26-2); Fawcett, paper, $8
> (0-449-90624-8).
>
> Gr. 8–12. "Only minutes after my daddy married Sarah Kate he was
> killed. So here we are. Two strangers in a house." Ten-year-old
> Clover tells how she and her new white stepmother try to make a
> life together while they struggle with their grief and differences. A
> warm, unsentimental story set in the contemporary South.

Sebestyen, Ouida.
Words by Heart.
> 1979. Little, Brown/Joy Street Books, $14.95 (0-316-77931-8);
> Bantam, paper, $3.50 (0-553-27179-2).

Gr. 5–10. As the first black family in a small southwestern town in 1910, the Sills make the white townspeople uneasy. Especially threatening is Lena, hungry for book-learning and at the head of the class.

Shange, Ntozake.
Betsey Brown.
1985. St. Martin's, $12.95 (0-312-07727-0); paper, $8.95 (0-312-07728-9).

Gr. 8–12. In St. Louis in the late 1950s, Betsey experiences the anguish of school busing as well as the conflict and joy within her middle-class family.

> "*If* I grow up, I'd like to be a bus driver."
>
> —Lafeyette Rivers

Smith, Mary Carter.
"Cindy Ellie." In Best Loved Stories Told at the National Storytelling Festival.
1991. National Storytelling Press, $19.95 (1-879991-01-2); paper, $11.95 (1-879991-00-4).

Gr. 4 and up. This wonderfully entertaining, tongue-in-cheek version of "Cinderella," told in a mixture of street vernacular and standard English, is set in East Baltimore, where Cindy Ellie rides to the mayor's inauguration ball in a white Cadillac, her hair in 100 shining braids.

Taylor, Mildred.
Roll of Thunder, Hear My Cry.
1976. Dial, $14.95 (0-8037-7473-7); Bantam, paper, $3.50 (0-553-25450-2).

Gr. 6–12. A strong family stands together against Klan violence in Mississippi during the Depression. Winner of the 1977 Newbery Medal. The sequel, *Let the Circle Be Unbroken,* includes a stirring civil-rights confrontation in which a woman insists on her right to register to vote.

Thomas, Joyce Carol.
Marked by Fire.
1982. Avon/Flare, paper, $2.95 (0-380-79327-X).

Gr. 7–12. Abby grows up strengthened by the affection of her black Oklahoma community. Then a tornado hits and drives her family apart, and a physical assault all but breaks her will.

Williams-Garcia, Rita.
Fast Talk on a Slow Track.
1991. Dutton/Lodestar, $14.95 (0-525-67334-2).

Gr. 8–12. Everything has always been too easy for valedictorian Denzel Watson. Fast and smooth, he skates through the high school social and academic scene "achieving the most while expending the least." When he fails at Princeton, he doesn't dare tell his middle-class parents. Yet his failure haunts him. Will he stay on the street or crawl back to college? Who is he?

Woodson, Jacqueline.
Maizon at Blue Hill.
1992. Delacorte, $14 (0-385-30796-9).

Gr. 5–10. Black and smart, seventh-grader Maizon wins a scholarship to a girls' boarding school in Connecticut, but she hates being an outsider, and though her grades are fine, she's lonely for her Brooklyn neighborhood. A candid story about a girl who suddenly finds herself a "minority."

VIDEOS

Black Americans of Achievement.
1992. Library Video Company. 12 titles (each 30min.). Each, $39.95.

Gr. 6–12. Straightforward productions effectively profile significant historical personalities and contemporary figures through chronicles of their accomplishments and helpful insights by historians.

The Friends.
1985. The Media Guild. 25min. $245.

Gr. 6–12. Dramatized scenes from Rosa Guy's novel are intercut with footage of teens interviewing the author about the effect of her life experiences on her writing, especially her move from the West Indies to Harlem.

In the Land of Jim Crow: Growing Up Segregated.
1991. Coronet. 26min. $250.

Gr. 8–12. This incisive and personalized account of everyday life before the civil-rights era uses news photos, stills, and adults' palpable recollections of their childhoods.

The Songs Are Free.
1991. Mystic Fire Video. 58min. $29.95.

Gr. 10–12. In interview segments and before workshop audiences, artist and folklorist Bernice Johnson Reagon muses on the African roots of the blues, gospel, and contemporary songs she movingly performs.

Visions of the Spirit.
1989. Women Make Movies. 58min. $295.

Gr. 9–12. This intimate video profile of Alice Walker in her home glimpses her in conversation with her elderly mother and includes on-location scenes from the movie *The Color Purple*.

Asian Americans

There are no inscrutable Orientals in the books on this list. These stories reveal the inner lives of all kinds of people, who speak in a range of American voices—wry, angry, funny, lyrical—many of them caught between two demanding cultures.

The Asian American experience includes memories and stories of the places left behind, past and contemporary. Cambodian political refugees bring with them memories of atrocity; they also bring an ancient heritage that includes folk stories. The same is true of the Hmong from northern Laos and of the Vietnamese boat people. Born in Shanghai, the great illustrator Ed Young draws on the richness of his Chinese roots to give us *Lon Po Po*, the version of *Red Riding Hood* that won the Caldecott Medal. But he has also illustrated dozens of stunning books from cultures he has found here: like the illustrations that capture the mystery of Coleridge's *Rime of the Ancient Mariner*, and his witty, exuberant pencil drawings for *Bo Rabbit Smart for True: Folktales from the Gullah*.

Some stories set in Asia have been included on this list, especially if the writers now live in the U.S. The harrowing refugee experiences dramatized in Sook Nyul Choi's *Year of Impossible Goodbyes* and Yoko Kawashima Watkins' *So Far from the Bamboo Grove* are each rooted in their particular time and place, but they are also about the refugee experience everywhere. Phoebe Yeh, consultant for this list, says that American kids reading about young people in a war-torn nation can see why the authors might have sought a new homeland, why people still care so much about immigrating to the United States, what life here means to immigrants, how their lives are different and sometimes even the same. On the other hand, books by Yoshiko Uchida and others personalize the suffering of those who were persecuted in this country during World War II: the Japanese American citizens who were interned in concentration camps and who struggled afterwards to rebuild their lives.

What's true of all the lists is especially evident here: Asian Americans are not in any way a homogenous group. This is just an arrangement for convenience. The closer you get, the more group and individual differences you see. Koreans, Japanese, Filipinos, Indians, and Chinese have very different cultures. What does Chinese mean? Which Chinese? Laurence Yep points out in the introduction to *The Rainbow People* that some Chinese folktales come from a common heritage and some are specific to a region. And yet, what Yep shows in *The Star Fisher* about a Chinese American girl in West Virginia is true of many immigrants, Chinese and non-Asian, who suddenly find themselves the "other."

The extraordinary success of books like Maxine Hong Kingston's *Woman Warrior* and Amy Tan's *Joy Luck Club* has little to do with our need to know about "other" cultures. These books are best-sellers because, rooted as they are in the Chinese American experience, they explore the complexity and conflict of people everywhere.

As Kingston put it in a recent interview with Lucinda Smith:

> I hope that by "women from *your* culture" you mean
> Americans of the twentieth century—women of *our*

culture. I do not want readers to think that I am writing about an exotic other world. The stories of an old country are in the background of every American. Some of my characters are trapped by history and by oppressive mores; others somehow break free. Women who were born and raised in slavery have been able to become feminists and to invent new roles and identities. They were able to do this by finding liberating myths, such as that of the woman warrior, by discovering heroines and role models, and by seeing through injustices that society takes for granted, and thus being strong enough to work hard to change the world.

NONFICTION

Ashabranner, Brent and Ashabranner, Melissa.
Into a Strange Land: Unaccompanied Refugee Youth in America.
1987. Putnam, $14.95 (0-399-21709-6).

Gr. 5–12. Based on interviews with young Asian Americans from Vietnam, Cambodia, and other countries, this is a compelling account of young people who have come here alone and had to learn a new language and a whole new way of life. They talk about how and why they were forced to leave family and country, what happened to them on the boats and then in the refugee camps, what it's like for them in the U.S., and how they see the future. One moving chapter is about the special plight of the Amerasian kids. With photographs of kids and their foster families, the stories are riveting. Brent Ashabranner and Paul Conklin also did *The New Americans,* which focuses on immigrants from Asia as well as those from Latin America and the Caribbean.

The Big Aiiieeeee!: An Anthology of Chinese American and Japanese American Literature.
Ed. by Jeffrey Paul Chan and others.
1991. NAL/Meridian, paper, $14.95 (0-452-01076-4).

Gr. 9–12. The title of this strong anthology is a play on the "whine, shout, or scream" uttered by the stereotypical Chinese or Japanese found in white-made movies, comic books, or TV shows. Candid, sometimes angry, this is a collection of memoir, fiction, essay, drama, and poetry from the 1850s to the present.

Bode, Janet.
New Kids on the Block: Oral Histories of Immigrant Teens.
1989. Watts, $12.90 (0-531-10794-9).

Gr. 6–10. Representing the more recent wave of immigrants from such countries as El Salvador and Cuba, as well as from several Asian nations, 11 teenagers describe what it's like to begin anew in America. In sometimes funny, sometimes poignant recollections, they remember their native countries and talk about their struggle to adapt to a new home, strange foods and language, and different customs. Von, who came here on a boat with his father from Vietnam, is thrilled to be going to college, but he's been waiting for nine years for his mother and brothers and sisters to come to America. Amitabh, from India, speaks Gujarati at home, "but now there's English mixed in a lot." The kids talk about American violence and crime and about discrimination, as well as the challenges and opportunities their new country offers.

Brown, Dee.
Hear That Lonesome Whistle Blow: Railroads in the West.
1977. Holt, $13.95 (0-03-016936-4).

Gr. 9–12. In his gripping account of the building of the great transcontinental railroads in the nineteenth century, Brown conveys the greed and corruption of the railroad companies, and he also describes the work of the Chinese and Irish laborers who dug the tunnels, laid the rails, and hewed the bridges.

Brownstone, David.
The Chinese-American Heritage.
1988. Facts On File, $16.95 (0-8160-1627-5).

Gr. 7–12. One of the best entries in the America's Ethnic Heritage series, this gives a candid picture of the fierce discrimination suffered by Chinese immigrants in the U.S., for whom the land of opportunity has also been a land of bigotry. Brownstone describes conditions in China that have led to emigration at various times. Then he focuses on the immigrants' early experiences from the gold rush days when prejudice drove them from the land, sea, and mines into laundries, restaurants and domestic work. Finally, he examines the recent easing of restrictions and shows how, with racism lessening, more American-educated Chinese have moved into the middle class.

Ca Dao Vietnam: A Bilingual Anthology of Vietnamese Folk Poetry.
Ed. by John Balaban.
1980. Unicorn, $19.95 (0-87775-128-5); paper, $8.95 (0-87775-129-3).

Gr. 8–12. A bilingual anthology of *ca dao*—short, lyric poems drawn from Vietnam's oral folk tradition.

Cambodian Folk Stories from the Gatiloke.
Retold by Muriel Paskin Carrison, from a translation by The Venerable Kong Chhean.
1987. Tuttle, $15.95 (0-8408-1518-6).

Gr. 6–12. The folk stories in this collection, many of them brought to the U.S. by recent refugees, are from an ancient literary tradition told by Cambodian Buddhist monks. They are stories of ordinary people, humorous stories, and fables that teach justice, wisdom, and compassion.

"I wanted to find my father. I was sure I could find him once I got to America. I did not know his name . . . but his face is in my mind clearer than any picture. . . . Someday I will find him, and he will be happy to see me."

—Vietnamese teenager living in the U.S.

Davis, Daniel S.
Behind Barbed Wire: The Imprisonment of Japanese Americans during World War II.
1982. Dutton, $15.95 (0-525-26320-9).

> Gr. 6–12. This sensitive treatment of the incarceration of Japanese Americans in U.S. internment camps during World War II discusses the history of anti-Asian prejudice in this country and the role played by the media, the politicians, the courts, and the president in the suspension of civil rights on such a grand scale. Davis describes conditions in the camps as well as the difficulties inmates encountered reentering society.

Dictionary of Asian American History.
Ed. by Hyung-Chan Kim.
1986. Greenwood, $75 (0-313-23760-3).

> Gr. 7–12. This is the best ready-reference source on Asian American history, according to *Reference Books Bulletin*. Seven topical essays highlight the history of particular groups in America. The main body of the work contains 800 dictionary entries on the major events, persons, places, and concepts related to the Asian American experience.

Fiffer, Sharon Sloan.
Imagining America: Paul Thai's Journey from the Killing Fields of Cambodia to Freedom in the U.S.A.
1991. Paragon House, $19.95 (0-55778-326-8).

> Gr. 8–12. In 1981, 17-year-old Cambodian refugee Paul Thai came to Dallas with his parents and seven siblings to remake their lives. By then Paul had coped with war and the callous disregard for human life it engenders. How Paul perceives his experiences and what he does now, as the first Asian-born member of the Dallas police force, is told with charm and insight.

Fritz, Jean.
Homecoming: My Own Story.
1982. Putnam, $13.95 (0-399-20933-6); Dell, paper, $3.25 (0-440-43683-4).

> Gr. 5–9. In her memoir of living in China until the age of 12 during the turbulent 1920s, Fritz captures the mutual misunderstanding across cultures. She always felt that she was American; then when she did come to the U.S., she worried she would be a stranger.

Hamanaka, Sheila.
The Journey: Japanese Americans, Racism, and Renewal.
1990. Orchard, $18.95 (0-531-05849-2).

> Gr. 6–12. The book is based on artist Hamanaka's 25-foot, 5-panel mural. She tells of the experience of Japanese Americans, focusing on their internment during World War II. Her parents, her two-year-old sister, and her six-year-old brother were all interned. She was born after the war, and for a long time she wasn't told that her

grandfather had died in the camps. It's a story of prejudice and injustice, personal and official, and Hamanaka is passionate about what happened to her people.

Houston, Jeanne Wakatsuki and Houston, James D.
Farewell to Manzanar.
1973. Bantam, paper, $3.50 (0-553-27258-6).

Gr. 8–12. In a spare, powerful memoir, a Japanese American woman remembers the three years she spent as a small child with her family in the internment camp at Manzanar, and she talks about growing up after the war.

Huynh, Quang Nhuong.
The Land I Lost: Adventures of a Boy in Vietnam.
1982. Harper, $12.89 (0-397-32448-0); paper, $3.50 (0-06-440183-9).

Gr. 5–8. A Vietnamese American remembers his youth in the central highlands of Vietnam before war disrupted his dreams.

Ishikawa, Yoshimi.
Strawberry Road: A Japanese Immigrant Discovers America.
Trans. by Eve Zimmerman. 1991. Kodansha, $18.95 (4-7700-1551-8).

Gr. 10–12. In an honest, sometimes disturbing memoir, Ishikawa remembers himself as a teenage Japanese immigrant in the 1960s, a student in high school, and a worker in the strawberry fields of California. He discovers prejudice (including his own), lust, and the meaning of America in his own mind.

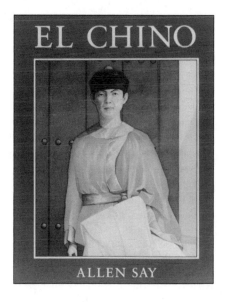

"I searched all over town, and finally found what I was looking for—a Chinese costume. I tried it on and hardly recognized myself in the mirror.

It was as if I were seeing myself for the first time. I looked like a *real* Chinese. And as I stared in the mirror, a strange feeling came over me. I felt powerful. I felt that I could do anything I wished—even become a matador! Could it be that I was wearing a magical costume?"

—Allen Say

Kingston, Maxine Hong.
China Men.
1980. Knopf, $22.95 (0-394-42463-8); Random/Vintage,
paper, $9.95 (0-679-72328-5).

Gr. 9–12. From family legends, history, and memories of her father, grandfathers, "uncles," and brothers, Kingston distills the experience of being a Chinese man outside of China, especially the emasculating role of underling where white people are the masters. Yet the promise of the Gold Mountain (be it Hawaii, Cuba, Canada, or the U.S.) never loses its luster, and masculinity adapts itself to ghosts of many shapes.

Kingston, Maxine Hong.
The Woman Warrior.
1976. Knopf, $24.95 (0-394-40067-4); Random/Vintage,
paper, $8.95 (0-679-72188-6).

Gr. 9–12. This exquisitely written memoir, candid and poetic, describes the conflict Kingston felt in growing up Chinese American, caught between the "ghosts" of her Chinese tradition and the alien values of the U.S.

Kitano, Harry.
The Japanese Americans.
1987. Chelsea House, $17.95 (0-87754-856-0).

Gr. 8–12. Part of the Peoples of North America series, this volume examines the history of Japanese immigration to and acculturation in the U.S. and Canada. Beginning with the waves of immigration in the 1860s, Kitano's study traces the lives of these people and their descendants through years of hardship and prejudice, culminating in the detention camps of World War II. The last chapters describe the increasing acceptance of Japanese people into the mainstream and their effect on that mainstream through contributions in science, politics, and the arts. The focus is mainly on the U.S., especially Hawaii and California.

Liang Heng and Shapiro, Judith.
Son of the Revolution.
1983. Random/Vintage, paper, $9.95 (0-394-72274-4).

Gr. 9–12. Liang Heng's autobiography, written with his American wife, describes his experiences as a Red Guard during the Cultural Revolution in China, when he was one of millions of teenagers caught up in the turmoil.

McCunn, Ruthanne Lum.
Chinese American Portraits: Personal Histories, 1828–1988.
1988. Chronicle, $29.95 (0-87701-580-5); paper, $16.95
(0-87701-491-4).

Gr. 8–12. This is vivid social history, told through informal family accounts, in text and fully captioned photographs, covering people from the East Coast to Alaska, from cities, farms, and the frontier.

McCunn also summarizes legislation affecting Chinese Americans from the nineteenth century through today.

Moore, David L.
Dark Sky, Dark Land: Stories of the Hmong Boy Scouts of Troop 100.
1989. Tessera Publications, paper, $14.95 (0-9623029-0-2).

Gr. 7–12. For the Hmong refugees who left their war-torn homeland in northern Laos and settled in the Minneapolis area, escape meant weeks of walking, months of starvation, years in refugee camps, and often the loss of parents or other family members. Moore, a high school teacher and Boy Scout leader, befriended these boys, gained their confidence, and formed Boy Scout Troop 100 to help them keep their sense of identity while adapting to America. "This collection of oral histories, filled with daring escapes and plans that failed as well as with courage and hope, will bring the Vietnamese conflict and the plight of refugees alive for readers," said *Booklist* reviewer Candace Smith. A chronology of the Hmong people is appended.

Morey, Janet Nomura and Dunn, Wendy.
Famous Asian Americans.
1992. Dutton/Cobblehill, $15 (0-525-65080-6).

Gr. 6–10. The treatment is adulatory, but this is a useful collective biography. The 14 Asian Americans included here represent a diversity of professions, backgrounds, and ages—from teenage tennis star Michael Chang and astronaut Ellison S. Onizuka to well-known television journalist Connie Chung and world-famous architect I. M. Pei. Some are recent immigrants from war-torn countries; others are members of families who have been in the U.S. for generations.

Mura, David.
Turning Japanese: Memoirs of a Sansei.
1990. Atlantic Monthly Press, $19.95 (0-87113-431-4).

Gr. 9–12. A third-generation Japanese American, the young poet Mura felt deeply rooted in the U.S. until his year-long visit to Japan put him in touch with a whole new experience of home, where he says he was part of the visual majority for the first time. This is a candid discussion of Japanese culture by someone who is both stranger and insider.

Say, Allen.
El Chino.
1990. Houghton, $14.95 (0-395-52023-1).

Gr. 3–8. Say's elegant watercolors are a compelling part of his picture book biography of a Chinese American civil engineer who became a matador. El Chino is Bong Way Wong, fourth child of immigrants from Canton, China. On a visit to Spain, he sees a bullfight and falls in love with the sport.

"I have written several short stories and books that tell of this wartime uprooting [of Japanese Americans], and each time I find it hard to believe that such a thing actually took place in the United States of America. But it did."

—Yoshiko Uchida

Uchida, Yoshiko.
The Invisible Thread.
1991. Messner, $12.95 (0-671-74164-0).

Gr. 6–9. In a moving autobiography, Uchida describes growing up in Berkeley, California, as a Nisei, second-generation Japanese American, her family's internment in a Utah concentration camp during World War II, and her pride in her heritage. This is part of the In My Own Words series of autobiographies that also includes Laurence Yep's *The Lost Garden.*

Yep, Laurence.
The Rainbow People.
1989. HarperCollins, $13.95 (0-06-026760-7); paper, $3.95 (0-06-440441-2).

Gr. 5–10. Twenty folktales collected in the Oakland, California, Chinatown community in the 1930s are retold here with vitality and humor and illustrated by David Wiesner. Yep's commentary places the stories in their historical context and relates them to cultural values. Another handsomely designed collection is Yep's *Tongues of Jade.*

Young, Ed.
Lon Po Po: A Red Riding Hood Story from China.
1989. Putnam/Philomel, $14.95 (0-399-21619-7).

All ages. Winner of the Caldecott Medal, this splendid picture book, filled with menace and foreboding, will appeal to older readers as a scary variant of a childhood story they know well. In a *Booklist* review, Carolyn Phelan pointed out that "the separation of some of the spreads into three or four vertical panels, as in

---

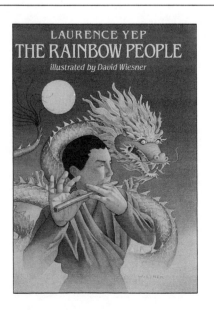

"When my father picked fruit in the Chinese orchards near Sacramento, the workers would gather in the shack after a hot, grueling day; one of the ways that the old-timers would pass the time before sleep came was to tell stories.

But these stories were far from escapist maneuvers. What Kenneth Burke said of proverbs is equally true of folktales: They are strategies for living. At the very least, the stories offered consolation and more often hope. But beyond that, the stories also expressed the loneliness, anger, fear, and love that were part of the Chinese American experience."

—Laurence Yep

Chinese screen or panel paintings, recalls the story's roots as well as the artist's own." Young dedicates the book "To all the wolves of the world for lending their good name as a tangible symbol for our darkness."

FICTION

Chang, Margaret and Chang, Raymond.
In the Eye of War.
> 1990. Macmillan/Margaret K. McElderry, $13.95
> (0-689-50503-5).
>
> Gr. 5–8. Based on Raymond Chang's boyhood in Shanghai during World War II, this tale describes the hated Japanese occupation through the eyes of a child and his family. To show how racism and exploitation can dehumanize any group, this novel can be read with Hamanaka's *The Journey* (see above) about the internment of Japanese Americans.

Chin, Fran.
Donald Duk.
> 1991. Coffee House, paper, $9.95 (0-918273-83-8).
>
> Gr. 9–12. Donald Duk hates his name; he'd much rather be Fred Astaire than an almost 12-year-old boy growing up in San Francisco's Chinatown. Chin's funny novel follows Donald's struggle to discover his place in his family and learn about his Chinese heritage.

Choi, Sook Nyul.
Year of Impossible Goodbyes.
> 1991. Houghton, $13.95 (0-395-57419-6).
>
> Gr. 6–10. A dramatic novel about a child in war-torn Korea—first, under Japanese military oppression; then after 1945, under Russian occupation; and finally, on the run across the border. Choi lived through this period as a child in North Korea. She now lives in the U.S.

Crew, Linda.
Children of the River.
> 1989. Doubleday, $14.95 (0-440-50122-9); paper, $5
> (0-385-29690-8).
>
> Gr. 6–10. Sundara Sovann wants to fit in at her Oregon high school. She likes blond football star Jonathan MacKinnon, and she'd like to say yes when he asks her to go to the movies. But Sundara's a refugee from Cambodia living with an immigrant family that sticks to the old ways—no dating allowed, no talking to white boys. She's also haunted by her memories of massacre in the country she left. Sundara tries to find a way to be American without giving up her Cambodian self.

Garland, Sherry.
Song of the Buffalo Boy.
   1992. HBJ, $16.95 (0-15-277107-7).

> Gr. 7–10. *Con-lai*—half-breed. *Con-hoang*—fatherless child. Loi, an Amerasian teenager in a small Vietnamese village, has heard these hateful names all her life. Her mother shuns any mention of her American father. Loi has secretly pledged to marry Khai, the "buffalo boy," the one person who seems to love her as she is, but their plans seem hopeless, and Loi runs away to Ho Chi Minh City. Should she seize a chance to find her father in America? The happy ending is contrived, but Loi is appealingly drawn, and the book's chief strength is its portrayal of a Vietnam village and big-city street life.

Garrigue, Sheila.
The Eternal Spring of Mr. Ito.
   1985. Bradbury, $13.95 (0-02-737300-2).

> Gr. 6–9. A young British girl evacuated to Vancouver, Canada, during World War II tells of the suffering of a Japanese Canadian family as they are shipped off to a remote settlement.

Ho, Minfong.
Rice without Rain.
   1990. Lothrop, $12.95 (0-688-06355-1).

> Gr. 7–12. In the revolutionary turmoil of Thailand in the 1970s, 17-year-old Jinda finds her love and personal commitment beset by politics and terror. Her father is imprisoned. She falls in love with a radical student leader and follows him to Bangkok. The novelist, a Thai teacher who now lives in New York, doesn't neatly resolve the tension between the personal and the political, and though she writes of atrocity and sorrow, the treatment is quiet.

Jen, Gish.
Typical American.
   1991. Houghton, $19.95 (0-395-54689-3); NAL/Plume,
     paper, $10 (0-452-26774-9).

> Gr. 10–12. In a touching, funny novel of the Chinese American immigrant experience, Ralph Chang (formerly Lai Fu) leaves Shanghai for America, marries his sister's friend, Helen (formerly Hailan), and the three of them love and quarrel and try to find their way in their new country.

Lee, Gus.
China Boy.
   1991. NAL, $19.95 (0-525-24994-X); Signet, paper, $5.99
     (0-451-17434-8).

> Gr. 9–12. Lee's autobiographical novel about growing up in San Francisco is funny, crude, sad, ugly, and wonderfully compelling, especially when the skinny loser Kai Ting, the American-born son of

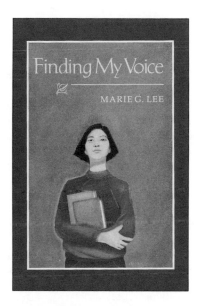

"When you leave a country it is like an animal caught in a trap that gnaws a limb off to free itself. You can't dwell on what you've lost—if you want to survive. You have to go on with what you have."

—Marie Lee

---

an aristocratic Mandarin family, finally learns to speak street language and to fight bullies, racists, and his abusive stepmother.

Lee, Marie G.
Finding My Voice.
   1992. Houghton, $13.95 (0-395-62134-8).

   Gr. 7–12. Pressured by her strict Korean immigrant parents to get into Harvard, high school senior Ellen Sung tries to find some time for romance, friendship, and fun in her small Minnesota town, but simmering racism from some of her classmates, and even from a teacher, is impossible to ignore. This YA novel tries to cram in too much, but Ellen's relationship with her father is the best part of the book. He never talks about the old country; she doesn't speak Korean; even their eating habits are different: she eats lasagna while he slurps his seaweed soup. When he finally does talk to her about why he doesn't mention the past, his words are powerful testimony to the cost of immigration.

Lord, Betty Bao.
In the Year of the Boar and Jackie Robinson.
   1984. HarperCollins, $12.95 (0-06-024003-2); paper, $3.50
     (0-06-440175-8).

   Gr. 4–7. Shirley Temple Wong, a 10-year-old Chinese girl, moves to Brooklyn in 1947 and learns about America through baseball, especially the Dodgers and their groundbreaking rookie, Jackie Robinson. As the Dodgers drive toward the pennant and Robinson stands his ground against racist taunts, Shirley finds the courage to make friends in her new world.

Namioka, Lensey.
Yang the Youngest and His Terrible Ear.
1992. Little, Brown/Joy Street Books, $13.95 (0-316-59701-5).

Gr. 4–7. Though the hero, Yingtao, is nine years old, teenage readers will identify with this warm, funny immigrant story that extends the meaning of outsider and home. The lighthearted, first-person narrative captures the bewilderment of the new immigrant, the confusion about customs and language, and also the longing for home in China and the sting of prejudice here.

Ng, Fae Myenne.
Bone.
1993. Hyperion, $19.95 (1-56282-944-0).

Gr. 9–12. Ng's piercing novel re-creates the generational barriers and the love within a Chinese American family in San Francisco. The young people are caught between wanting to get out of Chinatown and feeling disloyal about entering the mainstream.

Okimoto, Jean.
Molly by Any Other Name.
1990. Scholastic, $13.95 (0-590-42993-0).

Gr. 6–12. This docunovel about a teenage adoptee's search for her birth mother gives the facts of the process and also the complicated feelings of everyone involved. Molly is Asian; her adoptive parents are white. She's always suppressed her questions about who she is, but at age 18 she finds her birth mother, Karen, a third-generation Japanese Canadian who was shamed by her mother into giving up her illegitimate baby.

Paterson, Katherine.
Park's Quest.
1988. Dutton/Lodestar, $12.95 (0-525-67258-3);
Penguin/Puffin, paper, $3.95 (0-14-034262-1).

Gr. 6–8. Park can't understand why his mother won't tell him anything about his father, except that he was killed in the Vietnam War. Slowly Park learns the truth, that his father had an affair in Vietnam with the woman now married to Park's uncle and that the woman's daughter, Thanh (whom Park has labeled "geek"), is Park's half-sister. Great for reading aloud, this provocative story will stimulate discussion of "family values" and of racism.

Savin, Marcia.
The Moon Bridge.
1993. Scholastic, $13.95 (0-590-45873-6).

Gr. 5–7. During World War II in San Francisco, Ruthie Fox becomes best friends with Mitzi (Mitsuko) Fujimoto. Ruthie sees the racism directed against Mitzi and her Japanese American family, and then one day Mitzi isn't in school: she's interned for three years in a concentration camp. Told from the viewpoint of the sympathetic friend, this is sometimes overexplained, but readers will be caught by the joyful friendship story and the ugliness of prejudice close to home.

Tan, Amy.
The Joy Luck Club.
1989. Putnam, $18.95 (0-399-13420-4); Ivy, paper, $5.95 (0-8041-0630-4).

Gr. 8–12. Interwoven stories about Chinese American mothers and daughters caught between the old ways and their desperate need to succeed in America, loving each other but also cruel, manipulative, driven, afraid. "Mothers and daughters circle each other cautiously," said Donna Seaman in the *Booklist* review, "playing a game of love and fear, need and rejection. The older women are ambitious for their daughters, but while they want them to succeed in America, they want them to remain Chinese. The daughters consider themselves American and free to leave tradition behind, but they discover that their heritage is not something they can ignore." Teens will also enjoy *The Kitchen God's Wife*.

> "I had a whole different vocabulary of feeling in English than in Chinese, and not everything can be translated."
>
> —Fae Myenne Ng

Uchida, Yoshiko.
A Jar of Dreams.
1981. Macmillan/Margaret K. McElderry, $12.95 (0-689-50210-9); Macmillan/Aladdin, paper, $3.95 (0-689-71041-0)

Gr. 5–8. Rinko, an 11-year-old Japanese American girl in Oakland, faces prejudice in 1930s California. This is one of several stories in which Uchida draws on her own life. The others in the Rinko trilogy are *The Best Bad Thing* and *The Happiest Ending*. In *Journey to Topaz*, Uchida writes about a girl and her family who were among 120,000 West Coast Japanese Americans incarcerated in internment camps in Topaz, Utah. *Journey Home* is about their struggle to adjust in California after release from the camp.

Watanabe, Sylvia.
Talking to the Dead and Other Stories.
1992. Doubleday, $19 (0-385-41887-6).

Gr. 9–12. Watanabe sets these gently humorous and sensitive stories in her native Hawaii. Many of her characters, old and young, are Japanese. In one story, a son on leave from Vietnam weighs the option of fleeing to Canada while his father remembers his own anguished experiences during World War II. The mysterious and the mundane coexist in these tales, which *Booklist* reviewer Donna Seaman called "sweet with love and blossoms, salty with tears and the sea." The title story won an O. Henry Award.

Watkins, Yoko Kawashima.
So Far from the Bamboo Grove.
1986. Lothrop, $11.95 (0-688-06110-9); Penguin/Puffin, paper, $3.95 (0-317-62272-2).

Gr. 6–10. As World War II ends, an 11-year-old Japanese girl and her family, who have been living in North Korea, become refugees, in deadly danger from the soldiers of the new regime. A fictionalized autobiography, this is rooted in a vividly re-created place; it also evokes the refugee experience everywhere—homeless, separated, struggling for food, shelter, and safety. Watkins now lives in the U.S.

Yee, Paul.
Tales from Gold Mountain: Stories of the Chinese in the New World.
1990. Macmillan, $14.95 (0-02-793621-X).

Gr. 5–10. Romance, loyalty, and justice are among the themes Yee probes in eight original stories based on the Chinese immigrant experience in the U.S. and Canada. Simon Ng's brooding artwork provides controlled yet intense illustration.

Yep, Laurence.
The Star Fisher.
1991. Morrow, $12.95 (0-688-09365-5); Dell, paper, $3.50 (0-440-20433-X).

Gr. 6–10. Set in the 1920s and based on stories about Yep's own grandparents, this is a poignant, gently humorous novel about prejudice and courage. Fifteen-year-old Joan Lee was born in America, but when her family moves to open a laundry in a new town, the Lees become the first Chinese Americans whom the people in Clarksburg, West Virginia, have ever seen. Some kids at school cannot accept that Joan is American. Other fine YA novels by Yep include *Child of the Owl*, set in San Francisco's Chinatown, where a young girl finds her roots even as she loses faith in her compulsive

---

Lensey Namioka

Yang the Youngest and His Terrible Ear

Illustrated by Kees de Kiefte

"I greeted her in Chinese, but she just shook her head.

'I'm afraid I don't understand Japanese,' she said in English.

'I wasn't speaking Japanese,' I told her. 'I was speaking Chinese.'

'Sorry. I don't understand that either. My family is from Korea.'

I didn't know much about Korea, except that my country had once invaded her country. I hoped she didn't hold it against me."

—Lensey Namioka

gambler father. *Dragonwings*, a Newbery Honor book, is a sensitive novel about a Chinese American boy and his father who build a flying machine in early twentieth-century San Francisco.

VIDEOS

American Eyes.
> 1990. The Media Guild. 30min. $345.

> Gr. 8–12. Dealing with racial prejudice at school and emotionally charged conflicts within his supportive family, a Korean American teenager comes to appreciate the importance of his ancestry.

Becoming American.
> 1983. New Day Films. 30min. $295.

> Gr. 9–12. The adjustment of one Hmong refugee family from mountainous Thailand to urban American is incisively portrayed in this affecting documentary.

Family Gathering.
> 1989. PBS Video. 60min. $59.95.

> Gr. 10–12. Home movies, news clippings, and relatives' recollections personalize the treatment of Japanese Americans during World War II in this stirring portrait of the filmmaker's family.

Home from the Eastern Sea.
> 1989. Filmmakers Library. 57min. $445.

> Gr. 10–12. Personal recollections, stills, and documentary footage chronicle the settlement of the Pacific Northwest by Chinese, Japanese, and Filipino immigrants.

My Mother Thought She Was Audrey Hepburn.
> 1989. Filmmakers Library. 17min. $225.

> Gr. 10–12. A bittersweet exploration of one young Chinese American woman's conflict over her racial identity and her desire to emulate Caucasian role models.

Jewish Americans

Saul Bellow says of *Great Jewish Short Stories*: "Laughter and trembling are so curiously mingled that it is not easy to determine the relations of the two." Many books on this list, YA and adult, classic and contemporary, mix that "laughter and trembling," whether the setting is a village shtetl in Eastern Europe, a New York City immigrant slum, or an Indianapolis suburb. At the turn of the century in Czarist Russia, a bitter time in Jewish history, the great Yiddish writer Sholom Aleichem wrote about the shtetl with humanity and humor. He did it "without either ridiculing or rose-tinting," according to Hillel Halkin, a gifted translator from Yiddish and Hebrew into English. Halkin says of Aleichem: "It was consistently his method, for all the near-manic exuberance of his prose, to confront the reader with reality in its full harshness, laughter being for him the explosive with which he systematically undermined all escape routes away from the truth."

The immigrants who came to Ellis Island from the shtetl brought those stories with them. As with every ethnic group, they came with their language, their memories, and their stories. They changed in America, and they changed America, but all the while the old stories were being told and retold, transformed to reflect a new world. Take Judy Blume's popular contemporary novel *Are You There God? It's Me, Margaret,* about an 11-year-old girl in the suburbs of New Jersey. Like Aleichem's Tevye the Dairyman in the shtetl, half-Jewish Margaret chats to God, but her concerns are as much about when she's going to get her period as they are about whether she should join the temple or the church.

Of course there are some Jews who would say that Margaret can't be Jewish if her home isn't kosher and her mother is a Gentile. As with all the ethnic groups, the variety within the culture is enormous. Once you get close, "they" don't all look the same. There's a great gap between a fundamentalist Hasidic Jew and a secular Jew, between a Zionist and a non-Zionist, between a Sephardic Jew and an Ashkenazi. While some books on this list are about Jewish Americans whose dominant culture is much the same as the mainstream, the general focus is on titles in which Jewishness is important. Many of the books included show the raw memory of anti-Semitism, and especially the Holocaust, as an enduring part of Jewish identity, thus forming a natural link to the titles on the Holocaust list.

Milton Meltzer in his autobiography *Starting from Home* remembers how, as a first-generation child of Jewish Americans, he sometimes longed to be one of the "unhyphenated" people, a "real" American, and how he never asked—and his parents never told him—about life in the Old Country. In a bit of wry psychologizing, Susan Bloom, director of the Children's Literature Center at Simmons College, Boston, wonders if it's Meltzer's drive to connect with his parents' untold stories that has helped make him the committed writer he is. His passionate nonfiction is not only about the Holocaust and the Jews, but also about immigration and discrimination, about people everywhere who are outside. Many Jewish writers have drawn strength from their marginal status, from their wandering; they have been able to see Americans and Jews from outside, from what Ted Solotaroff calls "both sides of the hyphen." But Letty Pogrebin says a Jewish male can never be an outsider the way a Jewish woman is an outsider. Pogrebin's *Deborah, Golda, and Me*, like Alan Dershowitz's *Chutzpah*, represents a more militant confrontational style, where the self-deprecating joke, the apologetic tone, and the deflected anger have given way, in the 1990s, to the demand for full equality.

In the rich diversity of Jewish American writing today, the immigration conflicts are of less concern. As Jews feel more at home in America, there's an opening out to issues like feminism and gay identity, and at the same time, a return to tradition, both secular and religious.

NONFICTION

Allen, Woody.
  Getting Even.
    1971. Random, $10.95 (0-394-47348-5); paper, $5.95 (0-394-72640-5).

    Gr. 9–12. In this early collection of previously published pieces, Allen not only discourses humorously on such assorted subjects as a day in the life of Count Dracula, but also shares insights into his own background. His self-deprecating, earnest, guilt-ridden, nerdy, argumentative, comic persona draws strongly on Jewish tradition.

Antin, Mary.
  The Promised Land.
    1985. Princeton, $17.95 (0-691-00598-2).

    Gr. 8–12. First published in 1912, this is a poetic autobiography of a brilliant young Jew. She describes life in Russia, the difficulty of leaving her home, her years in a Boston slum, her education, and how she came to fit in in America.

Dershowitz, Alan M.
  Chutzpah.
    1991. Little, Brown, $22.95 (0-316-18137-4).

    Gr. 8–12. Dershowitz—lawyer, commentator, and author—is as famous for his unwavering focus on human rights as he is for his forceful personality. Here he relates his personal experience as a Jew to a general assessment of American Jews and their history in a violent century. He states that Jews need more chutzpah, i.e., assertiveness, a willingness to demand what is due, because many still think of themselves as second-class citizens, guests, if you will, of the "real" Americans.

Freedman, E. B. and others.
  What Does Being Jewish Mean? Read-Aloud Responses to Questions Jewish Children Ask about History, Culture, and Religion.
    1991. Prentice Hall, paper, $7.95 (0-139-62747-2).

"In New City, New York, a village largely inhabited by orthodox Jews, there is a sign advertising a Talmud course: TALMUD FOR EVERYONE—MEN ONLY."

—Letty Pogrebin

Gr. 6–12. Freedman, an orthodox rabbi, and his coauthors combine their experiences as parents, educators, and Jews in a sourcebook of answers to commonly asked questions. They talk about general topics such as Jewish customs, Bible stories, the synagogue, Israel, and Jewish history. Many questions clarify terms frequently heard, and there's a useful glossary that gathers them all together. The answers reflect a traditional Jewish perspective, but as Freedman clearly states, the text is not a dogmatic explication of do's and don'ts: rather, it is an introduction for curious and attentive young people.

Hentoff, Nat.
  Boston Boy.
    1986. Faber, paper, $7.95 (0-571-12951-X).

    Gr. 8–12. In humorous, poignant vignettes, writer and civil-rights activist Hentoff remembers growing up in 1940s Boston, where he encountered vicious anti-Semitism and immersed himself in the world of jazz.

Howe, Irving.
  World of Our Fathers.
    1976. HBJ, $34.95 (0-15-146353-0); Schocken, paper, $14.95 (0-8052-0928-X).

    Gr. 9–12. A great Jewish humanist tells of the journey of the Eastern European Jews to America and the life they found and made. Written with clarity and grace, this is superb social history, combining people's stories and general trends, and finding always ambiguity and conflict.

Lewis, Bernard.
  Semites and Anti-Semites: An Inquiry into Conflict and Prejudice.
    1986. Norton, $18.95 (0-393-02314-1); paper, $7.95 (0-393-30420-5).

    Gr. 9–12. Focusing on Middle Eastern politics, Lewis traces the religious, historical, and psychological ramifications of anti-Semitism, investigating prejudice both as political policy and cultural/ethnic hostility.

Mayer, Egon.
  Love & Tradition: Marriage between Jews and Christians.
    1985. Plenum, $19.95 (0-306-42043-0); Schocken, paper, $8.95 (0-8052-0828-3).

    Gr. 9–12. A sociologist looks at intermarriage, including discussion of the history and nature of marriage and the ongoing struggle to reconcile love and tradition.

Meltzer, Milton.
  The Jewish Americans: A History in Their Own Words.
    1982. HarperCollins, $13.89 (0-690-04228-0).

Gr. 7–12. Concentrating on people rather than events, Meltzer turns personal accounts into a living history of Jewish Americans from colonial times to the 1950s.

Meltzer, Milton.
Starting from Home: A Writer's Beginnings.
1988. Viking/Kestrel, $13.95 (0-670-81604-3); paper, $3.95 (0-14-032299-X).

Gr. 6–12. With understatement and candor, Meltzer's autobiography fuses his personal story—as a child of Jewish American immigrants in Worcester, Massachusetts, in the 1920s and 1930s—with an account of the sociopolitical conditions of the time.

Miller, Arthur.
Incident at Vichy.
1965. Penguin, paper, $4.95 (0-14-048193-1).

Gr. 7–12. In this play, Miller confronts directly issues of anti-Semitism and the Holocaust. Set in 1942 in "a place of detention" in Vichy, France, it's about a group of people who have been rounded up for interrogation. Are their papers in order? Are any of them Jews?

Miriam's Tambourine: Jewish Folktales from around the World.
Selected and Retold by Howard Schwartz.
1986. Free Press, $24.95 (0-02-929260-3); Oxford, paper, $10.95 (0-19-282136-9).

Gr. 7–12. Retold with simple power, these 50 tales from many times and places include stories of Elijah the Prophet, the Golem, Baal Shem Tov, and David's Harp. Included are extensive (though unobtrusive) notes.

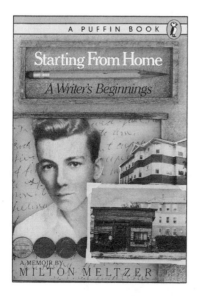

"'Learn, learn, learn!' Grandpa kept saying. 'You got to study hard to get anywhere in this America!' And sometimes, home late, eating the warmed-over supper with Rose, the table scattered with schoolbooks, he would mutter, 'Better they don't end up in the sweatshop, too.'

But they did."

—Milton Meltzer

Moline, Jack.
Growing Up Jewish; or, Why Is This Book Different from All Other Books?
1987. Penguin, paper, $5.95 (0-14-009836-4).

Gr. 8–12. A rabbi delivers wry, sometimes irreverent, perspectives on being Jewish, taking aim at everything from "chicken, the wonder food" to Jewish movie moguls to circumcision ("The Penile Code").

Moskowitz, Faye.
A Leak in the Heart: Tales from a Woman's Life.
1985. Godine, $13.95 (0-87923-551-9); paper, $9.95 (0-87923-659-0).

Gr. 8–12. These are plainspoken, moving, autobiographical stories about Moskowitz's growing up in an extended immigrant family in the 1930s and 1940s.

Pogrebin, Letty Cottin.
Deborah, Golda, and Me: Being Female and Jewish in America.
1991. Crown, $22 (0-517-57517-5); paper, Doubleday, $12 (0-385-42512-0).

Gr. 8–12. Pogrebin, best known as a founder of *Ms.* magazine, confronts head-on her struggles as a feminist to maintain a sense of Judaism. Ilene Cooper said in her *Booklist* review that this thought-provoking examination serves as a road map for others embarking on similar journeys. Pogrebin combs the Bible looking for role models; she also turns her feminist eye on Israel, and she considers a wide range of issues, from Christmas in America through race relations to the Palestinian question, viewing each as both a feminist and a Jew.

Rosenberg, Roy A.
The Concise Guide to Judaism: History, Practice, Faith.
1990. Mentor, paper, $4.99 (0-451-62832-2).

Gr. 7–12. This clear introduction discusses ancient history, philosophy and mysticism, the Rabbinic writings, and modern Judaism, and gives information about the Jewish household, the calendar, and the Holy Days.

Simon, Kate.
A Wider World: Portraits in Adolescence.
1986. HarperCollins, paper, $6.95 (0-06-091379-7).

Gr. 9–12. A detailed personal memoir of a girl's teenage years in Depression-era New York City vividly depicts her experiences with school, friends, mentors, work, family, and sex, including abortion. This is a sequel to *Bronx Primitive* about Simon's childhood.

Simon, Neil.
Brighton Beach Memoirs.
1984. Random, $11.95 (0-394-53739-4); NAL, paper, $3.95 (0-451-14765-0).

Arguably the most distinguished work of fiction ever written about immigrant life. —Lis Harris, *The New Yorker*

CALL IT SLEEP

HENRY ROTH

WITH AN INTRODUCTION BY ALFRED KAZIN

"Before her the grimy cupolas and towering square walls of the city loomed up. Above the jagged roof tops, the white smoke, whitened and suffused by the slanting sun, faded into the slots and wedges of the sky. She pressed her brow against her child's, hushed him with whispers. This was that vast incredible land, the land of freedom, of immense opportunity, that Golden Land. Again she tried to smile.

'Albert,' she said timidly, 'Albert.'

'Hm?'

'Gehen vir voinen du? In Nev York?'

'Nein. Bronzeville. Ich hud dir shoin geschriben.'

She nodded uncertainly, sighed . . .

Screws threshing, backing water, the *Peter Suyvesant* neared her dock—drifting slowly and with canceled momentum as if reluctant."

—Henry Roth

Gr. 8–12. Sex and baseball are the primary concerns of 15-year-old Eugene, protagonist of Simon's poignant, funny, autobiographical play about a lower-middle-class Jewish family coping during the Depression.

Singer, Isaac Bashevis.
  In My Father's Court.
    1966. Fawcett, paper, $2.50 (0-449-24074-6).

    Gr. 8–12. These candid autobiographical stories by the winner of the 1978 Nobel Prize for Literature are about Singer's growing up in early-twentieth-century Warsaw, where his father was a rabbi. Sequels include *A Young Man in Search of Love* and *Lost in America*.

Singer, Isaac Bashevis.
  Zlateh the Goat and Other Stories. Trans. by the author and Elizabeth Shub.
    1966. HarperCollins, $16 (0-06-025hub. 698-2); paper, $9.95 (0-06-44147-2).

    Gr. 2 and up. This is one of Singer's great collections of Yiddish folktales, masterfully retold with evocative illustrations by Maurice Sendak. Another one is *When Shlemiel Went to Warsaw and Other Stories*, illustrated by Margot Zemach.

Strom, Yale.
  The Expulsion of the Jews.
    1992. Shapolsky, $24.95 (0-56171-082-2).

    Gr. 7–12. A photo-history of the Sephardic Jews from the Inquisition to the present records 500 years of their lives in exile in places from Istanbul to Athens and Madrid.

Wiesel, Elie.
　Legends of Our Time.
　　1968. Schocken, paper, $12 (0-8052-0714-7).

　　　Gr. 7–12. Including his childhood memories of friends and teachers as well as his experience as a Holocaust survivor, Wiesel combines autobiography and story, as in the legend of "The Wandering Jew."

FICTION

Aleichem, Sholom.
　Tevye the Dairyman and the Railroad Stories.
　　Trans. by Hillel Halkin. 1987. Schocken, paper, $10.95
　　　(0-8052-0905-0).

　　　Gr. 7–12. In a fine new translation, this collection of realistic, marvelously entertaining portraits of shtetl life include the Tevye stories (some of which were popularized and sentimentalized in the musical *Fiddler on the Roof*) and also 21 railroad stories. The translator Halkin says that the character of Tevye, as he talks with God and tries to marry off his daughters, embodies the precarious existence of a Jew in Eastern Europe.

Aleichem, Sholom.
　The Nightingale; or, The Saga of Yosele Solovey the Cantor.
　　Trans. by Aliza Shevrin. 1985. Plume, paper, $8.95
　　　(0-452-25933-9).

　　　Gr. 9–12. This is a beautiful shtetl story about a poor, motherless boy whose heavenly voice transforms him into a great cantor—and also exposes him to gambling and womanizing and a world that can destroy him.

Angell, Judie.
　One-way to Ansonia.
　　1985. Bradbury, $11.95 (0-02-705860-3); Berkley, paper,
　　　$2.50 (0-425-08880-4).

　　　Gr. 6–10. Arriving in America in 1893, Rose Rogoff struggles toward womanhood, keeping her dreams alive until she can break free of the immigrant community that holds her back.

Arrick, Fran.
　Chernowitz!
　　1981. NAL, paper, $2.95 (0-451-12350-2).

　　　Gr. 6–10. When even longtime friends begin to bait him, Bob Cherno plots revenge against the anti-Semitic bully who started it all. This is a disturbing story of racism in an American school.

Bellow, Saul.
　The Victim.
　　1947. Penguin, paper, $6.95 (0-14-002493-X).

Gr. 10–12. Bellow tells a nightmare story of a Jewish man, Asa Leventhal, alone in New York, accused by a strange Gentile of having ruined him. Leventhal has always known how lucky he is to have escaped falling over the edge; now this stranger threatens him.

Blume, Judy.
Are You There God? It's Me, Margaret.
1970. Bradbury, $12.95 (0-02-710990-9); Dell, paper $3 (0-440-40419-3).

Gr. 5–7. When 11-year-old Margaret's family moves from the city to their new home in the suburbs, Margaret doesn't know whether to join the Y or the Jewish Community Center. Margaret's father is Jewish, and her mother's Christian. Her Jewish grandmother is always asking her if she has boyfriends and if they're Jewish. Her Christian grandparents disowned her mother for marrying a Jew. Margaret also worries about making friends and about not getting her period, and she asks God for help. This is an ever-popular, tender, funny story of contemporary life.

Cohen, Barbara.
People Like Us.
1987. Bantam, paper, $2.95 (0-553-27445-7).

Gr. 7–10. Fifteen-year-old Dinah is proud of her heritage and close to her family, but she finds her mother and grandparents' rejection of interfaith dating narrow-minded and unrealistic. Cohen captures an enduring conflict.

Doctorow, E. L.
The Book of Daniel.
1971. Random, $14.95 (0-394-46271-8); Fawcett, paper $4.95 (0-449-21430-3).

Gr. 8–12. Combining fact and fiction, Doctorow tells the story of the Rosenbergs through the memory of a fictional son, Daniel. The story sets their arrest, trial, and execution for espionage within the sociopolitical atmosphere of the early 1950s. Doctorow's *World's Fair* is a fictional memoir of life in New York City in the 1930s, written from the point of view of a child.

Girion, Barbara.
A Tangle of Roots.
1979. Putnam, paper, $2.25 (0-448-47747-5).

Gr. 7–10. When her mother unexpectedly dies, 16-year-old Beth Frankle, her father, and her grandmother must all come to terms with their grief.

Great Jewish Short Stories.
Ed. by Saul Bellow.
1963. Dell, paper, $5.99 (0-440-33122-6).

Gr. 7–12. Isaac Bashevis Singer's "Gimpel the Fool," Grace Paley's "Goodbye and Good Luck," and the Haggadah's "Hadrian and the Aged Planter" are among these eloquent stories, mainly modern, a few ancient. Later editions of Jewish short stories, edited by Irving Howe in 1977 and by Ted Solotaroff and Nessa Rapoport, are generally too sophisticated to be of interest to most young people.

Greenberg, Joanne.
I Never Promised You a Rose Garden.
1964. NAL, paper, $3.95 (0-451-16031-2).

Gr. 7–12. A powerful autobiographical novel describes a teenage schizophrenic girl's retreat from fear and lies and anti-Semitism into a private fantasy kingdom. She recovers with the help of a wise psychiatrist, who helps her face the harsh challenges of the real world. Greenberg originally published this perennially popular novel under the pseudonym Hannah Green.

Greene, Bette.
Summer of My German Soldier.
1973. Dial, $14.95 (0-8037-8321-3); Bantam, paper, $3.50 (0-553-27247-0).

Gr. 6–10. Set in a small town in Arkansas during World War II, this classic YA novel about racism disturbs many stereotypes. Twelve-year-old Patty Bergen befriends a German prisoner of war and helps him escape. Patty's private war is with her abusive Jewish father and the prejudiced people of her community.

Hesse, Karen.
Letters from Rifka.
1992. Holt, $14.95 (0-8050-1964-2).

Gr. 5–8. In letters to her cousin back "home" in Russia, 12-year-old Rifka tells of her journey to America in 1919: the dangerous escape over the border, the journey through Europe and across the sea to the new country. The best part of the book is about her time on Ellis Island, in limbo, waiting to see if the authorities will declare her infection-free. What's especially memorable is the emerging sense of Rifka's strong personality: she's brave and clever, and if she talks too much, so be it.

Hobson, Laura Z.
Gentleman's Agreement.
1947. Cherokee, $16.95 (0-87797-210-9).

Gr. 7–12. A famous novel with a simple premise: an investigative journalist on an assignment about anti-Semitism pretends to be Jewish and is shocked by the prejudice he encounters in society and even in himself.

Horowitz, Eve.
Plain Jane.
1992. Random, $20 (0-679-41261-1).

"The Jews' greatest contribution has been less what America has accepted than what it has resisted: such distinctive traits of the modern Jewish spirit at its best as an eager restlessness, a moral anxiety, an openness to novelty, a hunger for dialectic, a refusal of contentment, an ironic criticism of all fixed opinions."

—Irving Howe

Gr. 10–12. Growing up Jewish in Cleveland in the 1990s, 18-year-old Jane Singer calls herself an updated female Holden Caulfield. She loses her virginity, watches her sister marry an Orthodox Jewish doctor, and lives through her parents' divorce in this funny, sexy, sharp, compassionate, coming-of-age story.

Kemelman, Harry.
Sunday the Rabbi Stayed Home.
1969. Fawcett, paper, $4.95 (0-449-21000-6).

Gr. 7–12. Rabbi David Small plays detective in a popular mystery series. This time he's threatened with a split in temple membership and must deal with a murder involving a group of college students home for the Passover holidays.

Konecky, Edith.
Allegra Maud Goldman.
1976. Feminist Press, $9.95 (1-55861-022-7).

Gr. 8–12. This sensitive, funny, bittersweet, first-person narrative concerns the childhood trials and tribulations of precocious Allegra, growing up in 1930s Brooklyn.

Lasky, Kathryn.
Pageant.
1986. Four Winds, $14.95 (0-02-751720-9); Dell, paper, $3.95 (0-440-20161-6).

Gr. 6–12. With warmth and wit, Lasky describes Sarah's growing up in the early 1960s in a liberal, upper-middle-class family, frustrated and bored with her stuffy Indianapolis girls' school. She tries to accept her individuality without feeling like an outcast. Lasky also wrote the fine immigrant story *The Night Journey*.

"Are you there God? It's me, Margaret. I'm going to temple today—with Grandma. It's a holiday. I guess you know that. Well, my father thinks it's a mistake and my mother thinks the whole idea is crazy, but I'm going anyway. I'm sure this will help me decide what to be. I've never been inside a temple or a church. I'll look for you God."

—Judy Blume

Lehrman, Robert.
Juggling.
1982. Berkley, paper, $2.50 (0-425-11128-8).

Gr. 6–12. Howie Berger, affluent, arrogant soccer ace, has two principal goals: he wants to overcome his shyness around girls, and he wants to be accepted by the members of the Maccabiahs, a high-power soccer team composed largely of immigrant Jews.

Levitin, Sonia.
Journey to America.
1970. Aladdin, paper, $3.95 (0-689-71130-1).

Gr. 5–8. In a strong immigration story, Lisa Platt, the middle daughter, tells how her family is forced to leave Nazi Germany and make a new life in the United States. First their father leaves, then the others escape to Switzerland, where they endure harsh conditions. After months of separation, the family is reunited in New York.

Levoy, Myron.
Alan and Naomi.
1977. HarperCollins, $12.89 (0-06-023800-3); paper, $3.50 (0-06-440209-6).

Gr. 6–10. In New York City in 1944, duty gives way to real caring as Alan breaks through to troubled, fragile refugee Naomi, who can't forget her father's murder by the Nazis. Readers will be moved by the friendship story, by Alan's moral struggle with the evil of the Holocaust, and by the integrity of the bleak ending.

Malamud, Bernard.
The Assistant.
1957. Avon, paper, $4.95 (0-380-51474-5).

Gr. 9–12. A powerful story of love and daily struggle focuses on the family of poor storekeeper Morris Bober and his non-Jewish assistant, Frankie, who loves Bober's daughter. Another novel by Malamud of interest to teenagers is *The Fixer*, based on a true incident about a victim of anti-Semitic hysteria in Czarist Russia.

Mazer, Anne.
Moose Street.
1992. Knopf/Borzoi, $13 (0-679-83233-5).

Gr. 5–7. Eleven-year-old Lena Rosen lives on Moose Street in the 1950s but is not really of it. As the only Jewish child for blocks around, she's branded as different, even though she barely believes in the religion and doesn't observe many of the holidays. Being an outsider, though, she's able to see the neighborhood as others can't, and she discovers painful secrets.

Mazer, Harry.
The Last Mission.
1979. Dell, paper, $3.25 (0-440-94797-9).

Gr. 7–10. In 1944, a 15-year-old Jewish boy lies about his age, enlists in the U.S. Air Corps, and is taken prisoner by the Germans. Mazer also wrote *I Love You, Stupid!* about high school senior Marcus Rosenbloom, a virgin who's obsessed with girls and who tries to make sense of his feelings of friendship, lust, and love.

Mazer, Norma Fox.
After the Rain.
1987. Morrow, $12.95 (0-628-06867-7); Avon, paper, $3.50 (0-380-75025-2).

Gr. 6–12. In a candid family story, Rachel hates the rude, tyrannical behavior of her fiercely independent, 83-year-old grandfather, but her love for him grows in the last few months of his fatal illness.

Olshan, Joseph.
A Warmer Season.
1987. Ballantine, paper, $3.95 (0-318-33438-0).

Gr. 9–12. Olshan's story of family loss and friendship focuses on suburban high school senior Daniel, who loses his virginity and becomes close friends with his Italian Catholic classmate Gianni.

Ozick, Cynthia.
The Shawl.
1989. Knopf, $12.95 (0-394-57976-3); Random/Vintage, paper, $7.95 (0-679-72926-7).

Gr. 9–12. A short story of almost unbearable intensity and a novella are connected by the character of Rosa Lublin. In "The Shawl," she's cradling her baby in the death camps until a guard hurls the infant at an electrified fence. In "Rosa," she's a survivor in America, wild with anger and grief.

Potok, Chaim.
The Chosen.
1967. Knopf, $30 (0-679-40222-5); Fawcett, paper, $5.95 (0-449-21344-7).

Gr. 6–12. Rooted in Jewish culture, this story is also about the universals of friendship and competition and family. A relationship that starts in the fierce rivalry of a baseball game grows into a strong bond between two Orthodox boys, Danny and Reuven, as Reuven becomes involved in Danny's conflict with his austere, Hasidic rabbi father. The story continues in *The Promise.*

Raphael, Lev.
Dancing on Tisha B'av.
1990. St. Martin's, $15.95 (0-312-04862-9).

Gr. 10–12. Nineteen stories about gay men, Jews, young academics, and family deal with important and intriguing themes. Raphael writes about coming out gay and making love; about coming to terms with the Holocaust, especially from the perspectives of the children of survivors; and about the attraction traditional Judaism

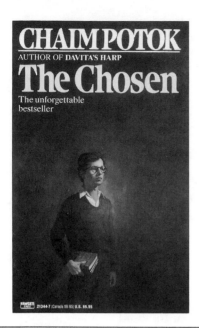

CHAIM POTOK
AUTHOR OF DAVITA'S HARP
The Chosen
The unforgettable
bestseller

"I felt more than saw the batter charging toward second, and as I was getting my glove on the ball he smashed into me like a truck. The ball went over my head, and I fell forward heavily onto the asphalt floor of the yard, and he passed me, going toward third, his fringes flying out behind him, holding his skullcap to his head with his right hand so it would not fall off. Abe Goodstein, our first baseman, retrieved the ball and whipped it home, and the batter stood at third, a wide grin on his face.

The yeshiva team exploded into wild cheers and shouted loud words of congratulations in Yiddish to the batter.

Sidney Goldberg helped me get to my feet.

'That momzer!' he said. 'You weren't in his way!'"

—Chaim Potok

exerts upon young, otherwise mainstream American Jews. Ray Olson said in his *Booklist* review that when Raphael sounds all these themes together in a story, the resultant harmonies are wonderfully resonant and compelling. The title story is beautifully told from the point of view of the sister of a young gay man.

Roiphe, Anne.
Lovingkindness.
  1987. Warner, paper, $4.50 (0-446-35274-8).

  Gr. 8–12. In a moving reversal of the conflict between the generations, a radical feminist mother is heartbroken when her daughter joins an Orthodox sect in Jerusalem and prepares to go through with an arranged marriage.

Roth, Henry.
Call It Sleep.
  1934. Farrar, $25 (0-374-11819-1); paper, $8.95
    (0-374-52292-8).

  Gr. 8–12. A lyrical novel that has become a classic immigration story focuses on a Jewish American boy in the slums of New York City in the early twentieth century. David Schearl is close to his gentle mother and terrorized by the towering anger of his father, who rages at his alienated immigrant life. When the family speaks English, their language is broken and ungrammatical; when they speak Yiddish, Roth translates it with eloquence and beauty.

Roth, Philip.
Goodbye, Columbus and Five Short Stories.
  1959. Bantam, paper, $4.50 (0-553-26365-X).

Gr. 9–12. In the sharp, funny novella *Goodbye, Columbus*, a poor young Jewish librarian has a passionate affair with a beautiful young woman whose newly rich family has recently moved to the suburbs.

Segal, Jerry.
The Place Where Nobody Stopped.
1991. Orchard/Richard Jackson, $14.95 (0-531-05897-2).

Gr. 6–10. Reminiscent of the stories of Sholom Aleichem, rich in Yiddish idiom, this gentle combination of Jewish folktale, historical fiction, and farce is set in turn-of-the-century Russia in a remote forest, a place where nobody stops and everything always happens the same way. Once a year the people have to hide from the brutal Cossacks who come thundering through the forest to force recruits into the czar's army. Meanwhile, the Jews wait for a crooked relative who's promised to get them passports to America.

Shalant, Phyllis.
Shalom, Geneva Peace.
1992. Dutton, $14 (0-525-44868-3).

Gr. 6–9. Feeling betwixt and between, Andi Applebaum turns her attention to her synagogue youth group, where she meets worldly and rebellious Geneva Peace. Except for a stereotypical portrait of a Jewish mother, this is an appealing story with its fine treatment of peer pressure, budding sexuality, and religious values.

Singer, Isaac Bashevis.
Yentl the Yeshiva Boy. Trans. by Marion Magid and Elizabeth Pollet.
1962. Farrar, $10.95 (0-374-29347-3).

Gr. 6–12. This great story about a girl who disguises herself as a boy appears in many Singer collections. It was made into a successful movie starring Barbra Streisand.

Singer, Marilyn.
The Course of True Love Never Did Run Smooth.
1983. HarperCollins, $12.95 (0-06-02573-9).

Gr. 7–12. Best friends since grade school, 16-year-olds Becky Weiss and Nemi Barish play a pair of lovers in their school production of *A Midsummer Night's Dream* and find that their relationship is changing.

Slepian, Jan.
Risk N' Roses.
1990. Philomel, $14.95 (0-399-22219-7).

Gr. 6–10. Set in the Bronx in the late 1940s, this is a very honest depiction of that age-old conflict—my family or my friend? Skip Berman thinks her mentally disabled sister, Angela, is a pain in the neck. Skip wants to be with Jean, the wild, attractive neighborhood

"The neighborhood had changed: the old Jews like my grandparents had struggled and prospered, and moved further and further west, towards the edge of Newark, then out of it, and up the slope of the Orange Mountains, until they had reached the crest and started down the other side, pouring into Gentile territory as the Scotch-Irish had poured through the Cumberland Gap."

—Philip Roth

205

leader. When Jean works out a plan to make Angela play a cruel trick on an old Holocaust survivor, Skip is caught between her loyalty to her sister, her strict moral upbringing, and the call of the street.

Wolff, Virginia Euwer.
  The Mozart Season.
    1991. Holt $15.95 (0-8050-1571-X).

    Gr. 5–9. Allegra Leah Shapiro, violinist and softball player in Portland, Oregon, confronts the Holocaust death of her Polish great-grandmother in Treblinka. Allegra finds—in her music, in her own experience, and in the feelings of close family and friends—that happiness is fragile, that suffering and joy are very close.

VIDEOS

Isaac in America: A Journey with Isaac Bashevis Singer.
    1986. Direct Cinema. 58min. $350.

    Gr. 10–12. Scenes of Isaac Bashevis Singer in his New York milieu, fond reminiscences of his Warsaw childhood, and readings and scenes from his works combine to form an intimate portrait of this Nobel Prize–winning writer.

Molly's Pilgrim.
    1985. Phoenix/BFA. 24min. $325.

    Gr. 5–7. A young Jewish Russian emigrée's very personal interpretation of the Thanksgiving story renews the meaning and spirit of the traditional American holiday. Based on a book by Barbara Cohen.

Mortimer Griffin and Shalinsky.
    1985. Beacon Films. 26min. $149.

    Gr. 9–12. An elderly Jewish student's questioning of his night-school teacher leads to a humorous and emotionally laden confrontation over the younger man's acceptance of his Jewish heritage. Based on a story by Mordecai Richler.

West of Hester Street.
    1983. Media Projects. 58min. $79.95.

    Gr. 10–12. The immigration of 10,000 Jewish "greenhorns" to Galveston, Texas, and into the heartland of America at the turn of the century is recounted in this you-are-there docudrama.

Latinos

The *border* is fact and metaphor for many Latino writers: the border of place, language, family, memory; the individual between two worlds. Much Latino writing captures that elemental immigration experience of moving to a new culture and finding suddenly that *you* are the *other*.

Until very recently, little was being published in English specifically for young adults about the Latino experience. There's some good YA nonfiction, especially in photo-essay form, about new immigrants in the fields and cities, about migrant workers, and about life on the Mexican border and the connections that barbed wire cannot sever. Except for the work of Gary Soto and Fran Leeper Buss, there's not much YA fiction; few characters are Latino, even in minor roles. Walter Dean Myers' *Scorpions* is a notable exception; in this fine interracial friendship story, the bond between African American Jamal and his Puerto Rican classmate Tito provides a funny, poignant counterpoint to the grim Harlem streets. And in Betsy Byars' popular *Bingo Brown's Guide to Romance*, Bingo's warm, clever English teacher, who stimulates Bingo to read *The Red Badge of Courage*, is Latino. Still, Latinos are hard to find in the YA novel.

Fortunately, many adult books do focus on the young Latino's coming-of-age. Sandra Cisneros is one of several contemporary women writers who speak with an exuberant lyricism about the immigrant experience, fusing the personal and the social with a strong sense of family intimacy. Her characters are rooted in the Mexican American community even as they transform themselves.

As with all the bibliographies in this book, there's always the question of whether stories set in the old country belong on one of the ethnic American lists in the Widening World section that concludes Part III. The answer is, they belong on both lists. People don't come to America blank: their memories and stories and poetry stay with them and enrich us all, even as new experience changes them, and they change us. And many Latinos go back often to the places and people they came from, and that return and leaving is part of their story.

The best stories aren't tidy. They don't fit neatly into categories *about* one subject. The arrangement here is just a matter of convenience. For example, in many ways, books about the Caribbean belong together, as well as on lists about the African American, Native American, and Latino experience. So this list should be used with books in the Widening World section.

All the Latino writers, whether they came to the U.S. from Mexico, Puerto Rico, Cuba, the Dominican Republic, or other Latin American countries, share the experience of bilingualism, however different their accents or culture. But the question of the "correct" terminology is an ongoing one. Some prefer *Hispanic.* Most writers I spoke to said that they generally identified with the term *Latino.* But then one of the advisers for this list, the poet Raúl Niño, laughed: "It's *Latino* until we decide on a new one," he said.

NONFICTION

After Aztlán: Latino Poets of the Nineties.
Ed. by Ray González.
1992. Godine, $24.95 (0-87923-931-X); paper, $15.95 (0-87923-932-8).

Gr. 8–12. In this collection of some of the best contemporary Latino poets who write primarily in English, many diverse voices speak of overcoming political barriers, preserving the traditions of culture and family, and relating to the "mainstream."

Anastos, Phillip and French, Chris.
Illegal.
1991. Rizzoli, $19.95 (0-8478-1367-3).

Gr. 6–12. Powerful photojournalism by two New York high schoolers who traveled to Texas to record the plight of illegal immigrants, many of them young boys of conscription age fleeing Central America.

Ashabranner, Brent.
The Vanishing Border: A Photographic Journey along Our Border with Mexico.
1987. Putnam, $14.95 (0-396-08900-3).

Gr. 6–12. With candor and humanity, this documentary photo-essay combines interviews, commentary, and history to show life in the 2,000-mile border country between the U.S. and Mexico. Both sides of the border are presented with immediacy in Paul Conklin's photos, which show individuals in all their variety and the connections between them. Also of interest is Ashabranner and Conklin's *Dark Harvest: Migrant Farmworkers in America,* which shows the exploitation of migrant farmworkers (most of them Latino) in a system that encourages child labor and holds people in harsh servitude and poverty.

Baca, Jimmy Santiago.
Black Mesa Poems.
1989. New Directions, $8.95 (0-8112-102-9).

Gr. 9–12. Winner of the 1989 International Hispanic Award, this poetry collection is rooted in New Mexico barrio and ranch experiences, including family, celebrations, the passing of the seasons, and love.

Brimner, Larry Dane.
A Migrant Family.
1992. Lerner, $12.95 (0-8225-2554-2).

Gr. 5–8. A spare photo-essay captures the daily life of 12-year-old Juan Medina and his migrant farm worker family, living in a makeshift camp in Southern California. We see what it's like to go to school, always a stranger, and to come home and find that bulldozers have demolished your shelter. "No one sheds tears. To be a migrant is to move." Brimner taught migrant students as a Title I teacher in El Centro, California.

Castillo, Ana.
My Father Was a Toltec.
1988. West End Press, $6.95 (0-931122-49-X).

Gr. 11–12. In poems that portray the harshness of barrio life, Castillo writes about her early Chicago years, her relation to her mother and womanizing father, her gang roots, ethnic warfare in the schools, and gender warfare in the neighborhoods, as she struggles to find another, better country that she can claim as her own.

Cockcroft, James D.
Outlaws in the Promised Land: Mexican Immigrant Workers and America's Future.
1986. Grove, $19.95 (0-8021-1206-4); paper, $14.95 (0-8021-5094-2).

Gr. 10–12. Using personal testimonies of the workers themselves and academic research, Cockcroft portrays the unjust and inhuman conditions Mexican migrant workers must face when they cross the border in search of jobs.

Drucker, Malka.
Frida Kahlo: Torment and Triumph in Her Life and Art.
1991. Bantam/Starfire, $16.50 (0-553-07165-3); paper, $7 (0-553-35408-6).

Gr. 8–12. The life of Frida Kahlo, Mexico's best-known woman artist, is vividly depicted in an absorbing biography. Drucker candidly and compassionately relates Kahlo's total absorption with

ILLEGAL
Seeking the American Dream

Photographs and Text by Phillip Anastos and Chris French

"We had to keep reminding ourselves that the unaccompanied minors were our age. Many of them come from countries ravaged by war. If that hasn't marked them, the journey to the United States, often hazardous in the extreme and filled with hardship after hardship, almost certainly has.

They flee from conditions we can barely imagine, and most of them would rather give up everything they know and everyone they love than be 'drafted' into the dreaded military, whose troops march through the streets, 'cherry picking' kids and telling them they've just 'volunteered' for the army. The guerrillas are no better, employing exactly the same tactics. A very real fear we heard voiced over and over was that you could end up fighting against your own brother!"

—Phillip Anastos

work and debunks the myths surrounding the strong sensual woman and artist.

Fernández-Shaw, Carlos M.
The Hispanic Presence in North America from 1492 to Today. Trans. by Alfonso Bertodano Stourton and others.
1991. Facts On File, $45 (0-8160-2133-3).

Gr. 8–12. This useful reference volume bridges the old and new. The first part, a general history of Spanish colonization, gives examples of Hispanic contributions in fields such as economics, the arts, and law. The rest of the book is arranged by region and discusses the Spanish presence in each area. There are also photos, maps, and numerous appendixes about everything from holidays to radio and TV stations.

Growing Up Latino: Memoirs and Stories.
Ed. by Harold Augenbraum and Ilan Stavans.
1993. Houghton, $22.95 (0-395-62231-X); paper, $12.95 (0-395-66124-2).

Gr. 9–12. Twenty-five diverse eloquent voices—from Sandra Cisneros and Edward Rivera to Julia Alvarez and Richard Rodriguez—detail what editor Stavans calls "the Hispanic journey from darkness to light, from rejection to assimilation, from silence to voice," and, in telling of their polarized identity, they change the culture of the U.S.

Harlan, Judith.
Bilingualism in the United States: Conflict and Controversy.
1991. Watts, $12.90 (0-531-13001-0).

Gr. 7–12. Is America a melting pot or a salad? Harlan looks at the controversies over bilingualism in terms of these two metaphors, showing that the arguments about language are both educational and political. The writing style and the design are dull, but Harlan has taken on a subject of crucial importance. The words we use affect how we see ourselves.

Inventing a Word: An Anthology of Twentieth Century Puerto Rican Poetry.
Ed. by Julio Marzán.
1980. Columbia, $37 (0-231-05010-0); paper, $15.50 (0-231-05011-9).

Gr. 7–12. A bilingual edition of 23 poets, some living in Puerto Rico and others in the U.S., some of whom write in the lyrical Spanish tradition and many of whom powerfully fuse politics with poetry.

Light, Ken.
To the Promised Land.
1988. Aperture/California Historical Society, $25 (0-89381-324-9).

"Ten years old, and old enough to know the hand shake of a father. August crossings over borders backwards into memory. The shock of it was he looked like me, only bigger with flesh and regrets. Back then when nopals were fat with red fruits of spring, a woman took her first steps north, a sleeping contraband tight to her breast. He asked me how I was doing, how old I was and if I was behaving myself; all I could do was sit on my hands and stare at his whiskered Adam's apple that bobbed in rhythm to his interrogation. . . . Yes and no was the extent of our first and only conversation. He fished inside his pants pocket and handed me some change, the last thing he said to me was 'be good.' "

—Raúl Niño

Gr. 7–12. The struggle of migrant workers on the U.S.-Mexican border is made palpable in Light's powerful photographs and in the oral histories compiled by Samuel Orozco.

Mora, Pat.
 Borders.
  1986. Arte Público, paper, $7 (0-934770-57-3).

  Gr. 8–12. In poems like "Bilingual Christmas," "Oral History," and "The Grateful Minority," El Paso poet Mora captures the immigrant experience, fusing the intimate and the political in language that's both colloquial and sharp. "Not fair," says the Mexican American girl looking at herself in the mirror.

Niño, Raúl.
 Breathing Light.
  1991. MARCH/Abrazo, paper, $6 (1-877636-10-X).

  Gr. 9–12. Niño, a young Chicago poet, is more individualistic and romantic than most Mexican American writers, and his casual, accessible voice will touch young readers. His autobiographical poems portray his experience growing up in Chicago, the only child of a Spanish-speaking housekeeper in a rich suburban area, where language and class separated him from other kids.

Ortiz-Cofer, Judith.
 Silent Dancing: A Partial Remembrance of a Puerto Rican Childhood.
  1990. Arte Público, paper, $8.50 (1-55885-015-5).

  Gr. 8–12. Through short autobiographical sketches and poems, Ortiz-Cofer relates her earliest memories of a lush Puerto Rican childhood and shares her feelings about her transient, Catholic adolescence, moving between the island and the States. She dramatizes the immigrant experience, loss of ethnicity, the battle of the sexes, crossing over into adulthood. She acts as translator for her mother, learning that English was the child's weapon and her power, and comes of age during the Cuban missile crisis. *Booklist* reviewer Kathryn LaBarbera called this "a delightful, thoughtful assessment of a bicultural, bilingual life, in which Spanish remains 'the language of fun, of summertime games.'"

Riding, Alan.
Distant Neighbors: A Portrait of the Mexicans.
1985. Knopf, $18.95 (0-394-50005-9); paper, $4.95 (0-394-74015-7).

Gr. 8–12. A *New York Times* journalist surveys Mexico's history and relates it to present social, political, and economic conditions, focusing also on the country's massive problems and its relations with the U.S.

"In the barrio, the police are just another gang."

—Luis J. Rodriguez

Rodriguez, Luis J.
Always Running: A Memoir of La Vida Loca, Gang Days in L.A.
1993. Curbstone, $19.95 (1-880684-06-3).

Gr. 10–12. Rodriguez's frank autobiography of his time with a barrio gang in the 1960s and early 1970s personalizes the crime statistics. He describes how gangs form, why he joined, his life of violence, his struggle to get away, and then his anguish at watching his teenage son run with a Latino gang on the Chicago streets.

Rodriguez, Richard.
Hunger of Memory: The Education of Richard Rodriguez.
1982. Bantam, paper, $4.95 (0-553-27293-4).

Gr. 8–12. Rodriguez takes a strong political stand against bilingual education and affirmative action, even as he's painfully honest about how much he has lost in attempting to succeed in the English-speaking white world. Teenagers everywhere will relate to his account of his lonely adolescence, his shame about not feeling "normal," his struggle for self-acceptance. He's the upwardly climbing scholarship boy, who works his way doggedly through a list of "the hundred most important books of Western Civilization," reading each word of each book but often having to check the book jacket to see what he's reading about. While Rodriguez's recently published *Days of Obligation: An Argument with My Father* will interest adults more than teens, many of the essays deal with the author's coming-of-age in California, a child of two cultures.

Roman, Joseph.
Pablo Neruda.
1992. Chelsea House, $17.95 (07910-1248-4).

Gr. 7–12. Pablo Neruda's father beat him for writing poetry and later cut off the boy's college money when he refused to pursue a conventional profession. This straightforward biography in the Hispanics of Achievement series traces the great poet's life in some detail and includes many quotes from Neruda, with one full poem with the translation facing the original Spanish. Roman shows how the poetry integrated everyday objects and private feelings with political ideals.

Shorris, Earl.
Latinos: A Biography of the People.
1992. Norton, $25 (0-393-03360-0).

Gr. 9–12. This compelling, journalistic account of the Latino experience, both historical and contemporary, tells the story through individual stories and general commentary and takes on crucial issues of ethnic identity, bilingualism, and assimilation.

Sinnott, Susan.
Extraordinary Hispanic Americans.
1991. Childrens Press, $30.60 (0-516-00582-0).

Gr. 5–10. A collective biography in chronological order and illustrated with black-and-white photos and line drawings, this includes two- to four-page biographies of well-known people from all fields, from the age of exploration in the 1400s through today.

Soto, Gary.
Home Course in Religion.
1991. Chronicle, paper, $8.95 (0-87701-857-X).

Gr. 7–12. There's anger and fragility in the casual idiom and rhythms of Soto's clear, intimate poems of growing up Catholic and Mexican in California: hanging out with a friend, suppressing anger at a mean-spirited adult, learning karate, searching for somewhere to go. Other collections by Soto include *The Elements of San Joaquin.*

POLITICS INVADES THE HOME

Thomas, Piri.
Down These Mean Streets.
　1967. Knopf, paper, $5.95 (0-685-02840-2).

　　Gr. 9–12. Poetic and brutal, Thomas' autobiography of growing up in Spanish Harlem during the Depression and after recounts his struggle to free himself of the effects of racial prejudice, drug addiction, and crime. Younger readers will enjoy his *Stories from El Barrio*.

"I have begun
my own quiet
war. Simple.
Sure. I am one
who leaves the
table like a man,
without putting
back the chair
or picking up
the plate."

　　—Sandra
　　Cisneros

FICTION

Alvarez, Julia.
How the García Girls Lost Their Accents.
　1991. Algonquin, $16.95 (0-945575-57-2).

　　Gr. 9–12. Fifteen interconnected stories portray with warmth and humor the life and loves of four sisters, daughters of a Dominican doctor, both on the island where they were born and in the U.S. where they now live. The stories expose the pangs and joys of being a woman and becoming an American.

Anaya, Rudolfo A.
Bless Me, Ultima.
　1972. Tonatiuh-Quinto Sol International, paper, $12
　　(0-89229-002-1).

　　Gr. 8–12. One of the most famous and best selling of all Mexican American novels tells the story of the initiation of a young boy, Antonio, through his relationship with Ultima, a wise *curandera* (mentor). The story blends oral traditions with a portrayal of rural life.

Buss, Fran Leeper and Cubias, Daisy.
Journey of the Sparrows.
　1991. Dutton/Lodestar, $14.95 (0-525-67362-8).

　　Gr. 7–12. Nailed into a crate in the back of a truck, 15-year-old María and her family endure the cruel journey across the border from Mexico and then north to Chicago. There they struggle to find work, always careful to remain "invisible" so that the authorities won't arrest them as illegal aliens and send them back. The story is told in restrained, simple prose through María's eyes, and there's no talk of heroes and no sensationalism. Readers will be caught by the facts of the survival struggle in our country now and by the lyrical account of the dangerous journey.

Cisneros, Sandra.
The House on Mango Street.
　1984. Arte Público. Vintage, paper, $9 (0-679-73477-5).

　　Gr. 8–12. This splendid book will touch teenagers deeply. A series of intense vignettes tells the story of a Mexican American girl's coming-of-age in Chicago. Esperanza confronts all the negative examples, role models, and problems of her neighborhood; dreams of a new home and a different life; and develops the knowledge and language that will help her both hold on to and transcend her environment. Stories like "My Name," "First Job," and "Papa Who Wakes Up Tired in the Dark" are great for reading aloud and will stimulate kids to write about their own lives with openness and spirit.

Cisneros, Sandra.
Woman Hollering Creek and Other Stories.
1991. Random, $18 (0-394-57654-3).

Gr. 10–12. These 22 stories are funny, revealing, poetic, and insightful. In "Barbie-Q," two little girls struggle with having only one outfit apiece for their Barbies and no Kens. Other stories leave humor behind; "Never Marry a Mexican" simmers with rage; "Eyes of Zapata" stands just on the border of realism.

Galarza, Ernesto.
Barrio Boy: The Story of a Boy's Acculturation.
1971. Univ. of Notre Dame, paper, $7.95 (0-268-00441-2).

Gr. 9–12. In fictionalized autobiography, Galarza moves from his childhood in Mexico through his family's attempt to make a new home in Sacramento, California. After his parents die, he finds himself in a migrant labor camp and begins to understand what has happened to his people.

Iguana Dreams: New Latino Fiction.
Ed. by Delia Poey and Virgil Suarez.
1992. HarperCollins, $25 (0-06-055329-4); paper, $12 (0-06-096917-2).

Gr. 10–12. This richly varied anthology brings together 29 short stories that reflect different aspects of Latino life, from the despair of the barrio to the unease of working within the Anglo status quo. At the same time, however, many of them embody universal themes of growing up. Judith Ortiz-Cofer's "American History," for example, captures the loneliness of a childhood shadowed by prejudice; Sandra Cisneros' "Salvador Late or Early" is a quiet, heartbreaking story about a boy who must take on too much. Not all the pieces are as good, and some are more adult in focus, but this is a fine introduction to some of the best contemporary Latino writers.

Jenkins, Lyll Becerra de.
The Honorable Prison.
1988. Dutton/Lodestar, $14.95 (0-525-67238-9);
Penguin/Puffin, paper, $3.95 (0-14-032952-8).

Gr. 7–12. In an unspecified Latin American country under military dictatorship in the 1950s, Marta and her family are placed under house arrest in a remote village guarded by an army post. The writer of this fine, partly autobiographical story grew up in Colombia and now lives in the U.S.

Baseball in April

AND OTHER STORIES

GARY SOTO

"'How come you're making a face?' asked Victor. 'I ain't making a face, *ese*. This *is* my face.'

Michael said his face had changed during the summer. He had read a *GQ* magazine that his older brother borrowed from the Book Mobile and noticed that the male models all had the same look on their faces. They would stand, one arm around a beautiful woman, and *scowl*. They would sit at a pool, their rippled stomachs dark with shadow, and *scowl*. They would sit at dinner tables, cool drinks in their hands, and *scowl*.

'I think it works,' Michael said. He scowled and let his upper lip quiver. His teeth showed along with the ferocity of his soul. 'Belinda Reyes walked by a while ago and looked at me,' he said."

—Gary Soto

Martínez, Max.
  Schoolland.
    1988. Arte Público, paper, $8.50 (0-934770-87-5).

    Gr. 10–12. Both harsh and loving, this autobiographical novel, set in rural Texas during the drought of the 1950s, is told from the point of view of a Mexican American teenager who learns about racism, sex, and hard times.

Mazzio, Joann.
  The One Who Came Back.
    1992. Houghton Mifflin, $13.95 (0-395-59506-1).

    Gr. 7–10. Friendship and prejudice in a multicultural school and community are well dramatized in this story about Alex Grant, who's suspected of having killed his best friend, Eddie Chavez. Eddie's been missing since the two teenagers ditched school to spend the day in the Sandia Mountains near their trailer park in New Mexico. The school counselor thinks that conflict is inevitable between Anglos and Mexicans and that Alex must have fought with Eddie. Even Alex's mother is racist ("You should never have hung around with ... Mexicans"). Some of this novel is heavy-handed, but kids will enjoy the mountain adventure, and they'll feel for Alex when no one believes his story.

Mohr, Nicholasa.
  In Nueva York.
    1977. Arte Público, paper, $8.50 (0-934770-78-6).

    Gr. 8–12. Seven interrelated stories vividly re-create experience in a New York City Puerto Rican barrio by focusing on the drama of individual lives. Also of note is Mohr's *El Bronx Remembered.* Full of character and humor, this story of the Puerto Rican community in New York's Lower East Side during the 1940s and 1950s is told mainly from the perspective of young people.

North of the Río Grande: the Mexican-American Experience in Short Fiction.
Ed. by Edward Simmen.
 1992. NAL/Mentor, paper $5.99 (0-451-62834-9).

 Gr. 7–12. An outstanding collection of more than 30 stories by both Anglo and Latino writers, from Stephen Crane in the nineteenth century to Sandra Cisneros today.

Perera, Hilda.
 Kiki: A Cuban Boy's Adventures in America. Trans. by Warren Hampton and Hilda Gonzalez.
 1992. Pickering Press, paper, $10.95 (0-940495-24-4).

 Gr. 4–8. This funny, poignant novel about a Cuban immigrant boy in Miami is candid about the conflicts of a young person caught between two cultures. At first Kiki struggles alone without his parents, but by the time they come to join him four years later he's reluctant to leave his comfortable Anglo foster home for the poverty and alienation of the immigrant community and their endless reminiscences of "home."

Rivera, Tomás.
 The Migrant Earth.
 1971. Trans. by Rolando Hinojosa. Arte Público, paper, $8 (0-934-77072-7).

 Gr. 9–12. Fourteen compelling vignettes interspersed with poetic moments and anecdotes capture the miseries of the Mexican American migrant farm worker: the Anglo and Chicano exploiters and con men, the trip north, the hard work in the fields, the problems at school, the search for selfhood and the possibility of redemption. Professor Mark Zimmerman, one of the advisers for this list, calls *The Migrant Earth* "perhaps the most acclaimed Chicano novel to date." A bilingual edition is available.

Santiago, Danny.
 Famous All Over Town.
 1983. NAL/Plume, paper, $8.95 (0-452-25944-6).

 Gr. 8–12. In a funny and moving adult novel about a Mexican American family in Los Angeles, 14-year-old Chato, gifted and sensitive, is pressured to act tough by his macho father and by the neighborhood gang.

Soto, Gary.
 Baseball in April and other Stories.
 1990. HBJ, $14.95 (0-15-205720-X); paper, $4.95 (0-15-205721-8).

 Gr. 5–9. Short stories about growing up Latino in Fresno, California, are funny and touching, candid about the conflicts among generations and within the individual. Several stories, such as "Seventh Grade," will be great for reading aloud.

Soto, Gary.
  Pacific Crossing.
    1992. HBJ, $14.95 (0-15-259187-7).

    Gr. 6–9. Lincoln Mendoza is selected for a summer exchange program to Japan, where he will continue the martial-arts training he began in San Francisco. His hosts and their son are as eager to learn about the U.S. and Lincoln's Mexican American heritage as 14-year-old Lincoln is to learn about Japan. Their cultural collisions are affable and gently humorous.

> "They want us to work. And they want us to disappear."
>
> —Juan Medina, 12 years old.

Where Angels Glide at Dawn: New Stories from Latin America.
  Ed. by Lori M. Carlson and Cynthia L. Ventura.
    1990. HarperCollins, $14 (0-397-32424-3).

    Gr. 6–8. With an introduction by Isabel Allende, these 10 stories for young people by modern Latin American writers from Mexico, El Salvador, Panama, Chile, Cuba, Peru, and Puerto Rico range from comedy and fantasy to stories of political repression.

VIDEOS

Chicano Park.
  1989. The Cinema Guild. 60min. $350.

  Gr. 9–12. The life of San Diego's Barrio Logan is examined in historical recollections and in its reemergence in recent decades through a focus on a people's park that symbolizes Chicano pride and heritage.

Living in America: One Hundred Years of Ybor City.
  1987. Filmmakers Library. 55min. $445. Also available in Spanish.

  Gr. 10–12. Attracting Italian, Cuban, and Spanish immigrants, the Tampa community of cigar factories and social clubs is fondly recalled in its pre–World War II heyday.

No Guitar Blues.
  1991. Phoenix/BFA. 27min. $365.

  Gr. 5–7. Fausto Sanchez wrestles with right and wrong in his quest for a longed-for guitar as this dramatization of a Gary Soto story portrays a strong and supportive family that fosters appreciation for its cultural heritage.

Victor.
  1989. Barr Films. 26min. $420.

  Gr. 5–7. Speaking English at school and Spanish at home, fifth-grader Victor bridges the two cultures with the help of his sympathetic teacher and his loving family.

Native Americans

The introduction to this resource list was written by Michael Dorris, a member of the Modoc tribe and the author of A Yellow Raft in Blue Water. *Dorris, who served as an adviser on title selection for the list, discusses the boredom that results when good intentions alone drive the creation of fictional characters. His preference as a child for the Hardy Boys over the reverent, humorless Indians populating much of children's literature is testament to the desperate need to move beyond political correctness. Fortunately, the books on this list do just that.*

THE WAY WE WEREN'T
by Michael Dorris

In the world of contemporary books dealing with American Indians, the road to the unhappy hunting ground is paved with good intentions. Perhaps in reaction to a previous generation's broad categorization of native peoples as savage, dangerous, or just plain odd, the modern approach to tribal societies seems a curious mixture of reverence and caution, with a heavy dollop of mysticism thrown in for ethnic flavor. The reader must search hard for portraits of aboriginal men and women, boys and girls, that afford a complex view or a matter-of-fact attitude toward everyday life, past or present.

Historical Indians seem always teetering on the verge of extrasensory perception. Their dreams prognosticate with an eerie accuracy that any weather reporter would envy. They possess the convenient ability to communicate freely with animals and birds, and they demonstrate a knack for nature-based simile. In the politically correct vocabulary of multiculturalism, Native Americans of whatever tribe or period tend to be an earnest, humorless lot, stiff and instructive as museum diorama.

In other words, quite boring.

As a child, I seldom identified with Indians in books because for the most part they were utterly predictable in their reactions to events. They longed for the past, were solemn paragons of virtue, and were, in short, the last people I would choose to play with. Personally, I preferred the Hardy brothers, Laura in the "Little House" books (though her mother's unrelenting racism toward Indians did give me pause), or other characters with pluck and a penchant for getting into trouble. Indian kids seemed far too busy making pots out of clay or being fascinated by myths about the origin of the universe to be much fun. They didn't remind me of anyone I knew, especially my cousins on the reservation.

The essential artistic issue is one of license. Any group of human beings who—in the opinion of editors, writers, illustrators, or readers—are *supposed* to be only one way or another are at a grave disadvantage as the subjects of literature. To be typecast in advance of introduction in a particular story is to be set in concrete. It's the antithesis of dynamic, the opposite of surprising, the denial of real life, and though young people who hear or read such tales may not be able to articulate this point, they validate it by their nightly reading preferences. If you really don't want to go to bed, you don't choose a book guaranteed to put you to sleep.

In fact, portraying non-Western peoples as dull is worse than bad entertainment: it's counter-productive to the intent of most parents and teachers. We seek to expose our children to other cultures in an effort to educate and encourage tolerance, to pique a lively curiosity, and to promote an appreciation for diversity. This is all fine, as long as the encompassing story is full of nuance and subtlety, as long as our attention is earned, not righteously presumed, and as long as the basic common denominator that underlies all individuals—the delight and dilemma of being complicatedly human—is not lost in the process. Indians in fiction must be people as much as they are *Indian*, for without some primal sense of identification, some attraction toward vicarious emotion, some invitation to shared imagination that spans all the obvious points of distinction between "us" and "them," what began as merely being foreign winds up as dutiful, even forbidding.

"From the pogroms suffered by the Navajo, to the pogroms suffered by the Armenians, to the pogroms suffered by my father's family in Hungary—it was all, essentially, the same. It was one suffering."

—Gerald Hausman

NONFICTION

America in 1492: The World of the Indian Peoples before the Arrival of Columbus.
Ed. by Alvin Josephy, Jr.
1992. Knopf, $35 (0-394-56438-3).

Gr. 9–12. A collection of 17 essays by experts, including Vine Deloria, Jr., N. Scott Momaday, and Peter Nabokov, depicts the diverse lives of the approximately 75 million people living in the Americas around the turn of the fifteenth century. The writers expose the stereotyping and the misshapen collection of largely false, distorted, or half-true images that have defined popular impressions about Indians. With 150 illustrations and maps.

American Indian Myths and Legends.
Ed. by Richard Erdoes and Alfonso Ortiz.
1984. Pantheon, paper, $16 (0-394-74018-1).

Gr. 7–12. To help keep Indian mythology alive, the editors have gathered a sampling of 160 Native American myths and legends, organizing them topically to reflect their cross-tribal connections.

Ashabranner, Brent.
Children of the Maya: A Guatemalan Indian Odyssey.
1986. Putnam, $14.95 (0-399-21707-X).

Gr. 5–12. This moving account, illustrated with photos by Conklin, portrays a group of Mayan Indians who fled oppression in Guatemala and settled in a small town in Florida.

Ashabranner, Brent.
To Live in Two Worlds: American Indian Youth Today.
1984. Putnam, $13.95 (0-396-08321-8).

Gr. 6–12. Words by Ashabranner and photographs by Paul Conklin vividly capture the hopes and fears of Native Americans of high school and college age who strive for success and happiness among a white majority. Also by Ashabranner and Conklin, *Morning Star, Black Sun* tells of the Northern Cheyennes' fight to preserve their land and their culture and their struggle against strip-mining coal companies.

Bierhorst, John.
The Mythology of North America.
1985. Morrow, $13 (0-688-04145-0); paper, $6.95 (0-685-09410-3).

Gr. 6–12. In an overview of Native American mythology, Bierhorst discusses characteristic patterns and themes, defines 11 mythological regions, and examines the sacred stories of each. He shows what unifies the North American myths (especially the sense of kinship between human and nonhuman beings) and identifies what they share with other world mythologies, including the concept of the world flood and the theft of fire. He looks at regional variations in motifs, gods, cultural heroes, and storytelling styles, always emphasizing how myths both reflect and influence people's lives. He also shows how scholarship has changed from the patronizing approach of some early folklorists.

Black Elk.
Black Elk Speaks: Being the Life Story of a Holy Man of the Oglala Sioux. As told through John G. Neihardt.
1932. Univ. of Nebraska, $19.95 (0-8032-3301-9); paper, $9.95 (0-8032-8359-8).

Gr. 8–12. In a book that has become a religious classic, Black Elk, warrior and medicine man of the Oglala Sioux, waiting out his last days on the Pine Ridge Reservation, blends his personal story (from his early boyhood through the Battle of Little Big Horn and the massacre at Wounded Knee) with his sacred vision and with the cry, "O make my people live!" Vine Deloria, Jr., says in his introduction to the recent edition that quite apart from its great effect on non-Indians, "for contemporary young Indians who have been aggressively searching for roots of their own in the structure of universal reality ... the book has become a North American bible of all tribes."

Brown, Dee.
Bury My Heart at Wounded Knee: An Indian History of the American West.
1971. Holt, $18.95 (0-03-085322-2); paper, $14.95 (0-8050-1730-5).

Gr. 9–12. A gripping chronicle of 30 years of conflict between Native Americans and whites. Amy Ehrlich has retold Brown's history in a simpler form for younger readers in *Wounded Knee: An Indian History of the American West.*

Brown, Virginia Pounds and Owens, Laurella.
The World of the Southern Indians.
1983. Beechwood, $15.95 (0-91222-00-3).

Gr. 6–9. Solidly informative, this systematic discussion of southeastern Indian groups (including the Cherokee, Chickasaw, Choctaw, Creeks, and Seminoles) is a good resource on the history and contributions of these peoples.

Bruchac, Joseph.
Native American Stories.
1991. Fulcrum, paper, $9.95 (1-55591-094-7).

Gr. 5–8. Abenaki storyteller Bruchac offers a rich collection of tales from many North American tribes. The stories are written with simplicity and directness, well honed for telling or reading aloud. Mohawk artist John Kohionhes Fadden illustrates each tale with a full-page ink drawing that captures the mystery and shows thematic motifs. A companion volume by the same author and artist is *Native American Animal Stories.*

Crow Dog, Mary and Erdoes, Richard.
Lakota Woman.
1990. Grove Weidenfeld, $18.95 (0-8021-1101-7);
HarperCollins, paper, $9.95 (0-06-097389-7).

Gr. 9–12. Born Mary Brave Bird on South Dakota's Rosebud reservation, the author of this compelling autobiography knew all too soon that to be a "woman of the Red Nation, a Sioux Woman," would not be easy. Raped at 14, she dropped out of school and became an alcoholic and a shoplifter until she found a place for herself in the American Indian Movement and began to rebuild her life. She traveled the trail of broken treaties and gave birth to her first child under fire at besieged Wounded Knee. Now married to the religious leader, Leonard Crow Dog, she continues her struggle for native self-determination. Her direct narrative speaks to the heart.

Curtis, Edward S.
The Girl Who Married a Ghost and Other Tales from the North American Indian.
1978. Macmillan, $12.95 (0-02-709740-4).

Gr. 7–12. Selecting examples from Edward Curtis' monumental 23-year project, *The North American Indian*, a work that has now virtually disappeared, John Bierhorst presents nine tales of varied origins, illustrating them with some of Curtis' own splendid photographs.

Dancing Tepees: Poems of American Indian Youth.
Ed. by Virginia Driving Hawk Sneve.
1989. Holiday, $14.95 (0-8234-0724-1); paper, $5.95
(0-8234-0879-5).

Gr. 5–9. This is a handsomely produced picture-book anthology of tribal songs and prayers as well as short poems by contemporary tribal poets. Illustrator Stephen Gammell draws from the art of native peoples for his detailed drawings and borders, which echo the art of each poet's cultural heritage.

LAKOTA VOICES

"I could never figure out why, in all those Western movies, the Indians are always shown riding around and around these wagons to get themselves shot instead of charging in and counting coup. If we really had been that stupid in those times, there wouldn't be any Sioux left."

—Archie Fire Lame Deer

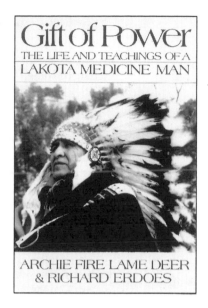

"But you can't live forever off the deeds of Sitting Bull or Crazy Horse. You can't wear their eagle feathers, freeload off their legends. You have to make your own legends now. It isn't easy."

—Mary Crow Dog

Deloria, Vine, Jr.
  Custer Died for Your Sins: An Indian Manifesto.
    1969. Univ. of Oklahoma, paper, $11.95 (0-8061-2129-7).

    Gr. 8–12. A highly critical, ironic attack on America's treatment of the Indians and on all those myths of noble savages and exotic primitives.

Dorris, Michael.
  The Broken Cord: A Family's Ongoing Struggle with Fetal Alcohol Syndrome.
    1989. HarperCollins, $18.95 (0-06-016071-3); paper, $9.95 (0-06-091682-6).

Gr. 7–12. In a heartfelt account, Dorris moves from his personal experience with his adopted son, brain-injured from fetal alcohol syndrome, to a general concern about the large numbers of babies, especially among Native Americans, being born to alcoholic mothers.

Fixico, Donald L.
Urban Indians.
1991. Chelsea House, $19.95 (1-55546-732-6).

Gr. 7–12. Part of the Indians of North America series, this book challenges myths that Indians are "curious vestiges of a distant past" with little role to play in modern civilization. Fixico points out that some Indians lived in cities long before whites came. He outlines the history of fluctuating government policy toward the reservations, especially the ongoing conflict between assimilation and traditionalism. He talks about various relocation programs: how, why, and when Indians have come to the cities; why some make it and some don't; and the stress of living in two worlds.

Freedman, Russell.
Indian Chiefs.
1987. Holiday, $16.95 (0-8234-0625-3).

Gr. 6–12. Haunting old photographs accompany biographical profiles of six renowned Indian chiefs, each of whom guided his people during a critical period in his tribe's history. Also by Freedman, *Buffalo Hunt* shows how the European decimation of the buffalo herds on the Great Plains was an ecological disaster that destroyed the traditional Native American way of life.

Freedman, Russell.
An Indian Winter.
1992. Holiday, $21.95 (0-8234-0930-9).

Gr. 6–12. Based on the 1830s accounts of the German prince/explorer Maximilian and illustrated with sketches and watercolors by his Swiss artist companion, Karl Bodmer, this handsome volume conveys the life and culture of the Mandan Plains Indians through the eyes of European strangers. The Mandan shared their stories and sat for their portraits and invited Maximilian and Bodmer to observe tribal life. Later a smallpox epidemic wiped out most of the tribe.

Goble, Paul.
Love Flute.
1992. Bradbury, $14.95 (0-02-736261-2).

Gr. 3 and up. Rooted in an exquisite legend of the Plains Indians, this picture book is a love story for everyone. A shy young man is given a flute that the birds and animals have made for him. When he plays it, he speaks with the music of nature. Words and pictures convey the lover's yearning and desire and also the thrilling power he gets from the living world around him. As in all Goble's work, his world is both precisely detailed and magically transformed, and fascinating notes and references will help readers to explore further.

"Throughout America, from north to south, the dominant culture acknowledges Indians as objects of study, but denies them as subjects of history. The Indians have folklore, not culture; they practice superstitions, not religions; they speak dialects, not languages; they make crafts, not arts."

—Eduardo Galeano

Green, Rayna.
  Women in American Indian Society.
    1992. Chelsea House, $17.95 (1-55546-734-2).

> Gr. 6–12. Green examines the changing role of women in Native American culture through history. She focuses on ordinary people, from pre-Columbian times through today. An excellent chapter looks at twentieth-century political activists and reformers who are working to restore the Indian culture and foster the artistic and literary voices of their peoples. Poems and other writings are interspersed throughout the text, and illustrations include black-and-white photos, line drawings, and color reproductions. Green is director of the American Indian Program at the National Museum of American History at the Smithsonian.

Hausman, Gerald.
  Turtle Island Alphabet: A Lexicon of Native American Symbols and Culture.
    1992. St. Martin's, $19.95 (0-312-07103-5).

> Gr. 7–12. From *arrow, basket,* and *eagle* to *wolf* and *zig-zag,* Hausman uses the alphabet arrangement to talk about Native American myth, story, symbol, art, theme, and history. The design, with photographs and line drawings, will lure readers to a most attractive collection. The eloquent introduction argues for the way that universal stories connect us all.

Hirschfelder, Arlene B.
  Happily May I Walk: American Indians and Alaska Natives Today.
    1986. Scribner, $13.95 (0-684-18624-1).

> Gr. 6–10. Writing in a clear, fluent style, Hirschfelder takes on a dual role: debunker of the many erroneous assumptions held about Indians, Aleuts, and Inuit and authoritative transmitter of a wealth of factual information about the complexities of contemporary Indian experience.

Hungry Wolf, Adolf and Hungry Wolf, Beverly.
  Children of the Sun: Stories by and about Indian Kids.
    1987. Morrow, paper, $7.95 (0-688-07955-5).

> Gr. 7–12. Recollections of the Hungry Wolf family tradition along with folklore and accounts of childhood adventures come together in a simple, elegant portrait.

Jacobs, Francine.
  The Tainos: The People Who Welcomed Columbus.
    1992. Putnam, $15.95 (0-399-22116-6).

> Gr. 6–9. A well-researched history of the culture and annihilation of the people who first welcomed Columbus in 1492. Without sensationalism, Jacobs describes how "discovery" led to the end of the Tainos' farming way of life and their eventual imprisonment, slavery, and decimation by disease.

Jennings, Francis.
The Invasion of America: Indians, Colonialism and the Cant of Conquest.
1976. Norton, paper, $9.95 (0-393-00830-4).

Gr. 9–12. This eye-opening discussion, both scholarly and lively, challenges European views of history and "savagery" and will make many rethink the accepted views of the encounter between the Puritans and the Indians.

Josephy, Alvin M.
Now That the Buffalo's Gone.
1982. Knopf, $25 (0-0394-46672-1); Univ. of Oklahoma, paper, $15.95 (0-8061-1915-2).

Gr. 8–12. Sensitive profiles of individual tribal groups illustrate the breadth and depth of the Native American struggle, from the early encroachment of whites to such contemporary concerns as racial stereotyping.

Katz, William.
Black Indians: A Hidden Heritage.
1986. Atheneum, $18.95 (0-689-31196-6).

Gr. 7–12. The special contributions and difficulties of individuals of dual Native American and African American heritage are revealed as Katz profiles black Indians in various roles—as soldiers, outlaws, explorers, and western scouts.

Koning, Hans.
Columbus, His Enterprise: Exploding the Myth.
1976. Monthly Review Press, paper, $8.95 (0-85345-825-1).

Gr. 9–12. In his no-holds-barred history of Columbus and his mission, Koning calls on us to abandon our comfortable but false myths and

love flute
Paul Goble

"The Elk Man said, 'All the birds and animals have helped make this flute for you. We have put voices inside it. When you blow it, our harmony will be in your melodies. With the music of this flute you will speak straight to the heart of the girl you love. Your life together will be long, and you will have children.'"

—Paul Goble

to face that the year 1492 opened an era of genocide, cruelty, and slavery on a larger scale than had ever been seen before.

Kroeber, Theodora.
Ishi in Two Worlds: A Biography of the Last Wild Indian in North America.
1976. Univ. of California, $32.50 (0-520-00674-7); paper, $10.95 (0-520-00675-5).

Gr. 9–12. First published in 1961, this is an account of the sole survivor of the California Yana tribe. Kroeber reconstructs the decimation of Ishi's people and his reluctant entry in 1911 into the world of his conquerors.

Lame Deer, Archie Fire and Erdoes, Richard.
Gift of Power: The Life and Teachings of a Lakota Medicine Man.
1992. Bear & Company, $21.95 (0-939680-87-4).

Gr. 7–12. With a rare combination of reverence and humor, and an awareness of both contemporary issues and the enduring Sioux traditions, Lame Deer's candid, chatty autobiography tells of his early life. He grew up with his beloved grandfather on the reservation; ran away from a miserable mission school at 14; had various jobs, including rattlesnake catcher, Hollywood stunt man, and soldier; spent years as an alcoholic and time in jail; and then recovered and worked with rehabilitating others. In the final third of the book, he talks without egotism about his role as medicine man and discusses tribal beliefs, from the sacred Sundance to the Vision Quest.

Lewis, Richard.
All of You Was Singing.
1991. Atheneum, $13.95 (0-689-31596-1).

All ages. A poetic version of an Aztec creation myth tells how music came to Earth; Caldecott-winner Ed Young's illustrations in geometric and swirling patterns utilize strong Aztec imagery.

Medicine Crow, Joseph.
From the Heart of the Crow Country: The Crow Indians' Own Stories.
1992. Crown/Orion, $17 (0-517-58839-0).

Gr. 8–12. An elder of the Crow tribe and the first Crow Indian to earn a graduate degree, Medicine Crow draws on his personal experience, his scholarship, and the stories of the oral tradition to tell the history of his people. This is part of the fine Library of the American Indian series, edited by Herman J. Viola.

Momaday, N. Scott.
The Way to Rainy Mountain.
1969. Univ. of New Mexico, paper, $8.95 (0-8263-0436-2).

Gr. 7–12. In a compelling personal voice, Momaday retells the Kiowa myths he learned from his grandmother and relates them to history, the life he knew as a child, and contemporary experience. Momaday also wrote the novel *House Made of Dawn*.

Native American Testimony: A Chronicle of Indian-White Relations from Prophecy to the Present, 1492–1992.
Ed. by Peter Nabokov.
1991. Viking, $25 (0-670-83704-0).

Gr. 7–12. This anthology of Indian responses to European invasion provides a dramatic perspective on the legacy of Columbus. Powerful narratives record various Indians' impressions of and experiences with whites, including attempts at living together, the travesty of treaty negotiations, and the long exile in their own land.

Ortiz, Simon J.
The People Shall Continue.
1988. Children's Book Press, $12.95 (0-89239-049-2).

Gr. 3 and up. Simply told, this visual history of North America from the point of view of the American Indian shows the continuing struggle against cultural genocide since 1492.

Ortiz, Simon J.
Woven Stone.
1992. Univ. of Arizona, $45 (0-8165-1294-9); paper, $18.95 (0-8165-1330-9).

Gr. 9–12. Ortiz's long introduction about growing up Native American will interest young adults as much as the fine, spare poetry in this large collection. In both, he talks of his pride in himself as a member of the Acoma people and his struggle to reconcile that with his sense of "otherness" in American culture.

Pijoan, Teresa.
White Wolf Woman: Native American Transformation Myths.
1992. August House, $17.95 (0-87483-201-2).

Gr. 7–12. Drawn from a wide range of Indian tribes, the 37 stories in this collection are about animal and human transformation and connection. There are stories about snakes, wolves, bears, and other animals. "Wolf Woman Running" is a powerful tale about a Sioux wife who runs away from her abusive husband and lives with the wolves through eight winters and summers. In "Spirit Eggs," a Cheyenne youth sees his friend changed into Snake Man, guardian of the Mississippi River. The introduction and notes are as good as the stories, with discussion of themes, origins, and where and from whom Pijoan heard each story.

Raven Tells Stories: An Anthology of Alaskan Writing.
Ed. by Joseph Bruchac.
1991. Greenfield Review Press, $12.95 (0-912678-80-1).

Gr. 8–12. A diverse collection of poetry, essays, plays, and short stories by 23 native Alaskan writers. Often the traditional storytelling forms are used with new variations in order to address modern problems. The need to preserve a distinct cultural heritage and the desire to develop personal and moral values are major themes.

Rising Voices: Writings of Young Native Americans.
  Ed. by Arlene B. Hirschfelder and Beverly R. Singer.
    1992. Scribner, $12.95 (0-684-19207-1).

> Gr. 5–8. The voices of young people will speak to readers about how it feels to be Indian "trying to be in harmony with both ways." Organized into sections on identity, family, homelands, ritual and ceremony, education, and harsh realities, the poems, brief essays, and testimonies convey a range of feelings, from pride in the old ways to conflict about the new. A few pieces flash with bitterness. There's a heartbreaking early account by a Chippewa sent away to school for seven years, who comes home a stranger.

The Sacred Path: Spells, Prayers and Power Songs of the American Indian.
  Ed. by John Bierhorst.
    1983. Morrow, $15.95 (0-688-01699-5); paper, $7.95 (0-688-02647-8).

> Gr. 7–12. Seneca, Arapaho, Blackfeet, and Netsilik Eskimo are just a few of the tribes represented in this rich, thematically ordered collection of chants, prayers, and magic spells.

Songs from This Earth on Turtle's Back: Contemporary American Indian Poetry.
  Ed. by Joseph Bruchac.
    1983. Greenfield Review Press, paper, $9.95 (0-912678-58-5).

> Gr. 8–12. Fifty contemporary Indian poets, both the well established and the lesser known—including Paula Gunn Allen, Diane Burns, Joy Harjo, Gordon Henry, N. Scott Momaday, Wendy Rose, Leslie Marmon Silko, and Gerald Vizenor—express a broad and varied view of their experience. Editor Bruchac provides a photograph and brief biography of each poet, and he shows that their sources range from old stories to contemporary political and social issues familiar to any citizen of the "global village."

Vaudrin, Bill.
  Tanaina Tales from Alaska.
    1981. Univ. of Oklahoma, paper, $7.95 (0-8061-1414-2).

> Gr. 9–12. Part of the Civilization of the American Indian series, this collection contains legends and stories told by the Tanaina Indians of southwestern Alaska and collected by a young Chippewa Indian. They are tales of foxes, beavers, wolverines, porcupines, and other animals, some of which disguise themselves as humans for sinister purposes and all of which have human desires and weaknesses.

Waldman, Carl.
  Atlas of the North American Indian.
    1985. Facts On File, $29.95 (0-87196-850-9).

> Gr. 7–12. This handsome, topically organized reference on Native American history and culture covers a wide range of subjects— among them, early explorers, ancient civilizations, life-styles, and land cessions.

Weatherford, Jack.
Indian Givers: How the Indians of the Americas
    Transformed the World.
    1988. Crown, $17.95 (0-517-56969-8); Fawcett, paper, $8.95
        (0-449-90496-2).

    Gr. 8–12. Weatherford talks about the contributions Native
    Americans have made to the modern world, stressing not only
    foods and medicines, but also concepts of egalitarian democracy
    and personal liberty. He elaborates on these ideas in *Native Roots:
    How the Indians Enriched America*, with specific focus on Indian
    contributions to the U.S.

FICTION

Borland, Hal.
When the Legends Die.
    1963. Bantam, paper $3.50 (0-553-25738-2).

    Gr. 9–12. In a powerful story, a Ute boy is separated from his native
    culture after his parents' death. He grows to manhood among
    whites, achieving success as a bronc rider but unable to find peace
    of mind in the non-Indian world.

Craven, Margaret.
I Heard the Owl Call My Name.
    1973. Dell, paper, $3.95 (0-440-34369-0).

    Gr. 7–12. Through his experience working with the Kwakiutl
    Indians of British Columbia, a young priest comes to an acceptance
    of his terminal illness and of the place of death in a universal cycle.

Dorris, Michael.
Morning Girl.
    1992. Hyperion, $12.95 (1-56282-284-5).

    Gr. 5–9. Morning Girl wishes she didn't have a brother, Star Boy,
    until in a moment of shared grief, she suddenly sees him as a
    person. This is a spare, beautiful story of two young people growing
    up in an island community—quarreling, coming together, grow-
    ing strong as they withstand tropical storm and public ridicule.
    Then Columbus "discovers" them.

Dorris, Michael.
A Yellow Raft in Blue Water.
    1987. Holt, $16.95 (0-8050-0045-3); Warner, paper, $8.95
        (0-446-38787-8).

    Gr. 9–12. The spirited voice of 15-year-old half-Indian, half-black
    Rayona leads off an engrossing three-part novel depicting three
    generations of contemporary Indian women who struggle to find
    lives for themselves both on and off the reservation. In his starred
    review of this book, *Booklist* Editor Bill Ott said that it is the women's
    stubbornness that both keeps them apart and allows them to survive.

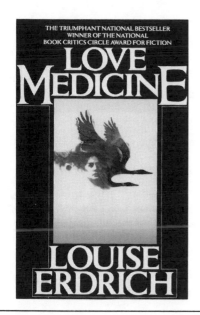

THE TRIUMPHANT NATIONAL BESTSELLER
WINNER OF THE NATIONAL
BOOK CRITICS CIRCLE AWARD FOR FICTION

LOVE MEDICINE

LOUISE ERDRICH

"Even when it started to snow she did not lose her sense of direction. Her feet grew numb, but she did not worry about the distance. The heavy winds couldn't blow her off course. She continued. Even when her heart clenched and her skin turned crackling cold it didn't matter, because the pure and naked part of her went on.

The snow fell deeper that Easter than it had for forty years, but June walked over it like water and came home."

—Louise Erdrich

animal theme

Erdrich, Louise.
Love Medicine.
1984. Holt, $13.95 (0-03-070611-4); Bantam, paper, $9.95 (0-553-34423-4).

Gr. 9–12. There's poetry in the casual talk and a rich sense of character in Erdrich's beautiful interconnected stories that tell of love, survival, loneliness, comedy, and suffering on a North Dakota reservation. *Love Medicine* is the first of a cycle of novels that includes *The Beet Queen* and *Tracks*. Erdrich spoke in a *Booklist* interview of the dark humor in her novels, "a humor about pain and about embarrassment."

George, Jean Craighead.
The Talking Earth.
1983. HarperCollins, $12.95 (0-06-021975-0); paper, $3.50 (0-06-440212-6).

Gr. 6–9. A Seminole girl, challenged by her tribal council for her modern ideas, spends three months alone in the Everglades and learns about herself and her people. The conservation message grows naturally out of the survival adventure story, which is told with simplicity and precision.

George, Julie Craighead.
Julie of the Wolves.
1972. HarperCollins, $15 (0-06-021943-2); paper, $3.95 (0-06-440058-1).

Gr. 6–10. This exciting, Newbery-winning novel tells of a contemporary 13-year-old Eskimo girl who is saved by a wolf pack when she's lost on the tundra.

Hamilton, Virginia.
Arilla Sundown.
 1976. Greenwillow, $13 (0-688-80058-0).

 Gr. 7–10. Twelve-year-old Arilla Adams of mixed black and Indian heritage finds her own importance within a family of unique, contrasting personalities.

Hill, Kirkpatrick.
Toughboy and Sister.
 1990. Macmillan/Margaret K. McElderry, $12.95 (0-689-50506-X).

 Gr. 4–8. Away on a fishing trip in the bush with their father, a young native Alaskan brother and sister learn to survive when their father dies in an alcoholic seizure and they are suddenly left on their own. The combination of survival adventure and family drama makes this a powerful story.

Hillerman, Tony.
Skinwalkers.
 1987. HarperCollins, $19.95 (0-06-015695-3); paper, $4.95 (0-06-080893-4).

 Gr. 8–12. Lieutenant Joe Leaphorn and Officer Jim Chee combine forces to determine if an attempt on Chee's life is related to three recent murders. The rich evocation of Navajo culture and the complex relationship between Leaphorn and Chee give depth and resonance to the novel, part of Hillerman's riveting mystery series.

Hogan, Linda.
Mean Spirit.
 1990. Atheneum, $19.95 (0-689-12101-6).

 Gr. 9–12. This intensely moving historical novel is set in Oklahoma during the 1920s, when the discovery of oil brought sudden wealth to the Osage tribe as well as exploitation by whites and an erosion of tribal cultural values.

Houston, James.
Frozen Fire: A Tale of Courage.
 1977. Macmillan/Margaret K. McElderry, $12.95 (0-689-50083-1); Aladdin, paper, $4.95 (0-689-70489-5).

 Gr. 5–9. Matthew and his friend must survive a struggle through 75 miles of whirling snow and bitter cold when they set out to locate Matt's father, who is lost in the Canadian Arctic. Based on a true ordeal of an Eskimo boy, this dramatic survival adventure also reveals contemporary Eskimo life in transition.

Jones, Douglas C.
Season of Yellow Leaf.
 1983. Tor, paper, $3.95 (0-8125-8450-3).

 Gr. 7–12. Carried off by Comanches at the age of 10, Morfydd is adopted by a chief, who renames her Chosen and instills in her the essence of being Indian.

La Farge, Oliver.
  Laughing Boy.
    1929. NAL, paper, $3.50 (0-451-52244-3).

    Gr. 7–12. Laughing Boy, brought up in the traditional Navajo way, falls in love with embittered Slim Girl, who has returned from the white world and is trying to find her way back to the heart of her people. This book won a Pulitzer Prize.

Lesley, Craig.
  Winterkill.
    1984. Dell, paper, $8.95 (0-685-31260-7).

    Gr. 9–12. In a quietly effective coming-of-age story, which flashes back and forth between generations, a Nez Perce rodeo rider, Danny Kachiah, rescues his son, Jack, from an abusive stepfather and sets out to reestablish their relationship. Lesley is also the author of *River Song*, which continues the story of Danny and Jack, and the coeditor of *Talking Leaves*, discussed below.

Lipsyte, Robert.
  The Brave.
    1991. HarperCollins, $14.95 (0-06-023915-8).

    Gr. 8–12. The fight scenes are great, but the moralizing is heavy-handed in this story about 17-year-old boxer Sonny Bear—part Moscondaga Indian, part white. On the run in New York City, Sonny is helped by Alfred Brooks, the hero of Lipsyte's acclaimed novel *The Contender*, who's now a Manhattan cop.

O'Dell, Scott.
  Sing Down the Moon.
    1970. Houghton, $13.95 (0-395-10919-1); Dell, paper, $3.25 (0-440-97975-7).

    Gr. 6–10. Fifteen-year-old Bright Morning tells of the harsh journey of her Navajo people, who were forced to leave their homes as prisoners in 1864 on the long march to Fort Sumner.

Richter, Conrad.
  A Light in the Forest.
    1953. Knopf, $17.95 (0-394-43314-9); Bantam, paper, $3.50 (0-553-26878-3).

    Gr. 7–12. Kidnapped at the age of four and raised by the Delawares, John Butler returns to his parents but remains irrevocably divided in his heart between his white family and the Indians who molded his youth.

Speare, Elizabeth.
  The Sign of the Beaver.
    1983. Houghton Mifflin, $12.95 (0-395-33890-5); Dell, paper, $3.50 (0-440-47900-2).

> "Chosen had learned by now that Comanche babies didn't cry much. They learned from the start that it did little good. They would be held by their elders when the elders felt it was time to hold them, and not before."
> —Douglas C. Jones

Gr. 5–8. In a survival story set in the Maine wilderness during colonial times, a white boy, Matt, is saved by an old Indian man, Saknis, and his grandson Attean. As friendship slowly grows between the two boys, Matt realizes that his beloved *Robinson Crusoe* story had it all wrong: it is Friday who would have known his way round and been the leader of the white man shipwrecked on the island.

Spider Woman's Granddaughters: Traditional Tales and Contemporary Writing by Native American Women.
Ed. by Paula Gunn Allen.
1989. Beacon, $19.95 (0-8070-8100-0); Fawcett, paper, $11.95 (0-449-90508-X).

Gr. 9–12. A fine Laguna/Sioux poet has collected traditional and contemporary stories by Indian women and organized the stories into sections on Warriors, Casualties, and Resistance. The collection includes great tales from the oral tradition, such as "The Warrior Maiden," and also stories by outstanding writers such as Leslie Marmon Silko, Linda Hogan, Louise Erdrich, and Allen herself.

Talking Leaves: Contemporary Native American Short Stories.
Ed. by Craig Lesley and Katheryn Stavrakis.
1991. Laurel, paper, $10 (0-440-50344-2).

Gr. 9–12. This is a wide-ranging, evocative collection of 38 stories by contemporary American Indian writers. The stories blend traditional and contemporary concerns, focusing on such values as respect for the land and honoring of elders, and the tension these values create in the lives of families torn by abuse, displacement, and despair. All are strikingly rich in narrative voice, as they

"A howl echoed out. A blood-curdling howl reverberated across the land. The howl of freedom flowed from her lips as her body changed into that of a white wolf. Her legs gained strength. Her eyes glowered silver-blue. She loped along the hills to her freedom."

—Teresa Pijoan

celebrate the survival of both tradition and individuality in a constantly shifting culture.

Welch, James.
Winter in the Blood.
1974. Penguin, paper, $7.95 (0-14-008644-7).

Gr. 8–12. A novel about a contemporary young Indian tells of his life shadowed by childhood memories of his brother's death. His soft-spoken but direct narrative avoids sentimentality even as he reveals the suffering of reservation life. Welch is the author of several other novels with Native American themes, including *Fools Crow.*

VIDEOS

Broken Treaties.
1989. Coronet. 33min. $250.

Gr. 7–12. Based on historical records but set in the present, this dramatization of an imaginary trial focuses on the conflict between the U.S. government and Native Americans over territorial treaties and treatment of the Indians.

Ghost Dance.
1990. New Day Films. 9min. $95.

Gr. 9–12. Stills and reproductions, poetic narration, and original music evoke the "ghost dance" performed by Native Americans at Wounded Knee prior to the onslaught of white troops.

The Right to Be Mohawk.
1989. New Day Films. 15min. $250.

Gr. 9–12. Seen on their tribal lands, one group of Mohawks in New York state is resisting the forces of assimilation in their determination to revitalize their cultural heritage.

Welcome Home Hero.
1991. Beacon. 26min. $149.

Gr. 9–12. A shooting accident reverberates through a Native American family as a young man comes to understand the brooding alcoholism and pain that afflicted his war-hero father.

Words on a Page.
1986. Beacon. 28min. $149.

Gr. 5–8. The tension between a talented young student who shows promise as a writer and her father with whom she shares a love of nature is examined in this dramatization set in a contemporary Native American community in Ontario.

THE WIDENING WORLD

In his poem, "Against Borders," the Russian poet Yevtushenko wants to know other places. He wants to use books to see "something else . . . like myself." That's the wonderful paradox of reading: books can tell you about the rich diversity of other people, yet learning about the widening world extends your view of yourself.

Each world area introduced in the various sections of this resource list really requires its own book, with its own multicultural complexities and connections. As with the titles in the Ethnic U.S.A. section, the closer you get, the more diverse each group is shown to be. It's only from very far away that Africa, for example, could ever appear to be one culture. Much more than in the previous chapters, the lists here can in no way be viewed as comprehensive or representative. Their function is simply to introduce a few of the best books by and about people outside the U.S.—books that will interest young readers and widen their worlds.

Because space is limited here and only a few titles can be included for each world area, no books—with the exception of Ashabranner's *Ancient Heritage*—that have already been discussed in the essays have been repeated on these lists. So, for example, *Shabanu* by Suzanne Fisher Staples is not listed with the books on Asia because it's discussed in detail in the essay on Family Matters. (Consult the theme index for a listing of world culture titles examined in the essays.) Note: the Racial Oppression and Ethnic U.S.A. resource lists do list books discussed in the essays.

Overlap, as has been stressed throughout this book, is an inevitability when one groups books around similar themes or characteristics. No book—and certainly no *good* book—is ever only one thing. Literature can't be filed in one place. The point is to make connections, to be fluid not rigid; making one connection should never preclude making another.

INTRODUCTION

A Book of Women Poets from Antiquity to Now.
  Ed. by Aliki Barnstone and Willis Barnstone.
   1980. Schocken, paper, $18 (0-8052-0997-2).

   Gr. 8–12. The many languages of India, China, the Middle East, Africa, Western Europe, and the Americas, among others, are represented in a beautiful, worldwide anthology of poetry written over a period of 4,000 years, starting with "the earliest known writer in the world," Sumerian princess Enheduanna.

Chandler, David P.
  The Land and People of Cambodia.
   1991. HarperCollins, $17.95 (0-06-021129-6).

   Gr. 7–12. This book is in the reliable Land and People series. Each volume in the series is written with verve and authority by someone who knows the country well and who discusses its geography, history, people, language, and culture. Other titles in the series include *The Land and People of Korea* by S. E. Solberg and *The Land and People of Bolivia* by David Nelson Blair.

The Family of Man.
   1955. Rev. ed. Simon & Schuster, $25 (0-671-55412-3); paper, $14.95 (0-671-55411-5).

   All ages. The classic collection of photography created by Edward Steichen for the Museum of Modern Art in New York shows people from birth to death in all parts of the world. In Steichen's words, the emphasis is on "daily relationships." These photographs mirror the "universal elements and emotions in the everydayness of life."

Giblin, James.
  From Hand to Mouth; or, How We Invented Knives, Forks, Spoons, and Chopsticks and the Table Manners to Go with Them.
   1987. HarperCollins, $11.95 (0-690-04660-X).

   Gr. 5–10. This look at eating customs forces you to see your own world like a foreigner; Giblin makes you laugh while he tells you the history of important customs. Kids love the discussion of how arbitrary such concepts as good table manners or proper behavior can be. Giblin has done several fine multicultural books, including *Let There Be Light,* in which he relates history, technology, culture, and design of windows with wit and clarity.

Hearne, Betsy.
  Beauties and Beasts.
   1993. Oryx, $23.50 (0-89774-729-1).

   Gr. 4–12. For kids, storytellers, and teachers, this is part of the fine Oryx Multicultural Folktale Series, which brings together international versions of well-known folktales. The beast can be a dog, a lizard, a bull, or just about any animal familiar to a geographic area. With each story there are notes about origin and culture, and

"Whenever someone suggests 'how much is lost in translation!' I want to say, Perhaps—but how much is gained! A new world of readers, for one thing."

—Naomi Shihab Nye

there's a general introductory essay. Others in the series include *A Knock at the Door* by George Shannon, and *Cinderella*, compiled and edited by Judy Sierra, which has stories from China, France, Germany, England, Ireland, Portugal, Norway, Iceland, Russia, Iraq, Africa, India, North America, Japan, the Philippines, and Vietnam.

Kronenwetter, Michael.
London.

1992. Macmillan/New Discovery, $13.95 (0-02-751050-6).

Gr. 6–12. This is one of the excellent photo-essays in the Cities at War Series. Others in the series are about Amsterdam, Berlin, Leningrad, Paris, and Tokyo. Each book is by a different author, and each concerns what happened to civilians during World War II. Much of kids' fascination with that war lies not in the campaigns and battles but in the lives of ordinary people. What was it like when a bomb fell on your street, or when you had to part from your parents? Each book begins with a background history of the city, and then gives a clear, direct account of the war years. The general overview is supported and enlivened by quotes from eyewitnesses and by stirring documentary photographs that range in subject from burning neighborhoods to individual, frightened faces.

Life Doesn't Frighten Me at All.
Ed. by John Agard.

1990. Holt, $14.95 (0-8050-1237-0).

Gr. 6–12. This highly accessible, contemporary poetry anthology has a strong multicultural focus, and each poet's ethnic identity is given. The great variety of colloquial voices ranges from Jamaican James Berry to Guyanese Agard ("Dem tell me bout Dick Whittington and he cat / But Touissant L'Ouverture / no dem never tell me bout dat"). Also included are such famous poets as Anne Sexton and Gwendolyn Brooks. The anthology will be a most joyful introduction to the lyricism of modern poetry, especially for those who love music.

Love Is Like the Lion's Tooth: An Anthology of Love Poems.
Ed. by Frances McCullough.

1984. HarperCollins, $13.89 (0-06-024139-X).

Gr. 7–12. The cornerstone of this unusual and evocative YA anthology is passion. The selections run the gamut—desire, the intense joy of falling and being in love, romance, ecstasy, jealousy, pain, the sorrow of love lost, adjustment, and, finally, a broader love for the world and its creatures. The scope is international, including several translations, with a range from Sappho to twentieth-century poets, among them Ted Hughes, Denise Levertov, Yehuda Amichai, Robert Bly, Sylvia Plath, and Natalya Gorbanyevskaya.

Meltzer, Milton.
The Amazing Potato: A Story in Which the Incas, Conquistadors, Marie Antoinette, Thomas Jefferson, Wars, Famines, Immigrants, and French Fries All Play a Part.

1992. HarperCollins, $15 (0-06-020806-6).

Gr. 5–8. The subtitle says it all. In clear, entertaining style, Meltzer shows how such an everyday object can be of such vast significance across the world.

Stories from the Days of Christopher Columbus.
Collected and retold by Richard Alan Young and Judy Dockrey Young.
1992. August House, $17.95 (0-87483-199-7); paper, $8.95 (0-87483-198-9).

Gr. 5–12. A good resource collection of stories that were being told in 1492, in Spanish, Taino, Aztec, and other languages across the world. This book includes notes on history, culture, and sources. The stories range from a Taino creation myth to a European folktale and an Aztec story of outcast lovers.

This Same Sky: A Collection of Poems from around the World.
Ed. by Naomi Shihab Nye.
1992. Four Winds, $15.95 (0-02-768440-7).

Gr. 6–12. This is an extraordinary anthology, not only in its range across the globe—129 contemporary poets from 68 countries, their work translated from a wide range of languages—but also in the quality of the selections and the immediacy of their appeal. From Palestine, Argentina, Latvia, Israel, and Lebanon to India, New Zealand, and El Salvador, these diverse voices connect us all. Browsers will dip into this enticing collection, and teachers will find its index by country useful for curriculum units. The brief notes on each contributor include some terse personal anecdotes that are nearly as stirring as the poetry. The translations are casual, even colloquial, getting away from the idea of poetry as something special and exotic.

Why Am I Grown So Cold? Poems of the Unknowable.
Ed. by Myra Cohn Livingston.
1982. Macmillan/Margaret K. McElderry, $14.95 (0-689-50242-7).

Gr. 6–12. Poetry of the eerie, the frightening, and the mysterious from many cultures and countries: fears, nightmares, spells, omens, curses, monsters, ghosts, and fiends that have always intrigued humankind. Use this with Virginia Hamilton's collection of stories *The Dark Way.*

AFRICA

Achebe, Chinua.
Things Fall Apart.
1959. Astor-Honor, $12.95 (0-8392-1113-9); paper, $7.95 (0-8392-5006-1).

Gr. 8–12. This celebrated Nigerian novel portrays traditional Igbo society at the turn of the century and then shows the disruption caused by the European missionaries and colonial officials.

African Folktales: Traditional Stories of the Black World.
Selected and retold by Roger D. Abrahams.
1983. Pantheon, paper, $16 (0-394-72117-9).

Gr. 9–12. From across sub-Saharan Africa, Abrahams has collected a wealth of creation myths, ghosts stories, trickster tales, riddles, and more, and he retells them in many different voices that capture the storytelling tradition. This is part of the excellent Pantheon Fairy Tale and Folklore Library.

African Short Stories.
Ed. by Chinua Achebe and C. L. Innes.
1985. Heinemann, paper, $7.50 (0-435-90536-8).

Gr. 8–12. Twenty stories by contemporary writers across the African continent, including Sembene Ousmane (Senegal), Eskia Mphalele (South Africa), Bessie Head (Botswana), and Ngugi wa Thiong'o (Kenya).

Bascom, William Russell.
African Art in Cultural Perspective.
1973. Norton, paper, $8.95 (0-393-09375-1).

Gr. 8–12. This well-illustrated handbook on the range and varieties of African arts focuses on the sculptural arts through a regional survey.

Dangarembga, Tsitsi.
Nervous Conditions.
1989. Seal Press, paper, $9.95 (0-931188-74-1).

Gr. 9–12. A frank, compelling novel of a young woman growing up in Southern Rhodesia (now Zimbabwe) in the 1960s and 1970s,

---

TWO ZIMBABWEAN AUTHORS

Tsiti Dangarembga

Doris Lessing

trying to escape poverty, sexism, and repressive authority in her family and in the racist society.

Davidson, Basil.
The African Slave Trade, Precolonial History, 1450–1850.
1988. Rev. ed. Little, Brown, paper, $10.95 (0-316-17438-6).

Gr. 8–12. Originally published as *Black Mother*, this classic account focuses on the course and growth of the slave trade and its consequences for Africa.

Emecheta, Buchi.
The Bride Price.
1976. Braziller, paper, $7.95 (0-8076-0951-X).

Gr. 9–12. The tragic story of a modern Nigerian girl, Aku-nna, who rebels against traditional marriage customs and elopes with the schoolmaster she loves, sets personal struggle within the problems of contemporary society.

Fage, J. D.
A History of Africa.
1989. 2d ed. Unwin Hyman, $65 (0-04-445388-4); paper, $21.95 (0-685-29290-8).

Gr. 9–12. A comprehensive history from prehistoric times to the present day, including sections on the impact of Islam and on Africa in the age of European expansion.

Laye, Camara.
The Dark Child.
Trans. by James Kirkup and Ernest Jones. 1954. Farrar, $17.95 (0-8090-1548-X); paper, $6.50 (0-374-50768-6).

Gr. 8–12. This spare, classic autobiography of a French-educated Malinke, whose culture harmonizes Islamic and ancient African traditions, tells of his childhood and youth in French Guinea.

Leakey, Richard E. and Lewin, Roger.
Origins: What New Discoveries Reveal about the Emergence of our Species and Its Possible Future.
1982. Dutton, paper, $8.95 (0-525-48246-6).

An informal, highly visual account of the archaeological research by the author's father, Louis, and others, which supports eastern Africa as the center of origin of the human species.

Lessing, Doris.
African Laughter.
1992. HarperCollins, $25 (0-06-016854-4).

Gr. 8–12. Lessing grew up in Rhodesia, now Zimbabwe, but was exiled from her home for 25 years by the white racist regime. In this memoir, she describes four journeys back to Zimbabwe since independence in 1982. Despite the country's huge problems, she

finds enormous optimism, growth, and commitment in a multiracial society that seems to be working. Also by Lessing is *African
Stories,* her magnificent collection of short fiction.

The Penguin Book of Modern African Poetry.
  Ed. by Ulli Beier and Gerald Moore.
    1984. Viking, paper, $9.95 (0-14-058573-7).

    Gr. 8–12. A valuable anthology of Africa's best-known poets, some
    writing in English, some in translation. Arranged by country.

"Look at Africa
as a continent of
people. They are
not devils, they
are not angels,
they're just
people."

—Chinua Achebe

Timberlake, Lloyd.
  Africa in Crisis: The Causes, the Cures of Environmental Bankruptcy.
    1986. New Society, $39.95 (0-86571-081-3); paper, $16.95
      (0-86571-082-1).

    Gr. 8–12. Bad land management, extreme population pressures,
    misguided foreign aid and development policies, and, in South
    Africa, apartheid's forced resettlements in barren "homelands" are
    among the causes of famine in Africa, states Timberlake, who sees
    in the African peasant the key to the continent's environmental
    health.

ASIA

Aikath-Gyaltsen, Indrani.
  Daughters of the House.
    1993. Ballantine, $16 (0-345-38073-8).

    Gr. 10–12. In a novel of contemporary India, 18-year-old tomboy
    Chchanda tells of her household of three generations of self-suffi-
    cient women and how love, lust, betrayal, and loyalty changes all
    of them.

Alexander, Lloyd.
  The Remarkable Journey of Prince Jen.
    1991. Dutton, $14.95 (0-525-44826-8).

    Gr. 6–9. Prince Jen learns to be a ruler and a man, in this breath-
    taking fantasy, chosen as *Booklist*'s Top of the List winner for
    Children's and Young Adult Fiction in 1991. In the style of Chinese
    storytelling, Alexander's story is rich in characterization and strong
    in lessons about the intricacies of life.

Chang, Margaret and Chang, Raymond.
  In the Eye of War.
    1990. Macmillan/Margaret K. McElderry, $13.95
      (0-689-50503-5).

    Gr. 5–8. Based on Raymond Chang's boyhood in Shanghai during
    World War II, this tells of the hated Japanese occupation through
    the eyes of a child and his family.

Endo, Shusaku.
  When I Whistle.
    Trans. by C. Van Gessel. 1979. Taplinger, paper, $6.95
      (0-8008-8244-X).

    Gr. 8–12. As he watches his son sell himself for success, a father
    remembers how he and a close friend loved the same girl in
    pre–World War II Japan.

Hayslip, Le Ly and Wurts, Jay.
  **When Heaven and Earth Changed Places: A Vietnamese Woman's
  Journey from War to Peace.**
    1989. Doubleday, $18.95 (0-385-24758-3).

    Gr. 10–12. Twenty years ago, living near Da Nang, Hayslip was a
    child guerrilla who endured imprisonment, rape, torture, and
    starvation while fighting for the Viet Cong. In a frank and frighten-
    ing memoir of those terrible times, Hayslip describes how her
    political loyalties came full circle.

Higa, Tomiko.
  **The Girl with the White Flag: An Inspiring Tale of Love and Courage
  in War Time.**
    Trans. by Dorothy Britton. 1991. Kodansha, $16.95
      (4-770-01537-2); Dell, paper, $3.50 (0-440-40720-6).

    Gr. 8–12. In this powerful memoir, Higa recounts her harrowing
    ordeal as a seven-year-old wandering through Okinawa alone in
    1945 at the end of World War II.

Hoobler, Dorothy and Hoobler, Thomas.
  Vietnam: Why We Fought.
    1990. Knopf, $17.95 (0-394-81943-8).

    Gr. 7–12. The Hooblers' abundantly illustrated volume looks at the
    Vietnam War from the broadest perspective. The lucid text is
    accompanied by dozens of dramatic, well-captioned photographs.
    Many are candid battlefield shots that show the war's tragedy on
    the faces of Vietnamese and Americans alike.

Lord, Bette Bao.
  Spring Moon: A Novel of China.
    1981. Avon, paper, $4.95 (0-380-59923-6).

    Gr. 8–12. Lord's novel spans some 80 years, from 1892 to the early
    1970s, and skillfully captures the rich fabric of traditional and
    revolutionary life in China. Spring Moon, though intelligent and
    educated, suffers the bound feet and other traditional bonds of
    Chinese women. Her rebellious daughter takes part in the Long
    March of 1934–35.

Markandaya, Kamala.
  Nectar in a Sieve.
    1954. NAL, paper, $4.95 (0-451-16836-4).

Gr. 8–12. A vivid picture of a changing rural India emerges in the story of Rukmani, a simple peasant girl. Married at the age of 12 to a tenant farmer she has never seen but comes to love, she struggles quietly and courageously against poverty and natural disasters.

Maruki, Toshi.
Hiroshima No Pika.
1982. Lothrop, $14.95 (0-688-01297-3).

Gr. 5–12. Impressionistic paintings and an eloquent realistic account express one child's suffering on the day the atom bomb was dropped on Hiroshima.

Mishima, Yukio.
The Sound of Waves.
Trans. by Meredith Weatherby. 1956. Putnam, paper, $6.95 (0-399-50487-7).

Gr. 9–12. On a remote island of Japan, a rich man forbids the love between his beautiful daughter and a poor, 19-year-old fisherman, Shinji, who eventually proves himself and shows up his spoiled, rich rival.

Paterson, Katherine.
Rebels of the Heavenly Kingdom.
1983. Dutton/Lodestar, $11.95 (0-525-66911-6); Avon/Flare, paper, $2.95 (0-380-68304-0).

Gr. 7–10. A 15-year-old peasant boy, Wang Lee, is caught up in the Taiping Rebellion in China in the 1850s, when hundreds of thousands of the poorest people, fiercely patriotic and imbued with their own version of Christianity, are fighting to free China from the weak and corrupt Manchu regime. The historic uprising is powerfully dramatized in all its fervor and conflict, and so is the individual's tragic perception that the demons are not all on the other side. Also by Paterson are several fine stories set in feudal Japan, including *The Master Puppeteer* and *Of Nightingales that Weep*.

Wang, Anyi.
Baotown.
Trans. by Martha Avery. 1989. Norton, $17.95 (0-393-02711-2).

Gr. 8–12. Baotown is a small, isolated farming village. By tracing the course of a friendship between a small boy named Dregs and an embittered old man named Fifth Grandfather, Wang deftly reveals the connections among all the villagers' lives and shows the reader how similar the world of Baotown is to our own.

Zhensun, Zheng and Low, Alice.
A Young Painter: The Life and Paintings of Wang Yani—China's Extraordinary Young Artist.
1991. Scholastic, $17.95 (0-590-44906-0).

Gr. 4–8. "I do not paint to get praise from others, but to play a game of endless joy," says young Wang Yani, whose life as a child prodigy is captured in this eye-catching book, filled with reproductions of her paintings and photos of the artist at work.

AUSTRALIA AND NEW ZEALAND

Conway, Jill Ker.
Road from Coorain: An Autobiography.
　　1989. Knopf, $19.95 (0-394-57456-7); Random, paper, $8.95
　　　(0-679-72436-2).

　　Gr. 9–12. Historian Conway, the first woman president of Smith College, spent her girlhood on a vast sheep ranch in Australia's outback. In her acclaimed autobiography, she focuses on an eight-year drought that killed her father and left her mother in ruin and hopelessness.

Duder, Tessa.
In Lane Three, Alex Archer.
　　1989. Houghton, $13.95 (0-395-50927-0).

　　Gr. 7–12. Tall, outwardly confident, and unconcerned for the properly feminine, New Zealand swimmer Alex Archer feels straightjacketed in a culture where being feminine means wearing Tangee lipstick and planning a wedding instead of a career. Recollections of her boyfriend's tragic death and her struggle to achieve success despite the strictures of a 1950s New Zealand mingle with a present that finds her swimming—thoughts whirling, heart pounding, muscles aching—toward a critical win that will take her to the 1960 Rome Olympics. Her story continues in *Alex in Rome.*

Klein, Robin.
Coming Back to Show You I Could Fly.
　　1990. Viking, $11.95 (0-670-82901-3).

　　Gr. 5–12. Two desperate misfits become friends: timid, lonely Seymour, 11, oppressed by adults and street bullies, and flamboyant Angie, 20, whose cheery vulgarity masks a helpless grief.

Mahy, Margaret.
Underrunners.
　　1992. Viking, $14 (0-670-84179-X).

　　Gr. 5–8. In a thrilling story of friendship and terror, Mahy makes daily life as weird and scary as science fiction. Every casual word builds a world so convincing that even coincidence seems inevitable. The setting is the end of a wild New Zealand peninsula, where two friends are kidnapped at gunpoint by a menacing stalker, elegant, crazy, and violent. This is a world of connection and disquiet, of innocence lost. Other books by this splendid writer include *The Changeover, Catalogue of the Universe,* and *Memory.*

"Everything around them was still, yet moving within its own stillness. The diving man dived, the underrunners opened grassy lips, crying silently into space, the hovering hawks hung there watching and waiting for prey. Tris galloped, flinging out his arms, breathing in. Winola galloped ahead of him. And in a way there were not one but two Selsey Firebones, set free for the moment to race under the open sky."

—Margaret Mahy

Park, Ruth.
 Playing Beatie Bow.
   1980. Atheneum, $13.95 (0-689-30889-2); Penguin/Puffin, paper, $3.95 (0-14-031460-1).

   Gr. 5–9. Abigail is furious with her divorced parents. She lives in a beautiful high-rise building in Sydney, Australia, designed by her architect father. It's a May evening (nearly winter on that side of the world), and as she wanders in the gathering dusk, forlorn and restless, she sees a scowling waif—as miserable as herself—and follows her through some strange alleyways. Suddenly, Abby finds herself trapped in her Sydney neighborhood 100 years before.

Shute, Nevil.
 A Town Like Alice.
   1950. Ballantine, paper, $4.95 (0-345-35374-9).

   Gr. 9–12. As a British prisoner of the Japanese in World War II Malaya, Jean Paget is helped by Malayans and by an Australian soldier. After the war, she returns to pay her debts and finds romance with the soldier in the Australian outback.

Southall, Ivan.
 Josh.
   1988. Macmillan, $12.95 (0-02-786280-1).

   Gr. 7–10. When 14-year-old Josh comes from Melbourne to visit his strict aunt in a country town, he has a hard time fitting in with her and with the local kids. A funny, poignant, and totally compelling story. Other great books by Southall include *Ash Road* about a huge bush fire.

Taylor, William.
  Agnes the Sheep.
    1991. Scholastic, $13.95 (0-590-43365-2).

    Gr. 5–8. An old woman dies, leaving Agnes—her ornery, con-
    stipated sheep—to Belinda and Joe, who have a hard time keeping
    the animal away from the various friends and relations who want
    to make it into sausages and blankets. A wry, off-the-wall original.
    Taylor's latest book, *Knitwits,* is just as funny.

Ward, Glenyse.
  Wandering Girl.
    1991. Holt, $14.95 (0-8050-1634-1); Ballantine, paper, $3.99
      (0-449-70414-9).

    Gr. 5–10. In her own words, aboriginal Ward remembers how at
    16 she was forced to work as a live-in servant for a wealthy, vicious
    white mistress. She suffers racism, social isolation, and endless
    drudgery until her final rebellion and escape. The oral history
    needs editing, but Ward's detailed account creates an authentic
    world. In a brief introduction and epilogue, she tells of her life
    before and after her years as a "dark servant," and she relates her
    personal experience to the struggle of her people.

Wrightson, Patricia.
  Balyet.
    1989. Macmillan/Margaret K. McElderry, $12.95
      (0-689-50468-3); Penguin/Puffin, paper, $3.95
      (0-14-034339-3).

    Gr. 5–9. Based on an aboriginal Australian legend, this tells of a
    contemporary teenager who falls under the spell of Balyet, a girl
    of the hills who was banished a thousand years ago.

CANADA

Atwood, Margaret.
  The Handmaid's Tale.
    1986. Fawcett, paper, $5.95 (0-449-21260-2).

    Gr. 10–12. In a terrifying novel of a near-future society ruled by
    racism, misogyny, and religious fundamentalism, a 33-year-old
    woman tells how she is forced to serve one of the ruling com-
    manders and bear his child.

Burnford, Sheila.
  The Incredible Journey.
    1961. Bantam, paper, $3.50 (0-553-27442-2).

    Gr. 5–12. This is a classic animal survival story about three pets—a
    Labrador retriever, an old bull terrier, and a Siamese cat—who
    make their way home through 250 miles of Canadian wilderness.
    Alone they wouldn't have made it, but, together, they survive.

Brooks, Martha.
Paradise Café and Other Stories.

1990. Little, Brown/Joy Street Books, $14.95 (0-316-10978-9).

Gr. 7–12. The title story and "A Boy and His Dog" are particularly strong in this fine YA short story collection. Also by Brooks is the YA novel *Two Moons in August*, which interweaves themes of friendship, grief, and love.

Craven, Margaret.
I Heard the Owl Call My Name.

1973. Dell, paper, $3.95 (0-440-34369-0).

Gr. 7–12. Through his experience working with the Kwakiutl Indians of British Columbia, a young priest comes to accept his terminal illness and the place of death in a universal cycle.

Eckert, Allan W.
Incident at Hawk's Hill.

1971. Little, Brown, $14.95 (0-316-20866-3); Dell, paper, $1.95 (0-440-94020-6).

Gr. 6–12. Based on a true story, this beautifully written survival adventure follows a six-year-old boy who gets lost on the Canadian prairie in 1870 and is cared for by a female badger in her burrow.

Ellis, Sarah.
Pick-up Sticks.

1992. Macmillan/Margaret K. McElderry, $13.95 (0-689-50550-7).

Gr. 5–8. "Why did you choose [to be a single mother] if you can't even do it right?" Polly feels embarrassed and anxious about her unconventional life-style with her single-parent, artist mother. Still, a few months spent with her rich relatives in their home humming

"He was one of the handsomest boys I'd ever seen. Somebody said he was part Indian, and with his powerful dark good looks and eyes blue and brooding as thunderclouds, I thought of him as some kind of bird god in disguise. . . . He didn't rent those metal skates the skinny key boys would fit, then clamp, to your runners. He wore his own boot skates made of richly glowing leather, and he was king of the roller rink."

—Martha Brooks

with both appliances and tension send Polly back to the shabby muddle of her mother's studio. With no simplistic messages, this is a sharp and affectionate novel of the way we live now.

Huggan, Isabel.
The Elizabeth Stories.
1987. Penguin, paper, $8.95 (0-14-010199-3).

Gr. 9–12. "I felt picked on, awkward, unloved, and ugly"—misfit Elizabeth discovers secrets, sex, and violence in herself as well as in those around her. Many of the stories in Huggan's frank, sophisticated collection about growing up in a small Canadian town have appeal for teenagers. Especially powerful is "Celia Behind Me," which captures the fear of being the outsider, a fear that can drive you to cruelty.

Malcolm, Andrew H.
The Land and People of Canada.
1991. HarperCollins, $17.95 (0-06-022494-0).

Gr. 6–12. In the fine Land and People series, this lively account by a dual citizen of Canada and the U.S. gives details of geography, way of life, politics, etc. Malcolm discusses how Canadians feel about their sometimes overbearing neighbor.

Paulsen, Gary.
Hatchet.
1987. Bradbury, $14.95 (0-02-770130-1); Penguin/Puffin, paper, $3.95 (0-14-032724-X).

Gr. 5–9. In one of the great survival adventure stories, Brian must cope alone in the Canadian wilderness with only a hatchet to help him find food and shelter. He finds strength he didn't know he had.

Robinson, Margaret A.
A Woman of Her Tribe.
1990. Scribner, $12.95 (0-684-19223-3).

Gr. 7–12. Half Nootka Indian, half English, 15-year-old Annette has lived all her life in her father's Nootka village on Vancouver Island. But when she receives a scholarship to an English-style academy in Victoria, she must try to reconcile the competing claims of her two heritages.

Wilson, Budge.
The Leaving.
1992. Putnam/Philomel, $14.95 (0-399-21878-5).

Gr. 6–10. The best of these short stories about teenage girls growing up in Nova Scotia capture turning points, sudden insights that kids will recognize—the moment when sexual attractiveness changes the power structure among girls, the rivalry between friends that leads to betrayal and self-betrayal, the blind rage against bossy authority.

CARIBBEAN AND SOUTH AMERICA

Allende, Isabel.
The House of the Spirits.
1985. Knopf, $24.50 (0-394-53907-9); paper, Bantam, $4.95 (0-553-25865-6).

Gr. 10–12. Rich in local detail, this family novel by the niece of the slain Chilean president tells of relatives, friends, and lovers split apart in the political turmoil as their country moves to military dictatorship.

Ashabranner, Brent.
Children of the Maya: A Guatemalan Indian Odyssey.
1990. Putnam/Philomel, $14.95 (0-399-21707-X).

Gr. 7–12. Ashabranner interviews the Mayan immigrants in a Florida community who discuss why they fled their country, how they endured the harsh journey through Mexico to the U.S., and how they struggle to maintain a sense of their culture and make a place for themselves. Paul Conklin's photographs intensify the humanity of the stories.

Berry, James.
When I Dance.
1991. HBJ, $15.95 (0-15-295568-2).

Gr. 5–9. This collection featuring the vernacular of two diverse places includes poems set in inner-city Britain, poems set in Jamaica, and poems that establish the close relationship between the two locations. Among the best are "Breath Pon Wind" about street gangs and "Let Me Rap You My Orbital Map."

Bierhorst, John.
The Mythology of South America.
1988. Morrow, $15.95 (0-688-06722-0).

Gr. 9–12. Dividing the continent into seven regions, Bierhorst discusses the types of myths (such as creation stories and trickster tales) common to the area, how they've traveled and changed, and their political significance throughout history. He includes handsome illustrations of masks, pottery, and other crafts. Bierhorst's other titles include *Black Rainbow: Legends of the Incas and Myths of Ancient Peru* and *The Mythology of Mexico and Central America.*

Blair, David Nelson.
Fear the Condor.
1992. Dutton/Lodestar, $15 (0-525-67381-4).

Gr. 7–12. Set in Bolivia in the 1930s, this novel concerns an Aymaran Indian girl, Bartolina, who is part of a community of tenant laborers forced to work for the ruling Hispanic *patron.* The historical details are sometimes hard to follow, but Bartolina is a

"That the native does not like the tourist is not hard to explain. For every native of every place is a potential tourist, and every tourist is a native of somewhere. . . . Every native would like to find a way out, every native would like a rest, every native would like a tour."

—Jamaica Kincaid

well-realized personality, rooted in her culture yet also questioning it. Blair also wrote *The Land and People of Bolivia*.

Hanmer, Trudy J.
Haiti.
1988. Watts, $12.40 (0-531-10479-6).

Gr. 5–9. In this impressive political history that examines the color, drama, comedy, and tragedy of the poorest nation in the Western Hemisphere, Hanmer looks at how poverty and racism pervade every aspect of daily life for the majority of Haitians.

Hauptly, Denis J.
Puerto Rico: An Unfinished Story.
1991. Atheneum, $13.95 (0-689-31431-0).

Gr. 6–10. A lawyer with the first circuit court, which includes Puerto Rico in its jurisdiction, Hauptly presents an astute history of the island from prehistoric times through the present day. He emphasizes how manipulation by colonial powers, most notably Spain and the U.S., has impeded the surge for Puerto Rican independence.

Hodge, Merle.
For the Life of Laetitia.
1993. Farrar, $15 (0-374-32447-6).

Gr. 5–9. Rooted in Caribbean culture and language in all their rich diversity, this novel celebrates place and community even as it confronts divisions of race, class, and gender. Laetitia is the first person from her rural extended family to make it to secondary

---

Isabel Allende

"In the U.S., writers are not supposed to mingle in politics. In my continent, in Latin America, that's impossible. I'm not talking just about recent events in Chile, not just about this generation that has lived through a military coup. Before all that things were the same. The situation in our continent is so terrible—the violence, the poverty, the inequality, the misery—that writers have necessarily assumed the voice of the people. What else can they write about? If they want to represent somebody, what else can they write about?"

—Isabel Allende

school. Everyone is jubilant for her, but she nearly breaks under the conflicts she must confront. The vivid characterization combines a sense of the ridiculous, which brings the pompous down to size, with a heartbreaking vision of lost potential.

Hoobler, Thomas and Hoobler, Dorothy.
Touissant L'Ouverture.
1990. Chelsea House, $17.95 (1-55546-818-7).

Gr. 6–12. This is a biography of L'Ouverture, a slave who, influenced by the ideals of the French Revolution, led his people to freedom in Saint Dominique (Haiti). The authors' style of this series volume is pedestrian, but the inherent drama of L'Ouverture's life will involve readers.

Joseph, Lynn.
A Wave in Her Pocket: Stories from Trinidad.
1991. Clarion, $13.95 (0-395-54432-7).

Gr. 3–8. Full of magic and suspense, six tales combine Trinidad's traditional folklore with a young person's view of island life. Joseph skillfully employs a tale-within-a-tale structure, and there's an understated tenderness between the girl and her grandaunt, who has a story for every occasion. Brian Pinkney's distinctive drawings in white crosshatch on a black background echo the mysterious side of the island stories.

Kincaid, Jamaica.
A Small Place.
1988. Farrar, $13.95 (0-374-26638-7).

Gr. 9–12. With her fury contained in spare, spitting prose, Kincaid, who was born and raised on the island of Antigua, attacks tourists who treat local people as exotica. Teenage readers will find this vitriolic essay both passionate and thought provoking.

The Magic Orange Tree and Other Haitian Folktales.
Collected by Diane Wolkstein.
1978. Schocken, paper, $14.95 (0-8052-0650-7).

Gr. 5–9. With zest and humor, Wolkstein tells 27 tales she collected while traveling through Haiti. She includes lively notes about each story, how she heard it, and its relation to European and African counterparts. "In almost every story in this collection," she says, "the background of hunger and survival exists, but there is also the humor."

Mohr, Nicholasa.
Going Home.
1986. Dial, $13.95 (0-8037-0269-8)); Bantam/Skylark, paper, $2.95 (0-553-15699-3).

Gr. 4–7. Twelve-year-old New Yorker Felita, on her first visit to her beloved Abuelita's town in the Puerto Rican mountains, struggles

"It takes you all your life to write the way you speak without faking it."

—Derek Walcott

with being an outsider. This is a convincing story that captures the universality of preteen relationships.

Rhys, Jean.
Wide Sargasso Sea.
1967. Norton, paper, $5.95 (0-393-00056-7).

Gr. 10–12. Set in Dominica and Jamaica during the 1830s, this small, searing novel tells the story of the first Mrs. Rochester, the mad wife in *Jane Eyre*. Rhys imagines what drove a sensitive Creole girl to her prison in the attic.

EASTERN EUROPE

Afanas'ev, Alexsandr.
Russian Folk Tales.
Trans. by Robert Chandler. 1980. Random, $14.95 (0-87773-195-0).

Gr. 4–12. Baba Yaga, Koschev the Deathless, and Vasilisa the Beautiful are some of the characters in this collection of traditional stories collected by a great nineteenth-century Russian folklorist. Drawing heavily on folk arts, the opulent color illustrations by Ivan Bilibin, a Russian illustrator of the late nineteenth century, extend the depth and drama of the stories.

Atkinson, Linda.
In Kindling Flame: The Story of Hannah Senesh, 1921–1944.
1985. Lothrop, $14.95 (0-688-02714-8).

Gr. 7–12. From her Hungarian childhood and life in Palestine to her return to her homeland and her death at the hands of Nazis, this biography of the brave young resistance fighter draws on her personal diary as well as giving historical background about the Holocaust and the war.

Degens, T.
Transport 7-41-R.
1974. Penguin/Puffin, paper, $3.95 (0-14-034789-5).

Gr. 6–8. This intense story is cast as a 13-year-old German girl's account of what it was like leaving the Russian front during World War II and traveling aboard a train packed with evacuees bound for Cologne.

Fluek, Toby.
Memories of My Life in a Polish Village, 1930–1949.
1990. Knopf, $19.95 (0-394-58617-4).

Gr. 7–12. Illustrating her text with her own luminous paintings and drawings, Fluek moves with powerful simplicity through the details of her Jewish prewar life, her struggle to survive Nazi occupation, and her eventual emigration.

Hautzig, Esther.
The Endless Steppe: Growing Up in Siberia.
1968. HarperCollins/Crowell, $13.95 (0-690-26371-6); paper,
$3.50 (0-06-447027-X).

Gr. 6–12. Written with powerful simplicity, this personal memoir
chronicles Hautzig's years from 10 to 14 as a Polish deportee with
her mother and grandmother in a remote, impoverished Siberian
village during World War II.

Holman, Felice.
The Wild Children.
1983. Scribner, $14.95 (0-684-17970-9); Penguin/Puffin,
paper, $4.95 (0-14-031930-1).

Gr. 7–10. The *bezprizoni* were packs of homeless young people who
roamed Russia in the early 1920s in the aftermath of world war,
revolution, civil war, and famine. In a fine novel, Holman focuses
on Alex, who becomes part of a gang that helps him to survive.

Singer, Isaac Bashevis.
The Certificate.
Trans. by Leonard Wolf. 1992. Farrar, $22 (0-374-12029-3).

Gr. 9–12. Poignant and comic, skeptical and passionate, Singer is
at his best in this story of 18-year-old David Bendiger, who arrives
in Warsaw from the shtetl penniless and lonely. David's search for
love, work, and meaning will touch teenage readers profoundly.

Solzhenitsyn, Alexander.
One Day in the Life of Ivan Denisovich.
Trans. by Ronald Hingley and Max Hayward. 1963. Farrar,
$24.95 (0-374-22643-1); paper, $12.95 (0-374-52195-6).

Gr. 9–12. Condemned by the Stalinist government to forced labor
in Siberia, a man suffers through a day at the camp, using various
rituals and devices to preserve his life and sanity. Translated from
the Russian, this famous autobiographical novel is told with an
almost humdrum simplicity that heightens the suffering.

Strom, Yale.
A Tree Still Stands: Jewish Youth in Eastern Europe Today.
1990. Putnam/Philomel, $16.95 (0-399-22154-9).

Gr. 6–12. An elegaic tone pervades these photo-essays of contemporary Jewish young people, age 7 to 20, in East Germany, Poland,
Czechoslovakia, Russia, Bulgaria, Yugoslavia, and Hungary. All are
descendants of parents and grandparents who somehow managed
to survive the Holocaust.

GREAT BRITAIN

Bawden, Nina.
Henry.
1988. Lothrop, $13.95 (0-688-07894-X); Dell, paper, $3.25
(0-440-40309-X).

Gr. 5–8. During World War II, a London family has escaped the Blitz
to live on a farm in Wales for three years. They love the farm, though
they miss their father, who is on dangerous patrol duty at sea. They
adopt a tiny squirrel, who's been tipped out of his nest, just as they've
been. They call him Henry, and he becomes their pet, sleeping in the
living-room and treating people like trees. Other great books by this
splendid writer include *Carrie's War* and *Humbug.*

Conlon-McKenna, Marita.
Under the Hawthorn Tree.
1990. Holiday, $13.95 (0-8234-0838-8).

Gr 5–7. Winner of the International Reading Association Children's
Book Award, this novel tells the story of Peggy O'Driscoll, whose
parents die during the Great Famine in Ireland in the late 1840s.
The potatoes are rotting; starvation and disease are everywhere.
Peggy walks with her older brother and sisters in search of food
and a home. The sense of the desperate time is strong and authentic.

Cross, Gillian.
On the Edge.
1984. Holiday, $13.95 (0-8234-0559-1); Dell, paper, $2.75
(0-440-96666-3).

Gr. 7–10. When this powerful thriller opens, Tug has been out
running. As he comes back to his London house and unlocks the
front door, he feels uneasy. "Dark! The house was too dark! . . . And
there was something else . . . He stretches out his hand towards the
light switch . . ." Tug is kidnapped and held captive by a strange couple
in a remote house on the moor. They tell him they're his mother and
father, and they play mind-games with him, so that he begins to doubt
his own perceptions and his memories. Also by Cross, *Chartbreaker.*

Howker, Janni.
The Nature of the Beast.
1985. Greenwillow, $10.25 (0-688-04233-3).

Gr. 7–12. Teenager Billy hunts a wild, marauding beast on the
moors near his home. But part of him secretly wants to be like the
beast: powerful, angry, and outside the society that has made his
unemployed father and grandfather raging and bitter. Howker's
books are all set in the north of England, including her fine story
collection *Badger on the Barge and Other Stories.*

Kronenwetter, Michael.
Northern Ireland.
1990. Watts, $13.90 (0-531-10942-9).

"The words had
magic in them,
the sound of
incantation and
harpsong . . . I
woke up, as
though I had
been dreaming,
and found my
own world not
quite the same
as it had been
before."

—Rosemary
Sutcliff

Gr. 7–12. With his usual combination of fairness and concern, Kronenwetter takes on the controversial subject of the Irish "Troubles." Stressing that the past is very much alive in Ireland now, he devotes several detailed chapters to the roots of the present bitterness and violence. Then he deals with contemporary religion, politics, and power; the role and support of the various terrorist groups; and the troubled relations with Britain. He offers no solutions but treats his subject with bleak candor.

Llewellyn, Richard.
How Green Was My Valley.
1940. Macmillan, $35 (0-02-573420-2); Dell, paper, $4.95 (0-685-53211-9).

Gr. 7–12. In a classic novel rooted in Wales, the son of a miner remembers how the mines destroyed the countryside and how unemployment and economic insecurity affected his family and community.

Mayne, William.
Gideon Ahoy!
1989. Delacorte, $13.95 (0-385-29692-4).

Gr. 5–12. This is a superb novel, both anguished and absurd. Seventeen-year-old Gideon, deaf and brain injured, has grown up happy and protected in his Yorkshire family, but when he takes off on a journey down the local canal, he goes through fire and water to remake himself—and nearly dies in the process. His story is told with humor and imaginative sympathy by his younger sister, Eva.

O'Brien, Edna.
The Country Girls Trilogy and Epilogue.
1986. Farrar, $18.95 (0-374-13027-2).

Gr. 10–12. These three novels were originally published in 1960, 1962, and 1964. Both comic and melancholy, they begin with the story of two friends growing up in Ireland. The young women leave their country village in search of love and freedom, but find themselves trapped by their dream.

Sutcliff, Rosemary.
The Shining Company.
1990. Farrar, $13.95 (0-374-36807-4); paper, $4.95 (0-374-46616-5).

Gr. 7–12. Sutcliff's lyrical war story of glory, comradeship, and betrayal draws readers into the desolate landscape of seventh-century Britain, where young Prosper and his companions ride out to meet and hold off the enemy Saxons. Sutcliff's historical novels of early Britain are all filled with poetry and action.

Townsend, Sue.
The Secret Diary of Adrian Mole, Aged 13 ¾.
1986. Avon, paper, $3.95 (0-380-86876-8).

Gr. 6–12. "There is a new girl in our class. She sits next to me in Geography. She is all right . . . I might fall in love with her." Adrian Mole would like to be an intellectual, but he has all kinds of problems, with his acne, his girlfriend, and his parents.

Ure, Jean.
You Win Some, You Lose Some.

1986. Delacorte, $14.95 (0-385-29434-4); Dell, paper, $2.95 (0-440-99845-X).

Gr. 7–10. Jamie Carr has come to London to win a place in a prestigious ballet school and to find a girlfriend, but his romantic dreams about the girls in his class don't quite work out.

Walsh, Jill Paton.
Grace.

1992. Farrar, $16 (0-374-32758-0).

Gr. 9–12. This dramatic novel is based on the life of Grace Darling, the young English woman who became a national celebrity in 1838 when she rowed out with her father from their lighthouse in a raging storm to save the survivors of a shipwreck. Walsh tells the story in Grace's voice, evoking both the physical reality of the cramped lighthouse and Grace's inner struggle against the beating storm of public attention that wrecks her life. Walsh also wrote *Fireweed,* about two teenagers who find each other when they refuse to evacuate from London during the World War II blitz.

Westall, Robert.
The Machine Gunners.

1976. Greenwillow, $11.88 (0-688-84055-8); McKay, paper, $3.50 (0-679-80130-8).

Gr. 5–9. After an air raid in the north of England during World War II, a group of young people take a machine gun from a crashed German plane; they build a secret place for the gun and prepare to use it. Other great World War II books by Westall include *Fathom Five* and *Children of the Blitz: Memories of Wartime Childhood.*

MIDDLE EAST

Abinader, Elmaz.
Children of the Roomje: A Family's Journey.

1991. Norton, $19.95 (0-393-02952-2).

Gr. 9–12. The author's parents immigrated to the U.S. from a small Lebanese village, and her memoir is about the memories of Lebanon, the journeys back, and the struggles in a new country. Abinader poetically evokes the Lebanese landscape with a great deal of feeling for the history of Lebanon and her people in the early part of the twentieth century.

Amichai, Yehuda.
The Selected Poetry of Yehuda Amichai.
Trans. by Chana Bloch and Stephen Mitchell. 1986.
HarperCollins, $22.95 (0-06-055001-5).

Gr. 9–12. Colloquial, sometimes direct, sometimes complex poems in translation by one of Israel's leading poets.

Arab Folktales.
Ed. by Inea Bushnaq.
1986. Pantheon, paper, $14 (0-394-75179-5).

Gr. 5 and up. Elegant, engaging prose, beautiful book design, and fastidious research of printed sources highlight this definitive collection for students of folklore, both teen and adult. Each group of tales is preceded by an informative and detailed introduction; groupings include Bedouin, Djinn (spirit), Djuha (fools), religious tales, and tales of magic, wit, and guile.

Ashabranner, Brent.
An Ancient Heritage: The Arab-American Minority.
1991. HarperCollins, $14.95 (0-06-020048-0).

Gr. 5–10. With a warming combination of personal involvement and unobstrusive background research, Ashabranner bases his book on informal interviews with a wide variety of Arab Americans. He includes a brief history of their culture and of their immigration to this country. (Since this is one of the few outstanding books about Arab Americans, it is discussed here as well as in the essay on The Perilous Journey.) Also by Ashabranner is *Gavriel and Jemal: Two Boys of Jeursalem* about one Palestinian and one Israeli boy who share a dedication to family learning and religion—and a heritage of suspicion and violence.

"I'm an American, but I let people know about my Lebanese background. Arab Americans are a part of the ethnic quilt that Jesse Jackson talks about, just like blacks and Hispanics, Indians and Asians, but the media has painted a terrible picture of Arabs—nothing but greedy oil billionaires, terrorists, playboy sheiks, and rug peddlers."

—Casey Kassem, disc jockey,
from *An Ancient Heritage*

Beshore, George.
  Science in Early Islamic Culture.
    1988. Watts, $10.40 (0-531-10596-2).

      Gr. 5–7. Throughout this straightforward and clearly written entry
      in the First Book series, Beshore emphasizes the role of Islamic
      scientists (Arab and non-Arab) in building upon the intellectual
      heritage of the Greeks and in developing the scientific method.
      Original, often brilliant contributions in astronomy, mathematics,
      medicine, geography, physics, and optics are duly noted.

Biographical Dictionary of the Middle East.
  Ed. by Yaacov Shimoni.
    1992. Facts On File $40 (0-8160-2458-8).

      Gr. 6–12. This ready-reference tool provides biographical sketches of
      approximately 500 major twentieth-century Middle Eastern figures.
      Included are heads of governments, party leaders, kings, and religious
      and military leaders, as well as a few writers and journalists. The focus
      is on political, rather than personal, information.

Farman Farmaian, Sattareh and Munker, Dona.
  **Daughter of Persia: A Woman's Journey from Her Father's Harem
    through the Islamic Revolution.**
    1992. Crown, $22 (0-517-58697-5).

      Gr. 9–12. Though Farman Farmaian was born and raised in a
      traditional Muslim family, her father was passionately committed
      to education and chose to ignore many of the Muslim restrictions
      for girls. Sattereh became a strong-willed, independent thinker,
      determined to help Iran's poor as her country was rocked by coups,
      bullied by oil-mad Westerners, and sucked dry by the shah. Even-
      tually her reform work angered Ayatollah Khomeini's followers,
      and she had to flee for her life.

Grossman, David.
  The Yellow Wind.
    Trans. by Haim Watzman. 1988. Farrar, $17.95
      (0-374-29345-7); Dell, paper, $9.95 (0-385-29736-X).

      Gr. 9–12. In a grim, melancholy account translated from the
      Hebrew, a young Israeli writer describes his 1987 journey to the
      Palestinian camps and Jewish settlements on the West Bank, as he
      probes his people's role in the occupied territories. Grossman says
      that he belongs to the generation that celebrated its bar mitzvah
      during the Six Day War.

Heide, Florence Parry and Gilliland, Judith Heide.
  Sami and the Time of Troubles.
    1992. Clarion, $14.95 (0-395-55964-2).

      Gr. 2 and up. A child caught up in the terror of civil war: that's the
      subject of this compelling picture book illustrated by Ted Lewin,
      which will have much to say to older readers. Firmly rooted in the lives
      of a family in Beirut, this quiet story reminds us of other "troubles,"
      whether in Northern Ireland or in Eastern Europe's ethnic crossfire.

Hiçyilmaz, Gaye.
Against the Storm.
　1992. Little, Brown/Joy Street Books, $14.95 (0-316-36078-3).

　　Gr. 6–12. In a story of contemporary Turkey, 12-year-old Mehmet's family moves from the village to the city in search of a better life, but they end up in a dusty shantytown where they slowly lose courage and hope. Mehmet breaks free and makes his way back to the village, holding on to his humanity and his sense of himself.

Laird, Elizabeth.
Kiss the Dust.
　1992. Dutton, $15 (0-525-44893-4).

　　Gr. 6–10. A fast-paced refugee adventure story about a Kurdish teenager, Tara Hawrami, and her family caught up in the Iran-Iraq war in 1984. When oppression touches their middle-class home, the Hawramis escape the secret police over the garden wall, live through bombing raids in the mountains, endure a series of harsh refugee camps, and finally find asylum in Britain.

Levitin, Sonia.
The Return.
　1987. Atheneum, $13.95 (0-689-31309-8); Fawcett, paper,
　　$2.95 (0-449-70280-4).

　　Gr. 6–10. In this vivid and compelling novel, Desta, a Falasha (Ethiopian Jew), despised and ill-treated by the local people, undertakes an arduous journey with her family toward a new home in Israel.

Mahfouz, Najib.
Palace Walk.
　Trans. by William M. Hutchins with Olive E. Kenny. 1990.
　　Doubleday, $22.95 (0-385-26465-8).

　　Gr. 10–12. Translated from the Arabic, this first volume of a trilogy will interest teens. The emotional and physical struggles of three generations of a Cairo middle-class family in the first half of the twentieth century are depicted with sympathy and honesty. There's a focus on the torments of adolescent love as well as on the banked passions of an established marriage. Nobel Prize–winner Mahfouz re-creates the daily life of his characters in rich detail.

Oz, Amos.
In the Land of Israel.
　Trans. by Maurie Goldberg-Bartura. 1983. Random, paper,
　　$9 ((0-394-72728-2).

　　Gr. 8–12. In a series of articles translated from the Hebrew, Israeli novelist Oz describes his two-month journey in 1982 through Israel and the West Bank, revealing the complex and tragic truth he found.

Shaaban, Bouthaina.
Both Right and Left Handed: Arab Women Talk about Their Lives.
　1991. Indiana Univ., $35 (0-253-35189-8); paper, $12.95
　　(0-253-20688-X).

Gr. 9–12. In this brave and eloquent book, Shaaban, a Syrian disowned by her family for marrying without their consent, weaves her own story together with those of other women of Syria, Lebanon, Palestine, and Algeria to form a tapestry of frustration and hope. A stereotype-shattering look at the lives of Arab women.

WESTERN EUROPE

Boissard, Janine.
Christmas Lessons.
 Trans. by Mary Feeney. 1984. Little, Brown, $15.95 (0-316-10097-8).

 Gr. 9–12. Told from the point of view of 18-year-old budding writer Pauline Moreau, the third of four daughters, this is a gentle, "slice-of-life" novel, one of a series about a warm, upper middle-class French family whose members sustain each other through some painful times.

Finkelstein, Norman H.
Captain of Innocence: France and the Dreyfus Affair.
 1991. Putnam, $15.95 (0-399-22243-X).

 Gr. 7–12. The persecution of Alfred Dreyfus—the Jewish French army officer who was falsely accused of treason in 1894, tried in secret, and imprisoned for years—still speaks to us today with its elements of racism and government cover-up. This account focuses on the suspense and drama of the trials and court martials, sets the affair against the widespread anti-Semitism of the time, and brings in the painstaking attempts by Dreyfus' supporters (including the great French writer Zola) to expose the truth. Finkelstein makes no attempt to glorify Dreyfus, showing rather that he was an ordinary officer and family man, fiercely loyal to his army and country, with little understanding of the wider issues of his case.

Frank, Rudolf.
No Hero for the Kaiser.
 Trans. by Patricia Crampton. 1986. Lothrop, $13 (0-688-06098-5).

 Gr. 6–12. First published in Germany in 1931, this was publicly burned by Hitler for its urgent antiwar message, and only translated into English in 1986. It's the story of 14-year-old Jan caught in the crossfire of World War I. Written in a spare beautiful style, several of the chapters begin with fascinating technical detail about weapons and tactics and then explode into slaughter.

Härtling, Peter.
Crutches.
 Trans. by Elizabeth D. Crawford. 1988. Lothrop, $12.95 (0-688-07991-1).

 Gr. 6–9. Translated from the German, this tells of a boy desperately looking for his mother in the shambles of Europe after World War

II. He is cared for by a one-legged war veteran who becomes his friend.

Hesse, Hermann.
  Demian: The Story of Emil Sinclair's Youth.
    Trans. by Michale Roloff and Michael Lobeck. 1919. Bantam, paper, $3.50 (0-553-26246-7).

    Gr. 9–12. In a classic coming-of-age story, a German boy picked on by a school bully finds wisdom and understanding through his relationship with the mysterious older boy, Max Demian. Also by Hesse, *Siddartha* and *Steppenwolf.*

Kazantzakis, Nikos.
  Zorba the Greek.
    1952. Simon & Schuster, paper, $9.95 (0-671-21132-3).

    Gr. 10–12. Zorba, a Greek workman in Crete, enjoys life to the full, tells wild stories of his erotic adventures, and teaches his boss—a rich young "bookworm"—to dance.

Lagerlöf, Selma.
  The Changeling.
    1992. Knopf, $15 (0-679-81035-8).

    Gr. 3 and up. The cruel stepmother, the lost child, the noble changeling: all these folktale motifs are reversed in this harsh and beautiful tale, translated from an old story by the Swedish Nobel Prize winner and illustrated with elaborate folk-art paintings by Jeanette Winter. This time the changeling is a monster, but the human mother shields him and refuses to abandon him, even when he burns her house down, even when her husband leaves her. The story has psychological and moral complexity to draw older readers.

First published in Germany in 1931, this story of a Polish boy caught between warring armies in World War I was burned for its antiwar message in 1933 when Hitler came to power. Frank was arrested, and on his release from prison, he fled to Switzerland. Shortly before his death in 1979, the book was republished in Germany. It was finally translated into English in 1986.

Lawson, Don.

The Abraham Lincoln Brigade: Americans Fighting Fascism in the Spanish Civil War.

1989. HarperCollins, $11.89 (0-690-04697-9).

Gr. 7–10. Lawson's accessible account of the young American volunteers who fought against fascism in Spain in the 1930s focuses on the military history. He also gives some sense of the political issues of the time and integrates brief sketches of the leaders and ordinary soldiers who fought and died for a cause they fervently supported. Lawson shows how the conflict was the testing ground for World War II, both militarily and ideologically. Another fine account is *The Lincoln Brigade* by William Katz and Marc Crawford.

Macaulay, David.

Cathedral: The Story of Its Construction.

1973. Houghton, $15.45 (0-395-17513-5); paper, $7.70 (0-395-31668-5).

Gr. 6–12. Macaulay describes, set by step, the construction of an imagined representative cathedral in France, and through his lively narrative and detailed architectural drawings, he makes you see the grandeur and intricacy of Gothic architecture. In all his splendid books, including *Castle* and *Pyramid,* Macaulay relates culture and history and technology with wit and beauty.

Newth, Mette.

The Abduction.

Trans. by Tina Nunnally and Steve Murray. 1989. Farrar, $13.95 (0-374-30008-9).

Gr. 8–12. Translated from the Norwegian, this quiet, brutal novel dramatizes the suffering of those who were "discovered" by the European explorers. In the 1600s, a Norwegian ship in Greenland abducts a teenage Inuit girl, Osuqo, and the young man she is soon to marry and takes them back to "civilization." The story is told in alternating chapters from Osuqo's point of view and that of Christine, a crippled young Norwegian drudge who is as outcast in her society as are the abused Inuit prisoners she cares for. The author's afterword unobtrusively fills in the historical context.

Preussler, Otfried.

The Satanic Mill.

Trans. by Anthea Bell. 1973. Peter Smith, $19 (0-8446-6196-1); Macmillan, paper, $3.95 (0-02-044775-2).

Gr. 5–9. A compelling fantasy translated from the German tells of Krabat, a 14-year-old boy in Germany 300 years ago. Between New Year's Day and Twelfth Night, he has a strange dream and finds himself following a voice to a mill, where he joins 11 others as slaves to a harsh master who practices black magic.

NOTES AND PERMISSIONS

The notes that follow comprise bibliographic citations for all works discussed in the text and sources (with permission statements where required) for all quoted material. Permission statements, supplied by publishers, vary in style and form throughout. Original publication dates are given in bibliographic citations except in the case of translations, where the date of the English translation is used. Shortened citations (author and title only) are used for works previously cited in the same chapter and for works cited in complete form in one of the resource lists. Picture credits follow the notes.

"Against Borders" by Yevgeny Yevtushenko. English version © 1962, 1991 by Anselm Hollo. First published in *Red Cats*, The Pocket Poets Series, Number Sixteen, City Lights Books, San Francisco, 1962. Used with permission of Anselm Hollo.

Preface: An Immigrant's Journey

p.9 · "In Praise of Exile." Leszek Kolakowski. From *Modernity on Endless Trial*. Univ. of Chicago, 1990, "we live in an age..." (p.59).

p.10 · Bharati Mukherjee. *Interview in Bill Moyers: A World of Ideas II: Public Opinions from Private Citizens*. Doubleday, 1990, paper, (p.3).

p.12 · *The Language of the Night: Essays on Fantasy and Science Fiction*. Ursula Le Guin. Ed. Susan Wood. Putnam, 1979, "we all have..." (p.79).
· *Other Peoples' Myths: The Cave of Echoes*. Wendy Doniger O'Flaherty. Macmillan, 1988, "primal echoes" (p.156).
· Parts of this discussion of myth are based on my article "Medusa in the Mall," *School Library Journal*, Feb. 1989.

p.13 · *The Power of Myth*. Joseph Campbell with Bill Moyers. Doubleday, 1988. This is the companion-guide to the PBS series in which Bill Moyers interviewed Campbell shortly before his death in 1987. "the quest to find..." (p.139).
· *Other Peoples' Myths*. O'Flaherty. "rites of passage..." (p.156–7).
· *I Am the Cheese*. Robert Cormier. Pantheon, 1977.
· *Annie John*. Jamaica Kincaid. Farrar, 1985.
· *Bingo Brown's Guide to Romance*. Betsy Byars. Viking, 1992.
· *One-Eyed Cat*. Paula Fox. Bradbury, 1984. Dell, paper, "little worm..." (p.70).

p.14 · "Abuelo: My Grandfather, Raymond Acuña." Michael Nava. From *A Member of the Family: Gay Men Write about Their Closest Relations*. Ed. John Preston. Dutton, 1992.
· *Other Peoples' Myths*. O'Flaherty. "kitsch mythology" (p.39).

p.15 · "Sirens, Knuckles, and Boots! Apartheid in South Africa." Diane Goheen and Mike Printz. *VOYA*, Oct. 1989.

Introduction: Beyond Political Correctness

p.17 · Parts of this chapter are based on speeches given at the YALSA President's Program of the ALA in San Francisco in June 1992; and at the 34th Allerton Institute of the Graduate School of Library and Information Science, University of Illinois, Oct. 25–7, 1992. Some material was originally published in "Booktalking: Going Global," *Horn Book*, Jan./Feb. 1989.
· Lucille Clifton. "note to my self" in *Quilting*. Copyright © 1991 by Lucille Clifton. Reprinted from *Quilting* by Lucille Clifton with the permission of BOA Editions, Ltd., 92 Park Avenue, Brockport, NY 14420.
· "P. C. labeling." My main source for these terms is *The Official Politically Correct Dictionary and Handbook*. Henry Beard and Christopher Cerf. Villard, 1992.
· "misnourishment," *New York Times*, Dec. 27, 1992.

p.18 · *Somehow Tenderness Survives: Stories of Southern Africa*. Ed. Hazel Rochman. HarperCollins/Charlotte Zolotow, 1988.
· "The Old Chief Mshlanga." Doris Lessing. *African Stories*. Simon & Schuster, 1965. Reprinted in *Somehow Tenderness Survives*, paper: "as remote..." (p.25);

"uncouth" (p.26); "opened it up" (p.30) "an easy gush..." (p.41).
· *Kaffir Boy: The Story of a Black Youth's Coming of Age in Apartheid South Africa.* Mark Mathabane. NAL/Dutton, 1986.

p.19 · *I Know Why the Caged Bird Sings.* Maya Angelou. Random, 1970. Bantam, paper, "People were those..." (p.21).

p.20 · "Why Do We Read?" Katha Pollitt. *The Nation,* Sept. 23, 1991. Reprinted in *Debating P. C.: The Controversy Over Political Correctness on College Campuses.* Ed. Paul Berman. Laurel/Dell, 1992.
· *My War with Goggle-Eyes.* Anne Fine. Joy Street/Little Brown, 1989.
· Susan Sontag. In introduction to *Best American Essays, 1992.* Ed. Susan Sontag. Ticknor & Fields, 1992, "literature is a party..." (p.xviii).
· E. L. Doctorow. Interview in *A World of Ideas: Conversations with Thoughtful Men and Women about American Life Today and the Ideas Shaping our Future.* Bill Moyers. Doubleday, 1989, "he gave the best..." (p.90).
· Margaret Atwood. Quoted in *Write to the Heart: Quotes by Women Writers.* Ed. Amber Coverdale Sumrall. Crossing Press, 1992, "It's amazing..." (p.76).

p.21 · *Year of Impossible Goodbyes.* Sook Nyul Choi. Houghton, 1991.
· *So Far from the Bamboo Grove.* Yoko Kawashima Watkins. Lothrop, 1986.
· *The Woman Warrior.* Maxine Hong Kingston. Knopf, 1976.
· Kingston quoted in *Write to the Heart.* Ed. Sumrall, "the expectation among..." (p.77).
· *The Journey: Japanese-Americans, Racism and Renewal.* Sheila Hamanaka. Orchard, 1990; *A Visit to Amy-Claire.* Claudia Mills. Illus. Hamanaka. Macmillan, 1992; *Sofie's Role.* Amy Heath. Illus. Hamanaka. Four Winds, 1992.
· *The Remarkable Journey of Prince Jen.* Lloyd Alexander. Dutton, 1991.
· Junko Yokota Lewis in speech, "Looking Beyond Literary and Visual Images to Raise the Level of Cultural Consciousness," Chicago Children's Reading Round Table Conference, Sept. 12, 1992. Lewis also discusses this issue in an article "Reading the World: Japan," *Book Links,* Mar. 1992.

p.22 · Nadine Gordimer. *Booklist* interview, Sept. 15, 1990.
· Virginia Hamilton. *Booklist* interview, Feb. 1, 1992.
· Roger Sutton, Executive Editor of the *Bulletin of the Center for Children's Books.* "What Mean We, White Man?" *VOYA,* Aug. 1992.

p.23 · Michael Dorris. "Indians in Aspic," *New York Times,* Feb. 24, 1991.
· *Through Indian Eyes: The Native Experience in Books for Children.* 3d ed. Ed. Beverly Slapin and Doris Seale. New Society, 1992.
· Lionel Trilling. "Greatness with One Fault in It," *Kenyon Review* 4 (1942). Quoted by John Hersey in introduction to the new edition of *Let Us Now Praise Famous Men.* James Agee. Houghton, 1988.

p.24 · *Somehow Tenderness Survives.* Ed. Hazel Rochman.
· Jamaica Kincaid. "I thought we..." *New York Times,* Oct. 9, 1992.
· Katha Pollitt. From *Debating P.C.* (p.205).
· *Kaffir Boy.* Mathabane (p.193).
· *Black Boy.* Richard Wright. HarperCollins, 1945, paper, "new ways of..." (p.272–3).
· "My Name." From *The House on Mango Street.* Sandra Cisneros. Arte Público Press, 1984. Rev. ed., Vintage, 1989, "looked out..." (p.10–11).

p.25 · *The Joy Luck Club.* Amy Tan. Putnam, 1989.
· *When Shlemiel Went to Warsaw.* Isaac Bashevis Singer. Farrar, 1968, "in our time...," opening note.
· Isaac Bashevis Singer. From *Children's Literature,* 6 (1977), "Unknown words..." (p.13–14).
· *E. B. White: Some Writer!* Beverly Gherman. Atheneum, 1992, "children are..." (p.93).

p.26 · *Shabanu: Daughter of the Wind.* Suzanne Fisher Staples. Knopf, 1989.
· *Somehow Tenderness Survives.* Ed. Rochman, Glossary (p.179).
· *The Autobiography of Malcolm X.* Malcolm X and Alex Haley. Ballantine, 1965, paper, "true African family..." (p.199).

p.27 · *Hide and Seek.* Ida Vos. Trans. Terese Edelstein and Inez Smidt. Houghton, 1991.
· *The Big Lie: A True Story.* Isabella Leitner. Scholastic, 1992.

Part One ◆ Themes: Journeys Across Cultures

THE PERILOUS JOURNEY

p.30 · Joseph Campbell. *The Hero with a Thousand Faces.* 2d ed. Princeton University/Bollingen Foundation, 1968, "And where we had..." (p.25).
· Walter de la Mare. In "The Listeners." From *Collected Poems.* Faber, 1979.

p.31 · *A Wrinkle in Time.* Madeleine L'Engle. Farrar, 1962.

Notes

     · *The Hitchhiker's Guide to the Galaxy.* Douglas Adams. Harmony, 1980.
     · *Where It Stops, Nobody Knows.* Amy Ehrlich. Dial, 1988.
     · *Somewhere in the Darkness.* Walter Dean Myers. Scholastic, 1992.
     · *In Summer Light.* Zibby Oneal. Viking, 1985.

p.32   "Saturday at the Canal." Gary Soto. From *Home Course in Religion.* Copyright © 1991. Used with permission of Chronicle Books.

p.33   · *Go Tell It on the Mountain.* James Baldwin. Knopf, 1953. Dell, paper, "What happen?..." (p.41).
     · *The Honorable Prison.* Lyll Becerra de Jenkins. Dutton/Lodestar, 1988. Penguin /Puffin, paper: "Today is a day..." (p.1); "Every individual..." (p.63).

p.34   · *Fast Talk on a Slow Track.* Rita Williams-Garcia. Dutton/Lodestar, 1991: "firstborn son..." (p.103); "achieving the most..." (p.158).
     · "Locked In." Ingemar Leckius. Trans. May Swenson. From *This Same Sky: A Collection of Poems from around the World.* Ed. Naomi Shihab Nye. Macmillan/Four Winds, 1992 (p.152).

p.35   · "Once Upon a Time." Nadine Gordimer. From *Jump and Other Stories.* Farrar, 1991.
     · "The Old Chief Mshlanga." Doris Lessing. First published 1965. Reprinted in *Somehow Tenderness Survives.* Ed. Hazel Rochman. HarperCollins/Charlotte Zolotow, 1988, paper, "an easy gush..." (p.41).
     · *In Summer Light.* Zibby Oneal. Viking, 1985. This quote is from her acceptance speech for the 1986 *Boston Globe–Horn Book* Award for Fiction; reprinted in *The Horn Book Magazine,* Jan./Feb. 1987 (p.30–3).
     · *Where It Stops, Nobody Knows.* Amy Ehrlich. Dial, 1988. Penguin/Puffin, paper: "We had secrets..." (p.35); "she turned off..." (p.158).

p.36   · "Where Are You Going, Where Have You Been?" Joyce Carol Oates. First published 1970. Reprinted in *Who Do You Think You Are? Stories of Friends and Enemies.* Ed. Hazel Rochman and Darlene McCampbell. Little, Brown/Joy Street, 1993.

p.37   · "Cinderella." *Trail of Stones.* Gwen Strauss. Illus. Anthony Browne. "Mother, no one..." (p.18). Text copyright © 1990 by Gwen Strauss. Reprinted by permission of Alfred A. Knopf, Inc.
     · *Annie John.* Jamaica Kincaid. Farrar, 1985. NAL/Plume, paper: "I wanted to go..." (p.103); "My heart just broke..." (p.105–6).
     · *The Joy Luck Club.* Amy Tan. Putnam, 1989. Ivy Books, paper: "My mother believed..." (p.141); "You want me..." (p.153); "It was not..." (p.154).

p.38   · *Choosing Sides.* Ilene Cooper. Morrow, 1990: "Is this really..." (p.189–91); "Basketball makes me..." (p.21618).

p.39   · *Wolf Rider: A Tale of Terror.* Avi. Bradbury, 1986, "The kitchen phone..." (p.1–2).

p.40   · *Woodsong.* Gary Paulsen. Bradbury, 1990.

p.41   · *Escape from Warsaw.* Ian Serraillier. First published 1956. Scholastic/Point, paper, "The noise in..." (p.37).
     · *Along the Tracks.* Tamar Bergman. Trans. Michael Swirsky. Houghton, 1991.

p.42   · *We Were Not Like Other People.* Ephraim Sevela. Trans. Antonina Bouis. HarperCollins, 1989: "I thought that..." (p.75); "We both decided..." (p.176); "Worthless child..." (p.57); "I know things..." (p.178); "the grass could..." (p.147); "It would have been..." (p.213).

p.43   · *Year of Impossible Goodbyes.* Sook Nyul Choi. Houghton, 1991.
     · *So Far from the Bamboo Grove.* Yoko Kawashima Watkins. Lothrop, 1986.
     · *Some of Us Survived: The Story of an Armenian Boy.* Kerop Bedoukian. Farrar, 1978.
     · *The Road from Home: The Story of an Armenian Girl.* David Kherdian. Greenwillow, 1979.
     · *The Man from the Other Side.* Uri Orlev. Trans. Hillel Halkin. Houghton, 1991.

p.44   · *Many Thousand Gone: African Americans from Slavery to Freedom.* Virginia Hamilton. Knopf, 1993: "Heard tell that..." (p.55); "I was soon put down..." (p.23).

p.45   · *Ajeemah and His Son.* James Berry. HarperCollins/Willa Perlman, 1992: "He didn't belong..." (p.39); "horror, awe, and dread" (p.11); "all beaten down..." (p.56).
     · *A Thief in the Village.* James Berry. Orchard, 1988.

p.46   · *Steal Away.* Jennifer Armstrong. Orchard/Richard Jackson, 1992.
     · *The People Could Fly: American Black Folktales.* Virginia Hamilton. Knopf, 1985: "They say the people..." (p.166–7); "had only their imaginations..." (p.173).

p.47   · "The Prison Cell." Mahmud Darwish. Trans. Ben Bennani. From *This Same Sky* (p.48–9).

p.48   · *Monkey Island.* Paula Fox. Orchard/Richard Jackson, 1991: "*away*" (p.38); "I can walk there..." (p.148).

p.49   · *Somewhere in the Darkness.* Walter Dean Myers. Scholastic, 1992: "I'm your father" (p.19); "Anything I could..." (p.86); "You don't even..." (p.156); "worse than being..." (p.28).
     · *Scorpions.* Walter Dean Myers. HarperCollins, 1988.

- *Wildflower Girl.* Marita Conlon-McKenna. Holiday, 1992, "five stinking, rotten…" (p.60).
- *Under the Hawthorn Tree.* Marita Conlon-McKenna. Holiday, 1990.
- *Immigrant Kids.* Russell Freedman. Dutton, 1980.

p.50 · *Letters from Rifka.* Karen Hesse. Holt, 1992, "You are bored?…" (p.39).
- *Kindertransport.* Olga Levy Drucker. Holt, 1992: "I was never…" (p.27); "what was real…" (p.99).

p.51 · *Kiki: A Cuban Boy's Adventure in America.* Hilda Perera. Trans. Warren Hampton and Hilda González. Pickering, 1992.
- *An Ancient Heritage: The Arab-American Minority.* Brent Ashabranner. Photos Paul Conklin. HarperCollins, 1991: "Most Americans think…" (p.88); "I left a country…" (p.112).
- *The Vanishing Border.* Brent Ashabranner. Putnam, 1987.
- "The Most Vulnerable People" from *Into a Strange Land: Unaccompanied Refugee Youth in America.* Brent and Melissa Ashabranner. Putnam, 1987, "Fran cried out…" (p.4–5).

p.52 · *Journey of the Sparrows.* Fran Leeper Buss with the assistance of Daisy Cubias. Dutton/Lodestar, 1991, "You're the one…" (p.38).

p.53 · "On the Rainy River." From *The Things They Carried.* Tim O'Brien. Houghton, 1990: "Driving up Main Street…" (p.47); "I loved baseball…" (p.53); "because I was embarrassed…" (p.62).
- Louise Erdrich. From *Write to the Heart: Quotes by Women Writers.* Ed. Amber Coverdale Sumrall. Crossing Press, 1992, "Going home for most…" (p.64).

THE HERO AND THE MONSTER

p.54 · "I went up one step…" I learned this traditional rhyme in the school playground in South Africa. One version of it is powerfully illustrated by Maurice Sendak in *I Saw Esau: The Schoolchild's Pocket Book.* Ed. Iona & Peter Opie. Candlewick, 1992. *Booklist* interview with Sendak about *I Saw Esau,* June 15, 1992.
- *Lon Po Po: A Red Riding Hood Story from China.* Ed Young. Putnam/Philomel, 1989.

p.55 · *The Dark Way: Stories from the Spirit World,* Virginia Hamilton. HBJ, 1990, "our most secret fearful heart" (p.xiv).
- *Bingo Brown's Guide to Romance.* Betsy Byars. Viking, 1992: "quiet manhood" (p.80); "In the old days…" (p.4); "mixed sex conversation" (p.59); "for eternity" (p.23).
- *The Trojan Horse.* Warwick Hutton. Macmillan/Margaret K. McElderry, 1992.
- *Freedom's Children.* Ellen Levine. Putnam, 1993, "You would have thought…" (p.61).

p.56 · *Freedom Songs.* Yvette Moore. Orchard, 1991. Penguin/Puffin, paper: "Do it…" (p.46); "I'd like a Coke…" (p.158); "The singing…" (p.166).
- "Notes of a Native Son." From *Notes of a Native Son,* 3d ed. James Baldwin. Beacon, 1955.

p.57 · Frederick Douglass to Harriet Tubman, Aug. 29, 1868. Appendix in *Harriet Tubman: The Moses of Her People.* Sarah H. Bradford. Introduction by Butler A. Jones. Citadel Press, 1961.
- *"Who Was That Masked Man, Anyway?"* Avi. Orchard/Richard Jackson, 1992, "ruthless, clear-eyed…" (p.11).

p.58 · *A Yellow Raft in Blue Water.* Michael Dorris. Holt, 1987. Warner, paper: "bound for something…" (p.171); "who's lived for…" (p.297); "I've been looking…" (p.29–30).

p.59 · *Celine.* Brock Cole. Farrar, 1989. Sunburst, paper: "I do know…" (p.63); "we will never…" (p.55); "seems to bulge…" (p.122).

p.60 · *In Summer Light.* Zibby Oneal. Viking, 1985.
- "My Name." From *The House on Mango Street.* Sandra Cisneros. Random/Vintage, 1989 (p.10–11). Copyright © 1989 by Sandra Cisneros. Published in the United States by Vintage Books, a division of Random House, Inc., New York, and distributed in Canada by Random House of Canada Limited, Toronto. Originally published in somewhat different form by Arte Público Press in 1984 and revised in 1989. Reprinted by permission of Susan Bergholz Literary Services, New York.

p.61 · *The Woman Warrior: Memoirs of a Girlhood among Ghosts.* Maxine Hong Kingston. Knopf, 1976. Random/Vintage, paper: "Perhaps women were…" (p.19); "The girls said…" (p.194).

p.62 · *Probably Still Nick Swansen.* Virginia Euwer Wolff. Holt, 1988. Scholastic/Point, paper: "The prom was…" (p.20–2); "He felt as…" (p.172).

p.63 · *One-Eyed Cat.* Paula Fox. Bradbury, 1984. Dell, paper: "as if his…" (p.8); "The cat was gray…" (p.66); "Hunting will be hard…" (p.70).

p.64 · *Cyclops.* Leonard Everett Fisher. Holiday, 1991, "The stories they..." (unpaged).

p.65 · *Eva.* Peter Dickinson. Delacorte, 1988. Dell, paper, "Eva willed her..." (p.17).
· *The Secret House.* David Bodanis. Simon & Schuster, 1988.

p.66 · *Mary Reilly.* Valerie Martin. Doubleday, 1990, "Are you ever..." (p.131).
· *Beauty.* Robin McKinley. HarperCollins, 1978. Pocket, paper: "I caught a gleam..." (p.114); "If you wanted..." (p.118).

p.67 · *Amycus. The Hydra.* Bernard Evslin. Chelsea House, 1989. Monsters of Mythology Series. "And Scylla, burning..." *Scylla and Charybdis* (p.8).
· *The Dark Way.* Virginia Hamilton: "whether it be..." (p.xi); "frightful fun" (p.xii). *Booklist* interview with Hamilton, Feb. 1, 1992.
· *In the Beginning: Creation Stories from around the World.* Virginia Hamilton. HBJ, 1988.

p.68 · *Cousins.* Virginia Hamilton. Putnam/Philomel, 1990, "You look like..." (p.30–1).

OUTSIDERS

p.69 · "Pied Beauty." Gerard Manley Hopkins (1844–89). *Poems and Prose.* Penguin Classics (p.30).
· *Shane.* Jack Schaefer. Houghton. 1949.
· *The Runner.* Cynthia Voigt. Atheneum, 1985.
· "Wolf Woman Running." From *White Wolf Woman and Other Native American Transformation Myths.* Retold Teresa Pijoan. August House, 1992.
· *Sojourner Truth: Ain't I a Woman?* Patricia C. McKissack and Fredrick McKissack. Scholastic, 1992.
· *Jane Eyre.* Charlotte Brontë. 1847. Many editions available.
· *The Goats.* Brock Cole. Farrar, 1987.
· *Hide and Seek.* Ida Vos. Trans. Terese Edelstein and Inez Smidt. Houghton, 1991.
· *The Invisible Thread.* Yoshiko Uchida. Messner, 1992.
· *Ajeemah and His Son.* James Berry. HarperCollins/Willa Perlman, 1992.
· Paula Fox. Introduction to 1984 paperback edition of *Tell Me that You Love Me, Junie Moon.* Marjorie Kellogg. Farrar, 1968.
· *The House on Mango Street.* Sandra Cisneros. Arte Público Press, 1984. Rev. ed., Random/Vintage, 1989.
· *Frankenstein; or The Modern Prometheus.* Mary Wollstonecraft Shelley. 1818. Many editions available.
· *There's a Girl in My Hammerlock.* Jerry Spinelli. Simon & Schuster, 1991.

p.70 · *Jane Eyre.* Brontë. Bantam, paper, "My heart beat..." (p.11).

p.71 · *Rebecca.* Daphne du Maurier. Doubleday, 1938.
· *Wide Sargasso Sea.* Jean Rhys. Norton, 1967.
· *Summer of My German Soldier.* Bette Greene. Dial, 1973.
· *Stepping on the Cracks.* Mary Downing Hahn. Clarion, 1991.
· *Don't Say a Word.* Barbara Gehrts. Trans. Elizabeth D. Crawford. Macmillan/Margaret K. McElderry, 1986.
· *Children of the River.* Linda Crew. Delacorte, 1989.

p.72 · *Maizon at Blue Hill.* Jacqueline Woodson. Delacorte, 1992: "minority" (p.103); "We have to..." (p.83).
· *The Bluest Eye.* Toni Morrison. Holt, 1970.
· *Black Ice.* Lorene Cary. Knopf, 1991.
· *Fell.* M. E. Kerr. HarperCollins/Charlotte Zolotow, 1987. Dell, paper: "Heir to a fortune..." (p.4); "Jazzy's game was..." (p.28).

p.73 · *There's a Girl in My Hammerlock.* Spinelli: "Can a boy..." (p.97); "Classes? Subjects?..." (p.11); "Don't even drink..." (p.131).

p.74 · "Sure You Can Ask Me a Personal Question." Diane Burns. Burns is Anishinabe (Ojibwa) and Chemehuevi Indian. From *Songs from This Earth on Turtle's Back: Contemporary American Indian Poetry.* Ed. Joseph Bruchac. Greenfield Review Press, 1983 (p.35). Used with kind permission of the author.
· "Observations." From *Stories I Ain't Told Nobody Yet: Selections from the People Pieces.* Copyright © 1989 by Jo Carson. Used with permission of the publisher, Orchard Books, New York.

p.75 · *Lily and the Lost Boy.* Paula Fox. Orchard/Richard Jackson, 1987, "She and Mr. Kalligas..." (p.124).
· *The Remarkable Voyages of Captain Cook.* Rhoda Blumberg. Bradbury, 1991, "he told one..." (p.87).

p.76 · *Yoruba Girl Dancing.* Simi Bedford. Viking, 1992: "She motioned me..." (p.84); "By and by..." (p.91).

p.77 · *The Runner.* Voigt. Fawcett, paper: "he ran himself" (p.90); "young at a..." (p.175).
· *The Goats.* Cole. Sunburst, paper, "She found him..." (p.98).

FRIENDS AND ENEMIES

p.79 · "Poem." Langston Hughes. From *The Death Keeper and Other Poems.* © 1932 by Alfred A. Knopf, Inc., and renewed 1960 by Langston Hughes. Reprinted by permission of the publisher, Alfred A. Knopf, Inc.

· *The Power of Myth.* Joseph Campbell with Bill Moyers. Doubleday, 1988, "When I take..." (p.149).

· *The Goats.* Brock Cole. Farrar, 1987.

p.80 · *Bridge to Terabithia.* Katherine Paterson. HarperCollins, 1977.

· *"Who Was That Masked Man, Anyway?"* Avi. Orchard/Richard Jackson, 1992.

· Walter Dean Myers. Columbia Children's Literature Institute, July 1990.

· *Fast Sam, Cool Clyde, and Stuff.* Walter Dean Myers. Viking, 1975.

· *Scorpions.* Walter Dean Myers. HarperCollins, 1988; paper, "Every thought..." (p.213).

· "We Real Cool." From "BLACKS," by Gwendolyn Brooks. © 1991. Published by THIRD WORLD PRESS, Chicago, 1991. Reprinted by permission of the author.

p.81 · "Song in the Front Yard." Gwendolyn Brooks. From *I Am the Darker Brother: An Anthology of Modern Poems by Black Americans.* Ed. Arnold Adoff. Macmillan/Collier, paper, 1968 (p.11).

· *There Are No Children Here: The Story of Two Boys Growing Up in the Other America.* Alex Kotlowitz. Doubleday, 1991, "struggle with school..." (p.xi).

· *Fallen Angels.* Walter Dean Myers. Scholastic, 1988; paper: "hours of boredom..." (p.132); "I looked up into the face..." (p.251).

· *All Quiet on the Western Front.* Erich Maria Remarque. Trans. A. W. Wheen. Little, Brown, 1929. Fawcett, paper, "There was indeed..." (p.15–17).

p.82 · *Grapes of Wrath.* John Steinbeck. Viking, 1939.

· *A Tree Grows in Brooklyn.* Betty Smith. HarperCollins, 1943.

· *Roll of Thunder, Hear My Cry.* Mildred Taylor. Dial, 1976.

p.83 · *Forever Nineteen.* Grigory Baklanov. Trans. Antonina W. Bouis. HarperCollins, 1989.

· *Alan and Naomi.* Myron Levoy. HarperCollins, 1977, paper, "I won't do it..." (p.20).

· *Bad Times, Good Friends: A Personal Memoir.* Ilse-Margret Vogel. HBJ, 1992.

p.84 · *Waiting for the Rain.* Sheila Gordon. Orchard, 1987.

· *A Hand Full of Stars.* Rafik Schami. Trans. Rika Lesser. Dutton, 1990. Penguin/Puffin, paper, "poverty smothers . . . " (p.95). Original written in German.

p.85 · "How I Learned English." Gregory Djanikian. From *The Music of What Happens: Poems That Tell Stories.* Sel. Paul B. Janeczko. Orchard/Richard Jackson, 1988 (p.19). Originally appeared in *Poetry,* Jan. 1987. Reprinted by permission of the author.

· *The Chosen.* Chaim Potok. Knopf, 1967. Fawcett, paper: "You're looking good..." (p.15); "Standing on the field..." (p.31).

p.86 · *The Thanksgiving Visitor.* Truman Capote. Random, 1968.

p.87 · "The Poison Tree." William Blake. From *Songs of Experience.* 1794. *The Complete Poems.* Penguin Classics (p.129).

· *The Fire-Raiser.* Maurice Gee. Houghton, 1992: "Flame filled the..." (p.10); "silent, quick and mad" (p.73); "witch and spider" (p.39).

p.88 · *Risk N' Roses.* Jan Slepian. Based on review in the *New York Times Book Review,* Jan. 20, 1991.

· *Cat's Eye.* Margaret Atwood. Doubleday, 1989. Bantam, paper: "On the window ledge..." (p.123); "Once I'm outside..." (p.127); "With enemies..." (p.127); "You don't have..." (p.167).

p.89 · *Queen of the Sixth Grade.* Ilene Cooper. Morrow, 1988, "Then, when the class..." (p.62–3).

p.90 · *The Agony of Alice.* Phyllis Reynolds Naylor. Atheneum, 1985. Dell, paper: "I didn't even..." (p.71); "an entire conversation..." (p.75).

· *All but Alice.* Phyllis Reynolds Naylor. Atheneum, 1992.

p.91 · *Yang the Youngest and His Terrible Ear.* Lensey Namioka. Little, Brown/Joy Street, 1992.

· *Remembering the Good Times.* Richard Peck. Delacorte, 1985. Dell, paper, "Rusty leaned back..." (p.112).

LOVERS AND STRANGERS

p.92 · Rumi. "2195. In the Arc of Your Mallet." Trans. from the Persian John Moyne and Coleman Barks. From *Open Secret: Versions of Rumi.* Published by Threshold Books. Printed by permission of Threshold Books, R.D. 4, Box 600, Putney, Vermont 05301.

· "Waiting." From *The Leaving.* Budge Wilson. Putnam/Philomel, 1992.

Notes

· *Under All Silences: Shades of Love: An Anthology of Poems.* Comp. Ruth Gordon. HarperCollins/Charlotte Zolotow, 1987.

p.93 · "love is the air…" In "being to timelessness as it's to time." From *Complete Poems, 1913–1962.* e. e. Cummings. By permission of Liveright Publishing Corporation, Copyright © 1923, 1925, 1931, 1935, 1938, 1939, 1940, 1944, 1945, 1946, 1947, 1948, 1949, 1950, 1951, 1952, 1953, 1954, 1955, 1956, 1957, 1958, 1959, 1960, 1961, 1962 by the Trustees for the e. e. cummings Trust. Copyright © 1961, 1963, 1968 by Marion Morehouse Cummings.

· "There was your voice…" From *Letters from Maine: New Poems.* May Sarton. Used with the permission of W. W. Norton & Company, Inc. Copyright © 1984 by May Sarton.

· *West Side Story.* Leonard Bernstein. 1957.

· *Romeo and Juliet.* William Shakespeare: "What's Montague?…" (Act I, Scene 5); "Prodigious birth of…" (Act I, Scene 5).

· "The Smoking Mountain." From *Stories from the Days of Christopher Columbus.* Retold Richard Alan Young with Judy Dockrey Young. August House. 1992: "the painted boundary pole" (p.57); "I cannot change…" (p.61).

p.94 · "Country Lovers." Nadine Gordimer. First published 1975. Reprinted in *Somehow Tenderness Survives.* Ed. Hazel Rochman. HarperCollins/Charlotte Zolotow, 1988; paper, "The verdict on…" (p.75).

· Susan Moran. "Creative Reading: Young Adults and Paperback Books." *Horn Book,* July/Aug. 1992 (p.493).

· "American History." Judith Ortiz-Cofer. From *Iguana Dreams: New Latino Fiction.* Ed. Delia Poey and Virgil Suarez. HarperCollins, 1992. Reprinted in *Who Do You Think You Are?* Ed. Hazel Rochman and Darlene McCampbell. Little, Brown/Joy Street, 1993, "you people…" (p.45).

p.95 · *Taste of Salt: A Story of Modern Haiti.* Frances Temple. Orchard/Richard Jackson, 1992.

· *Rice without Rain.* Minfong Ho. Lothrop, 1990: "grow things and…" (p.218); "strong and sweet…" (p.227).

p.96 · *Daniel and Esther.* Patrick Raymond. Macmillan/Margaret K. McElderry, 1990: "Was it very…" (p.48); "as if she's…" (p.26); "I looked down…" (p.160); "I just wanted…" (p.124).

· "Distances of Longing." Fawziyya Abu Khalid (Saudi Arabia). Trans. May Jayyusi. From *This Same Sky.* Ed. Naomi Shihab Nye. Macmillan/Four Winds, 1992 (p.24).

· *Love Flute.* Paul Goble. Bradbury, 1992.

p.97 · "Marie Jolie." From *Cajun Folktales.* Retold J. J. Reneaux. August House, 1992.

· *White Wolf Woman: Native American Transformation Myths.* Teresa Pijoan. August House, 1992, "A blood-curdling howl…" (p.59).

· *Women Who Run with the Wolves.* Clarissa Pinkola Estes. Ballantine, 1992.

· *The King's Equal.* Katherine Paterson. HarperCollins, 1992.

p.98 · *Wuthering Heights.* Emily Brontë. 1847. Bantam, paper, "My great miseries…" (p.74).

· *The Owl Service.* Slan Garner. Walck, 1968.

p.99 · *The Ballad of the Sad Café and Other Stories.* Carson McCullers. Houghton, 1951. Bantam, paper: "lonesome, sad, and…" (p.3); "bold and fearless…" (p.29); "There are the lover…" (p.26).

· *Pygmalion.* George Bernard Shaw. 1913. Many editions available.

· *The Fat Girl.* Marilyn Sachs. Dutton, 1983.

p.100 · *Just Friends.* Norma Klein. Knopf, 1990.

· *I Love You, Stupid!* Harry Mazer. HarperCollins, 1981.

· *The Course of True Love Never Did Run Smooth.* Marilyn Singer. Delacorte, 1983.

· *Permanent Connections.* Sue Ellen Bridgers. HarperCollins, 1987: "You expect too…" (p.167); "You have seen…" (p.140). This discussion based on my review in the *New York Times Book Review,* July 26, 1987.

· *A Yellow Raft in Blue Water.* Michael Dorris. Holt, 1987.

· *Downstream.* John Rowe Townsend. HarperCollins, 1987: "I never want…" (p.168); "You've broken up…" (p.170).

p.101 · *The Catalogue of the Universe.* Margaret Mahy. Macmillan/Margaret K. McElderry, 1986. Scholastic/Point, paper: "All right!…" (p.122); "I'd rather be tall." (p.47).

· *The Arizona Kid.* Ron Koertge. Little, Brown/Joy Street, 1988. Avon/Flare, paper: "Let's face it…" (p.13); "That was one…" (p.6); "I forget sometimes…" (p.161).

p.102 · *Weetzie Bat.* Francesca Lia Block. HarperCollins/Charlotte Zolotow, 1989, "He wore his hair…" (p.4).

p.103 · Norma Klein. *Something about the Author: Autobiography Series,* Vol. I. Gale, 1986.

FAMILY MATTERS

p.104 · Gloria Steinem. "Ruth's Song (Because She Could Not Sing It)." From *Outrageous Acts and Everyday Rebellions*. Holt, 1983. Signet, paper (p.145).
· "My Lucy Friend…" From *Woman Hollering Creek and Other Stories*. Sandra Cisneros. Random, 1991 (p.4).
· *Sons and Lovers*. D. H. Lawrence. 1913. Many editions available.
· *I Know Why the Caged Bird Sings*. Maya Angelou. Random, 1970.
· *Beloved*. Toni Morrison. Knopf, 1987.
· *Morning Girl*. Michael Dorris. Hyperion, 1992.
p.105 · *The Joy Luck Club*. Amy Tan. Putnam, 1989.
· *Weetzie Bat*. Francesca Lia Block. HarperCollins/Charlotte Zolotow, 1989.
· *Memory*. Margaret Mahy. Macmillan/Margaret K. McElderry, 1987.
· "Those Winter Sundays." Reprinted from *Angle of Ascent, New and Selected Poems*, by Robert Hayden, by permission of Liveright Publishing Corporation. Copyright © 1975, 1972, 1970, 1966 by Robert Hayden.
· "Papa Who Wakes Up Tired in the Dark." From *The House on Mango Street*. Sandra Cisneros. Arte Público Press, 1984. Rev. ed., Random/Vintage, 1989.
p.106 · *Shabanu: Daughter of the Wind*. Suzanne Fisher Staples. Knopf, 1989.
· *The Moonlight Man*. Paula Fox. Bradbury, 1986. Dell, paper: "where was he?…" (p.1); "Catherine wanted to…" (p.17); "splendid journey" (p.25); "See you…" (p.179). This discussion based on my review in the *New York Times Book Review*, Mar. 23, 1986.
p.107 · *One Fat Summer*. Robert Lipsyte. HarperCollins/Charlotte Zolotow, 1977: "He's always afraid…" (p.53); "I always hated…" (p.1); "I hit the…" (p.120).
p.108 · *What Hearts*. Bruce Brooks. HarperCollins/Laura Geringer, 1992.
· *Midnight Hour Encores*. Bruce Brooks. HarperCollins/Laura Geringer, 1986.
· *I Only Made Up the Roses*. Barbara Ann Porte. Greenwillow, 1987: "My Real Father…" (p.50); "Daddy stood me…" (p.52–3).
p.109 · *The Boy in the Moon*. Ron Koertge. Little, Brown/Joy Street, 1990. Avon, paper: "The good thing…" (p.41); "get out there…" (p.41).
· *At the Crossroads*. Rachel Isadora. Greenwillow, 1991.
p.110 · *A Leak in the Heart*. Faye Moskowitz. Godine, 1985, "Yet my mother's…" (p.69).
· *Beloved*. Toni Morrison. Knopf, 1987. NAL/Plume, paper, "That anybody…" (p.251).
p.111 · *Prairie Songs*. Pam Conrad. HarperCollins, 1985; paper, "'Momma?'…" (p.102).
· "Ruth's Song (Because She Could Not Sing It)." Steinem (p.165).
p.112 · *This Boy's Life: A Memoir*. Tobias Wolff. Atlantic, 1989. Harper Perennial, paper: "I was my…" (p.142); "The human heart…" (p.143).
· "A Deep-Sworn Vow." W. B. Yeats. Macmillan. From *The Poems of W. B. Yeats*. Macmillan. First published 1919, "to the heights…"
· *My War with Goggle-Eyes*. Anne Fine. Little, Brown/Joy Street, 1989. Bantam, paper, "So [Goggle-Eyes] said…" (p.31).
p.113 · "Abuelo: My Grandfather, Raymond Acuña." Michael Nava. From *A Member of the Family: Gay Men Write about Their Closest Relations*. Ed. John Preston. Dutton, 1992: "He represented a…" (p.17); "It isn't necessary…" (p.20).
p.114 · *Granny Was a Buffer Girl*. Berlie Doherty. Orchard, 1986, "snotty-nosed" (p.30).
· *Gentlehands*. M. E. Kerr. HarperCollins, 1978, "She's not our…" (p.1).
p.115 · "Brother." Mary Ann Hoberman. From *Hello and Good-by*. 1959. Little, Brown. Reprinted in *Sunflakes: Poems for Children*. Ed. Lillian Moore. Clarion, 1992 (p.65). Reprinted by permission of Gina Maccoby Literary Agency Copyright © 1959, renewed 1987 by Mary Ann Hoberman.
· *Tales from the Bamboo Grove*. Yoko Kawashima Watkins. Bradbury, 1992.
· *Boots and His Brothers*. Eric Kimmel. Holiday, 1992.
· *Howl's Moving Castle*. Diana Wynne Jones. Greenwillow, 1986.
p.116 · "The Red Convertible." Louise Erdrich. First published 1974. From *Love Medicine*. Holt, 1984, "When he came home…" (p.147).
· *Brothers Like Friends*. Klaus Kordon. Trans. Elizabeth D. Crawford. Putnam/Philomel, 1992.
· *The Changeover: A Supernatural Romance*. Margaret Mahy. Macmillan/Margaret K. McElderry, 1984. Scholastic/Point, paper, "an inexplicable tremble" (p.3). One of the best annotations for this book appears on the YALSA genre list on Horror, published by ALA: "Would you become a witch to save your little brother?"
· *Sweet Whispers, Brother Rush*. Virginia Hamilton. Putnam/Philomel, 1982.
p.117 · *Barry's Sister*. Lois Metzger. Atheneum, 1992: "Barry would never…" (p.71); "only wrecked him" (p.75); "now playing at…" (p.77); "You don't get…" (p.80); "blind and dead…" (p.144); "somewhat handicapped" (p.212). This discussion based on a review in the *New York Times Book Review*, May 17, 1992.

· *The Man Who Mistook His Wife for a Hat.* Oliver Sacks. Simon & Schuster, 1985.
· *Morning Girl.* Michael Dorris. Hyperion, 1992: "I watched the…" (p.40); "that we…" (p.74); "a people very…" (p.71).
· *A Yellow Raft in Blue Water.* Michael Dorris. Holt, 1987.

FINDING THE WAY HOME

p.119 · Parts of this chapter were published in the *Chicago Children's Reading Round Table Bulletin,* Jan. 1990 and in *Horn Book,* May/June 1990.
· Tobias Wolff. *This Boy's Life: A Memoir.* Atlantic, 1989. Harper Perennial, paper, "The human heart…" (p.143).
· *A Member of the Family.* Ed. John Preston. Dutton, 1992.
· *Tell Freedom.* Peter Abrahams. Knopf, 1954 (p.222–36).
· *Memories of a Catholic Girlhood.* Mary McCarthy. HBJ, 1957, paper, "My own…" (p.5).

p.120 · "A Soft Spring Night in Shillington." From *Self-Consciousness: Memoirs.* John Updike. Knopf, 1989, "I loved doorways…" (p.33).
· *One Writer's Beginnings.* Eudora Welty. Harvard, 1984. Warner, paper, "Where do babies…" (p.17).

p.121 · "Doctor." From *Love Lines: Poetry in Person.* Betsy Hearne. Macmillan/Margaret K. McElderry, 1987 (p.29). Used with permission of the author.

p.122 · *Hunger of Memory: The Education of Richard Rodriguez.* Richard Rodriguez. Godine, 1982. Bantam, paper, "Thirteen years old…" (p.125).
· *Starting from Home: A Writer's Beginnings.* Milton Meltzer. Viking, 1988, paper, "unhyphenated" (p.78).
· "The Konk." From *Stories from El Barrio.* Piri Thomas. Knopf, 1978, "I walked slowly…" (p.59–60). Used with permission of the publisher.

p.123 · *But I'll Be Back Again: An Album.* Cynthia Rylant. Orchard/Richard Jackson, 1989: "I was ashamed…" (p.32); "I wanted…" (p.34).
· "The Story of My Life." Anna Bender. From *Rising Voices: Writings of Young Native Americans.* Ed. Arlene B. Hirschfelder and Beverly R. Singer. Scribner's, 1992, "I had no reason…" (p.75–6). Used with permission, courtesy of Hampton University Archives.

p.124 · *A Girl from Yamhill: A Memoir.* Beverly Cleary. Morrow, 1988, "My father kissed…" (p.279).

p.125 · *Boy.* Roald Dahl. Farrar, 1984: "totally idyllic…" (p.51); "We hated her…" (p.33); "I couldn't get…" (p.131); "scabs and when…" (p.31); "me seven months…" (inside cover). This discussion based on my review in the *New York Times Book Review,* Jan. 20, 1985.
· "Crackling Day." Peter Abrahams. From *Tell Freedom.* Knopf, 1954. Reprinted in *Somehow Tenderness Survives.* Ed. Hazel Rochman. HarperCollins/Charlotte Zolotow, 1988, paper, "Uncle Sam flung…" (p.21–2).
· *Black Boy.* Richard Wright. Harper, 1945.

p.126 · "The Toilet." Gcina Mhlope. First published 1987. From *Somehow Tenderness Survives,* "Then one morning…" (p.110).

p.127 · *The Invisible Thread.* Yoshiko Uchida. Messner, 1992: "Long after Tanforan…" (p.90); "There had yet been…" (p.79).
· *Anne Frank: The Diary of a Young Girl.* Anne Frank. Trans. B. M. Mooyaart. Doubleday, 1952. Rev. ed. 1967. Pocket/Washington Square, paper, "Wednesday, 13 January…" (p.57); "Sunday, 27 February…" (p.144).

p.128 · *Hide and Seek.* Ida Vos. Trans. Terese Edelstein and Inez Smidt. Houghton, 1991.

p.129 · *Survival in Auschwitz: The Nazi Assault on Humanity.* Primo Levi. Trans. from the Italian by Stuart Woolf. 1959. Macmillan/Collier, paper: "in the middle…" (p.14); "true initiation"… (p.23); "They think…" (p.109); "I believe…" (p.111).

p.130 · *The Autobiography of Malcolm X.* Malcolm X and Alex Haley. 1965. Ballantine, paper: "Thicker each year…" (p.379).
· *Malcolm X: By Any Means Necessary.* Walter Dean Myers. Scholastic, 1993.
· "The Autobiography of Dedre Bailey: Thoughts on Malcolm X and Black Youth." As told to Marpessa Dawn Outlaw and Mathew Countryman. From *Malcolm X: In Our Own Image.* Ed. Joe Wood. St. Martin's, 1992, "Just look at…" (p.235).
· *I Know Why the Caged Bird Sings.* Maya Angelou. Random, 1970. Bantam, paper: "It was Shakespeare…" (p.11); "I have often…" (p.84).

p.131 · "A Long Line of Cells." Lewis Thomas. From *Inventing the Truth: The Art and Craft of Memoir.* Ed. William Zinsser. Houghton, 1987: "To begin personally…" (p.128); "What sticks…" (p.131).

Part Two ◆ Resources: Going Global

RACIAL OPPRESSION

The Holocaust

p.134 · "A Four-Hundred-Year-Old Woman." Bharati Mukherjee. From *The Writer on Her Work II: New Essays in New Territory.* Ed. Janet Sternburg. Norton, 1991 (p.38).

p.135 · This resource guide draws on the *Booklist* special issue "Remembering the Holocaust," June 15, 1989.
· Bruno Bettelheim. In "The Holocaust—One Generation Later." From *Surviving and Other Essays.* Vintage, 1980: "unimaginable" (p.91); "by average..." (p.84).

p.136 · Ida Fink. "I thought one..." *New York Times Book Review* July 12, 1987.
· *The Journey.* Ida Fink. Farrar, 1992.

p.137 · *The Other Way Round.* Judith Kerr. Putnam/Coward-McCann, 1975.

p.138 · *Fateless.* Imre Kertész. "Buchenwald's weather was..." (p.90).

p.139 · The Big Lie. Isabella Leitner. Scholastic, 1992.
· *The Reawakening.* Macmillan/Collier, 1965. *Survival in Auschwitz.* Macmillan/Collier, 1959. Primo Levi.

p.140 · *David and Jonathan.* Cynthia Voigt. "It's not who..." (p.241).

p.141 · *Hide and Seek.* Ida Vos. "This is Mrs...." (p.36).

p.143 · From the last speech of Martin Luther King, Jr., Memphis, Tennessee, Apr. 1968. "The first question..." Quoted as frontispiece in *Rescue,* Milton Meltzer.
· Martin Niemoller (1892–1984), German theologian. "The Nazis came..." *Congressional Record* Oct. 14, 1968 (p.31636).

p.144 · Heinrich Heine. "Wherever they burn..." *Almansor.* 1823. I.245. Trans. from German.
· *The Short Life of Sophie Scholl.* Hermann Vinke. HarperCollins, 1984.

Apartheid

p.146 · Besides the specific quotes and facts documented, the introduction is based on several of the fine historical and political analyses included in the bibliography, especially Allister Sparks' *Mind of South Africa* and Leonard Thompson's *History of South Africa,* as well as on the excellent up-to-date information prepared by the South African Institute of Race Relations in their annual *Race Relations Survey.*
· Archbishop Desmond Tutu. "They say that..." Used by permission of John Allen, press secretary to Archbishop Tutu.

p.147 · Children tortured. Sources for this include "Children in Detention in South Africa." Audrey Coleman. United Nations Centre against Apartheid. July 1987. Coleman was a founding member of the Johannesburg-based Detainees' Parents Support Committee. The government banned the Committee in 1988.
· Dr. Jonathan Gluckman. Interview with the *Sunday Times,* Johannesburg, July 1992.

p.150 Xhosa proverb. Sparks. *Mind of South Africa* (p.3).
· Nadine Gordimer. *Burger's Daughter.* Viking, 1979: "It's about suffering..." (p.332).

p.151 · *A Separate Development.* Christopher Hope. Scribner's, 1981.
· *Black Child.* Peter Magubane. Knopf, 1982.

p.152 · *Kaffir Boy.* Mark Mathabane. "A huge throng..." (p.24)

p.153 · *Love in Black and White.* Gail and Mark Mathabane. HarperCollins, 1991.
· Nelson Mandela, leader of the African National Congress. "I have fought..." Rivonia Trial, 1964, before being sentenced to life in prison. He said it again in 1990, Cape Town, upon his release after 27 years. *No Easy Walk to Freedom.* Heinemann, paper (p.189).

p.154 · *Sophiatown.* Don Mattera. "Bulldozers like the..." (p.20).
· *Nelson Mandela.* Fatima Meer, "I felt I was..." (p.376).

p.155 · Nadine Gordimer. "In my writing..." *Booklist* interview, Sept. 15, 1990.
· "The Old Chief Mshlanga." Doris Lessing. From *Somehow Tenderness Survives,* p.41.

p.156 · *Children under Apartheid.* Africa Fund, 1980.
· *Tell Freedom.* Peter Abrahams. Knopf, 1954.

p.157 · *My Son's Story.* Nadine Gordimer. "what was there..." (p.230).

p.159 · *At the Crossroads.* Rachel Isadora. "A rooster crows..." unpaged.

ETHNIC U. S. A.

African Americans

p.161 · Deborah Taylor, Young Adult Services Specialist at Enoch Pratt Free Library in Baltimore, acted as special consultant for this list. Her contribution is also more direct because the list incorporates many titles from her *Booklist* bibliography, "The Black Experience in Books for Young Adults," Dec. 1,

1989. I have also drawn on several other *Booklist* bibliographies, children's, young adult, and adult, including my list "Growing Up Black," Aug. 1984.

· Dick Gregory. "Feb." From *Talk that Talk* (p.424). I am grateful to Melrita Bonner, Librarian and Branch Manager in Little Rock, Arkansas, who first introduced me to this beautiful anthology. She read aloud the heartrending "Ibo Landing Story," retold by Frankie and Doug Quimby (p.139).

p.162 · Sojourner Truth. "I have ploughed…" *Many Thousand Gone.* Virginia Hamilton (p.72).

p.164 · *The Big Sea.* Langston Hughes. "I began to…" (p.310).

· Nowhere to Run. Gerri Hirshey. "a restless music…" (p.xiii).

· *Black Out Loud.* Macmillan, 1970. *Celebrations.* Follett, 1977. Ed. Arnold Adoff.

p.165 · *What a Morning!* John Langstaff. Macmillan/Margaret K. McElderry, 1987.

· "No more auction…" Hamilton says in *Many Thousand Gone* that when the black soldiers in the Union army marched to war they sang this "joyous anthem of freedom written by some nameless, inspired former slave, most likely in the year of jubilee" (p.143). This version reprinted from *Children of Promise* (p.28).

p.166 · Zora Neale Hurston, "How It Feels To Be Colored Me," originally published in *World Tomorrow II* May 1928: "sobbing school of…" (p.215). Reprinted in *I Love Myself When I Am Laughing…: A Zora Neale Hurston Reader.* Ed. Alice Walker. Feminist Press, 1979.

· *Their Eyes Were Watching God.* Zora Neale Hurston. Lippincott, 1937.

p.167 · *I Love Myself.* Walker. "Sometimes, I feel discriminated against…" (p.216).

· *Sojourner Truth: Ain't I a Woman?* Patricia and Fredrick McKissack. Scholastic, 1992.

p.168 · *Second Wind.* Bill Russell. "If Shakespeare can…" (p.104).

p.169 · *Fallen Angels.* Walter Dean Myers. "Captain Stewart…" paper (p.77).

p.170 · *A Hero Ain't Nothin' but a Sandwich.* Alice Childress. Avon, 1973.

p.172 · *The Contender.* Robert Lipsyte. "It's the climbing…" (p.27).

· *Anne Frank: The Diary of a Young Girl.* Anne Frank. Trans. B. M. Mooyaart. Doubleday, 1952. Rev. ed. 1967.

· *Brown Girl, Brownstones.* Paule Marshall. Feminist Press, 1959.

p.174 · *Fallen Angels.* Myers. "hours of boredom…" (p.132).

· *Clover.* Dori Sanders. "Only minutes after…" (p.100).

p.175 · Lafeyette Rivers, a 10-year-old boy in a Chicago public housing complex. *There Are No Children Here.* Alex Kotlowitz. "If I grow up…" (p.x).

· *Let the Circle Be Unbroken.* Mildred Taylor. Dial, 1981.

· *Fast Talk on a Slow Track.* Rita Williams-Garcia. "achieving the most…" (p.158).

p.176 · *Maizon at Blue Hill.* Jacqueline Woodson. "minority" (p.103).

Asian Americans p.177 · Phoebe Yeh, children's book editor at Scholastic, acted as special consultant for this resource guide.

· *Bo Rabbit Smart for True: Folktales from the Gullah.* Retold Priscilla Jaquith. Drawings Ed Young, Philomel. 1981. *Rime of the Ancient Mariner.* Samuel Taylor Coleridge. Illus. Ed Young. Atheneum, 1992.

· Maxine Hong Kingston. *Women Who Write: From the Past and Present to the Future.* Lucinda Irwin Smith. Messner, 1989, "I hope that…" (p.87). Reprinted by permission of the publisher, Julian Messner / A Division of Simon & Schuster, New York.

p.178 · *The New Americans.* Brent Ashabranner. Putnam, 1983.

p.179 · Vietnamese teenager. *Into a Strange Land.* Brent Ashabranner. "I wanted to find…" (p.70).

· *New Kids on the Block.* Janet Bode. "but now there's…" (p.25).

p.181 · *El Chino.* Allen Say. "I searched all…" (p.22).

p.183 · *The Invisible Thread.* Yoshiko Uchida. "I have written…" (p.133).

p.184 · *The Rainbow People.* Laurence Yep. "When my father…" (p.x).

· *The Lost Garden.* Messner, 1991. *Tongues of Jade.* HarperCollins, 1991. Laurence Yep.

p.187 · *Finding My Voice.* Marie Lee. "When you leave…" (p.143).

p.189 · *Bone.* Fae Myenne Ng. "I had a…" (p.18).

· *The Kitchen God's Wife.* Amy Tan. Putnam, 1991.

· *The Best Bad Thing.* Macmillan/Margaret K. McElderry, 1983. *The Happiest Ending,* 1985. *Journey Home,* 1978. *Journey to Topaz.* Scribner, 1971. Yoshiko Uchida.

p.190 · *Yang the Youngest.* Lensey Namioka. "I greeted her…" (p.20).

· *Child of the Owl.* HarperCollins, 1977. *Dragonwings.* HarperCollins, 1975. Laurence Yep.

Jewish Americans p.192 · Saul Bellow. Introduction to *Great Jewish Short Stories,* "Laughter and trembling…" (p.12).

· Hillel Halkin. Introduction to his new translation of Aleichem's stories, *Tevye the Dairyman and the Railroad Stories,* "without either ridiculing…"

· *Starting from Home.* Milton Meltzer. "unhyphenated" (p.78).

p.193 · Ted Solotaroff. Quoted by Letty Cottin Pogrebin in *Deborah, Golda, and Me* "both sides of..." (p.xvi).
· *Deborah, Golda, and Me.* Letty Cottin Pogrebin. "In New City..." (p.49).
p.195 · *Starting from Home.* Meltzer. "Learn, learn, learn!..." (p.18).
p.196 · *Bronx Primitive.* Kate Simon. HarperCollins, 1982.
p.197 · *Call It Sleep.* Henry Roth. "Before her the..." (p.16).
· *A Young Man in Search of Love.* Doubleday, 1978. *Lost in America.* Doubleday, 1981. *When Shlemiel Went to Warsaw.* Farrar, 1968. Isaac Bashevis Singer.
p.199 · *World's Fair.* E. L. Doctorow. Random, 1985.
p.200 · *Writing Our Way Home.* Ed. Ted Solotaroff and Nessa Rapoport. Schocken, 1992.
· *World of Our Fathers.* Irving Howe. "The Jews' greatest..." (p.646).
p.201 · *Are You There God? It's Me, Margaret.* Judy Blume. "Are you there..." (p.56).
· *The Night Journey.* Katherine Lasky. Viking, 1981.
p.202 · *The Fixer.* Bernard Malamud. Farrar, 1966.
p.203 · *I Love You, Stupid!* Harry Mazer. HarperCollins, 1981.
· *The Promise.* Chaim Potok. Knopf, 1969.
p.204 · *The Chosen.* Chaim Potok. "I felt more..." (p.20).
p.205 · *Goodbye, Columbus.* Philip Roth. "The neighborhood had..." (p.64).

Latinos

p.207 · Raúl Niño and Marc Zimmerman acted as special consultants for this list, which also draws on a bibliography, "Growing Up Hispanic," prepared by Sally Estes in *Booklist,* June 15, 1985.
· *Scorpions.* Walter Dean Myers. HarperCollins, 1988.
· *Bingo Brown's Guide to Romance.* Betsy Byars. Viking, 1992.
p.208 · *Dark Harvest.* Brent Ashabranner. Putnam, 1985.
p.209 · *A Migrant Family.* Larry Dane Brimner. "No one sheds..." (p.36).
· *Illegal.* Philip Anastos. "We had to..." (p.57).
p.210 · *Growing Up Latino.* Ed. Harold Augenbraum and Ilan Stavans, "the Hispanic journey..." (p.xiii).
p.211 · *Breathing Light.* Raúl Niño. "Ten years old..." (p.31).
· *Borders.* Pat Mora. "Not fair," in "Same Song" (p.41).
p.212 · *Days of Obligation.* Richard Rodriguez. Viking, 1992.
· *Always Running.* Luis Rodriguez. "In the barrio..." (p.72).
p.213 · *The Elements of San Joaquin.* Gary Soto. Univ. of Pittsburgh, 1977.
p.214 · From "Beautiful & Cruel." *The House on Mango Street.* Sandra Cisneros. "I have begun..." (p.89). Copyright © 1989 by Sandra Cisneros. Published in the United States by Vintage Books, a division of Random House, Inc., New York and distributed in Canada by Random House of Canada Limited, Toronto. Originally published in somewhat different form by Arte Público Press in 1984 and revised in 1989. Reprinted by permission of Susan Bergholz Literary Services, New York.
p.216 · *Baseball in April.* Gary Soto. In "Seventh Grade." "How come you're..." (p.53). Copyright © 1990 by Gary Soto, reprinted by permission of Harcourt Brace Jovanovich, Inc.
· *The One Who Came Back.* Joann Mazzio. "you should never..." (p.113).
· *El Bronx Remembered.* Nicholasa Mohr. Arte Público Press, 1975.
p.218 · *A Migrant Family.* Brimner. "They want us..." (p.18).

Native Americans

p.219 · Michael Dorris acted as special consultant for this resource guide, which also draws on a list, *Growing Up Native American,* by Stephanie Zvirin that appeared in *Booklist,* Nov. 1, 1987, and on the *Booklist* multimedia special issue, *Dealing with Columbus,* Oct. 15, 1991.
p.220 · *Turtle Island Alphabet.* Gerald Hausman. "From the pogroms..." (p.xiii).
p.221 · *Morning Star, Black Sun.* Brent Ashabranner. Putnam, 1982.
· *Wounded Knee.* Amy Ehrlich. Dell, 1975.
p.222 · *Native American Animal Stories.* Joseph Bruchac. Fulcrum, 1992.
p.223 · *Gift of Power.* Archie Fire Lame Deer. "I could never..." (p.95).
· *Lakota Woman.* Mary Crow Dog. "But you can't..." (p.11).
p.224 · Eduardo Galeano. Quoted in *Spider Woman's Granddaughters.* Ed. Paula Gunn Allen: "Throughout America, from..." (p.1).
· *Buffalo Hunt.* Russell Freedman. Holiday, 1989.
p.226 · *Love Flute.* Paul Goble. "The Elk Man said..." unpaged.
p.227 · *House Made of Dawn.* N. Scott Momaday. HarperCollins, 1977.
p.229 · Carla Willeto. Quoted in *Rising Voices.* "trying to be..." (p.86).
p.230 · *Native Roots: How the Indians Enriched America.* Crown, 1991.
p.231 · *Love Medicine.* Louise Erdrich. "Even when it..." (p.6). *The Beet Queen,* 1986. *Tracks,* 1988. *Booklist* interview with Erdrich and Michael Dorris, Mar. 15, 1989.

Notes

p.233 · *Season of Yellow Leaf.* Douglas Jones. "Chosen had learned…" (p.219).
· *River Song.* Craig Lesley. Houghton, 1989.
· *The Contender.* Robert Lipsyte. HarperCollins, 1967.
p.234 · *White Wolf Woman.* Retold Teresa Pijoan. "A howl…" (p.59).
p.235 · *Fools Crow.* James Welch. Viking, 1986.

THE WIDENING WORLD

p.236 · "Against Borders." Yevgeny Yevtushenko. See p.i.
p.237 · *This Same Sky.* Ed. Naomi Shihab Nye. "Whenever someone…" (p.xiii).
· *Land and People of Korea.* HarperCollins, 1991. *Land and People of Bolivia.* HarperCollins, 1990.
· *Family of Man.* Edward Steichen: "daily relationships…" (p.2).
· *Let There Be Light.* James Giblin. HarperCollins, 1988.
p.238 · *A Knock at the Door.* 1992; *Cinderella.* 1992.
· *Life Doesn't Frighten Me at All.* John Agard. "checking out me history" (p.64).
p.241 · *Black Mother.* Basil Davidson. 1961.
p.242 · *African Stories.* Doris Lessing. Simon & Schuster, 1965.
· Chinua Achebe. Interview with Bill Moyers. *Bill Moyers: A World of Ideas.* Doubleday, 1989. "Look at Africa…" (p.343).
· Some titles were taken from the bibliography *Other Voices: Fiction by Chinese Women*, by Elizabeth D. Gray in *Booklist*, Jan. 1, 1991, and from her excellent pamphlet, *All the Other Voices: An Annotated Bibliography of Fiction by African, Asian and Latin American Women.* 1987.
p.244 · *The Master Puppeteer.* HarperCollins, 1976. *Of Nightingales that Weep.* HarperCollins, 1974. Katherine Paterson.
p.245 · Zhensun. "I do not paint…" back cover.
· *The Catalogue of the Universe.* Macmillan/Margaret K. McElderry. 1985. *The Changeover* 1974. *Memory.* 1987. Margaret Mahy.
p.246 · *Underrunners.* Margaret Mahy. "Everything around them…" (p.169).
· *Ash Road.* Ivan Southall. St. Martin's, 1966.
p.247 · *Knitwits.* William Taylor. Scholastic, 1992.
p.248 · *Paradise Café.* Martha Brooks. In "King of the Roller Rink" (p.18).
· *Two Moons in August.* Martha Brooks. Little, Brown/Joy Street, 1991.
· *Pick-up Sticks.* Sarah Ellis. "Why did you…" (p.55).
p.249 · *The Elizabeth Stories.* Isabel Huggan. "I felt picked on…" (p.104).
· This draws on Julie Corsaro's bibliography on the Caribbean, published in *Book Links*, Sept. 1992.
p.250 · *A Small Place.* Jamaica Kincaid. "That the native…" (p.18).
· *Black Rainbow.* Farrar, 1976. *The Mythology of Mexico and Central America.* Morrow, 1980. John Bierhorst.
p.251 · *The Land and People of Bolivia.* HarperCollins, 1990.
· Isabel Allende. "In the U.S.…" *Booklist* interview, June 15, 1991.
p.252 · Derek Walcott. *Bill Moyers: A World of Ideas.* "It takes you…" (p.434).
· *The Magic Orange Tree.* Diane Wolkstein. "In almost every…" (p.11).
p.255 · Rosemary Sutcliff. *The Shining Company.* "The words had…" (p.22–3).
· *Carrie's War.* HarperCollins, 1973. *Humbug.* Clarion, 1992. Nina Bawden.
· *On the Edge.* Gillian Cross. "Dark! the house…" (p.1).
· *Chartbreaker.* Gillian Cross. Holiday, 1987.
· *Badger on the Barge.* Janni Howker. Greenwillow, 1985.
p.257 · *The Secret Diary of Adrian Mole.* Sue Townsend. "There is a…" (p.8).
· *Fireweed.* Jill Paton Walsh. Farrar, 1969.
· *Fathom Five.* Greenwillow, 1979. *Children of the Blitz.* Viking, 1985. Robert Westall.
· The bibliography, "Arab Culture: Books for Children and Young Adults," by Julie Corsaro, in *Booklist* Sept. 1, 1989, was extremely helpful in compiling this list. Many of the annotations were critical, and I did not find enough good books to recommend for a separate bibliography on Arab Americans.
p.258 · *An Ancient Heritage.* Casey Kassem. "I'm an American…" (p.6).
· *Gavriel and Jemal.* Brent Ashabranner. Putnam, 1984.
p.262 · *Siddartha.* New Directions, 1951; original German edition, 1923. *Steppenwolf.* Holt, 1929; original German edition 1927. Hermann Hesse.
p.263 · *The Lincoln Brigade.* Atheneum, 1989
· *Castle.* Houghton, 1977. *Pyramid.* Houghton, 1975. David Macaulay.

Picture Credits

Part Two, Racial Oppression: Warsaw Uprising, German photographer unknown; photo courtesy of Bettmann Archives • Cover illustrations for *Maus: A Survivor's Tale* and *Maus: A Survivor's Tale II: And Here My Troubles Began* by Art Spiegelman used by permission of Pantheon Books • Cover illustration from *Hide and Seek*, written by Ida Vos © 1991, published by Houghton Mifflin Company • People of Mogopa, photo by Paul Weinberg; Houses set on fire, photo by Guy Tillim; Women who lost their homes at Crossroads, photo by Guy Tillim; Thembalihle School, photo by Rafs Mayet; all used by permission of SouthLight (formerly Afropix), Johannesburg • Jacket from *Kaffir Boy: An Autobiography* by Mark Mathabane used by permission of New American Library, a division of Penguin USA Inc. • *Mandela: The Man, the Struggle, the Triumph* by Dorothy and Thomas Hoobler; cover illustration used with permission of Franklin Watts • Jacket illustration by Rachel Isadora from her *At the Crossroads;* copyright © 1991 by Rachel Isadora; reprinted by permission of Greenwillow Books, a division of William Morrow & Co. Inc. **Part Two, Ethnic U.S.A.:** From *Many Thousand Gone* by Virginia Hamilton; illustration by Leo and Diane Dillon; used with permission of Knopf, 1993 • Cover photograph from *Sorrow's Kitchen* by Mary Lyons © 1990; used with permission of Charles Scribner's Sons/Macmillan Publishing Company • Cover art from *Fallen Angels* by Walter Dean Myers (Scholastic Hardcover), copyright © 1988 by Jim Dietz; reprinted by permission of Scholastic Inc. • *Fast Talk on a Slow Track* by Rita Williams-Garcia; jacket illustration by Bob Marstall; photograph of jacket; copyright © 1991 by Rita Williams-Garcia; used by permission of Lodestar Books, an affiliate of Dutton Children's Books, a division of Penguin USA Inc. • Cover art from *Talk That Talk: An Anthology of African-American Storytelling*, ed. by Linda Goss and Marian E. Barnes; cover art by Julie Metz; cover painting by Jacob Lawrence, courtesy of the North Carolina Museum of Art; copyright © 1989 by Simon & Schuster, Inc.; used by permission • Photograph of James Baldwin by Michael Zide/Hampshire College; used with permission of Beacon Press • Photograph of Malcolm X used with permission of Michael Ochs Archives, Venice, Cal.; © 1992 • Cover illustration for *El Chino* by Allen Say used by permission of Houghton Mifflin • Cover illustration for *The Rainbow People* by Laurence Yep; illustrated by David Wiesner, used by permission of HarperCollins Children's Books • Cover illustration for *Finding My Voice* by Marie Lee used by permission of Houghton Mifflin • *Yang the Youngest and His Terrible Ear* by Lensey Namioka; cover illustration by Kees de Kiefte; used by permission of Little, Brown/Joy Street • *Starting from Home* by Milton Meltzer; cover illustration by Viqui Maggio; copyright © 1988 by Viqui Maggio; used by permission of Viking Penguin, a division of Penguin Books USA Inc. • Cover illustration for *Call It Sleep* by Henry Roth used by permission of Farrar • Cover illustration for *Are You There God? It's Me, Margaret* by Judy Blume, Dell Yearling Edition, used by permission of Dell, a division of Bantam, Doubleday, Dell Publishing • Cover illustration for *The Chosen* by Chaim Potok used by permission of Fawcett Crest • Photograph of Raúl Niño by Diana Solis • *Journey of the Sparrows* by Fran Leeper Buss; jacket illustration by Stephen Johnson; copyright © 1991 by Stephen Johnson for jacket illustration; used by permission of Lodestar Books, an affiliate of Dutton Children's Books, a division of Penguin USA Inc. • *The Honorable Prison* by Lyll Becerra de Jenkins; jacket illustration by Judy Pedersen; copyright © 1988 by Lyll Becerra de Jenkins; used by permission of Lodestar Books, an affiliate of Dutton Children's Books, a division of Penguin USA Inc. • Cover photo for *Illegal* by Phillip Anastos used with permission of Rizzoli Publishers copyright © 1991 • Cover illustration for *Baseball in Apr.* by Gary Soto; used with permission of Harcourt Brace Jovanovich, Inc. • Cover illustration for *Gift of Power* by Richard Erdoes and Archie Fire Lame Deer; copyright © 1992, Bear & Co., P.O. Drawer 2860 Santa Fe, NM 87504; used with permission • Jacket photograph for *Lakota Woman* by Mary Crow Dog; Harper Perennial Edition; used with permission • *Love Flute* by Paul Goble copyright © 1992 used with permission Bradbury Press/Macmillan Publishing Company • Cover illustration for *Love Medicine* by Louise Erdrich used by permission of Bantam Books, a division of Bantam, Doubleday, Dell Publishing Group, Inc. • *White Wolf Woman* by Teresa Pijoan; cover photograph used by permission of the publisher, August House. **Part Two, The Widening World:** Photo of Tsitsi Dangarembga courtesy of Seal Press • Photograph of Doris Lessing by Miriam Berkley © 1993 • From *Underrunners* by Margaret Mahy; copyright © 1992 by Linda Thomas for jacket illustration; used by permission of Viking Penguin, a division of Penguin Books USA Inc. • *Paradise Café* by Martha Brooks; jacket art © 1990 by Judy Pederson; reprinted by permission of Little, Brown and Company • Photograph of Isabel Allende; copyright © Marcia Lieberman; used with permission • *An Ancient Heritage: The Arab-American Minority;* cover photo by Paul Conklin used with permission of HarperCollins • Cover illustration by Klaus Steffens from *No Hero for the Kaiser* by Rudolf Frank; illustration copyright © 1983 by Klaus Steffens; cover reprinted by permission of Lothrop, Lee & Shepard Books, a division of William Morrow & Company, Inc. **Back cover:** Photograph of Hazel Rochman by Art Plotnik.

THEME INDEX TO PART ONE

Good books are not about one subject. Following are suggested categories that may help you in thinking about various themes and links for combining the titles in this book as well as those from your own wide reading. Only those books discussed in Part One or quoted in Part Two have been included in this index. In some cases, when *all* of the books in a chapter pertain to a specific theme, references are supplied to an entire essay rather then listing the individual titles discussed within it. Titles in quotes without italics are short stories, poems, or essays. For page citations, refer from the titles listed here to the author-title index.

.   .   .   .

REFUGEES

Along the Tracks
An Ancient Heritage
Children of the River
Escape from Warsaw
Into a Strange Land
Journey of the Sparrows
Kiki
Kindertransport
Letters from Rifka
The Man from the Other Side
Many Thousand Gone
So Far from the Bamboo Grove
Some of Us Survived
Steal Away
The Road from Home
The Trojan Horse
We Were Not Like Other People
Year of Impossible Goodbyes

RELIGION

Alan and Naomi
Are You There, God? It's Me, Margaret
Autobiography of Malcolm X
The Chosen
Freedom Songs
Gift of Power
Go Tell It on the Mountain
The Man from the Other Side
Many Thousand Gone
Memories of a Catholic Girlhood
Shabanu
This Boy's Life

SCHOOL

All But Alice
Bingo Brown's Guide to Romance
Bridge to Terabithia
Children of the River
Choosing Sides
Daniel and Esther
Fast Talk on a Slow Track
The Fat Girl
Fell
Hunger of Memory
Maizon at Blue Hill
Probably Still Nick Swansen
Queen of the Sixth Grade
Remembering the Good Times
The Runner
"Seventh Grade"
"The Story of My Life"
There's a Girl in My Hammerlock
Yang the Youngest and His Terrible Ear
Yoruba Girl Dancing

SECRETS

"Country Lovers"
Cousins
Gentlehands
Jane Eyre
The Man from the Other Side
Mary Reilly
One Writer's Beginnings
One-Eyed Cat
Scorpions

The Secret House
Stepping on the Cracks
Summer of My German Soldier
Sweet Whispers, Brother Rush
The Things They Carried
Where It Stops, Nobody Knows
Wolf Rider
Wuthering Heights

SCIENCE FICTION AND FANTASY

Beloved
The Changeover
Eva
Howl's Moving Castle
Mary Reilly
Sweet Whispers, Brother Rush
A Wrinkle in Time

SHORT STORIES

"American History"
"The Ballad of the Sad Café"
"Country Lovers"
"My Lucy Friend Who Smells Like Corn"
"My Name"
"The Old Chief Mshlanga"
"On the Rainy River"
"Once Upon a Time"
"The Red Convertible"
"Seventh Grade"
"The Smoking Mountain"
Somehow Tenderness Survives
"The Toilet"
"Where Are You Going, Where Have You Been?"
What Hearts
Who Do You Think You Are?

THE SIXTIES

Autobiography of Malcolm X
But I'll Be Back Again
Fallen Angels
Freedom Songs
Freedom's Children
Kiki
"The Red Convertible"
The Runner
The Things They Carried

SOUTH

"The Ballad of the Sad Café"
Beloved
"Doctor"
Freedom's Children
Freedom Songs
I Know Why the Caged Bird Sings
Kiki
Many Thousand Gone
"Marie Jolie"
"My Lucy Friend Who Smells Like Corn"
One Writer's Beginnings
Permanent Connections
Somewhere in the Darkness

Summer of My German Soldier
The Thanksgiving Visitor

SPORTS

Baseball in April
Bridge to Terabithia
Brothers Like Friends
Choosing Sides
The Chosen
"How I Learned English"
The Runner
There's a Girl in My Hammerlock
Yang the Youngest and His Terrible Ear

WESTERN EUROPE

All Quiet on the Western Front
Anne Frank
Bad Times, Good Friends
Brothers Like Friends
Don't Say a Word
El Chino
Hide and Seek
Lily and the Lost Boy
"Locked In"

WOMEN'S ROLES

Beauty
Beloved
Cat's Eye
The House on Mango Street
I Know Why the Caged Bird Sings
Jane Eyre
The Joy Luck Club
The King's Equal
Lakota Woman
Maizon at Blue Hill
The Moonlight Man
Prairie Songs
"Ruth's Song"
Shabanu
Sojourner Truth
There's a Girl in My Hammerlock
White Wolf Woman
The Woman Warrior
A Yellow Raft in Blue Water

WORLD WAR II

Alan and Naomi
Along the Tracks
Bad Times, Good Friends
The Chosen
Daniel and Esther
Don't Say a Word
Escape from Warsaw
Forever Nineteen
The Invisible Thread
Kindertransport
The Man from the Other Side
So Far from the Bamboo Grove
Stepping on the Cracks
Summer of My German Soldier
We Were Not Like Other People
"Who Was That Masked Man, Anyway?"

AUTHOR/TITLE INDEX